Get the eBook FREE!

(PDF, ePub, Kindle, and liveBook all included)

We believe that once you buy a book from us, you should be able to read it in any format we have available. To get electronic versions of this book at no additional cost to you, purchase and then register this book at the Manning website.

Go to https://www.manning.com/freebook and follow the instructions to complete your pBook registration.

That's it!
Thanks from Manning!

Code Like
a Pro in C#

JORT RODENBURG

MANNING

SHELTER ISLAND

For online information and ordering of this and other Manning books, please visit
www.manning.com. The publisher offers discounts on this book when ordered in quantity.
For more information, please contact

  Special Sales Department
  Manning Publications Co.
  20 Baldwin Road
  PO Box 761
  Shelter Island, NY 11964
  Email: orders@manning.com

Manning Publications Co.
20 Baldwin Road
PO Box 761
Shelter Island, NY 11964

Development editor:	Marina Michaels
Senior technical development editors:	Eric Lippert and Enrico Buonanno
Technical developmental editor:	Jean-François Morin
Review editor:	Mihaela Batinic
Production editor:	Andy Marinkovich
Copy editor:	Pamela Hunt
Proofreader:	Katie Tennant
Technical proofreader:	Tanya Wilke
Typesetter:	Dennis Dalinnik
Cover designer:	Marija Tudor

ISBN: 9781617298028
Printed in the United States of America

contents

preface

My first introduction to C# came when I joined Fujifilm Medical Systems in 2016. I had previous experience in Java and Python, but when C# came around, I did not look back. I loved its low barrier of entry and (at first excruciatingly infuriating) focus on explicit typing. Throughout my time at the company, I annoyed my coworkers with questions about C# and how to best use it. Getting started was easy, but becoming proficient was another matter altogether. Everybody can write a "Hello, World" application within 10 minutes, no matter their background, but using a language to its fullest strengths while knowing why certain things are implemented the way they are simply takes time. After a while, I felt like I had plateaued in my C# knowledge and was looking for resources to take me to the next level. Quickly, I realized that there were three major types of books dealing with .NET and C#: books about language-transcending topics (clean code, architecture, infrastructure, and the like) that happened to use C#, books on how to start programming using C#, and books that are so advanced that you might just be qualified to become the CTO of Microsoft after reading them. I wanted there to be a book that sat in the middle of all three: a book that deals with clean code and bridges the gap between beginner and advanced topics. That book did not exist, so I wrote it. This is that book.

If you are a software engineer (or developer, or coder, or whatever your title may be) with previous experience in a (preferably object-oriented) programming language and want to jump into C#, this is the book for you. You will not have to learn how to write an `if` statement, nor will I explain what an object is to you. What you will find in this book are skills and topics that prepare you for deeper study into the language and platform. Of course, I can't promise to cover everything a more difficult resource assumes you know, but within the limited page count of this book, I sure tried. I very much hope you enjoy this book and learn a thing or two. And if not, well, it never hurts to go over things you know again.

acknowledgments

When I first started talking with Manning about writing this book, I had little idea of how it would take over my life for about a year or so. To be fair, I was warned on multiple occasions that authors tend to underestimate the time needed to write a book. I, being stubborn, thought I would be the exception. I was not. From December 2019 to March 2021, I put many hours into this book. On multiple occasions, I thought to myself that "this will surely be the end." Every single time (but one, obviously), it was not. Luckily, I have a very patient wife and plenty of time to kill.

It is with that in mind that I would first like to thank my wife for sticking by me on this roller coaster and to apologize to her for disappearing from her life for a year. I could not have written this book without her unwavering support. She was the rock on which this book was built. I also want to thank my family, who were always very excited to hear about new developments and updates. I took the liberty of naming the CEO of the company in the business case we follow through the book by combining the first name of my maternal grandfather (Aljen) and the surname of my paternal grandmother (van der Meulen).

I also have to thank the exceptional team at Manning. In particular, I want to single out Marina Michaels. As my editor, she shaped this book into something more than a random collection of incoherent rants. Thanks to Marina, I have developed a healthy fear of using the word *will* anywhere in writing. I also had a very valuable team in Jean-François Morin, Tanya Wilke, Eric Lippert, Rich Ward, Enrico Buonanno, and Katie Tennant. This intercontinental team of superheroes/ninjas/rockstars provided amazing feedback and caught an immense amount of (often very embarrassing) technical mistakes. I also want to thank all the reviewers and MEAPers who read the manuscript before publication and gave fantastic feedback, often in no uncertain terms. I do not claim this book to be a masterpiece, but I do hope you will get something useful out of it.

To all the reviewers, thanks: Arnaud Bailly, Christian Thoudahl, Daniel Vásquez Estupiñan, Edin Kapic, Foster Haines, George Thomas, Goetz Heller, Gustavo Filipe Ramos Gomes, Hilde Van Gysel, Jared Duncan, Jason Hales, Jean-François Morin, Jeff Neumann, Karthikeyarajan Rajendran, Luis Moux, Marc Roulleau, Mario Solomou, Noah Betzen, Oliver Korten, Patrick Regan, Prabhuti Prakash, Raymond Cheung, Reza Zeinali, Richard B. Ward, Richard DeHoff, Sau Fai Fong, Slavomir Furman, Tanya Wilke, Thomas F. Gueth, Víctor M. Pérez, and Viktor Bek. Your suggestions helped make this a better book.

And finally, there are a few people I want to thank for either having helped me with some part of this book or my career in general. First up are David Lavielle and Duncan Henderson: thank you for taking a chance on me and giving me my first job in software development. Jerry Finegan: thanks for introducing me to C# and letting me ask one dumb question after the other. Your patience and feedback were much appreciated. Michael Breecher: you had a hand in shaping some of the content around congruence in this book (forced by my late-night texts asking weird math questions about notation), and the book is better for it. Szymon Zuberek: the first draft of chapter 2 was written in your New York apartment. Thanks for letting us crash on your couch any time we wanted to visit and, as always, for providing conversational fodder. And I thank the wonderful people at Acronis and Workiva, who have had to listen to me drone on about "this book I am writing" for what feels like forever. They've been good sports (mostly).

about this book

This book builds on your existing programming skills to help you seamlessly upskill your coding practice or transition to C# from Java or another object-oriented language. You'll learn to write the kind of idiomatic C# code that's essential for enterprise development. This book discusses essential backend skills and puts them into practice with a common career challenge: refactoring a legacy codebase to be secure, clean, and readable. By the time you're done, you'll have a professional-level understanding of C# and be ready to start specializing with advanced-level resources.

There's no "Hello, World" or Computer Science 101 basics—you'll learn by refactoring an out-of-date legacy codebase, using new techniques, tools, and best practices to bring it up to modern C# standards. Throughout this book, we take an existing codebase (written in the .NET Framework) and refactor it, with a simplified API, to .NET 5.

Who should read this book

If you are a developer proficient in an object-oriented programming language, be it Java, Dart, C++, or what have you, this book can help you get up to speed in C# and .NET without completely starting over. A lot of your knowledge carries over, so why learn how to write an `if` statement for the 500th time?

Similarly, if you are proficient in a programming language like Go, C, JavaScript, Python, or any other mainstream language, after reading this book you can write clean, idiomatic C#. You may want to read up on some object-oriented design principles, but this should not prove to be a steep barrier to entry (if you're coming from

Go, make sure to pay extra attention whenever we use interfaces; they do not work the same).

Lastly, if you are a developer who has been using C# for a while now and is wondering how to "level-up" your knowledge: this book is for you. A lot of advanced C# resources assume knowledge that is not covered in introductory or beginner resources. This book aims to bridge that gap.

How this book is organized: A roadmap

This book has a somewhat unconventional approach to its structure compared to a regular technical book. Most technical books are reference books or can be read in any order. This book is not a reference book, and to get the most out of it, you need to read the chapters in order. The book is structured around the following six parts, as shown in figure figure 1:

1   "Using C# and .NET"—In chapter 1 we discuss what this book is, what it teaches, and what it does not teach. Chapter 2 is a brief tour of the C# language and .NET ecosystem, focusing on what sets .NET apart from other platforms and the C# compilation story.

2   "The existing codebase"—In this part, I guide you through the exploration of the codebase we inherit. This part is a detailed walk-through of the existing codebase, with a discussion on potential improvements and design flaws.

3   "The database access layer"—Following part 2, we start to rewrite the entire service. In part 3, we focus on creating a new .NET Core project and learn how we can use Entity Framework Core to connect to a cloud (or local) database. Other discussed topics include the repository/service pattern, virtual methods and properties, and sealed classes.

4   "The repository layer"—In part 4, we step into the land of the repository/service pattern and implement five repository classes. You also learn about dependency injection, multithreading (including locking, mutexes, and semaphores), custom equality comparisons, test-driven development, generics, extension methods, and LINQ.

5   "The service layer"—The next step is to implement the service layer classes. In part 5, we write four service layers from the ground up and talk about reflection, mocking, coupling, runtime assertions and type checks, error handling, structs, and yield return.

6   "The controller layer"—Part 6 is the final step in our rewrite of the service we initially inherited in part 2. This part sees us writing two controller classes and has us perform acceptance testing. Besides those topics, we also broach ASP.NET Core middleware, HTTP routing, custom data binding, data serialization and deserialization, and generating an OpenAPI specification at runtime.

A lot of chapters in this book (and some sections within chapters) have exercises designed to test your knowledge of the material. You can complete these exercises

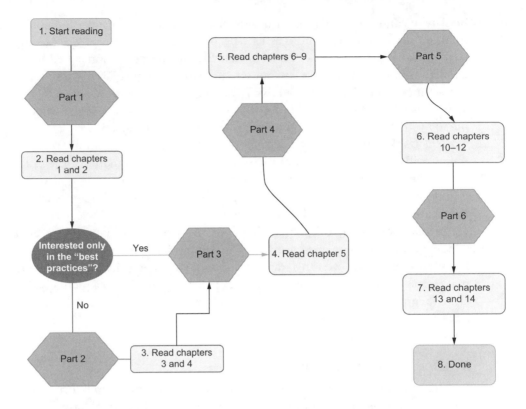

Figure 1   A flowchart of suggested routes to read this book. Follow the steps, and answer the questions to achieve your ideal reading experience. This flowchart is inspired by the book structure flowcharts in Donald Knuth's *The Art of Computer Programming series*.

quickly. I encourage you to complete these when you encounter them and to revisit sections you may have skimmed or misunderstood.

About the code

At the time of writing, the .NET landscape can be divided into three major pieces: .NET Framework 4.x, .NET Core 3.x, and.NET 5. The entire book uses .NET 5, except for chapters 3 and 4 (for reasons you will understand after reading those chapters).

The C# language versions used are C# 3 and C# 9 (we do not use any C# 9–specific features in most of the book, so an installation of C# 8 works as well). Because C# languages are backward compatible, you just need to install the latest version (at the time of writing, either C# 8 or C# 9 preview). The chapters with provided source code are 2, 3 and 4 (combined), 5, 6, 7, 8, 9, 10, 11, 12, 13, and 14.

To run the code, you need to install a version of .NET Framework higher than 3.5 (if you want to run the code in chapters 3 and 4) and .NET 5. If you want to run the database used in the book locally or have trouble installing anything needed in this book, you can find installation instructions in appendix C ("Installation guides"). This book mostly uses Visual Studio as its IDE, but you can use any IDE that supports C# (or none at all) if you please. Visual Studio 2019 has a free version called Visual Studio 2019 Community. When we encounter things that require Visual Studio, the book notes this as such. The code and .NET 5 should run on Windows, macOS, and Linux. The book uses the command line (or terminal, for you macOS users) wherever possible to avoid a reliance on any particular IDE or operating system.

This book contains many examples of source code both in numbered listings and in-line with normal text. In both cases, source code is formatted in a `fixed-width` `font` `like` `this` to separate it from ordinary text. Sometimes code is also **`in bold`** to highlight code that has changed from previous steps in the chapter, such as when a new feature adds to an existing line of code.

In many cases, the original source code has been reformatted; line breaks were added, and indentation was reworked to accommodate the available page space in the book. In some cases, even this was not enough, and listings include line-continuation markers (➥). Code annotations accompany many of the listings, highlighting important concepts. Also note that curly braces typically have been placed on the preceding lines for new code blocks. This is not the appropriate real-world C# convention but was done to preserve space. The source code itself does not use this convention.

liveBook discussion forum

Purchase of *Code Like a Pro in C#* includes free access to a private web forum run by Manning Publications where you can make comments about the book, ask technical questions, and receive help from the author and from other users. To access the forum, go to https://livebook.manning.com/book/code-like-a-pro-in-c-sharp/welcome/v-9/. You can also learn more about Manning's forums and the rules of conduct at https://livebook.manning.com/#!/discussion.

Manning's commitment to our readers is to provide a venue where a meaningful dialogue between individual readers and between readers and the author can take place. It is not a commitment to any specific amount of participation on the part of the author, whose contribution to the forum remains voluntary (and unpaid). We suggest you try asking him some challenging questions lest his interest stray! The forum and the archives of previous discussions will be accessible from the publisher's website as long as the book is in print.

about the author

JORT RODENBURG is a software engineer, author, and public speaker. He specializes in C# and has worked on software in a variety of fields, such as financial compliance and reporting, inkjet printing, medical imaging, distributed systems, and cyber security. Jort has mentored engineers proficient in a different programming language to help them get up to speed in C# and .NET. Jort also speaks on all things C#, .NET, and programming at conferences and meetups.

about the cover illustration

The figure on the cover of *Code Like a Pro in C#* is captioned "Homme Samojede," or "Samojede Man." The illustration is taken from a collection of dress costumes from various countries by Jacques Grasset de Saint-Sauveur (1757–1810), titled *Costumes de Différents Pays*, published in France in 1797. Each illustration is finely drawn and colored by hand. The rich variety of Grasset de Saint-Sauveur's collection reminds us vividly of how culturally apart the world's towns and regions were just 200 years ago. Isolated from each other, people spoke different dialects and languages. In the streets or in the countryside, it was easy to identify where they lived and what their trade or station in life was just by their dress.

The way we dress has changed since then and the diversity by region, so rich at the time, has faded away. It is now hard to tell apart the inhabitants of different continents, let alone different towns, regions, or countries. Perhaps we have traded cultural diversity for a more varied personal life—certainly for a more varied and fast-paced technological life.

At a time when it is hard to tell one computer book from another, Manning celebrates the inventiveness and initiative of the computer business with book covers based on the rich diversity of regional life of two centuries ago, brought back to life by Grasset de Saint-Sauveur's pictures.

Part 1

Using C# and .NET

In this first part of the book, we'll take a brief tour of the C# language and talk about some of its features. Chapter 1 covers what C# and .NET are and why you would (and would not) use them for your projects. Chapter 2 dives deeper into the various iterations of .NET and takes a C# method through its compilation process, stopping at each major step along the way.

Although this part is truly the introduction of this book, it still provides invaluable information to somebody familiar with C#. Some of the knowledge introduced in these first two chapters are things you need to know before moving on to more advanced topics.

Introducing C# and .NET

This chapter covers

- Understanding what C# and .NET are
- Learning why you would use C# for your projects (and why you wouldn't)
- Switching to C# and how to get started

Another book on C#, you say? Yes, another one. Plenty of books are written about C# and .NET, but this book has one fundamental difference: I wrote this book to help you develop clean, idiomatic C# code in your day-to-day life. This book is not a reference book but rather a practical guide. This book does not cover things like how to write an `if` statement, what a method signature is, or what an object is. We are not concerned about syntax but instead focus on concepts and ideas. There is a difference between knowing the syntax of a language and being able to write clean, idiomatic code. After going through this book, that is exactly what you will be able do. Whatever your background is and whatever programming languages you know, as long as you understand object-oriented programming, this book helps you shift into the C# and .NET ecosystem, as shown in figure 1.1.

What do organizations like Microsoft, Google, and the US government have in common? They all use C#—and for good reason. But why? C# is just another

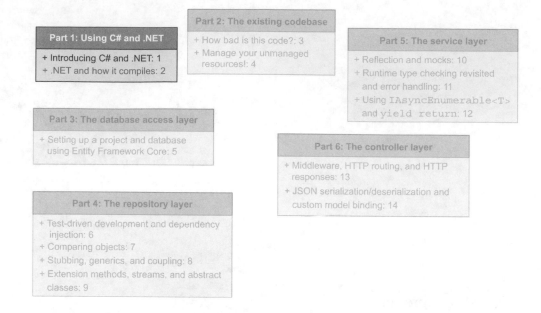

Figure 1.1   Every chapter introduction contains a progress diagram, which allows you to quickly figure out where you are in the book.

programming language. It bears similarities to Java and C++, allows for both object-oriented and functional programming, and enjoys wide support from a large open source community. Great. Now, why should you care? In this chapter, we'll explore that question in depth, but let me reveal a couple of spoilers: C# excels at allowing you to create scalable software. To start writing C#, all you need is the .NET SDK of your choice (more on that in chapter 2) and perhaps an IDE. The language and runtime are open source.

Any time you look online for C#, chances are, you come across the .NET Framework. You can think about the .NET Framework as your warm blanket, a warm fire, and a mug of hot chocolate on a winter day, providing you with everything you need: libraries that encapsulate low-level Windows APIs, expose commonly used data structures and provide wrappers for complicated algorithms. Daily development in C# almost certainly involves the .NET Framework, .NET Core, or .NET 5, so we'll explore these frameworks where appropriate.

Figure 1.2 shows where this book's topics fit in a general .NET web architecture. It also shows the architecture we use to completely rewrite an existing application, which we'll start in chapter 5 (the green/dashed arrows indicate this path).

For those of you with prior experience in C#: this book sits between beginner and advanced resources. With the skills taught in this book, you can bridge the knowledge gap and prepare yourself for advanced skills. The first two chapters may

A typical web architecture on a Microsoft stack

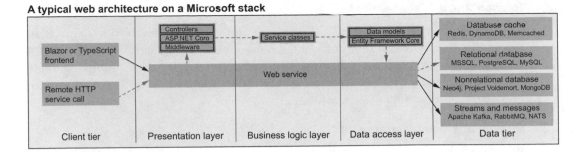

Figure 1.2 An example of a typical web service architecture on a Microsoft stack. This book follows the approach shown by the green/dashed arrows. This book covers the presentation, business logic, and data access layers.

seem a bit basic to you, but I invite you to not skim over these. It is always good to refresh your knowledge.

1.1 Why work in C#?

If you are already familiar with a programming language other than C# and like using it, why should you use C#? Perhaps you were hired by a company that uses only C#. Or maybe you just want to see what all the fuss is about.

I promise not to repeatedly tell you that C# is a "strongly typed object-oriented programming language that enables cross-platform development of scalable enterprise software." You are likely aware of that, and it is hardly the most exciting sentence to dissect. In this section, we cover the buzzwords in that definition once and do not touch on it again. At the risk of sounding like I'm employed by Microsoft's marketing department, for the rest of this section, we'll focus on the following highlights and use cases of C#:

- C# (and the .NET ecosystem) enables the development of software in an economical way. Economical solutions are important because enterprise development is the bread and butter of C#.
- C# can improve code stability and is maintainable because of its support for self-documenting code, secure libraries, and ease of use.
- C# is developer friendly and easy to use. There's nothing worse than discovering that the programming language you want to use does not have good support for the things you love (such as a stable package manager, good support for unit testing, and a cross-platform runtime).

Of course, writing scalable, maintainable, and developer-friendly "clean code" can be done in most (if not all) programming languages. The difference lies in the developer experience. Some languages are really good at guiding you in writing clean code, whereas others are not. C# is not perfect, but it does try to help you in this regard.

1.1.1   *Reason 1: C# is economical*

C# is free to use and develop in. The language and platform are fully open source, all documentation is free, and most tooling has free options. For example, a common C# setup includes an installation of C# 8, .NET 5, and Visual Studio Community. All these are free and used in this book. No license fee is required for the runtime, and you can deploy the end product wherever you want.

1.1.2   *Reason 2: C# is maintainable*

When we talk about maintainability in this book, we mean the ability to fix bugs, change functionality, and address other issues without unintended side effects. This sounds like an obvious requirement for any programming language, but it is very hard to implement. C# has features that improve the maintainability (and, therefore, safe extensibility) of large codebases. Think, for example, about generics and Language-Integrated Query (LINQ). We'll discuss these two things throughout the book, but they are examples of the platform exposing functionalities that can help you write better code.

For a company, maintainability might not be the number one priority on the surface, but if you develop code that is maintainable (meaning clean code that is easily extendable and backed by tests), development costs drop. Development costs dropping when writing maintainable code may seem counterintuitive at first: maintainable code takes longer to write and architect, driving up the initial costs of development. However, imagine what happens after a little while when a user discovers a bug or they want an additional feature. If we write maintainable code, we can quickly and easily find the bug (and fix it). Adding the feature is simpler because the codebase is extensible. If we can easily extend and fix a codebase, development costs go down.

Open/Closed Principle

In 1988, the French computer scientist Bertrand Meyer (creator of the Eiffel programming language) released a book called *Object-Oriented Software Construction* (Prentice Hall, 1988). The release of Meyer's book was a pivotal moment in the history of object-oriented programming and design, because in it, he introduced the Open/Closed Principle (OCP). The OCP is aimed at improving the maintainability and flexibility of software designs. Meyer says the OCP means that "software entities (classes, modules, functions, etc.) should be open for extension, but closed for modification."

But what does the OCP mean in practical terms? To examine that, let's apply the OCP to a class: we deem a class "open" for extension and "closed" to modification if we can add functionality to the class without changing the existing functionality (and, therefore, potentially breaking parts of our code). If you abide by that rule, the odds of you introducing a regression (or new bug) in the existing code are much smaller than if you try to force in the bug fix or new feature with no regard for maintainability and extensibility. When you work with code that is more complicated (and coupled; discussed in chapter 8), you are more likely to introduce new bugs due to misunderstanding the side effects of your changes. This is what we want to avoid at all costs.

1.1.3 *Reason 3: C# is developer friendly and easy to use*

Enterprise development is the bread and butter of C# development and where C# and .NET shine. What would your ideal codebase look like in an enterprise environment? Perhaps you would like a codebase that is easily navigable with a solid package manager and backed by tests (unit, integration, and smoke). Let's also throw in excellent documentation and cross-platform support.

> **DEFINITION** *Self-documenting code* means code that is written clearly enough that we need no comments to explain the logic. The code documents itself. For example, if you have a method called `DownloadDocument`, others can have some inkling of what it does. There is no need to add a comment saying that the logic inside the method downloads a document.

To top things off, perhaps we can have good integration with a cloud service for continuous integration and delivery (CI/CD). A pragmatic view tells us that the likelihood of you having such a codebase is not very high. Of course, this wish list is unrealistic for most scenarios. However, if you want to do some of these things (or all of them, if you are adventurous), C# does not work against you. It offers existing workflows, functionalities, and native libraries to get you 99% of the way there.

Developers coming from a language such as Java should see some similarities in the project structure. Although some differences exist, they are not large. We'll discuss the C# project structure in depth throughout the book.

.NET also has support for several popular testing frameworks. Microsoft provides the Visual Studio Unit Testing Framework, which contains (and by extension is sometimes called) MSTest. MSTest is just the command-line runner for the Visual Studio Unit Testing Framework. Other commonly used testing frameworks are xUnit and NUnit. You can also find support for mocking frameworks such as Moq (Moq is similar to Java's Mockito or Go's GoMock. We'll learn more about using Moq with unit tests in section 10.3.3.), SpecFlow (behavior-driven development similar to Cucumber), NFluent (a fluent assertion library), FitNesse, and many more.

Last, you can run C# on a host of platforms, albeit with some limitations (some older platforms are restricted to older versions of C# and the .NET Framework). With .NET 5, you can run the same code on Windows 10, Linux, and macOS. This functionality got its start as .NET Core, a spinoff of the .NET Framework that has since merged with .NET Framework (and other frameworks) to create .NET 5. You can even run C# code on iOS and Android through Xamarin and on PlayStation, Xbox, and Nintendo Switch platforms through Mono.

1.2 *Why not work in C#?*

C# isn't the best choice for everybody under every circumstance. It is imperative that you choose the best tool for the job. C# works well in a wide variety of situations, but a few use cases you might not want to use C# and .NET for follow:

- Operating system development
- Real-time operating system–driven code (embedded development)
- Numerical computing

Let's examine briefly why C# might not be an ideal fit for these use cases.

1.2.1 Operating system development

Operating system (OS) development is an incredibly important corner of software engineering, yet not many people develop OSes. Developing an OS takes a lot of time and commitment, with codebases routinely going into millions of lines of code, developed and maintained over many years and sometimes decades.

The main reason C# is not suitable for OS development comes down to spotty support for manual memory management (unmanaged code) and C#'s compilation process. Although C# allows the use of pointers when using "unsafe" mode, it does not rival a programming language like C in ease of use for manual memory management.

Another problem with using C# to develop an OS is its partial reliance on a just-in-time (JIT) compiler (more on this in chapter 2). Imagine having to run your operating system through a virtual machine. Performance would be a problem because the virtual machine has to play catch-up all the time to run the JIT-compiled code, which is similar to what happens when .NET code runs on your machine. This critique means that a fully statically compiled language is a better fit for OS development.

Yet, examples of OSes developed in higher-level languages do exist. For example, Pilot-OS (created by Xerox PARC in 1977) was written in Mesa,[1] a predecessor of Java.

If you want to learn more about operating system development, the wiki for the osdev.org community is an excellent resource (wiki.osdev.org). There you can find guides to get started, tutorials, and reading suggestions. Resources for learning C include Jens Gustedt's *Modern C* (Manning, 2019) and the classic book, *The C Programming Language*, by Brian Kernighan and Dennis Ritchie (Prentice Hall, 1988).

1.2.2 Real-time operating system embedded development in C#

Similar to OS development (section 1.2.1), real-time operating system (RTOS)–driven code, which you most often find in embedded systems, experiences large performance issues when run through a virtual machine. An RTOS scans code linearly, in real time, and executes the instructions at a configurable interval ranging from one operation per second to many times per microsecond, depending on the wishes of the developer and the capabilities of the microcontroller or programmable logic controller (PLC) the code runs on. A virtual machine gets in the way of true real-time execution due to added latency and overhead at run time.

If you want to learn more about RTOS-driven code and embedded development, you can check out several highly regarded books, such as David E. Simon's *An Embedded*

---

[1] The name "Mesa" is a pun, referring to the programming language being high level, just like an isolated, elevated hill with a flat top.

Software Primer (Addison-Wesley Professional, 1999), or Elecia White's *Making Embedded Systems: Design Patterns for Great Software* (O'Reilly Media, 2011).

1.2.3 Numerical computing and C#

Numerical computing (also called *numerical analysis*) concerns the study, development, and analysis of algorithms. People (usually computer scientists or mathematicians) working in numerical computing use numerical approximation to solve problems in just about every branch of science and engineering. From a programming language perspective, it presents unique challenges and considerations. Every programming language can evaluate mathematical statements and formulas, yet some are specifically built for this purpose.

Consider plotting graphs. C# can absolutely handle plotting, but what performance and ease of use does C# offer when compared with something like MATLAB? (MATLAB is both a computing environment and a programming language created by MathWorks.) The short answer is that it doesn't compare. Graphics programming in C# sees you working in either something like WPF (which uses Direct3D), OpenGL, DirectX, or a different third-party graphics library (usually aimed at video games). With MATLAB, you have a language that ties into an environment built to render complicated 3-D graphs. You can literally call `plot(x, y)`, and MATLAB plots your graph for you.

So, C# can do numerical computing but does not offer the same ease of use as a language with high-level libraries and abstractions dealing with graph plotting as MATLAB does. If it interests you to learn more about MATLAB or numerical computing, some available resources on these topics include Richard Hamming's *Numerical Methods for Scientists and Engineers* (Dover Publications, 1987), Amos Gilat's *MATLAB: An Introduction with Applications* (Wiley, 2016), and the Cody tutorial program for MATLAB (https://www.mathworks.com/matlabcentral/cody).

1.3 Switching to C#

Because of the similarity among languages, developers with a good understanding of the syntax of a Java virtual machine (JVM) language (most notably Java, Scala, and Kotlin) or C++ may have an easier time with this book than somebody coming from a non-C-style language, non-virtual-machine-esque-based language, or web and cloud-focused languages such as Dart, Ruby, or Go. Coming from a non-C-style language background does not mean that C# is impossible to understand. You may find yourself rereading some passages twice, but in the end, you'll get there just fine.

If you come from an interpreted language such as Python, the .NET compilation process may seem odd at first. Languages within the confines of .NET use a two-step compilation process. First, code is compiled statically to a lower-level language called Common Intermediate Language (CIL, IL, or MSIL for short; MS for Microsoft—it is somewhat similar to Java bytecode, for the Java developers among us), which in turn compiles just-in-time (JIT) to native code when the .NET runtime executes the code on the host. All this might sound like a lot to digest suddenly, but in a few chapters, you will understand it all.

If you come from a scripting language such as JavaScript, static typing might seem to limit and frustrate you. But once you get used to knowing what your type is at all times, I think you'll like it.

And if you come from a language such as Go or Dart, where native libraries are sometimes hard to find, .NET 5 may surprise you with its rich store of libraries. By providing functions for most things you can think of, the .NET libraries are your primary source for functionality. A lot of applications written with .NET never use any third-party libraries.

To get the housekeeping out of the way, let's discuss tooling. We will not dive into how to install an IDE or the .NET SDK in this chapter. If you have not installed a .NET SDK or an IDE and want some help, you can find a couple of quick installation guides in appendix C. To follow along with this book, you need to install the latest versions of the .NET Framework and .NET 5. In this book, we'll start with an old codebase that uses the .NET Framework. Because of that, we'll use the .NET Framework to run that old codebase as we migrate the code to .NET 5.

As mentioned earlier, C# is open source and maintained by the community with help from Microsoft. You don't need to pay for a runtime, SDK, or IDE license. Concerning IDEs, Visual Studio (the IDE we'll use in the examples in this book) has a free Community edition that you can use to develop personal projects and open source software. If you like your current IDE, chances are you can find a C# plugin for it. You can also use the command line to compile, run, and test C# projects, although I encourage you to give the dedicated C# tooling (Visual Studio) a chance because it provides the smoothest experience and easiest route to writing idiomatic C# code.

Many concepts and techniques you have picked up elsewhere transfer to C#, but some don't. C# has matured more on the backend than it has on the frontend, because it is traditionally mostly used for that purpose. A historical focus on backend development for C# does not mean that the frontend experience is any less impressive. You can write a full-stack application in C# without the need to touch JavaScript. Although this book focuses on backend development, many of the concepts taught here help you on the frontend as well.

Have you ever come across a monster method with five nested for loops, a bunch of hardcoded numbers (so-called magic numbers), and more comments than code? Imagine you are a new developer who just joined a team. How would you feel when you boot up your IDE, pull down the source code, and see this method? Despair would not quite cover it. Now imagine that you placed all the individual actions in your monster method in their own small methods (perhaps fewer than 5 to 10 lines of code). What would your monster method look like? Instead of being a bunch of difficult-to-follow conditionals and assignments, with no clear path to understanding unless you have specific domain knowledge, the code almost reads like a narrative. If you name your methods well, your main method should read like a recipe that even the worst cooks can follow.

When I mention "clean code," I am referring to the coding practices evangelized by Robert C. Martin in his videos (https://cleancoders.com/videos) and books *Clean Code* (Prentice Hall, 2008), *Clean Architecture* (Prentice Hall, 2017), and, with Micah Martin, *Agile Principles, Patterns, and Practices in C#* (Pearson, 2006), and as well as through his compilation of the "SOLID" principles (Single Responsibility Principle, Open/Closed Principle, Liskov Substitution Principle, Interface Segregation Principle, and Dependency Inversion Principle). I explain clean code principles fully when they come up in the book along with practical information on how to actually use them.

At the end of the day, why bother writing clean code? Clean code works like a washing machine for bugs and incorrect functionality. If we put our codebase in the clean code washing machine, as shown in figure 1.3, we see that once you refactor something to be more "clean," bugs come out and incorrect functionality stares at you with no place to hide. After all, "it all comes out in the wash." Of course, it is also risky to refactor production code; often unintended side effects are introduced. This makes it difficult for management to approve big refactors without added functionality. However, with the right tools (some of which are discussed in this book), you can minimize the chances of negative side effects and improve the quality of the codebase.

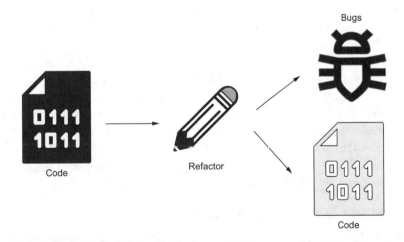

Figure 1.3 Clean code is like a washing machine for your code. It takes your dirty laundry (your code), adds soap and water (clean code principles), and separates the dirt from the clothes (separates the bugs from the code). What it leaves you with are clothes (code) with less dirt (bugs) than you started with.

This book contains sidebars with information on clean code topics. If the sidebars are clean code related, I denote them as such and explain both the concepts and how to apply them to the real world. Appendix B contains a clean code checklist. You can use the checklist to determine whether you need to refactor existing code. The checklist serves as a reminder for some of the more forgettable (but still important) concepts.

1.4   *What you will learn in this book*

This book will teach you to write idiomatic and clean C# code. It does not teach the C# language, .NET 5, or programming from the ground up. We follow a pratical approach: a business scenario in which we refactor an old API to be more clean and secure. Along the way, you'll learn many things. A few highlights follow:

- Taking an old codebase and refactoring it for security, performance, and cleanliness
- Writing self-documenting code that can pass any code review
- Using test-driven development to write unit tests alongside your implementation code
- Safely connecting to a cloud database through Entity Framework Core
- Introducing clean code principles into an existing codebase
- Reading Common Intermediate Language and explaining the C# compilation process

So, what do you need to know to get the most out of this book? The expectation is that you understand the basic principles of object-oriented programming (inheritance, encapsulation, abstraction, and polymorphism) and are familiar with another programming language that supports developing code through an object-oriented approach (be it C++, Go, Python, or Java).

After reading this book, you'll write clean, secure, testable C# code that follows good object-oriented design principles. Additionally, you'll be ready to further deepen your knowledge in C# through advanced resources. Some suggested readings for after this book are Jon Skeet's *C# in Depth*, 4th edition (Manning, 2019), Jeffrey Richter's *CLR via C#*, 4th edition (Microsoft Press, 2012), Bill Wagner's *Effective C#*, 2nd edition (Microsoft Press, 2016), Dustin Metzgar's *.NET Core in Action* (Manning, 2018), John Smith's *Entity Framework Core in Action*, 2nd edition (Manning, 2021), and Andrew Lock's *ASP.NET Core in Action*, 2nd edition (Manning, 2021).

1.5   *What you will not learn in this book*

This book aims to fill the gap between beginner and advanced C# resources. With that goal come some consequences regarding what assumptions I make about your understanding of C# and programming. As briefly discussed here, I expect you to have some professional programming experience and that you are comfortable with either the basics of C# or a different object-oriented programming language.

What do I mean by that? To get the most out of this book, you should understand object-oriented principles and be able to develop basic applications or APIs in your favorite programming language. As a result, this book does not teach you some of the following topics often present in a beginner programming book:

- The C# language itself. This is not a book along the lines of Code C# from Scratch. Instead, I teach you how to take your existing C# or object-oriented programming knowledge to the next level.
- Syntax around conditionals and branching statements not specific to C# (if, for, foreach, while, do-while, etc.).
- What polymorphism, encapsulation, and inheritance are (although we use these concepts regularly in this book).
- What a class is and how we model real-world objects through classes.
- What a variable is, or how to assign a value to one.

If you are new to programming, I highly recommend going through a book such as Jennifer Greene's *Head First C#*, 4th edition (O'Reilly, 2020) or Harold Abelson, Gerald Jay Sussman, and Julie Sussman's *Structure and Interpretation of Computer Programs*, 2nd edition (The MIT Press, 1996)[2] before reading this book.

This book also doesn't cover these more specialized ways to use C#:

- Microservice architecture. This book does not go into depth on what microservices are and how to use them. Microservice architecture is very much the trend and is useful in many use cases but is not related to C# or how you code like a pro. Three wonderful resources to learn more about microservices are Chris Richardson's *Microservices Patterns* (Manning, 2018), Prabath Siriwardena and Nuwan Dias's *Microservices Security in Action* (Manning, 2019), and Christian Horsdal Gammelgaard's *Microservices in .NET Core* (Manning, 2020).
- How to use C# with containerized environments such as Kubernetes and/or Docker. Although very practical and used in many enterprise development environments, knowing how to use Kubernetes or Docker does not guarantee you can "code like a pro" in C#. To learn more about these technologies, see Marko Lukša's *Kubernetes in Action*, 2nd edition (Manning, 2021), Elton Stoneman's *Learn Docker in a Month of Lunches* (Manning, 2020), and Ashley Davis's *Bootstrapping Microservices with Docker, Kubernetes, and Terraform* (Manning, 2021).
- Concurrency with C# beyond multithreading and locks (discussed inchapter 6). We often find this topic in highly threaded and performance-critical scenarios. Most developers don't work with such code much. If you do find yourself in that position, an excellent resource to learn more about concurrent programming in C# is Joe Duffy's *Concurrent Programming on Windows* (Addison-Wesley, 2008).
- The deep internal details of either the CLR or the .NET Framework themselves. Although the CLR and .NET 5 are interesting, knowing every little detail about them is of little practical use for most developers. This book covers the CLR and .NET Framework in some detail but stops where things get unpractical or unwieldy. The "bible" for the CLR and .NET Framework is Jeffrey Richter's *CLR via C#*, 4th edition (Microsoft Press, 2012).

---

[2] Available for free from The MIT Press at https://mitpress.mit.edu/sites/default/files/sicp/index.html.

You have two ways to read this book. The recommended way is to read the entire book, front to back and in order. If you are interested only in refactoring and best practices, you can just read parts 3 through 6.

Summary

- This book doesn't cover "Programming 101." It assumes knowledge of object-oriented programming. This allows us to focus on practical concepts.
- C# and .NET 5 shine at scalable enterprise development with a focus on stability and maintainability. This makes C# and .NET a perfect platform of choice for both companies and individual developers.
- C# and .NET 5 do not shine at operating system development, RTOS-embedded development, or numerical computing (or analysis). For those tasks, C and MATLAB fit better.

.NET and how it compiles

2

This chapter covers

- Compiling C# to native code
- Reading and understanding Intermediate Language

In 2020, Microsoft released .NET 5, an all-encompassing software development platform. Before that, in the late 1990s and early 2000s, Microsoft created the .NET Framework, which was the precursor to .NET 5. The original use case for the .NET Framework was developing enterprise Windows applications. In fact, we'll use the .NET Framework to examine exactly such a codebase in chapters 3 and 4. The .NET Framework ties together a large collection of libraries. Although the .NET Framework and C# are frequently used together, we do encounter use cases for the .NET Framework without C# (most notably, using a different .NET language). The two most important pillars of the .NET Framework are the Framework Class Library (FCL; a humongous class library that is the backbone of the .NET Framework) and the Common Language Runtime (CLR; the runtime environment of .NET that contains the JIT compiler, garbage collector, primitive data types, and more). In other words, the FCL contains all the libraries you are likely to use, and the CLR executes the code. Later on, Microsoft introduced .NET Core, aimed at multiplatform development. See figure 2.1 for where this chapter falls in the book's scheme.

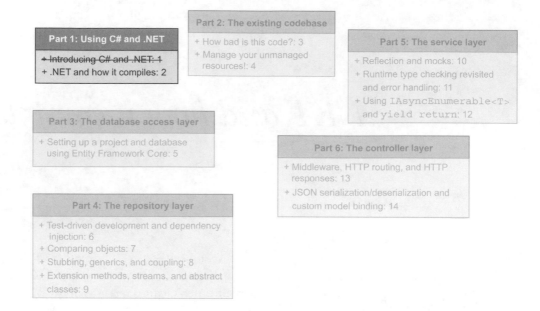

Figure 2.1   So far, you've learned about what to expect in this book. In this chapter, we'll dive into what .NET and its flavors are. By discussing the .NET ecosystem, we'll gain a baseline understanding that will serve us well in the rest of the book.

In this chapter, we'll discuss a couple of features of .NET 5 and contrast them against implementations (and sometimes the lack thereof) in other platforms such as Java, Python, and Go. After that, we'll learn about the C# compilation process by showing how a C# method is translated from C# to Common Intermediate Language (CIL) to native code. These fundamental building blocks allow us to have a solid foundation in our knowledge of the C# language and the .NET ecosystem. If you are already familiar with C# and .NET, this chapter is bound to have some repetition for you. If nothing else, I suggest you read through section 2.3. The discussion on the C# compilation process is deeper than what you find in most resources and is assumed knowledge in some advanced C# resources. To test your knowledge of the respective topics, sections 2.2 and 2.3 have exercises for you to try.

2.1   *What is the .NET Framework?*

In the beginning . . . there was the .NET Framework—the old-school way of using .NET. The .NET Framework was introduced in the early 2000s by Microsoft. Developers could use C# with it to write enterprise desktop applications. Because Microsoft had an intrinsic interest in targeting Windows, the .NET Framework works only on Windows and relies on many Windows APIs to perform graphic operations. If you work on any desktop application written in C# before late 2020 (and the introduction of .NET 5), I guarantee you it was written using .NET Framework.

The .NET Framework has gone through various iterations over time, but the most recent release (July 2019) is 4.8.0. There will be no further releases of the .NET Framework because it's been replaced with .NET 5, but its many legacy applications will live on. A lot of the material covered in this book applies to .NET Framework. In fact, we'll see a .NET Framework application in chapters 3 and 4.

2.2 What is .NET 5?

In this section, we'll talk about what .NET 5 is and why it exists. Since 2016, .NET has existed as two major streams: .NET Framework and .NET Core. The new .NET 5 combines these two streams (as well as different auxiliary streams such as Xamarin and Unity), as shown in figure 2.2. In effect, .NET 5 is a rebranding of .NET Core as it forms the basis for a new .NET. We should therefore see .NET 5 as not just another iteration of the .NET Framework or .NET Core but rather as a reboot and merger of previous technologies.

Housing all .NET technologies under one umbrella gives you access to all the tools and use cases you want. You can develop enterprise software, websites, video games, Internet of Things (IoT), embedded applications running on Windows/macOS/Linux, ARM processors (ARM32/64), machine learning services (ML.NET), applications, cloud services, and mobile apps, all throughout the same framework. And because the .NET Framework adheres to the .NET Standard, all existing codebases and libraries should be compatible with .NET 5 (as long as .NET 5 supports the underlying packages and features used by the codebase).

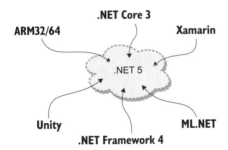

Figure 2.2   .NET 5 merges .NET Framework 4 with ARM32/64, Xamarin, .NET Core 3, Unity, and ML.NET. This allows us to use all those .NET variations under one umbrella: .NET 5.

.NET 5, just like the .NET Framework and .NET Core, is an implementation of the .NET Standard—a specification that has been used to develop a variety of implementations of .NET: .NET 5, .NET Framework, .NET Core, Mono (the cross-platform technology that .NET Core is built on), Unity (video game development), and Xamarin (iOS and Android development). These have different use cases but are inherently very similar. Developing an implementation against the .NET Standard means that code sharing between implementations is as seamless as possible.

The .NET Standard contains information on what APIs are available for use when interacting with the CLR (the runtime on which C# depends). Before the .NET

Standard, we had no real way of making sure that our code or library would work across .NET implementations, besides using Portable Class Libraries (PCL). PCLs are libraries that can be shared among projects but can target only a specific version of a .NET implementation (or "profile"). Today we call these PCLs "profile-based PCLs." Libraries targeting a .NET implementation adhering to the .NET Standard are also PCLs, but instead of targeting a specific implementation, they target a version of the .NET Standard. To differentiate between profile-based PCLs, we call these ".NET Standard-based PCLs." The .NET Standard encapsulates a lot of the Windows APIs used by libraries written in the pre–.NET Standard era (and, therefore, profile-based PCLs). As a result, we can use those libraries in any .NET Standard implementation of .NET without a problem. The first version of the .NET Framework to implement the .NET Standard was 4.5.

In keeping with Microsoft's push for open source software, .NET 5 and all its related repositories are open source and available on GitHub (https://github.com/dotnet). For more information on new features slated to be included in new versions of .NET, see the CoreFX roadmap at https://github.com/dotnet/corefx/milestones. You can access the .NET Standard at https://github.com/dotnet/standard.

Exercises

EXERCISE 2.1

Which one of the following operating systems is not supported by .NET 5?

- a Windows
- b macOS
- c Linux
- d AmigaOS

EXERCISE 2.2

What does the term "CLR" stand for?

- a Creative License Resources
- b Class Library Reference
- c Common Language Runtime

EXERCISE 2.3

Fill in the blanks: The .NET Standard is a(n) _____, which dictates implementation details for all .NET platforms to enable code sharing.

- a implementation
- b precursor
- c tool
- d specification

2.3   *How CLI-compliant languages are compiled*

In this section, you'll get an in-depth look at how C# (and other Common Language Infrastructure–compliant languages; see section 2.3.2) compiles. Knowing the entire compilation story prepares you to take advantage of all of C#'s features while understanding some of the pitfalls related to memory and execution. The C# compilation process knows three states (C#, Intermediate Language, and native code) and two stages, as shown in figure 2.3: going from C# to Common Intermediate Language and going from Intermediate Language to native code.

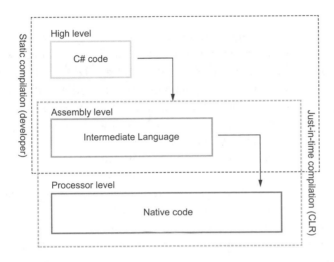

Figure 2.3   **The complete C# compilation process. It goes from C# code to Common Intermediate Language to native code. Understanding the compilation process gives us knowledge about some of the internal choices made around C# and .NET.**

NOTE   Native code is sometimes referred to as *machine code.*

By looking at what it takes to go from one step to the other and follow a method as the compiler and CLR compile the high-level C# code down to runnable native code, we gain an understanding of the complex machine that is C# and .NET 5. A good understanding of this process is often a resource gap found in beginner resources, but advanced resources require you to understand this.

We use a combination of static compilation and JIT compilation to compile C# to native code as follows:

1   After a developer writes the C# code, they compile their code. This results in Common Intermediate Language stored within Portable Executable (PE for 32 bit, PE+ for 64 bit) files such as .exe and .dll files for Windows. These files are distributed or deployed to users.

2   When we launch a .NET program, the operating system invokes the Common Language Runtime. The Common Language Runtime JIT compiles the CIL to the native code appropriate for the platform it is running on. This allows CLI-compliant languages to run on a lot of platforms and compiler types. However,

it would be amiss not to mention the major negative implication of using a virtual machine and JIT compiler to run your code: performance.

A statically compiled program has a leg up at execution time because you don't need to wait on a runtime to compile the code.

> **DEFINITION**   Static and JIT compilation are two commonly used ways of compiling code. C# uses a combination of static compilation and JIT compilation. This entails that the code is compiled down to bytecode at the last possible moment. Static compilation compiles all the source code ahead of time.

2.3.1   Step 1: C# code (high-level)

The first time I encountered the Pythagorean theorem was in 2008. I was in the Dutch version of high school and saw in the mathematics textbook that we would cover the Pythagorean theorem that year. A couple of days later, late at night, I was in the car with my father. We had been driving for a while, so the conversation had reached a natural slow point. In a completely out-of-character moment, I asked him, "What is the Pythagorean theorem?" The question clearly took him aback because I had shown little academic interest, especially in mathematics, at that point in time. For the next ten minutes, he attempted to explain to me, somebody with the mathematical abilities of a grapefruit, what the Pythagorean theorem was. I was surprised I actually understood what he was talking about, and now, years later, it has proven to be an excellent resource to show you the first step in the C# compilation process.

In this section, we'll look at the first step in the C# compilation process: compiling C# code, as shown in figure 2.4. The program we'll follow through the compilation process is the Pythagorean theorem. The reason for using a program representing the Pythagorean theorem to teach you that the C# compilation process is straightforward: we can condense the Pythagorean theorem to a couple of lines of code that are understandable with a high school level of mathematical knowledge. This lets us focus on the compilation story instead of on implementation details.

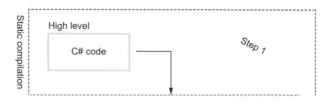

Figure 2.4   The C# compilation process, step 1: C# code. This is the static compilation phase.

> **NOTE**   If a quick refresher is in order, the Pythagorean theorem states that $a^2 + b^2 = c^2$. We commonly apply the Pythagorean theorem to discovering the length of a right-angled triangle's hypotenuse by taking the square root of the resulting value, which is the sum of the squared lengths of the two sides adjacent to the right-angled triangle.

We'll start by writing a simple method that proves the Pythagorean theorem when given two arguments, as shown in the next listing.

Listing 2.1 Pythagorean theorem (high level)

```
public double Pythagoras(double sideLengthA, double sideLengthB) {
    double squaredLength = sideLengthA * sideLengthA + sideLengthB * sideLengthB;
    return squaredLength;
}
```

We declare a method with a public access modifier, returning a floating-point number, called Pythagoras, that expects two floating-point (double) arguments: sideLengthA and sideLengthB.

We perform the Pythagorean theorem and assign the result to a variable called squaredLength.

If we run this code and give it the arguments of [3, 8], we see that the result is 73, which is correct. Alternatively, because we are using 64-bit floating-point numbers (doubles), we can also test argument sets like. The result is 12037.7057.

Access modifiers, assemblies, and namespaces

C# knows six access modifiers (from most open to most restrictive): public, protected internal, internal, protected, protected private, and private. The two you use the most in daily life are public and private. *Public* signifies availability across all classes and projects (this is the concept of "exported" in some languages; unlike some of those programming languages, the capitalization of a method name does not matter when it comes to access modifiers in C#), and *private* means visible only from the current class.

The other four (internal, protected, protected internal, and private protected) are used less often but good to know. *Internal* gives access to all classes in its own assembly, and *protected* limits access to only classes that derive from the original class. That leaves *internal protected*. This access modifier is a combination of the internal and protected access modifiers. It grants access to derived classes and its own assembly. *Private protected* gives access within its own assembly but only to the code in the same class or in a derived class.

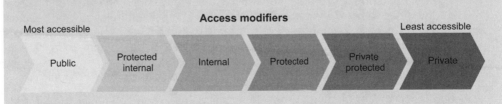

C# access modifiers from open to restricted. Using the correct access modifier helps with encapsulating our data and protecting our classes.

Now we compile the code. Let us assume that the method in listing 2.1 is part of a class called `HelloPythagoras`, which is part of a project and solution also called `HelloPythagoras`. To compile a .NET 5 (or .NET Framework/.NET Core solution) to

Intermediate Language stored in a PE/PE+ file, you can either use the build or compiler button in your IDE or run the following command in your command line:

```
dotnet build [solution file path]
```

A solution file ends with the file extension .sln. The command to create our solution follows:

```
dotnet build HelloPythagoras.sln
```

After we run the command, the compiler launches. First, the compiler restores all the required dependency packages through the NuGet package manager. Then the command-line tool compiles the project and stores the output in a new folder called bin. Within the bin folder are two potential options for further folders, debug and release, depending on the mode we set the compiler to (you can define your own modes if you want to). By default, the compiler compiles in debug mode. Debug mode contains all the debug information (stored in .pdb files) that you need to step through an application with breakpoints.

To compile in release mode through the command line, append the `--Configuration release` flag to the command. Alternatively, in Visual Studio, select debug or release mode from the drop-down list. This is the easiest, quickest, and the likeliest way you will compile your code.

Debug and release build modes

In daily life, the practical difference between the debug and release modes are performance and security. By including references to the .pdb files in the debug build's output code, the runtime has to iterate over more code to do the same logic than you would in a release mode where those references are not present. As a result, the Intermediate Language required to model that code is larger and takes longer to compile when compared to release mode.

Additionally, if you include debugging information, somebody with malicious intent could potentially use that information to their advantage and have an easier window into your codebase. This is not to say that compiling in release mode removes any need for good security practices. Intermediate Language can easily be decompiled (whether originally compiled in debug or release mode) to something similar to the original source code. If you want to appropriately protect your source code, consider looking into obfuscators (Dotfuscator, .NET Reactor) and threat models.

A good rule of thumb is to develop using debug mode and test with both debug and release modes. Often this takes the form of testing locally under debug mode and doing user acceptance testing in a dedicated environment with a release build. Because the code between modes is slightly different, you may find bugs in the release mode that you don't find in the debug mode. You do not want to be in a situation where you tested only the debug build and find a blocking bug in the release build right before your deadline.

At this point, the C# high-level code is compiled into an executable file containing the Intermediate Language code.

2.3.2 *Step 2: Common Intermediate Language (assembly level)*

From a day-to-day perspective, your job is done. The code is in an executable form, and you can wrap up your ticket or user story. From a technological perspective, the journey is just getting started. The C# code is statically compiled down to Common Intermediate Language, as shown in figure 2.5, but IL cannot be run by the operating system.

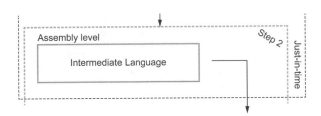

Figure 2.5 The C# compilation process, step 2: Intermediate Language. Here we go from static to just-in-time compilation.

But how do you get from IL to native code? The missing piece is the Common Language Runtime (CLR). This part of .NET 5 translates Common Intermediate Language to native code. It is the "runtime" of .NET. We can compare the CLR to the Java Virtual Machine (JVM). The CLR has been part of .NET since the very beginning. It is also good to note that with the movement toward .NET Core and .NET 5, a new implementation of the CLR is taking the place of the old CLR: CoreCLR. The explanations in this book regarding the CLR are valid for both the traditional CLR and CoreCLR, and the term CLR is used for both the regular Common Language Runtime and CoreCLR.

Any code that is written using an implementation of a technical standard called Common Language Infrastructure (CLI), such as .NET 5, can be compiled down to Common Intermediate Language. The CLI describes the infrastructure behind .NET, whose specific flavors are implementations of the CLI themselves, and gives languages a basis around which to form their type system. Because the CLR can take any piece of Intermediate Language (IL), and the .NET compiler can generate this IL from any CLI-compliant language, we can have IL code generated from mixed-source code. C#, Visual Basic, and F# are the most common .NET programming languages, but a bunch more are also available. See table 2.1 for a roundup of these acronyms.

Until 2017, Microsoft also supported J#, a CLI-compliant implementation of Java. Theoretically, you could download the compatible compiler and use J#, but you would miss out on some modern Java features in exchange for developing on the .NET platform.

NOTE   The CLR is an immensely complicated piece of software. If you want to know more about the (traditional, Windows-based) CLR, see Jeffrey Richter's *CLR via C#* (4th edition; Microsoft Press, 2012).

Because the compiler embeds IL in files, we need to use a disassembler to view the CIL. All .NET flavors come with Microsoft's own dissembler called ILDASM (Intermediate Language Disassembler). To use ILDASM, we need to run the Developer Command Prompt for Visual Studio, which is installed alongside Visual Studio. This is a command-prompt environment that gives us access to .NET tools. Be aware that ILDASM is available only for Windows.

Table 2.1   .NET acronyms summarized

Acronym	Expansion	Description
CLR	Common Language Runtime	The .NET virtual machine runtime. The CLR manages critical things like code execution, garbage collection, threads, and memory allocations.
CLI	Common Language Infrastructure	A specification describing what executable code in the .NET ecosystem looks like and how it should be executed.
CIL	Common Intermediate Language	A language that can be JIT compiled by the CLR to execute CLI-compliant code. This is what C# compiles down to in the first compilation stage.
IL	Intermediate Language	Another term for CIL.
MSIL	Microsoft Intermediate Language	Another term for CIL.

Once in the developer command prompt, we can invoke ILDASM on our compiled file and specify an output file as follows:

```
>\ ildasm HelloPythagoras.dll /output:HelloPythagoras.il
```

If we do not specify an output file, the command-line tool launches the GUI for ILDASM. In there, you can also view the IL code of the disassembled executable. The output file can be of whatever file extension you want, because it is a simple binary text file. Note that in the .NET Framework, ILDASM operates against the .exe file, not the .dll. .NET 5 and .NET Core use the .dll file.

When we open the HelloPythagoras.il file in a text editor or look at the ILDASM GUI, a file filled with mysterious code opens. This is the IL code. We focus on the IL for the Pythagoras method (if compiled in debug mode), as shown next.

Listing 2.2   Pythagorean theorem (Common Intermediate Language)

```
.method public hidebysig static float64
  Pythagoras(float64 sideLengthA,
            float64 sideLengthB) cil managed {
```

```
.maxstack 3
.locals init ([0] float64 squaredLength,
              [1] float64 V_1)
IL_0000:    nop
IL_0001:    ldarg.0
IL_0002:    ldarg.0
IL_0003:    mul
IL_0004:    ldarg.1
IL_0005:    ldarg.1
IL_0006:    mul
IL_0007:    add
IL_0008:    stloc.0
IL_0009:    ldloc.0
IL_000a:    stloc.1
IL_000b:    br.s        IL_000d
IL_000c:    ldloc.1
IL_000e:    ret
}
```

If you have ever worked in or seen assembly-level programming, you might notice some similarities. Common Intermediate Language is definitely harder to read and more "close to the metal" than regular C# code, but it is not as mysterious as it might look. By stepping through the IL line by line, you see that this is just a different syntax for programming concepts you already know. The IL code generated by the compiler on your machine may look slightly different (especially the numbers used with the `ldarg` opcode), but the functionality and types of opcodes should be the same.

The very first thing we see is the method declaration, shown next:

```
.method private hidebysig static float64
       Pythagoras(float64 sideLengthA,
                  float64 sideLengthB) cil managed
```

We can easily see that the method is private, static, and returns a 64-bit floating-point number (known as a *double* in C#). We can also see that the method is named Pythagoras and takes in two arguments called sideLengthA and sideLengthB, both 64-bit floating-point numbers. The two terms that seem odd are hidebysig and cil managed.

First, the term hidebysig tells us that the Pythagoras method hides every other method with the same method signature. When omitted, the method hides all methods with the same name (not limited to signature match). Second, cil managed means that this code is Common Intermediate Language and that we are running in managed mode. The other side of the coin would be unmanaged. This refers to whether the CLR can execute the method, potentially has manual memory handling, and has all the metadata that the CLR requires. By default, all your code runs in managed mode unless you explicitly tell it not to by enabling the compiler "unsafe" flag and designating code as "unsafe."

Moving on to the method itself, we can split the method into two parts: the setup (constructor) and execution (the logic). First, let's look at the constructor, shown next:

```
.maxstack 3
  .locals init ([0] float64 squaredLength,
                [1] float64 V_1)
```

There are some unfamiliar terms here. To start, `.maxstack 3` tells us that the maximum allowed elements on the memory stack during execution is three. The static compiler automatically generates this number and tells the CLR JIT compiler how many elements to reserve for the method. This part of the method code is important—imagine not being able to tell the CLR how much memory we need. It may decide to reserve all available stack space on the system, or not reserve any at all. Either scenario would be catastrophic.

Next up is

```
.locals init (…)
```

When we declare a variable in a CLI-compliant programming language, the compiler assigns the variable a scope and initializes the variable's value to a default value at compile time. The `locals` keyword tells us the scope of the variables declared in this code block are local in scope (scoped to the method, not the class), whereas `init` means that we are initializing the declared variables to their default values. The compiler assigns it to `null` or a zeroed-out value, depending on whether the variable is a reference or value type.

Expanding the `.locals init (…)` code block reveals the variables we are declaring and initializing as follows:

```
.locals init (
  [0] float64 squaredLength,
  [1] float64 V_1
```

The IL declares two local variables and initializes them to zero values: `squaredLength` and `V_1`.

Now, you might say, hang on a second! We only declared one local variable in our C# code: `squaredLength`. What is this `V_1` business? Have a look at the following C# code again:

```
public double Pythagoras(double sideLengthA, double sideLengthB) {
  double squaredLength =
➡ sideLengthA * sidelengthA + sideLengthB * sideLengthB;
  return squaredLength;
}
```

We explicitly declared only one local variable. However, we are returning `squaredLength` by value rather than by reference. This means that under the hood, a new variable is declared, initialized, and assigned the value of `squaredLength`. This is `V_1`.

To summarize, we looked at the method signature and the setup. Now we can dive into the weeds of the logic. Let's also split the following part up into two sections—the evaluation of the Pythagorean theorem and the returning of the resulting value:

```
IL_0000:      nop
IL_0001:      ldarg.0
IL_0002:      ldarg.0
IL_0003:      mul
IL_0004:      ldarg.1
IL_0005:      ldarg.1
IL_0006:      mul
IL_0007:      add
IL_0008:      stloc.0
```

To start, we see an operation (we also call these operations *opcodes*) called nop. This is also called the "Do Nothing Operation" or "No Operation" because, on its own, a nop operation does nothing. They are widely used in IL and assembly code to enable breakpoint debugging. Along with the PDB file that is generated in debug builds, the CLR can inject instructions to stop program execution at a nop operation. This allows us to "step through" code at runtime.

Next up, we look at the evaluation of the Pythagorean theorem itself, as follows:

```
    double squaredLength =
➡ sideLengthA * sideLengthA + sideLengthB * sideLengthB;
```

The following two operations are a doubleheader: two ldarg.0 operations. The first operation (IL_0001) loads the first sideLengthA occurrence onto the stack. The second operation (IL_0002) loads the second sideLengthA occurrence onto the stack as well.

After we have loaded the first mathematical evaluation's arguments onto the stack, the IL code calls the following multiplication operation:

```
IL_0003:      mul
```

This results in the two arguments loaded during IL_0001 and IL_0002 being multiplied and stored into a new element on the stack. The garbage collector now purges the previous (now unused) stack elements from the stack.

We repeat this process for the squaring of the sideLengthB arguments as follows:

```
IL_0004:      ldarg.1
IL_0005:      ldarg.1
IL_0006:      mul
```

So now we have elements in the stack containing the values of $sideLengthA^2$ and $sideLengthB^2$. To fulfill the Pythagorean theorem, and our code, we have to add these two values and store them in squaredLength. This is done in IL_0007 and IL_0008, as shown next:

```
IL_0007:      add
IL_0008:      stloc.0
```

Similar to the `mul` operations (`IL_0003` and `IL_0006`), the `add` operation (`IL_0007`) evaluates the addition of the previously stored arguments and places the resulting value into an element on the stack. The IL takes this element and stores it into the `squaredLength` variable we initialized in the setup (`[0] float64 squaredLength`) through the `stloc.0` command (`IL_0008`). The `stloc.0` operation pops a value from the stack and stores it at the variable on index 0.

We have now fully evaluated and stored the Pythagorean theorem result into a variable. All that remains is to return the value from the method, as shown next, just like we promised in our original method signature:

```
IL_0009:      ldloc.0
IL_000a:      stloc.1
IL_000b:      br.s         IL_000d
IL_000c:      ldloc.1
IL_000e:      ret
```

First, we load the value of the variable at location 0 into memory (`IL_0009`). In the previous segment, we ended with storing the value of the Pythagorean theorem into the variable at location 0, so that must be `squaredLength`. But, as mentioned earlier, we are passing the variable by value, not by reference, so we create a copy of `squared-Length` to return out of the method with. Luckily, we declared and initialized a variable just for this purpose at index 1: `V_1` (`[1] float64 V_1`). We store the value into index 1 through the `stloc.1` operation (`IL_000a`).

Next up, we see another strange operation: `br.s IL_000d` (`IL_000b`). This is a branching operator that signifies that the return value is calculated and stored away for returning. The IL uses a branching operator for debugging purposes. A branching operator is similar to a `nop` operation. All different branches of your code (conditionals with other return values) jump to the `br.s` operator when return is called. The `br.s` operator takes up two bytes and, therefore, has two IL locations (`IL_000b` and `IL_000d`); one opcode usually takes up one byte. Because the `br.s` operator has a size of two bytes, `IL_000c` (`ldloc.1`) is wrapped in the branching operator. This allows the debugger to stop executing at the loading of the stored return value and manipulate it, if necessary.

Finally, we are ready to return out of the method through `IL_000c` and `IL_000e` as follows:

```
IL_000c:      ldloc.1
IL_000e:      ret
```

The `ldloc.1` (`IL_000c`) operation loads the previously stored return value. This is followed by the `ret` operator, which takes the value we loaded at `IL_000c` and returns it from the method. See the entire code sample in listing 2.3.

That brings us to the end of the section. Hopefully, you are now a bit more comfortable with the nitty-gritty parts of the static compilation step of C# and .NET.

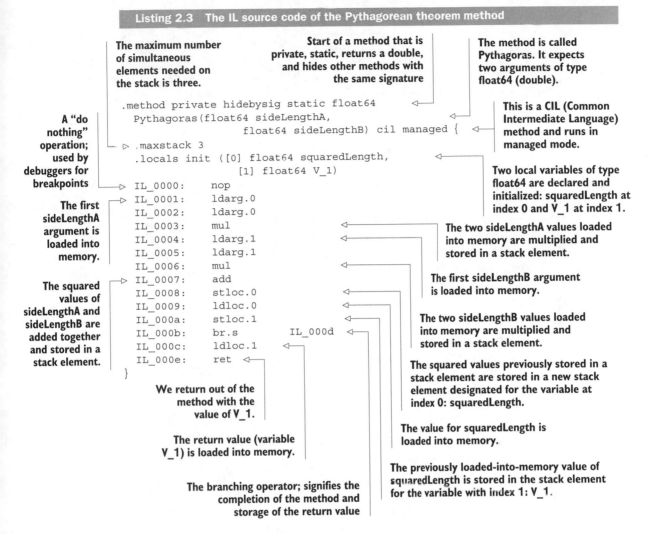

Listing 2.3   The IL source code of the Pythagorean theorem method

The maximum number of simultaneous elements needed on the stack is three.

Start of a method that is private, static, returns a double, and hides other methods with the same signature

The method is called Pythagoras. It expects two arguments of type float64 (double).

```
.method private hidebysig static float64
    Pythagoras(float64 sideLengthA,
                float64 sideLengthB) cil managed {
    .maxstack 3
    .locals init ([0] float64 squaredLength,
                  [1] float64 V_1)
    IL_0000:    nop
    IL_0001:    ldarg.0
    IL_0002:    ldarg.0
    IL_0003:    mul
    IL_0004:    ldarg.1
    IL_0005:    ldarg.1
    IL_0006:    mul
    IL_0007:    add
    IL_0008:    stloc.0
    IL_0009:    ldloc.0
    IL_000a:    stloc.1
    IL_000b:    br.s        IL_000d
    IL_000c:    ldloc.1
    IL_000e:    ret
}
```

This is a CIL (Common Intermediate Language) method and runs in managed mode.

A "do nothing" operation; used by debuggers for breakpoints

The first sideLengthA argument is loaded into memory.

The squared values of sideLengthA and sideLengthB are added together and stored in a stack element.

Two local variables of type float64 are declared and initialized: squaredLength at index 0 and V_1 at index 1.

The two sideLengthA values loaded into memory are multiplied and stored in a stack element.

The first sideLengthB argument is loaded into memory.

The two sideLengthB values loaded into memory are multiplied and stored in a stack element.

The squared values previously stored in a stack element are stored in a new stack element designated for the variable at index 0: squaredLength.

The value for squaredLength is loaded into memory.

The previously loaded-into-memory value of squaredLength is stored in the stack element for the variable with index 1: V_1.

We return out of the method with the value of V_1.

The return value (variable V_1) is loaded into memory.

The branching operator; signifies the completion of the method and storage of the return value

2.3.3   Step 3: Native code (processor level)

The last step in the compilation process is the conversion from Common Intermediate Language to native code, shown in figure 2.6, which the processor can actually run. Until now, the code has been statically compiled, but that changes here. When .NET 5 executes an application, the CLR launches and scans the executable files for the IL code. Then, the CLR invokes the JIT compiler to convert the IL into native code as it runs. Native code is the lowest level of code that is (somewhat) human-readable. A processor can execute this code directly because of the inclusion of predefined operations (opcodes), similar to how Common Intermediate Language includes the IL operation codes.

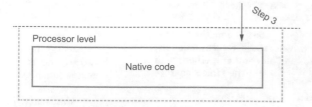

Figure 2.6   The C# compilation process, step 3: native code. This is the JIT phase of the process.

JIT compiling our code comes at a performance cost, but also means that we can execute .NET-based code on any platform supported by the CLR and a compiler. We can see this in practice with .NET Core and the new CoreCLR. The CoreCLR can JIT-compile Intermediate Language to Windows, macOS, and Linux, as shown in figure 2.7.

Because of the JIT nature of this compilation step, viewing the actual native code is a bit tricky. The only way to view native code generated from your Intermediate Language would be to use a command-line tool called ngen, which comes preinstalled with .NET 5. This tool allows you to generate so-called native images containing native code from the Common Intermediate Language stored in a PE file ahead of time. The CLR stores native code output in a subfolder of %SystemRoot%/Assembly/ NativeAssembly (only available on Windows). Be aware, however, that you cannot use the regular file explorer to navigate here, nor would the resulting output be legible. After running ngen, the CLR sees that the IL is already compiled (statically) to native code and executes based on that. This comes with the expected performance boost; however, the native code and IL code can get out of sync when a new build is released and have unexpected side effects if the CLR decides to use the older statically compiled native image instead of recompiling the new, updated code.

Figure 2.7   CoreCLR can JIT-compile for targets such as Linux, Windows, and macOS. This allows for cross-platform execution of C# code.

In day-to-day operations, you likely don't touch IL all that much or are overly concerned about the IL-to-native-code compilation. However, understanding the compilation process is a fundamental block of knowledge because it sheds light on design decisions in .NET 5 that we'll encounter throughout the book.

Exercises

EXERCISE 2.4

What are the steps and order of the .NET compilation process?

- a .NET code -> Intermediate Language -> Native code
- b Intermediate Language -> .NET code -> Native code
- c .NET code -> Native code
- d Java -> JVM

EXERCISE 2.5

Fill in the blanks: A _____ compiler compiles the code right before it is needed, whereas code compiled ahead of time was done through a _____ compiler.

- a static
- b JIT
- c dynamic

EXERCISE 2.6

Where is Intermediate Language stored?

- a DOCX files
- b Text files
- c HTML files
- d Font files
- e Portable Executable files

EXERCISE 2.7

Fill in the blank: If we have to make a copy of a stack element to pass around a variable, that variable is a _____ type.

- a reference
- b pirate
- c value
- d nullable

EXERCISE 2.8

Fill in the blank: If we can manipulate a variable value through a pointer to an element on the heap, that variable is a _____ type.

- a reference
- b pirate
- c value
- d nullable

Summary

- .NET 5 consumes and rebrands .NET Core and .NET Framework (and other .NET implementations) and effectively becomes .NET Core 4 in all but name.
- .NET uses a combination of static and JIT ("just-in-time") compilation. This allows for faster execution when compared to a fully JIT language and cross-platform execution.
- The C# compilation process has three states of being: (1) C# code, (2) Intermediate Language code, and (3) native code.
- The C# compilation process has two steps: C# to Intermediate Language (static compilation) and Intermediate Language to native code (JIT compilation).
- Intermediate Language is stored in portable executable files (such as .exe and .dll on Windows). The CLR scans these files for the embedded IL and executes it, JIT compiling it to the appropriate native code.
- The Common Language Runtime is invoked on the launch of a .NET application and JIT compiles the Intermediate Language code to native code.
- A 64-bit floating-point number is of type "double" in C#.
- C# has six separate access modifiers: public, protected internal, internal, protected, protected private, and private. These are used to control access to your methods.
- The command line can compile C# through the `dotnet build [solution file path]` command. You can also compile through an IDE such as Visual Studio.
- The Common Language Infrastructure is a technical standard that provides a base for all languages targeting .NET. This allows us to use languages such as F# and VB.NET along with C#.
- Intermediate Language commands translate roughly to bytecode opcodes.

Part 2

The existing codebase

After reading part 1, you are familiar with C# and the various flavors of the .NET Framework. You know how C# is compiled and why you would (or would not) want to use it for your own projects. In this part, I'll introduce you to Flying Dutchman Airlines. This company acts as our business case throughout the rest of the book.

In the next two chapters, we'll work on an existing codebase and examine it in depth, taking stock of where we can make improvements and why.

How bad is this code?

3

This chapter covers
- HTTP routes, resources, and endpoints
- Auto-properties and init-only setters
- Configuring an ASP.NET service

In this chapter, we'll meet Flying Dutchman Airlines, who have hired us to refactor their legacy codebase. Flying Dutchman has told us their business needs and given us their requirements for the refactor. Their legacy application, which we'll examine in this (and the next) chapter, is a backend web service developed on the .NET Framework following the Model-View-Controller (MVC) pattern. The code has many readability and security issues, so don't be surprised if there are pieces of code in this chapter that you don't like. The point of this chapter is for us to determine where we can change the existing codebase. We'll look in-depth at the models, views, and configuration of the (messy) codebase in this chapter to prepare for refactoring the code in later chapters. Figure 3.1 shows where we are in the scheme of the book.

Flying Dutchman Airlines, whose logo is shown in figure 3.2, is a low-cost airline based in Groningen, the Netherlands. The airline serves 20 destinations, including London, Paris, Prague, and Milan. Established in 1977, the company has had its

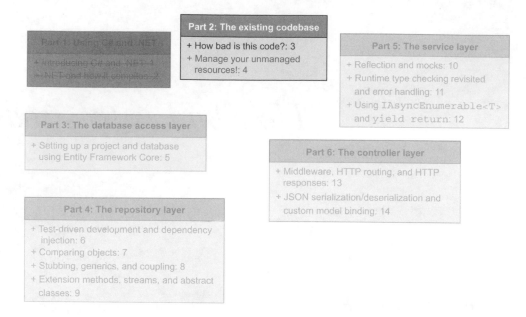

Figure 3.1   In this chapter, we'll start part 2: The existing codebase. We'll look at what requirements are laid out for us to address in the rest of the book and what models and views the existing codebase contains.

difficulties in the marketplace. Flying Dutchman Airlines markets itself as an "ultra-low-cost airline." Now that we are in the middle of the twenty-first century, management has decided it is time to bring the business into this century as well. This is where you come in. In this section, we'll meet our new boss and get the specifications for the product we are to create.

3.1   *Introducing Flying Dutchman Airlines*

It is the first day at your new job, and you pull up ten minutes early into the parking lot. Your button-down shirt is washed, steamed, ironed, and pressed. You are ready for your first day at work. Your arrival is heavily anticipated, and the first order of the day, after the obligatory HR paperwork and ID badge photos, is to meet with the CEO. You are the first in-house software engineer they have hired in a long time and expectations are high.

Flying Dutchman Airlines

Figure 3.2   The Flying Dutchman Airlines logo. Flying Dutchman Airlines is the company we are working for in this book.

The CEO strikes up a conversation and points you to a chair. He tells you that his name is Aljen van der Meulen and that he joined Flying Dutchman Airlines only recently, but he sees room for a lot of potential improvements at the airline, especially in the technology department. The Flying Dutchman Airlines website works fine, but there is no way for people to book a flight through a search aggregator. (An aggregator is a type of search engine that collects, or aggregates, information from specific sources. In this case, FlyTomorrow aggregates available flights for booking from airlines.)

As a result, Aljen signed a contract with the flight aggregator FlyTomorrow.com. FlyTomorrow is the most-visited airline-related website over the last year and has some specific requirements for airlines to abide by if they want to integrate with their search engine. The existing codebase for the airline's internal systems does have an API for searching and booking flights, but it is a big mess and needs thorough refactoring. Aljen slides over a piece of paper and motions for you to take a look. As shown in figure 3.3, it is the part of the contract between FlyTomorrow and Flying Dutchman Airlines that highlights the technological requirements needed to fulfill the contract.

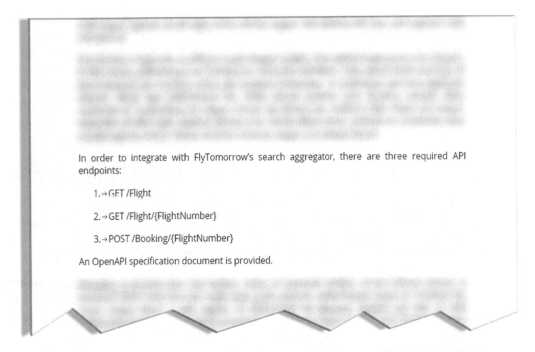

In order to integrate with FlyTomorrow's search aggregator, there are three required API endpoints:

1.→ GET /Flight

2.→ GET /Flight/{FlightNumber}

3.→ POST /Booking/{FlightNumber}

An OpenAPI specification document is provided.

Figure 3.3 Some of the API-related language in the contract between Flying Dutchman Airlines and FlyTomorrow. The contract contains information about the endpoints we need to implement to fulfill the requirements.

The two most important requirements are the presence of HTTP GET and HTTP POST endpoints in the current API. FlyTomorrow uses these to query for available flights (GET) and book them (POST). Furthermore, the API has to return error codes where appropriate.

NOTE If you are unfamiliar with HTTP actions such as POST and GET, or HTTP and web development in general, you should consider exploring those topics a bit further. A fine resource is Mozilla's documentation on HTTP request methods: https://developer.mozilla.org/en-US/docs/Web/HTTP/Methods.

3.2 *Pieces of the puzzle: Taking a look at our requirements*

George, the CTO, steps into the office. Not wasting time, he launches into a discussion on the codebase. The existing codebase is small but messy. Everything is written in a prehistoric version of C# (C# 3.0, to be precise), and the version of .NET Framework used is 4.5. The database runs on a locally hosted Microsoft SQL Server and is queried without an object-relational mapping (ORM) framework. George would love for the refactored version to run on .NET 5 and use the latest version of C#. Although we cannot change the database schema, we do have access to it. In fact, George has gone ahead and deployed it to Microsoft Azure.

3.2.1 *Object-relational mapping*

When you want to make changes to a database, you often use a database management tool such as SQL Server Management Studio (SSMS), MySQL Workbench, or Oracle SQL Developer. You can use these tools to write SQL queries and execute them against a database, as well as do things like set up stored procedures and perform backups. How can we query and interact with the database through the code at runtime? We can use a tool for object-relational mapping. ORM is a technique for mapping data from a database to a representation in your codebase and vice versa. In practical terms, imagine you have a database called BookShop. This database might have tables such as Books, Customers, and Orders. How would you model those in an object-oriented codebase? Likely by using models called Books, Customers, and Orders.

> **DEFINITION** An *entity* refers to a definition in a database that models the real world, whereas a *model* is a class representation of such a model (or any other real-world object). Just remember, entity is database, and model is code.

It is also a fair assumption that the developers have synchronized the fields to be the same in both the database and in the code. This does not mean that they are of the same type, however. Take Books, for example: when queried for a particular book, the database returns a record in Book as some sort of stream, often in JSON or binary. The model in the code is of the type Book, but we defined this class ourselves. The database does not know of the existence of this class. The database table and codebase model representations are not inherently compatible but do map to each other. This is an isomorphic relationship, something we'll explore further in section 3.3.3.

George and Aljen see the contract with FlyTomorrow as an opportunity to revamp the existing codebase because the company intends to grow its user base and increase its scalability. FlyTomorrow has even provided the airline with an OpenAPI specification to check the endpoints against (an endpoint is an entry point for a different service calling our service into our codebase). FlyTomorrow requires the following three endpoints:

- `GET /flight`
- `GET /flight/{flightNumber}`
- `POST /booking/{flightNumber}`

> **DEFINITION** OpenAPI (formerly Swagger) is an industry-standard way of specifying APIs. Within an OpenAPI specification, you often find the endpoints an API has and guidance on how to interact with an API.

3.2.2 *The GET /flight endpoint: Retrieving information on all flights*

In this section, we'll explore the first endpoint: `GET /flight`. The `/flight` endpoint accepts a `GET` request and returns information about all flights in the database. Figure 3.4 tells our endpoint requirements story.

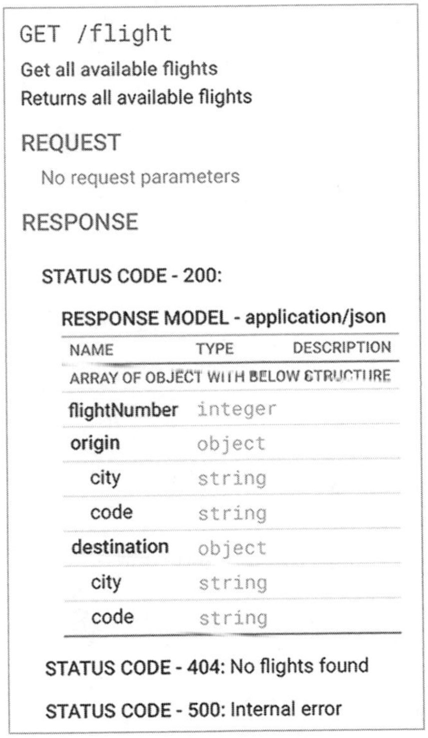

```
GET /flight

Get all available flights
Returns all available flights

REQUEST
    No request parameters

RESPONSE

    STATUS CODE - 200:

        RESPONSE MODEL - application/json

        NAME            TYPE        DESCRIPTION
        ARRAY OF OBJECT WITH BELOW STRUCTURE

        flightNumber    integer
        origin          object
            city        string
            code        string
        destination     object
            city        string
            code        string

    STATUS CODE - 404: No flights found

    STATUS CODE - 500: Internal error
```

Figure 3.4 A screenshot of a generated OpenAPI `GET /flight` endpoint specification. It accepts a `GET` response and can return an HTTP status of 200 (along with information on all available flights), 404, or 500.

According to the OpenAPI specification from FlyTomorrow, the `GET /flight` endpoint should return a list of all available flights. The flight data should contain the flight number and two pieces of airport metadata. The airport model contains the city the airport serves and the International Air Transport Association (IATA) airport code. When no flights are found (meaning no flights are in the database), we should return an HTTP code of 404 (not found). If an error occurred, whatever it may be, the return value should be an HTTP code 500 (internal server error) response.

3.2.3   The GET /flight/{flightNumber} endpoint: Getting specific flight information

The second endpoint that FlyTomorrow requires is `GET /flight/{flightNumber}`. In figure 3.5, the OpenAPI specification shows us the expected input and outputs of the endpoint.

Figure 3.5   A screenshot of a generated OpenAPI specification for the `GET /flight/{flightNumber}` endpoint. This endpoint returns detailed information about a specific flight in the database when given a flight number.

This endpoint has a path parameter of {flightNumber}, specifying which flight's details are returned to the caller.

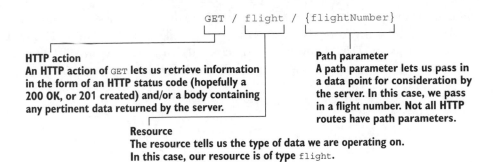

HTTP action
An HTTP action of GET lets us retrieve information in the form of an HTTP status code (hopefully a 200 OK, or 201 created) and/or a body containing any pertinent data returned by the server.

Path parameter
A path parameter lets us pass in a data point for consideration by the server. In this case, we pass in a flight number. Not all HTTP routes have path parameters.

Resource
The resource tells us the type of data we are operating on. In this case, our resource is of type flight.

The API should return an HTTP code 400 (bad request) if an invalid flight number is provided in the path. An invalid flight number could be a negative number or a string that contains only letters. If a requested flight number does not map to a flight in the database, then an HTTP code 404 (not found) is returned.

3.2.4 The POST /booking/{flightNumber} endpoint: Booking a flight

The last required endpoint is a POST endpoint with the path /booking/{flightNumber}, as shown in figure 3.6.

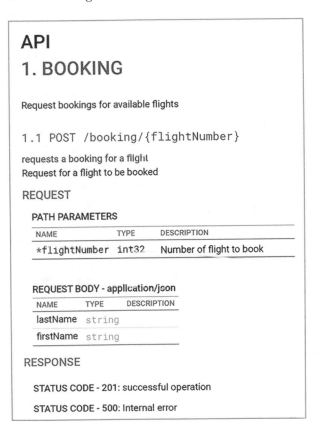

Figure 3.6 The OpenAPI specification for the POST /booking/{flightNumber} endpoint. The endpoint requires us to pass in a first and last name, as well as use the flight number we wish to book as a path parameter. It returns an HTTP status code value 201 along with booking information on success. On failure, it returns an HTTP status code value of 404 or 500.

The POST endpoint has a URL path parameter of {flightNumber} and requires a request body with two fields: firstName and lastName, both strings. The endpoint either returns an HTTP status code 201 (created) on success or an HTTP status code 500 on failure to book due to a logical or database error. See figure 3.7.

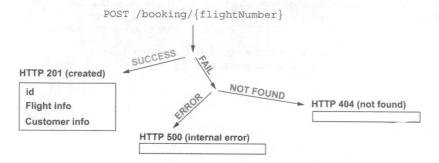

Figure 3.7 The request-return life cycle of the POST /booking/{flightNumber} endpoint. On success, the endpoint returns an HTTP status of 201 along with a booking ID, flight information, and customer information. In case the service cannot find the appropriate flight, it returns an HTTP status 404. When there is an internal error, it returns HTTP status 500.

NOTE The full OpenAPI file can be viewed (in YAML format) in appendix D.

The workflow, as shown in figure 3.8, that FlyTomorrow uses to search and book flights is as follows:

1 FlyTomorrow queries our GET /flight endpoint to list all the flights to the consumer.
2 When the consumer selects a flight to get details for, FlyTomorrow queries our GET /flight/{flightNumber} endpoint with the flight number.
3 When the customer is ready to book the flight, FlyTomorrow sends a POST request to POST /booking/{flightNumber} to book the flight.

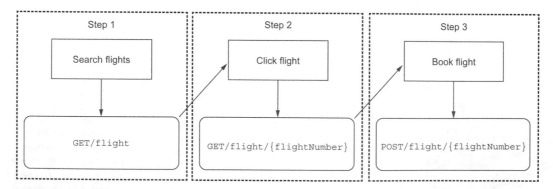

Figure 3.8 The Search -> Click -> Book workflow and API calls. This is the workflow used by our client and the one around which we model our codebase.

3.3 Coming to terms with the existing codebase

For the remainder of this chapter, we'll walk through the part of the code we inherited: the models, views, and configuration code. We'll discuss points of improvement, clean code, and security. We'll also touch on the database schema and how the inherited code's models compare to the schema.

> **WARNING** The rest of this chapter (and the next) deals with the existing codebase. This means that we will see sloppy and incorrect code, diversions from the given requirements, and all-around bad things. We will fix them all in later chapters.

This chapter serves as the foundation on which we can build our improved service. After reading this chapter and the next, you'll be intimately familiar with the codebase we are trying to improve and itching to start refactoring in part 3.

3.3.1 Assessing the existing database schema and its tables

Now that we have our OpenAPI file and know what is expected of us, it is time to look at the existing codebase and database. The code we have inherited has a lot of pain points that we can improve on. We can change anything we want, according to George and Aljen, but not the database. Because it is our only rock-solid foundation block, let's start by looking at the database schema. The database is deployed to Microsoft Azure and is a regular, run-of-the-mill SQL database with only a couple of tables, as follows:

- Airport
- Booking
- Customer
- Flight

In this section, we'll look at the database schema, shown in figure 3.9, and dissect the key constraints the schema provides us.

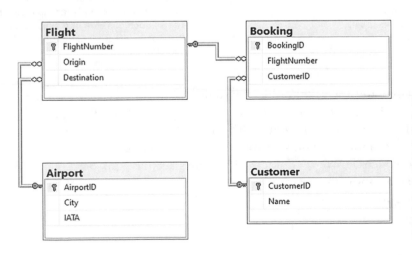

Figure 3.9 The database schema and foreign key constraints of the Flying Dutchman Airlines database hosted in Microsoft Azure. This schema shows the tables we use throughout the book.

As George told us, no ORM is used in the existing codebase, but even without one, you would expect to see some objects modeled after these tables.

> **NOTE** If you are unfamiliar with databases and/or SQL in general, you may want to read up on the basics. Two good resources are Cornell University's *Relational Databases Virtual Workshop* at https://cvw.cac.cornell.edu/databases/ and *The Manga Guide to Databases* (No Starch Press, 2009) by Mana Takahashi, Shoko Azuma, and Trend-Pro Co., Ltd.

3.3.2 The existing codebase: Web service configuration files

Looking at the solution's structure gives us some insight into how the project was laid out. In this section, we are looking at the source files dealing with the configuration of the service, as shown in figure 3.10.

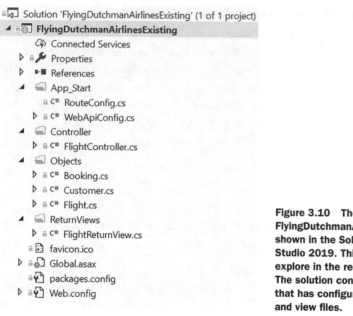

Figure 3.10   **The folder structure of FlyingDutchmanAirlinesExisting.sln, as shown in the Solution Explorer in Visual Studio 2019. This is the structure we'll explore in the remainder of the chapter. The solution consists of a single project that has configuration, controller, object, and view files.**

C# uses a hierarchical relationship for solutions and projects to organize its codebases. A solution can have many projects, but a project typically is part of only one solution. It is very much a parent (solution) -child (project) pattern. Note, however, that a project cannot contain subprojects. Figure 3.10 gives us a clear look at the layout of the codebase. We see folders with names such as App_Start, Controller, and Objects. These show the use of a Model-View-Controller pattern, albeit with slightly different terms.

The Model-View-Controller design pattern

One of the most used design patterns in software development, the Model-View-Controller (MVC) pattern distances any user and external interfaces from the business logic and the stored data. The MVC pattern has grown in popularity in the last decade because it is immensely useful for both desktop and web development.

When using MVC, the model layer does most of the work. We store all our data in models and perform most necessary business logic in the models themselves. To interact with this data, we usually want some kind of user interaction. That is where the controller and view layers come in. A controller acts as a funnel, routing user requests to the model layer. The view layer consists of objects that represent specific "views" of the data in the model layer. The controller layer returns these views to the user.

Throughout this book, bit by bit, you will gain an in-depth understanding of how to use MVC-like patterns and models. After reading this book, you will be intimately familiar with models, views, and controllers.

Another good resource on the MVC pattern (and other design patterns) is Eric Freeman, Elisabeth Robson, Bert Bates, and Kathy Sierra's *Head First: Design Patterns* (O'Reilly, 2004).

Looking from the top, we see that the solution name is FlyingDutchmanAirlines-Existing and that it contains a project with the same name. That brings us to our first source code file: AssemblyInfo.cs. This file is in the project's root folder, but Visual Studio visualizes it in a separate Properties category.

The AssemblyInfo file is not a file you venture into very much in daily life. It contains metadata about your assembly, such as the assembly title and version.

In contrast to AssemblyInfo.cs, the next file is of much interest. Because we are dealing with a web service, we need to have some kind of routing for our endpoints. This is served by the RouteConfig class in the App_Start folder.

OPENING UP THE ROUTECONFIG FILE

As shown in the next listing, opening up RouteConfig, we see that the class only has one method: RegisterRoutes.

Listing 3.1 RouteConfig.cs

```
public class RouteConfig {
  public static void RegisterRoutes(RouteCollection routes) {
    routes.MapRoute(
      "Default",
      "{controller}/{action}/{id}"
    };
  }
}
```

Listing 3.1 shows the `RouteConfig` class minus routine things such as a namespace declaration and package imports.

NOTE   Most source code listings in this book do not include the required imports because they would take up a lot of space in every listing.

The `RegisterRoutes` method allows us to specify a pattern for mapping incoming HTTP routes to endpoints in our code. `RegisterRoutes` returns no value (`void`) and takes in an instance of `RouteCollection`, a class of the ASP.NET Framework.

DEFINITION   ASP.NET is a web framework that ties deeply into the .NET Framework, .NET Core, and .NET 5. ASP.NET adds web development capabilities to C# such as WebAPI support and URL routing. Because of its deep integration into the .NET ecosystem, people sometimes do not realize they are calling libraries from ASP.NET. Throughout this book, we'll use ASP.NET but won't explicitly call out when we do. For more information on ASP.NET, see Andrew Lock's excellent *ASP.NET Core in Action* (2nd edition; Manning, 2020).

Should you avoid static?

Being able to access your methods or fields without having to create an instance of the class can be very useful. It certainly is easy to access your code wherever you want and whenever you want (assuming what you are trying to access is also public). But before you mark everything as static, I would urge you to reconsider.

Yes, you can access a static method or field without creating an object instance, but so can somebody else. You are unlikely to be the only developer working in a given codebase, and as a result, you can't predict their needs and assumptions.

For example, consider the following code found in an imaginary video game:

```
public record Player {
  public static int Health;
}
```

We have a record type called `Player` and a public static string field representing the player's `health`. When the player's health is damaged, the game loop logic calls as follows:

```
Player.Health--;
```

This decreases the health of the player by 1. All is well for a single-player adventure, but what if we want multiple players, perhaps for a local co-op or split-screen feature? We'll just instantiate another `Player`! But now we have two instances of `Player`, both using the same static Health field. When we now decrease health for one player, it's decreased for all. This could be a neat game-play twist, but in general, we want to avoid changing the state across instances through `static`.

The only operation executed in the `RouteConfig.RegisterRoutes` method is the call to the `MapRoute` method, which is part of the `RouteCollection` instance passed into the `RegisterRoutes` method. `MapRoute` takes in two things: what we want to call the routing pattern (Default) and what the actual routing pattern is (`{controller}`/`{action}`/`{id}`). When you add an ID to a routing pattern, as we have done, it becomes a URL path variable parameter. A common use case for a URL path variable is using them with HTTP GET calls to specify a specific resource to get by a resource ID, as shown in the next listing.

Listing 3.2   Setting up HTTP routes

```
routes.MapRoute(          ◁──┐  MapRoute scans the codebase
  "Default",                 │  for matching routes.
  "{controller}/{action}/{id}"   ◁────   We specify the name of
};                                       the route as Default.
     The route we scan for is determined here.
```

We'll see more of this routing pattern and how it works in action when we look at the `FlightController` in chapter 4.

LOOKING AT THE WEBAPICONFIG FILE

The next file we see is WebApiConfig.cs. When we open the file, we see something peculiar: there is another class inside of `WebApiConfig`, as shown in the next code sample.

Listing 3.3   WebApiConfig.cs and its nested class, `Defaults`

```
public class WebApiConfig {
  public class Defaults {
    public readonly RouteParameter Id;

    public Defaults(RouteParameter id) {        Defaults is
      Id = id;                                  a nested
    }                                           class.
  }

  public static void Register(HttpConfiguration config) {    Calling
    config.MapHttpAttributeRoutes();                         MapHttpAttributeRoutes
                                                             enables attribute
    config.Routes.MapHttpRoute(                              routing.
      "DefaultApi",                         We map routes following
      "api/{controller}/{id}",              the API/Controller/ID
      new Defaults(RouteParameter.Optional) pattern.
    );

    GlobalConfiguration.Configuration.Formatters.JsonFormatter.Add(
      new System.Http.Formatting.RequestHeaderMapping(
        "Accept",                                            Allows
        "text/html",                                         for JSON
        StringComparison.InvariantCultureIgnoreCase,         responses
        true,                                                to be
        "application/json")                                  returned
      );
  }
}
```

The register method is part of the WebApiConfig class, not Defaults.

In C#, you can have nested classes and access them just like regular classes (depending on their access modifier). Nested classes come in handy when creating a dedicated class file would bring more confusion to the overall project structure than you want. Sometimes, a "throw-away" class inside the only class you use the nested class in can be cleaner than creating a new file. We'll discuss how to improve this code in section 5.2.3.

> **DEFINITION** The code in listing 3.3 has a keyword we haven't seen yet: `readonly`. When something is designated as read-only in C#, it means the value is immutable after assignment.

To access a public nested class from outside the class it is nested in, use the enclosing class to access it. For example, we can access the nested defaults class by using `WebApi-Config.Defaults`. You can use a nested class with any access modifier, but you are still at the mercy of the outer class's access modifier. If the outer class has an access modifier of `internal` and the nested class is `public`, you still need to meet the access requirements of the outer class before accessing the nested class.

> **NOTE** For developers coming from Java: nested classes in C# do not have an implicit reference to the outer class. This is a difference in the practice of static nested classes in Java and nested classes in C#. C# also allows multiple non-nested classes in one file, as opposed to Java. This is not good practice, but it is allowed.

The `Register` method requires a parameter of type `HttpConfiguration`. It uses the `HttpConfiguration` instance to do the following two things:

- The runtime scans and maps all endpoints with route method attributes.
- The runtime allows for routes with optional URL parameters.

A method attribute (called a method annotation in Java) can mark any method and is used to give it some metadata. Some examples of when we would use attributes follow:

- To mark which fields should be serialized
- To mark which methods are obsolete
- To mark whether the method has a specific HTTP route assigned to it

In the case of the existing code, we see method attributes with routing in the `Flight-Controller` class. A method attribute comprises two enclosing brackets with the respective attribute sandwiched in (e.g., `[MyMethodAttribute]`).

The `config.Routes.MapHttpRoute` is similar to the `routes.MapRoute` method in `RouteConfig` (listing 3.1). The code in `RouteConfig` configured the routes for endpoints with URL path parameters, but now we need to also configure routes to allow for routes without them. Once again, we pass in a name (`DefaultApi`) and a template (`api/{controller}/{id}`), but this time we also pass in a new `Defaults` object with the `Id` set to `RouteParameter.Optional`. This allows us to route both endpoints with and without the parameter (because it is now optional).

Finally, we set the accepted `MediaTypeMappings` to application/json in the call to `GlobalConfiguration.Configuration.Formatters.JsonFormatter.MediaTypeMappings`.

CHARTING ASP.NET AND CONFIGURATION FILES: GLOBAL.ASAX, PACKAGES.CONFIG, AND WEB.CONFIG
Let's skip the folders called Controller, Objects, and ReturnViews, and look at the three source files at the bottom of the solution in the next listing: Global.asax, packages.config, and Web.config.

Listing 3.4 Global.asax

```
namespace FlyingDutchmanAirlinesExisting {
  public class WebApiApplication : System.Web.HttpApplication {
    protected void Application_Start() {
      GlobalConfiguration.Configure(WebApiConfig.Register);
      RouteConfig.RegisterRoutes(RouteTable.Routes);
    }
  }
}
```

What is this strange file extension .asax? We have not seen this extension before. An .asax file indicates a global application class. These classes are used in an ASP.NET application to execute code in response to lower-level system events such as the launching or ending of the service. The logic inside a global application class is the very first piece of code executed that we can manipulate. We can execute code at the start of our application by creating an `Application_Start` method, as in listing 3.4. To execute code at the end of an application, put it in an `Application_End` method.

The `Application_Start` method has an access modifier state of `protected` and returns nothing. The `GlobalConfiguration.Configure` call registers a callback to where the `WebApiConfig` registers its routes.

> **DEFINITION** A *callback* is a function that is slated to be executed after the execution of the current function. You can think of it as a queuing system where the callback is enqueued (or cuts in line, depending on your perspective) for execution right after the current method's processing is done. A caller calls the callee, passing it back a callback, which the callee invokes after its work completes.

Following the registration of the callback to register the routes, `RegisterRoutes` is called on the `RouteConfig`, and the `RouteTable`'s routes are passed in. This results in the areas of the routes (things between slashes, e.g., "`/flight/`" means flight is an area) that are defined in the `RouteTable` being registered and usable. We need to register the callbacks and call `RouteConfig` at launch because we could not execute them otherwise. Because the routes would not be registered, we could not kick off any execution by triggering an endpoint.

Two other files remain that we can square into the configuration camp: packages.config and Web.config. Packages.config is a file tied to the NuGet package manager. The NuGet package manager is the default package manager for .NET and is deeply integrated with Visual Studio. The packages.config file specifies what packages (and versions of said packages) are referenced and installed in solutions and projects. A target ASP.NET Framework is also specified. For example, this being an ASP.NET application and ASP.NET being a framework separate from .NET (but with heavy integration and mostly automatic installation support), it is referenced in the packages .config file as follows:

```
<package id="Microsoft.AspNet.WebApi" version="5.2.7"
  ➥ targetFramework="net45" />
```

Web.Config provides us with settings that configure how the application is supposed to run, what version of the .NET Framework to use (remember, this codebase runs on the .NET Framework), and compiler settings. For example, the compile mode we are running under is debug (the default mode). This is defined in the following line:

```
  <compilation debug="true" targetFramework="4.5"/>
```

That brings us to the end of the configuration files. We'll skip the `FlightController` class for now and look at the models and views we were provided: Booking.cs, Customer.cs, Flight.cs, and FlightReturnView.cs.

3.3.3 *Considering models and views in the existing codebase*

In the MVC pattern, models should mirror the structure of database tables, whereas views are driven by clients. Views act as a representation of the data, determined by the client. We'll discuss what that means further in section 10.1.1. In this section, we'll look at the models and views that the inherited codebase contains. The project has the following three models:

- Booking
- Customer
- Flight

The code also has one view: `FlightReturnView`. In an ideal world, the models closely resemble what is present in the database, but it looks like the existing code is not quite there yet.

UNCOVERING THE BOOKING MODEL AND ITS INTERNAL DETAILS

Models represent an important cornerstone of a web service. They hold data that we can spin and twist into perspectives and show different angles through views. The first model we'll look at is the `Booking` model. The idea behind this model is to provide an object to hold data about the booking of a flight, as shown in the next code sample:

```
namespace FlyingDutchmanAirlinesExisting.Objects {
  public class Booking {
    public string OriginAirportIATA;
    public string DestinationAirportIATA;
    public string Name;
  }
}
```

We see that the `Booking` model is fairly simple and contains three fields (`Origin-AirportIATA`, `DestinationAirportIATA`, and `Name`), all with a public access modifier. This would be an opportunity to introduce some encapsulation by adding a backing field, getter, and setter.

WHY GETTERS AND SETTERS MATTER (AUTO-PROPERTIES AND INIT-ONLY SETTERS)

Encapsulation: you've heard the term many times before, but it is tricky to do it right. A major motivation for encapsulation is to provide controlled access to your code. You can fine tune how you want others to interact with your work and provide access guidelines through access modifiers. Opponents of getters and setters say it bloats the code and that it is time consuming to write getters and setters for every property. Proponents would counter by pointing out that controlling access to a property is not code bloat and that it increases speed in the long run.

Imagine having a codebase like the one we are considering right now. Perhaps you are getting the `Booking.Name` string in 50 places by directly accessing it. What would happen if you need to change the original property's name to `Booking.NewName`? You would have to change the call in 50 different locations, making your life miserable. Some IDEs do have functionality that can automate this process for you, but then you are relying on an IDE to fix your code smell. I prefer having the code be clean so we don't have to use a tool to automate a fix for us.

Now imagine you write a (what some people call "Java-style") getter (`Booking.GetName`) and a setter (`Booking.SetName(string name)`) and use those to access and change your property? You would need to change things in only one place: the original class. Getters and setters have another critical purpose: they control access to your property and dictate who can do what with it. Another use case for getters and setters is making your property `readonly` but only to outside classes. If you were to apply the `readonly` modifier to the field, it would hold for everybody. Instead, you can accomplish the same thing by being strategic with getters and setters. If you make the setter private but the getter public, code outside of the encapsulating class can access but not edit the property. You can also add logic inside the setters and getters. For example, do you need to do some validation of the passed-in arguments before setting the property to a new value? Add the logic in the setter.

Some of the ways you can use getters and setters in C# include the following:

- The traditional dual-method technique where you create two new methods (a dedicated getter and a dedicated setter method) and use those
- Auto-properties
- Init-only setters[1]

---

[1] Init-only setters were introduced as part of C# 9. Only .NET 5 (and later versions) support C# 9. Init-only setters (and C# 9) are not supported on .NET Framework or .NET Core.

With auto-properties, you can inline the getters and setters and let the compiler do the work of creating the methods under the hood. This is one place where you can take the abstraction .NET provides and use it to your advantage.

Let's compare and contrast the two approaches by applying them to a name field. First up is the traditional dual-method option, shown here:

```
private string _name;
public string GetName() {
  return _name;
}

protected void SetName(string value) {
  _name = value;
}
```

The field containing the value is private (in C#, private fields are often prefixed with an underscore) and named _name. This field is sometimes called a "backing field" because the field "backs" the getter and setter. Two methods are created to regulate setting and getting _name: GetName and SetName. In this example, everybody can get the name, but only this class and classes inheriting from this class can set the name field (protected). To better regulate access (and improve readability), we can use an auto-property as follows:

```
public string Name { get; protected set; }
```

The auto-property is only one line, yet it provides the same functionality as the dual-method technique. If no access modifier is provided, the getter or setter defaults to the property's method accessor, as seen with get in this example. You can also provide method bodies to the getter and setter just by adding curly braces and a body.

 With C# 9, a new way of using setters was introduced: init-only setters. This technique allows you to create immutable properties (often wrapped in an object) by using the init keyword. We start as if we create an auto-property, but instead of specifying a getter, we use init. Let's say the Name property we've been using is part of a class called Person and uses an init-only setter as follows:

```
class Person {
  public string Name { get; init; }
}
```

We can create an instance of Person pretty easily, but because we used the init-only setter for Name, we can't come back and set a value for Name after instantiation, as shown here:

```
Person p = new Person();
p.Name = "Sally";
```

This puts us in a bit of a bind. If we try to assign a value to Name, we get a compiler error telling us we cannot assign to the init-only property unless we are in an object initializer, a constructor, or an init accessor. We'll look at object initializers much further in section 6.2.5, but to give you a little preview, we can assign the initial value to Person.Name with an object initializer as follows:

```
Person p = new Person() {
  Name = "Sally"
};
```

This sets the value for Name to "Sally" at object creation rather than attempting to set the value after the object is created. This restriction forces you to assign to an init-only setter in a very specified way, and it stops people from overwriting the values after they are set.

COMPARING THE BOOKING MODEL AND TABLE

If we compare the Booking model with the Booking table in the database, we see some discrepancies, including one that would have a security engineer cry foul. None of the fields in the Booking model match the Booking table in the database. There even seem to be some erroneous additions, as shown in figure 3.11.

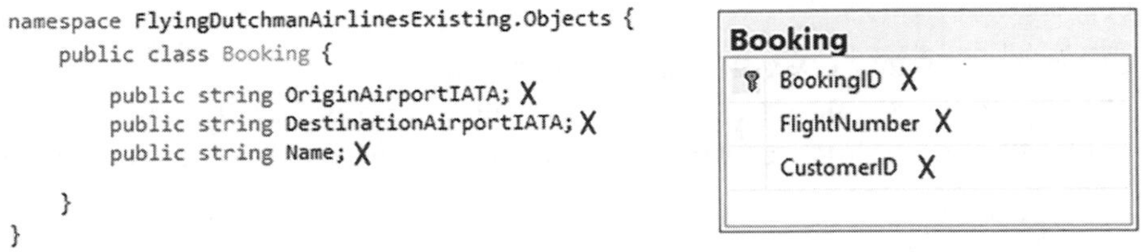

```
namespace FlyingDutchmanAirlinesExisting.Objects {
    public class Booking {
        public string OriginAirportIATA; X
        public string DestinationAirportIATA; X
        public string Name; X

    }
}
```

Booking

| 🔑 BookingID X |
| FlightNumber X |
| CustomerID X |

Figure 3.11 The isomorphic relationship between the Booking class and dbo.Booking. Every field is incorrect; this is not good. The Xs indicate fields with an incorrect isomorphic relationship.

There is one positive thing to say about the Booking class: it has the right name. But that is about it. As we can see, the model contains no representations of Flight-Number, BookingID, or CustomerID. Looking back at figure 3.9, we see that those fields are involved with key constraints (BookingID is a primary key. FlightNumber and CustomerID have foreign key relationships). The model contains fields for the origin airport IATA code, destination airport IATA code, and the customer name.

THE CUSTOMER MODEL AND ITS INTERNAL DETAILS

With some hesitation, we look at the next model, which follows—Customer:

```
namespace FlyingDutchmanAirlinesExisting.Objects {
  public class Customer {
    public int CustomerId;
    public string Name;

    public Customer(int customerID, string name) {
      CustomerID = customerID;
```

```
            Name = name;
        }
    }
}
```

The damage is fairly controlled in the `Customer` class. `Customer` also has good isomorphism between database tables, as shown in figure 3.12.

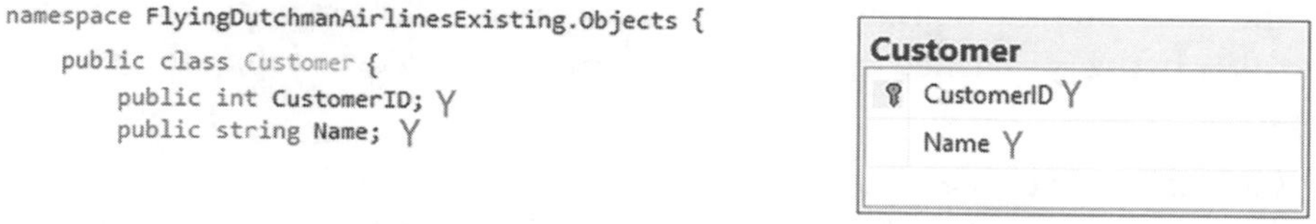

```
namespace FlyingDutchmanAirlinesExisting.Objects {
    public class Customer {
        public int CustomerID; Y
        public string Name; Y
```

Customer
⚷ CustomerID Y
Name Y

Figure 3.12   The isomorphic relationship between the (abbreviated) `Customer` class and dbo.Customer. CustomerID and Name map correctly.

From what we can tell, no changes are needed to get `Customer` up to date with the database table.

BOARDING THE FLIGHT CLASS AND ITS INTERNAL DETAILS

Turning to the `Flight` class, we see in the following code sample that `Flight` has three fields, all of them integers, which almost map completely to the database table Flight:

```
namespace FlyingDutchmanAirlinesExisting.Objects {
  public class Flight {
    public int FlightNumber;
    public int OriginID;
    public int DestinationID;

    public Flight(int flightNumber, int originID, int destinationID) {
      FlightNumber = flightNumber;
      OriginID = originID;
      DestinationID = destinationID;
    }
  }
}
```

Comparing the `Flight` class's fields to the database table, we see that, in essence, the model is correct. But we are in the business of writing *clean code*, and that also means that we have consistency across the codebase and database when it comes to field names. It is also worth mentioning that the whole foundation of having database models in your codebase (be it through ORM or manually) relies on the practice of the closest interpretation of the isomorphic relationship between a database row and a class.[2] It's important

---

[2] For more information on isomorphic relationships and how they map true statements to interpreted theorems (e.g., database schemas to models), see chapter 2 ("Meaning and Form in Mathematics") of Douglas R. Hofstadter's Pulitzer Prize–winning *Gödel, Escher, Bach: An Eternal Golden Braid* (Basic Books, 1977) and Richard J. Trudeau's *Introduction to Graph Theory* (2nd edition; Dover Publications, 1994).

to keep in mind that even though the name of a field might be the same as the name of a column in the database, it is still an abstraction. They are not the same; yet to us, they are as close as they can get.

Applying an isomorphic relationship to database and codebase communication makes a strong case for always using ORM, because you get the closest match between representation in code and representation in the database.

As designated in figure 3.13 by the "?!" icons, we have a mismatch in two field names:

- OriginID versus Origin
- DestinationID versus Destination

```
namespace FlyingDutchmanAirlinesExisting.Objects {
    public class Flight {
        public int FlightNumber; Y
        public int OriginID; ?!
        public int DestinationID; ?!
```

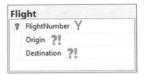

Figure 3.13 The isomorphic relationship between the (abbreviated) Flight class and dbo.Flight. The Origin/OriginID and Destination/DestinationID are very close matches. FlightNumber is a solid match.

In situations like this, the database rules. When we start our work on the refactored version of the API, Entity Framework Core makes sure that these discrepancies do not occur.

Flight, Booking, and Customer make up the contents of the Models folder. But wait a second, let's have another look at our database schema. It looks like there may be something missing . . .

As we can deduce from figure 3.14, we did not encounter any class that could be said to model the Airport table. So, does the code work?

If we had some tests, we may have been able to say one way or the other, or if coverage was spotty and not in the right places, we could at the very least attempt a sort of proof by induction[3] based on the tests that do exist to prove the correct functionality of the methods. It might be very true that without the Airport class we can still perform all the functions we want and provide value to the customer. It is also true that the developers of this code have likely made their life harder by not sticking to the format of their source data.

---

[3] If you want to learn more about proof by induction, I recommend two resources. First, watch the initial three video lectures (*Introduction and Proofs, Induction,* and *Strong Induction*) of MIT's *Mathematics for Computer Science 6.042J* course (MIT OpenCourseWare, 2010) at https://ocw.mit.edu/courses/electrical-engineering-and-computer-science/6-042j-mathematics-for-computer-science-fall-2010/index.htm. Second, I recommend section 1.2.1 ("Mathematical Preliminaries / Mathematical Induction") in Donald Knuth's *The Art of Computer Programming, Volume 1: Fundamental Algorithms* (3rd edition; Addison Wesley Longman, 1977).

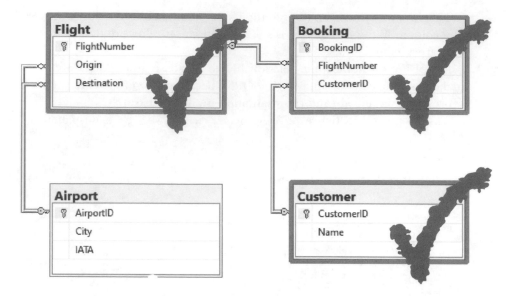

Figure 3.14   The database schema when contrasted to the codebase's models. Models representing the tables Flight, Booking, and Customer are present in the codebase; Airport is not. This means there is an incomplete isomorphic relationship between the codebase and the database.

THE FLIGHTRETURNVIEW VIEW AND ITS INTERNAL DETAILS

Having thoroughly explored the models and how they match up with the database, we turn our view to the ReturnViews folder. A `View` allows us to represent the data encapsulated in a model (or many models) in any way that we want. As shown next, there is only one view in the ReturnViews folder—`FlightReturnView`:

```
namespace FlyingDutchmanAirlinesExisting.ReturnView {
  public class FlightReturnView {
    public int FlightNumber;
    public string Origin;
    public string Destination;
  }
}
```

`FlightReturnView` is a very simple class with just three fields: `FlightNumber` (integer), `Origin` (string), and `Destination` (string). A view is a slice of an object(s) molded to reflect only a subsection of details or a combination of details from many models (a denormalized view). Here, the developers wanted to return `FlightNumber`, `Origin`, and `Destination` fields to the user. Returning the `Flight` class would not be sufficient because that does not contain `Origin` or `Destination`. Likewise, returning the `Booking` class also would not have sufficed as it only contains `FlightNumber`, and not `Origin` or `Destination`. Using views to return data is a powerful design pattern often used in API development. It can be construed as having powers similar to the JOIN SQL operation, because you can join multiple datasets in any way you want. That being said, if we can get away with not using one, that would be better, because it increases the complexity of the codebase.

Summary

- An object-relational mapping tool allows us to deal with databases at a higher abstraction level than querying them directly with SQL.
- A C# repository usually contains one solution, which in turn contains multiple projects. Keeping with this pattern makes your codebase easier to navigate for seasoned C# developers.
- The ASP.NET Framework is a framework aimed at developing web services and is part of the .NET ecosystem. We can use ASP.NET in the .NET Framework, .NET Core, and .NET 5. We use ASP.NET to create web services.
- We need to define and register HTTP routes through the use of a `RouteConfig`. If we do not do this, we cannot reach our endpoints.
- We can attach attributes to methods, fields, and properties. An example of an attribute is `[FromBody]`.
- A callback is a function that is to be executed after the current function. We can use callbacks to queue certain methods to execute when we want them instead of immediately.
- The NuGet package manager is C#'s premier package manager. We can use it to install third-party packages or the packages of .NET that are not part of the regular SDK, such as ASP.NET.

Manage your unmanaged resources!

This chapter covers

- Discovering the underlying type of an object at compile time and run time
- Writing code that uses `IDisposable` and `using` statements to dispose of unmanaged resources
- Using method and constructor overloading
- Using attributes
- Accepting a JSON or XML input in an endpoint and parsing it into a custom object

In chapter 3, the CEO of Flying Dutchman Airlines, Aljen van der Meulen, assigned us a project to revamp Flying Dutchman Airlines' backend service so that the company can integrate with a third-party system (a flight aggregator called FlyTomorow). We were given an OpenAPI specification and took a look at the database schema and the configuration, model, and view classes. Figure 4.1 shows where we are in the scheme of the book.

> **WARNING** This chapter deals with the existing codebase written in the .NET Framework. This means that we will see sloppy and incorrect code,

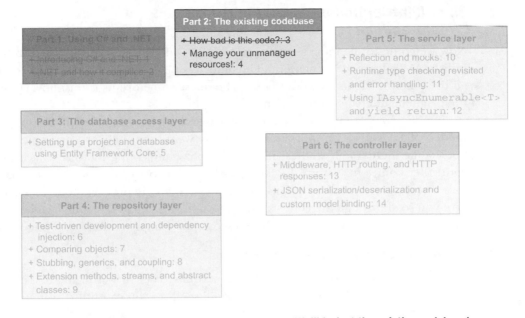

Figure 4.1 In this chapter, we'll bring part 2 to a close. We'll look at the existing codebase's controller class and discuss potential improvements we can make to the code.

diversions from the given requirements, and all-around bad things. We will fix them all in later chapters and migrate to .NET 5.

Our understanding of the existing codebase is gradually increasing, and we have almost covered the entirety of it. In this chapter, we'll look at the last remaining part (the only controller in the codebase) and dive into the endpoints one by one as follows:

- GET /flight—This endpoint allows users to get information on all flights in the database.
- GET /flight/{flightNumber}—This endpoint allows users to retrieve information about a specific flight, given a flight number.
- POST /flight/{flightNumber}—This endpoint allows users to book flights when given a flight number.
- DELETE /Flight/{flightNumber}—This endpoint allows the user to delete a flight from the database when given a flight number.

We'll also discuss connection strings, enumerable types, garbage collection, method overloading, static constructors, method attributes, and much more. After reading this chapter, you should have a clear idea of where we can make improvements, what improvements we can make, and why.

4.1   The FlightController: Assessing the GET /flight endpoint

Now we come to the meat and potatoes of the codebase we are supposed to fix and polish. As we learned in chapter 3, FlyTomorrow plans to use this endpoint to display all the possible flights users can book. The question before us is this: how close does the original codebase get to that intent?

The previous chapter covered the database schema, configuration, and supporting models. That's all very important stuff, but we want to actually process some data (or book some flights) with all these models, schemas, and configurations. This is where a controller comes in (within the context of an MVC pattern), and this codebase has only one: FlightController.cs. This code is larger than the previous code files, so make sure you read through the code carefully. Combing through the code in this way gives us a very clear understanding of where we can make improvements and bug fixes.

4.1.1   The GET /flight endpoint and what it does

In this section, we'll explore the `FlightController` class by way of the first endpoint: the GET flight, as shown in listing 4.1. We'll see how you can utilize a method attribute to generate documentation on the fly, how we can determine the type of an object at run time and compile time, why you may not want to hardcode a database connection string, and how to return an HTTP status from a controller. Hopefully, after looking over the existing code, we'll get a sense of where we can make improvements and why we would want to make them.

> **Listing 4.1   FlightController.cs** `GET /flight`

```
// GET: api/Flight                                              A comment that attempts
[ResponseType(typeof(IEnumerable<FlightReturnView>))]          to describe the code. We
public HttpResponseMessage Get() {                             should remove comments
  var flightReturnViews = new List<FlightReturnViews>();       like this.
  var flights = new List<Flight>();

  var connectionString =
     "Server=tcp:codelikeacsharppro.database.windows.net,1433;Initial
     Catalog=FlyingDutchmanAirlines;Persist Security Info=False;User
     ID=dev;Password=FlyingDutchmanAirlines1972!;
     MultipleActiveResultSets=False;Encrypt=True;
     TrustServerCertificate=False;Connection Timeout=30;";

  using (var connection = new SqlConnection(connectionString)) {
    connection.Open();

  // Get Flights
    var cmd = new SqlCommand("SELECT * FROM flight", connection);

    using (var reader = cmd.ExecuteReader()) {
      while (reader.Read()) {
        flights.Add(new Flight(reader.GetInt32(0),
  reader.GetInt32(1), reader.GetInt32(2)));
```

Generates documentation on the fly → (points to `[ResponseType...]`)

This connection string is hardcoded, which is a security problem. → (points to connection string)

The using statement is used for disposing of disposable objects. ← (points to `using (var connection...`)

Opens the connection to the database ← (points to `connection.Open();`)

Sets up a GET SQL query → (points to `var cmd = new SqlCommand...`)

Reads the database return ← (points to `using (var reader = cmd.ExecuteReader())`)

```
      }
    }                          An alternative
                              method to dispose
  cmd.Dispose();      ⟵──┘    of objects


  foreach (var flight in flights) {
    // Get Destination Airport details
    cmd = new SqlCommand("SELECT City FROM Airport WHERE AirportID =
➡ " + flight.DestinationID, connection);

    var returnView = new FlightReturnView();
    returnView.FlightNumber = flight.FlightNumber;

    using (var reader = cmd.ExecuteReader()) {
      while (reader.Read()) {
        returnView.Destination = reader.GetString(0);
        break;
      }
    }

    cmd.Dispose();


    // Get Origin Airport details
    cmd = new SqlCommand("SELECT City FROM Airport WHERE AirportID =
➡ " + flight.OriginID, connection);

    using (var reader = cmd.ExecuteReader()) {
      while (reader.Read()) {
        returnView.Origin = reader.GetString(0);
        break;
      }
    }

    cmd.Dispose();                      Adds the resulting
                                        view to an internal
    flightReturnViews.add(returnView);  collection
  }                               ⟵──┘


  return Request.CreateResponse(HttpStatusCode.OK,
➡ flightReturnViews);        ⟵───┐ Returns an HTTP
}                                  200 and the flights
```

For every flight, gets the destination Airport details

For every flight, gets the origin Airport details

4.1.2 Method signature: The meaning of ResponseType and typeof

Welcome to the deep end. Listing 4.1 is a fair bit of code with a lot of things that may be new to us. All endpoints in the controller look similar to this one. They all use the same patterns to get and return the data, so after we fully understand what is happening here, the other endpoints are going to be a breeze.

In this section, we'll look at the method signature of the /flight's Get method. We'll start by examining the ResponseType attribute, followed by a discussion on the typeof keyword and what it does. Last, we'll glimpse how the ResponseType attribute uses the IEnumerable interface and typeof operator. What does the method signature look like? See the following:

```
[ResponseType(typeof(IEnumerable<FlightReturnView>))]
public HttpResponseMessage Get()
```

The ResponseType attribute is used to generate documentation on the fly and is not often used in a situation where we deal with OpenAPI (or Swagger) specifications. This attribute is very helpful if you do not use some kind of automatic OpenAPI generation. The ResponseType attribute has no impact on what type we can return from the method but does require us to specify the type. The attribute then wraps our returned data into an HTTPResponseMessage type and returns out of the method. To figure out what type an instance is, we can use the typeof operator, into which we can pass an argument to be tested. The typeof operator returns an instance of System.Type, which contains data that describes the type you passed into the typeof operator. This is done by the compiler at compile time.

 READONLY AND CONST Expression and statement values determined at compile time can be assigned to both readonly and const properties. Values determined dynamically at run time cannot be assigned to a const property because a constant cannot change after compile time, whereas a readonly property can be written to once (either at the declaration or in a constructor). Using readonly and const prevents reassignment at run time. In effect, this allows you to prohibit unwanted changes to your code, which enforces the intention that a value should not change at run time and could minimize the number of unintended side effects stemming from changes made by other developers.

If we wanted to get the type of an instance at run time (through reflection,[1] discussed in section 6.2.6), we could use the GetType method that the object type exposes (and because object is the base class of all types, as shown in figure 4.2, it is exposed on all types). If we were to omit the typeof operator, the attribute would cause a compiler error because ResponseType expects an instance of System.Type.

NOTE You often encounter data structures that implement the IEnumerable interface directly or indirectly. The IEnumerable interface allows you to create enumerators to loop over collections in a variety of ways (most notably the foreach construct). If you want to create your own data structure that has an enumerator, just implement the IEnumerable interface.

---

[1] Even though the Object.GetType method is not part of the reflection namespace, I do consider it part of the "reflection" workflow. Reflection invariably starts by using Object.GetType, and it is used to get data from an instance at run time. This a very "reflection"-like operation. For more information, see section 6.2.6 or Jeffrey Richter's *CLR via C#* (4th edition; Microsoft Press, 2012).

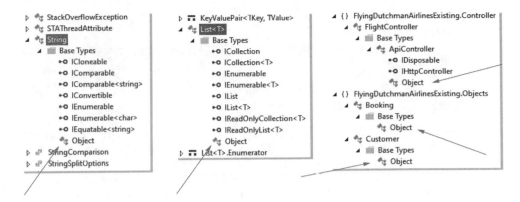

Figure 4.2 **The common denominator of all types is** `Object`**. These screenshots were produced using Visual Studio's Object Browser, which lets you inspect any object for its base types.**

The `Get` method returns an instance of type `HttpResponseMessage`. This type contains the data used to return an HTTP response, including an HTTP status code and a JSON body.

4.1.3 Collecting flight information with collections

We are ready to dive into the `FlightController`'s `GET` method. In this section, we'll take our first steps to return information on every flight in the database to our users. We'll discuss the method instance collections we'll use to achieve this goal, as well as the connection string that is hardcoded into the source code and why this is less than ideal.

Looking at the following first line of code, we see something that we could change:

```
var flightReturnViews = new List<FlightReturnView>();
```

The code declares a variable called `flightReturnViews` and assigns it to an empty instance of type `List` of `FlightReturnView`.

> **NOTE** I prefer using explicit types instead of the `var` keyword. To me, it makes the code more readable because I can easily spot what type I am working with. In this book, I use explicit typing, but you could definitely use the `var` keyword if you'd like. The code will generally run fine whether you use explicit typing, implicit typing, or a mix of both. Opinions vary greatly, and discussions inevitably heat up on whether to use the `var` keyword. It's up to you to pick which one to use in what scenario.

The var keyword

Using the `var` keyword is a quick and easy way to declare variables. The compiler infers the type and you can move on. The other side of the story is that using the `var`

(continued)

keyword can lead to unnecessary ambiguity. For example, compare the following two statements:

```
var result = ProcessGrades();
List<Grades> result = ProcessGrades();
```

If you were to use the `var` keyword, you would have to look into the `ProcessGrades` method to find out what the return type is. This promotes the idea of not needing to know any implementation details on the code you call. On the other hand, if you explicitly write down the return type as part of the variable declaration, you always know what type you are operating on. Knowing the type could allow us to make different decisions on how to implement a certain piece of code.

The `var` keyword can help you write code faster and, depending on your background, more intuitively. Sometimes, you don't need to know the underlying type—you just want to get on with writing your code.

The next two lines share a similar story:

```
var flights = new List<Flight>();
var connectionString =
    "Server=tcp:codelikeacsharppro.database.windows.net,1433;Initial
    Catalog=FlyingDutchmanAirlines;Persist Security Info=False;User
    ID=dev;Password=FlyingDutchmanAirlines1972!;MultipleActiveResultSets=False;
    Encrypt=True;TrustServerCertificate=False;Connection Timeout=30;";
```

Take a minute to look over the two variables `flights` and `connectionString`, and think about ways to improve the code.

4.1.4 Connection strings, or how to give a security engineer a heart attack

When considering the hardcoded connection string in section 4.1.3, what went through your mind? Did you see any problems with this? If so, what were they? The problem is not with the actual content of the connection string. The connection details are correct, and we want to have a list holding objects of type `Flight`. The problem is that we have a hardcoded connection string in our controller.

A hardcoded connection string is usually a major security and operational vulnerability. Imagine committing this code to a source control system and having it accidentally available for the public to see. It may be an unlikely scenario, but I have seen it happen once or twice (and may have caused it myself once). Now you have opened yourself up to all kinds of nasty things when it comes to your database. If that doesn't convince you, let me try this: you've hardcoded your connection string instead of pulling it from some central storage (be it a config file or an environment variable injected in a containerized environment), and a different developer accidentally backspaces one too many times and deletes part of the connection string. Of course, the developer didn't run any tests, and the code was reviewed and merged when you were on vacation. Now everything is broken. The moral of the story is this: it's a small effort to not hardcode your connection strings (we'll see how to use local environment variables for connection strings in section 5.3.3).

> **NOTE** The connection string listed in this chapter is, in fact, the correct connection string for use with our database. The database is deployed through Microsoft Azure and publicly accessible. If you cannot connect (or do not want to) to the database, a local SQL version of the database is provided with the source code files of this book. Instructions on installing and spinning up a local version of the deployed database are in appendix C.

Instead of hardcoding a connection string, it would be better to either

- Store the connection strings in some kind of configuration file, or
- Access them through an environment variable

We'll explore the trade-offs between these two approaches when it comes time for us to fix this security issue.

4.1.5 *Using IDisposable to release unmanaged resources*

The next code block is a statement that wraps some logic, and we have seen something like it before. This section deals with the using statement, shown next, and the IDisposable interface. We'll learn how they tie into garbage collection and how to use them.

```
using (var connection = new SqlConnection(connectionString)) {
    …
}
```

When we use a using statement in this way, we scope the enclosing variable to the using code block and automatically dispose of it when we are through with the using block. So, in this example, the connection variable of type SqlConnection is designated as ready for garbage collection once we reach the closing bracket of the using statement.

But why is this important? C# is a managed language with a garbage collector that is supposed to handle this for us. This means we do not have to do manual memory allocation and deallocation like you would do in an unmanaged language like C. Sometimes, though, we need to help the garbage collector out a little bit when it could get confused. For example, how does the garbage collector know when it can collect on something if that something may need to live on beyond the current code block or variable scope?

The .NET garbage collector scans the code during run time for objects that no longer have any "links" to them. These links can be things like method calls or variable assignments. To do this, it uses so-called generations. These generations are running "lists" of objects that are either ready for collection or may be ready for collection in the future. The longer the object has lived, the higher its generation (the garbage collector uses three generations in total). Objects in the third generation are visited less often by the garbage collector than earlier generations. Let's say we have an object that holds a property of type integer, assigned a value of 3. This property acts as a counter in a conditional. If this variable lives on for a while after the method is over (its variable scope is longer than the code block) waiting for the garbage collector to collect on it, it is no big deal. The amount of memory taken by the variable is small, and it is not blocking any other execution. When an object such as this has no remaining links (often because its variable scope has expired), the garbage collector flags the object as safe for collection, frees up the appropriate memory on its next iteration, and removes the corresponding entry from its generation lists.

Now imagine we have a connection to a SQL database, as in the code on the previous page. If that connection were to "live on" beyond its intended use case, it could prove to be an issue. We may run into issues where the connection remains open, blocking other code to execute on the same database, or we may even open ourselves up to buffer overflow hacks. To combat such a memory leak, we dispose of resources that are "unmanaged." Unlike managed resources, which are garbage-collected anytime after the variable scope has concluded, we need to deal with unmanaged resources more directly. Yet, disposing of unmanaged resources correctly is an easy thing to forget. Typically, we want to dispose of an unmanaged resource whenever we are done with it as opposed to when all references (or links) to the object have disappeared and the garbage collector says we are done with it. Unmanaged resources typically implement the IDisposable interface, so to free an unmanaged resource, we call the Dispose method.

Freeing an unmanaged resource can take the form of calling the Dispose method at the end of the method. But what if you have branching code with multiple return opportunities? You would have to have multiple Dispose calls. That may work for small methods but can quickly get confusing when dealing with large code blocks of conditionals and multiple paths of traversal through your code. The using statement is a solution for that. Under the hood, the compiler converts the using statement to a try-finally code block. An example of this is shown in figure 4.3.

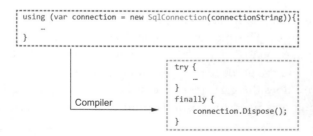

Figure 4.3   A using statement is converted to a try-finally block by the compiler. Using a try-catch allows us to abstract the manual Dispose call.

A try-finally is a subset of the try-catch-finally construct we often use when dealing with error handling. When we wrap code in a try code block, followed by a catch code block, if an exception is thrown, it is caught in the `catch` code block versus having our code hard-crash. A `finally` is an optional code block attached to the end of the `catch` that executes code as it leaves the code block, whether or not there was an error caught. We could call the `Dispose` method in the `finally` code block, ensuring that the `Dispose` method is always called after the method has been executed, no matter what the outcome is or if any errors were thrown.

> **NOTE** Calling `Dispose` on a resource implementing `IDisposable` does not cause an immediate garbage collection to happen. We are merely flagging it safe for collecting and requesting for it to happen at the next opportunity to do so. No impromptu garbage collection is initiated, but we take the management of when the resource is determined safe for collection into our own hands as opposed to letting the garbage collector decide.

4.1.6 Querying a database with SqlCommand

The constructor for `SqlConnection` takes in a parameter of type `string` that represents the connection string for us to connect to. After entering the `using` block, we can now operate on our newly created `SqlConnection` and query the database. In the next code listing, the code opens a connection to the database.

> **Listing 4.2 FlightController.cs GET Flight: inside the SqlConnection using statement**

```
connection.Open();              ◁── Opens the database
                                    connection
// Get Flights
var cmd = new SqlCommand("SELECT * FROM Flight", connection);   ◁── Creates a
                                                                   SqlCommand
using (var reader = cmd.ExecuteReader()) {                          with a SQL
  while (reader.Read()) {                                           query to select
    flights.Add(new Flight(reader.GetInt32(0), reader.GetInt32(1),  all flights
➥   reader.GetInt32(2)));       ◁── Creates new
  }                                 flight instances
}
cmd.Dispose();       ◁── Disposes of the
                         cmd instance
```

If the database cannot be reached through the provided connection string, the code throws an exception (which is unhandled). Following that, a `SqlCommand` is created with a query to select all records from the `Flight` table (`"SELECT * FROM Flight"`). The eagle-eyed reader might have spotted that a couple of lines down, `cmd.Dispose` is called. We would have to call `Dispose` on `reader` as well if we did not use a `using` statement. It looks like our predecessors were not consistent in using `using` statements or manual disposal requests. We are going to fix that. The code in listing 4.2 has a `using` statement that creates a `reader` object, rendered from the `cmd.ExecuteReader()` method.

The `reader` allows us to parse the database response into a more manageable form. We can see this in action if we step inside the `using` statement, where we create a new `Flight` object, as shown in figure 4.4.

```
// Get Flights
var cmd = new SqlCommand( cmdText: "SELECT * FROM Flight", connection);
```

Scope of reader

```
using (var reader = cmd.ExecuteReader()) {
    while (reader.Read()) {
        flights.Add(new Flight(reader.GetInt32( i: 0), originID: reader.GetInt32( i: 1),
            destinationID: reader.GetInt32( i: 2)));
    }
}
```

```
cmd.Dispose();
```

Figure 4.4 The scope of a variable created in a `using` statement. The `reader` instance is scoped to the `using` statement and is not accessible when the code leaves the `using` code block.

The `Flight` object takes three parameters, all 32-bit integers (int): `flightNumber`, `originID`, and `destinationID`. These also are the columns of our Flight table (if we take into account the slight misnaming we discussed earlier in this chapter). We know the order the columns are returned in, because we know the database schema. It probably would have been cleaner to specify what columns the query should return. If we explicitly say what columns we want to be returned, we can control the data flow better and know exactly what we are going to get. It does not require a developer unfamiliar with the code or database schema to do more research to find out what the expected returns are.

The code in listing 4.2 calls the reader's `GetInt32` method and passes in the value's index we are looking for. Once the `Flight` object is created, it is added to the `flights` collection. Moving on, take a minute to look over the code in listing 4.3. Hopefully, you'll see some very familiar things.

Listing 4.3 FlightController.cs `GET Flight`: getting the `Origin Airport` details

```
// Get Origin Airport details
cmd = new SqlCommand("SELECT City FROM Airport WHERE AirportID = " +
➡   flight.OriginID, connection);

using (var reader = cmd.ExecuteReader()) {
    while (reader.Read()) {
        returnView.Origin = reader.GetString(0);
        break;
    }
}
cmd.Dispose();

flightReturnViews.Add(returnView);
```

Creates a SQL query to select the City column of a specific Airport

Executes the SqlCommand

Assigns the first element of the database response to returnView.Origin

Reads the response from the database

The code in listing 4.3 creates a new `SqlCommand` to select the `City` column from the Airport table, where `AirportID` is equal to `flight.OriginID` (last time around it was the `flight.destination`). The code executes the `SqlCommand` and reads the return value into the `returnView.Origin` field. Then the code disposes of `SqlCommand` and adds the `returnView` to the `flightReturnViews` collection. And with that, we've finally come to the end of this endpoint. There's only one more line of code to consider:

```
return Request.CreateResponse(HttpStatusCode.OK, flightReturnViews);
```

Remember when we looked at the method signature? We discovered that we are supposed to return a `HttpResponseMessage`, and that is exactly what `Request.Create-Response` gives us.

> **TIP**   If you ever want to find out more about specific namespaces or classes of the .NET Framework, .NET Core, or .NET 5, the Microsoft online documentation is excellent and can be found at https://docs.microsoft.com/en-us/. For example, the .NET Framework documentation for `HttpRequest` is at https://docs.microsoft.com/en-us/dotnet/api/system.web.httprequest?view=netframework-4.8.

The `CreateResponse` method has several method overloads we can use, but for this, we want to pass in both an HTTP status code and an object to be serialized and returned to the caller.

Method overloading and static constructors

Method overloading, also called *function overloading*, allows multiple methods with the same name (but different parameters) in the same class. This means that we can have the methods `public uint ProcessData(short a, byte b)` and `public uint ProcessData(long a, string b)` in the same class with no problem. When we call the `ProcessData` method, our request is routed by the CLR to the appropriate method based on the input parameter types. What we cannot do is have two (or more) methods with the same name and input parameters. The reason for this is that the method call then becomes ambiguous. How is the CLR supposed to know where to direct our call? This also means that if we have the methods `internal void GetZebra(bool isReal-Zebra)` and `internal bool GetZebra(bool isRealZebra)`, we get a compiler error. Just changing the return type does not make the call less ambiguous to the CLR.

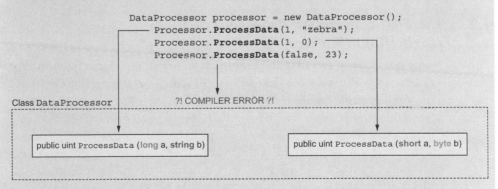

Overloading `ProcessData`. The compiler routes the `ProcessData` calls to the appropriate overloaded methods at compile time. A compiler error is generated if no overloaded method is matched.

(continued)

We can also overload constructors. We call this *constructor overloading*, but it is the same principle as method overloading. We can use overloaded constructors to have multiple paths to object instantiation. For constructors, there is also the `static` constructor. Because we are dealing with `static`, there can be only one static constructor, and, therefore, it cannot be overloaded. When instantiating a class or calling a static member on a class, a `static` constructor is always called before instantiation or static member access. We can have `static` constructors and regular constructors, but the runtime always calls the `static` (once) before the very first regular constructor you use. Consequently, a `static` constructor is always parameterless, and `static` constructors do not contain access modifiers (a static constructor is always public).

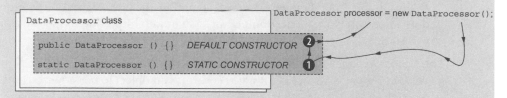

Static and default constructors. The static constructor is called first before any other constructor. Step 1: static constructor; step 2: default (or explicitly declared) constructors.

For the Java programmers out there, note that Java's anonymous static initialization block is equivalent to a static constructor in C#. C# can have only one static constructor, however, whereas Java can have multiple anonymous static initialization blocks.

To pass in a status code, we cannot simply pass in an integer. The `CreateResponse` method requires us to pass in our selection of the `HttpStatusCode` enum field, in this case, `HttpStatusCode.OK` (which maps to a status code of 200). And with the return executed, our job in this method is done.

In summation: although the `GET Flight` endpoint had some good things about it, we saw plenty of opportunities to refactor and improve.

4.2   *The FlightController: Assessing GET /flight/{flightNumber}*

Now that we have looked at the endpoints to get all the flights from the database, let's examine how the previous developers implemented the logic to get a specific flight from the database. In this section, we'll explore the `GET flight/{flightNumber}` endpoint and consider its strengths and flaws. We'll also consider whether we can remove extraneous comments and see an example of code as a narrative.

In listing 4.4, we'll lift the veil on the `GET /flight/{flightNumber}` endpoint and see familiar non-optimal practices, such as a hardcoded connection string. A lot of the code in listing 4.4 is code you should be able to read without a problem. The differences are in the details: we'll discuss the abundance of comments, the `HttpResponse-Message` class, and assigning `null` to implicit types (denoted by the `var` keyword).

Listing 4.4   FlightController.cs `GET flight/{flightNumber}`

```
// GET: api/Flight/5
[ResponseType(typeof(FlightReturnView))]
public HttpResponseMessage Get(int id) {
  var flightReturnView = new FlightReturnView();
  Flight flight = null;

  var connectionString =
  "Server=tcp:codelikeacsharppro.database.windows.net,1433;Initial
  Catalog=FlyingDutchmanAirlines;Persist Security Info=False;User
  ID=dev;Password=FlyingDutchmanAirlines1972!;MultipleActiveResultSets=False;
  Encrypt=True;TrustServerCertificate=False;Connection Timeout=30;";

  using(var connection = new SqlConnection(connectionString)) {
    connection.Open();

    // Get Flight
    var cmd = new SqlCommand("SELECT * FROM Flight WHERE FlightNumber =
  " + id, connection);

    using (var reader = cmd.ExecuteReader()) {
      while (reader.Read()) {
        flight = new Flight(reader.GetInt32(0), reader.GetInt32(1),
  reader.GetInt32(2));
        flightReturnView.FlightNumber = flight.FlightNumber;
        break;
      }
    }

    cmd.Dispose();

    // Get Destination Airport Details
    cmd = new SqlCommand("SELECT City FROM Airport WHERE AirportID = "
  + flight.DestinationID, connection);

    using (var reader = cmd.ExecuteReader()) {
      while (reader.Read()) {
        flightReturnView.Destination = reader.GetString(0);
        break;
      }
    }

    cmd.Dispose();

    // Get Origin Airport Details
    cmd = new SqlCommand("SELECT City FROM Airport WHERE AirportID = "
  + flight.OriginID, connection);

    using (var reader = cmd.ExecuteReader()) {
      while (reader.Read()) {
        flightReturnView.Origin = reader.GetString(0);
        break;
      }
    }
```

```
    cmd.Dispose();
  }

  return Request.CreateResponse(HttpStatusCode.OK, flightReturnView);
}
```

As you can see, 99% of the endpoint logic comprises patterns and code from the previous endpoint (listing 4.1), but there are some differences. The first is something we can find in the method signature, as shown next:

```
public HttpResponseMessage Get(int id)
```

The `Get flight/{flightNumber}` endpoint takes in an argument of type `integer`, stored in a variable called `id`. This maps directly to the `{flightNumber}` in the API path: `"/flight/{flightNumber}"`. The other difference is the following declaration of a `Flight` object instead of a list of flights. This makes sense because we want to deal with only an individual flight, not a whole bunch.

```
Flight flight = null;
```

It may look strange at first that the developers did not use the `var` keyword here, but that would not have compiled correctly. You cannot assign `null` to a variable declared with the `var` keyword, because when using `var`, the type is implicitly deduced from the assigned expression. Because `null` does not contain any type information, the developers had to declare the type for `flight` explicitly.

The code being very similar allows us to take a step back and uncover some other unclean bits of code without having to focus on what we already know. Foremost, what is up with the comments describing the logic? They are undoubtedly meant to act like breadcrumbs for you to follow as you struggle your way through the method:

- `// Get Flight`
- `// Get Destination Airport Details`
- `// Get Origin Airport Details`

Wouldn't it be nice if we put those in little small methods that could be reused by other endpoints? I have done exactly that in listing 4.5. Imagine a method that reads like a narrative or list of steps, containing only a couple of small methods, instead of the gigantic mess we have now. Listing 4.5 takes the code from listing 4.4 and imagines a world where a developer has extracted out internal details into separate methods, calling them in one public method. Compare listings 4.5 and 4.4. The difference in complexity is enormous. Of course, we are now using multiple database connections to retrieve the data related to one item. There's always a drawback, and that is one that may be too much for some people to bear. All the logic dealing with the *how* of getting things from the database has been abstracted away into private methods. A developer who is not intimately familiar with this class can now look at this method and instantly know what it does without knowing all the implementation details. Knowing the general flow of the method is often more than enough knowledge for a developer to gain. Notice that there is no code dealing with connection strings, opening database connections, and disposing of objects in the public method.

Listing 4.5   Example of a cleaned-up FlightController.cs `GET flight/{flightNumber}`

```
[ResponseType(typeof(FlightReturnView))]
public HttResponseMessage Get(int id) {
  Flight flight = GetFlight(id);                    ← Gets flight details from database

  FlightReturnView flightReturnView = new FlightReturnView();      ← Creates a new instance of FlightReturnView
  flightReturnView.FlightNumber = flight.FlightNumber;            ← Populates the returnView's FlightNumber field

  flightReturnView.Destination =
  GetDestinationAirport(flight.DestinationID);
  flightReturnView.Origin = GetOriginAirport(flight.OriginID);    ←

  return Request.CreateResponse(HttpStatusCode.OK, flightReturnView);   ←
}
```

Gets flight details from database

Creates a new instance of FlightReturnView

Populates the returnView's FlightNumber field

Populates the returnView's Destination field

Returns an HTTP 200 and the returnView

Populates the returnView's Origin field

In listing 4.5, I extracted all the nitty-gritty details into their own private methods. The method in listing 4.5 is far from perfect (there is no error handling, for starters), but it is an improvement.

The next endpoint is a POST endpoint that creates a booking in the database. It is also similar but sees us dealing with JSON deserialization.

4.3 *The FlightController: POST /flight*

We have seen logic to get flights in two ways: get all of them at once, or get a single one based on the flight number. But what if we want to book a flight? This section examines the POST /flight endpoint, shown in the next listing, which allows users to book a flight. It is similar to the previous endpoints but sees us dealing with JSON deserialization for the first time. Besides JSON deserializing, this section touches on the Don't Repeat Yourself (DRY) principle and the ModelState static class. One thing to note, however, is that FlyTomorrow's OpenAPI specification said we needed a POST /booking endpoint, not a POST /flight endpoint. Let's make a note of that, and fix it when the time comes.

Listing 4.6   FlightController.cs `POST /flight`

```
[ResponseType(typeof(HttpResponseMessage))]
public HttpResponseMessage Post([FromBody] Booking value) {
  var connectionString =
  "Server=tcp:codelikeacsharppro.database.windows.net,1433;Initial
  Catalog=FlyingDutchmanAirlines;Persist Security Info=False;User
  ID=dev;Password=FlyingDutchmanAirlines1972!;MultipleActiveResultSets=False;
  Encrypt=True;TrustServerCertificate=False;Connection Timeout=30;";
```

```
using (var connection = new SqlConnection(connectionString)) {
  connection.Open();

    // Get Destination Airport ID
  var cmd = new SqlCommand("SELECT AirportID FROM Airport WHERE IATA
= "'" + value.DestinationAirportIATA + "'", connection);
  var destinationAirportID = 0;

  using (var reader = cmd.ExecuteReader()) {
    while (reader.Read()) {
      destinationAirportID = reader.GetInt32(0);
      break;
    }
  }

  cmd.Dispose();

  // Get Origin Airport ID
  var cmd = new SqlCommand("SELECT AirportID FROM Airport WHERE IATA
= '" + value.OriginAirportIATA + "'", connection);
  var originAirportID = 0;

  using (var reader = cmd.ExecuteReader()) {
    while (reader.Read()) {
      originAirportID = reader.GetInt32(0);
      break;
    }
  }

  cmd.Dispose();

  // Get Flight Details
  cmd = new SqlCommand("SELECT * FROM Flight WHERE Origin = " +
originAirportID + " AND Destination = " + destinationAirportID,
connection);

  Flight flight = null;

  using (var reader = cmd.ExecuteReader()) {
    while (reader.Read()) {
      flight = new Flight(reader.GetInt32(0), reader.GetInt32(1),
reader.GetInt(2));
      break;
    }
  }

  cmd.Dispose();

  // Create new customer
  cmd = new SqlCommand("SELECT COUNT(*) FROM Customer",
connection);
  var newCustomerID = 0;

  using (var reader = cmd.ExecuteReader()) {
    while (reader.Read()) {
```

Gets the destination Airport from the database

Gets the origin Airport from the database

Gets the details of the flight we want to book

SQL query to count all customers in the database

```
            newCustomerID = reader.GetInt32(0);
        }
    }

    cmd.Dispose();

    cmd = new SqlCommand("INSERT INTO Customer (CustomerID, Name)
    VALUES ('" + (newCustomerID + 1) + "', '" + value.Name + "')",
    connection);
    cmd.ExecuteNonQuery();
    cmd.Dispose();

    var customer = new Customer(newCustomerID, value.Name);

    // Book flight
    cmd = new SqlCommand("INSERT INTO Booking (FlightNumber,
    CustomerID) VALUES (" + flight.FlightNumber + ", '" +
    customer.CustomerID + "')", connection);
    cmd.ExecuteNonQuery();
    cmd.Dispose();

    return Request.CreateResponse(HttpStatusCode.Created), "Hooray! A
    customer with the name \"" + customer.Name +
    "\" has booked a flight!!!");
    }
}
```

- Assigns the count of all customers in the database to newCustomerID
- SQL command to insert a new customer into the database
- Executes the command
- Creates an internal Customer object that mimics the in-database one
- Creates a booking in the database
- Returns an HTTP Status 201 and a message with sensitive customer data

That has got to be the longest, most convoluted endpoint we have seen yet. Because our previous approach proved somewhat successful, let's rinse and repeat. Once again, we see a method signature with the ResponseType attribute applied:

```
[ResponseType(typeof(HttpResponseMessage))]
public HttpResponseMessage Post([FromBody] Booking value)
```

This is a mostly familiar story to us by now. We also return an HttpResponseMessage. But there is a difference in this method signature when compared to the endpoints we looked at before: the Post method takes in a parameter of type Booking, and there's an attribute applied to this parameter as well.

> **NOTE** You can apply attributes not only to methods but also to variables, classes, delegates, interfaces, and much more. You can't use attributes on variables because all data related to an attribute must be known at compile time. This cannot be guaranteed for a variable.

You can use the FromBody attribute to automatically parse an XML or JSON body into any class you want (as long as the properties match between the input and the specified class). Here, the sent-in JSON body is mapped by the CLR to an instance of the Booking class. This magical little attribute is one of the most time-saving things you encounter in C#. A valid JSON payload for this endpoint would be as follows:

```
{
  "OriginAirportIATA": "GRQ",
  "DestinationAirportIATA": "CDG",
  "Name" : "Donald Knuth"
}
```

These values map directly to the fields in the Booking class. The .NET Framework takes the JSON and spits out our new Booking instance with those values, as shown in figure 4.5. Because this process binds a parameter to a model, we call the mapping process *model binding*. We'll dive deep into model binding in chapter 14.

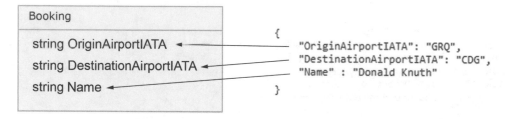

Figure 4.5   **Deserializing a JSON payload into a C# class. The [FromBody] attribute takes a JSON or XML body and parses it to a model.**

With model binding, we still rely on the quality of the input data. If the input data is missing a field, the underlying code for [FromBody] throws an exception, and the method automatically returns an HTTP status code of 400. If all the fields are in the JSON body, but the CLR cannot parse one of the fields for whatever reason, the CLR sets the global ModelState.IsValid property to false. It is therefore always a good thing to check for this, and we'll do that when we go to refactor this method.

As we scan through the method, we quickly realize that we have seen this all before. In fact, until we hit the last code block of the method, everything is old news—an enormous warning sign that this code violates the DRY principle.

The Don't Repeat Yourself principle

Previously, we discussed refactoring methods into small pieces. This results in methods that read like narratives, following a couple of simple steps to produce the output. We do this to increase readability, but there is another angle to examine: the DRY principle.

DRY stands for "don't repeat yourself" and was coined in the book *The Pragmatic Programmer* (Addison-Wesley, 1999), written by Andrew Hunt and Dave Thomas. Hunt and Thomas defined the DRY principle to mean that "Every piece of knowledge must have a single, unambiguous, authoritative representation within a system (27)." In practical terms, this often means that you write the same code only once. In other words: don't duplicate code.

> If you find yourself, for example, copying and pasting the same `foreach` loop (perhaps with a different collection to iterate over) multiple times in the same method, class, or even codebase, extract it out into a dedicated method and call it. This does two things: first, it makes the methods calling this extracted method much easier to read because you have encapsulated implementation details. Second, if you ever need to change the implementation of this `foreach` loop, you have to do it in only one spot versus everywhere in your codebase. So, as with comedy, keep it DRY!

The last code block of the method, shown in the next listing, is short and almost surprisingly to the point.

Listing 4.7 FlightController.cs POST `/flight`: **Inserting a** `Booking` **object in the database**

```
// Book Flight
cmd = new SqlCommand("INSERT INTO Booking (FlightNumber, CustomerID) VALUES
  (" + flight.FlightNumber + ", '" + customer.CustomerID + "')",
  connection);
cmd.ExecuteNonQuery();
cmd.Dispose();

return Request.CreateResponse(HttpStatusCode.Created, "Hooray! A customer
  with the name \"" + customer.Name + "\" has booked a flight!!! ");
```

Executes the command

Disposes of the SqlCommand object

SQL Query command to insert a booking into the database

Returns an HTTP status 201 along with sensitive customer data

The code in listing 4.7 creates a new `SqlCommand` to insert a new record into the `Booking` table, then executes on that query and disposes of the `SqlCommand`. Finally, it returns a response with an HTTP status code of 201 and a text blurb containing `customer.Name`.

4.4   The FlightController: DELETE /flight/{flightNumber}

We have looked at most of the endpoints in the `FlightController` class throughout this chapter and have found many ways in which we could improve the code. We have only one more endpoint to go in the controller: DELETE `flight/{flightNumber}`. Perhaps mercifully and appropriately, this method is less than 20 lines long. We can trim it down by extracting the connection string, but overall, we have seen much worse code in this chapter.

There is nothing new in this DELETE method (besides a different query passed into the `SqlCommand` constructor), and I am not going to take too much of your time going over it in detail in the next listing. There are two peculiarities, however: the OpenAPI specification we received from FlyTomorrow in chapter 3 did not specify we need a DELETE `/flight/{flightNumber}` endpoint at all. After all, why would we want to allow users to delete flights from the database? This endpoint is therefore not something we improve upon and not part of the requirements. Instead, we omit it and don't bother refactoring it in the coming chapters.

> **Listing 4.8   FlightController.cs** DELETE flight/{flightNumber]

```
[ResponseType(typeof(HttpResponseMessage))]
public HttpResponseMessage Delete(int id) {
  var connectionString =
➡ "Server=tcp:codelikeacsharppro.database.windows.net,1433;Initial
➡ Catalog=FlyingDutchmanAirlines;Persist Security Info=False;User
➡ ID=dev;Password=FlyingDutchmanAirlines1972!;MultipleActiveResultSets=False;
➡ Encrypt=True;TrustServerCertificate=False;Connection Timeout=30;";

  using (var connection = new SqlConnection(connectionString)) {
    connection.Open();

    var cmd = new SqlCommand("DELETE FROM Booking WHERE BookingID = '"
➡ + id + "'", connection);
    cmd.ExecuteNonQuery();
    cmd.Dispose();

    return Request.CreateResponse(HttpStatusCode.OK);
  }
}
```

And with that, we have finished our exploration of the existing codebase. We can improve on a lot of things, and we also have some security problems that we *must* fix.

Exercises

EXERCISE 4.1

True or false? You can apply attributes only to methods.

EXERCISE 4.2

True or false? You can't apply attributes to variables.

EXERCISE 4.3

True or false? The IEnumerable interface allows us to create new enums.

EXERCISE 4.4

What are *bad* practices with database connection strings?

- a Commit hardcoded connection strings to an SCM.
- b Never hardcode connection strings.
- c Store connection strings in a configuration file or environment variable.
- d Write connection strings on a sticky note and place it in your favorite copy of Harry Potter and the Chamber of Connection Strings.

EXERCISE 4.5

Why do we need to dispose of a class implementing the IDisposable interface?

- a Otherwise, it becomes indisposed.
- b Classes implementing IDisposable typically hold on to some resources that can cause a memory leak if not disposed of.
- c You don't have to dispose of a class implementing the IDisposable interface.

EXERCISE 4.6

If we call `Dispose` on a class, when does the garbage collector collect on the resource?

- a The next time it encounters the respective resource during its garbage collection rounds
- b Immediately
- c At the end of the method

EXERCISE 4.7

Which one of these is *not* an appropriate technique for disposing of objects?

- a Wrap the object creation in a `using` statement code block.
- b Call `Dispose` at every exit point in your method.
- c Remove the `IDisposable` implementation from the object's source code.

EXERCISE 4.8

True or false? A static constructor is run before default or defined (regular) constructors.

EXERCISE 4.9

True or false? A static constructor is run every time an object is instantiated.

Summary

- We can use the `typeof` operator to determine the type of an object at compile time or the `GetType` method (from the `object` base type) at run time.
- `Object` is the base type for all types in C#. This means that, through polymorphism, all the methods that `object` exposes are useable on all types (such as `GetType`). This allows us to use a basic set of methods on every type in C#.
- By implementing the `IEnumerable` interface, we can create classes with enumerators. We can use these classes to represent collections and perform operations on the elements they contain. This comes in useful when we want to create a collection that is not provided by the .NET ecosystem.
- We should never hardcode a connection string. This is a security problem. Instead, store connection strings in a configuration file or environment variable.
- The .NET garbage collector scans memory at run time for resources that have no remaining "links," flags them, and frees up their memory the next time the garbage collector runs. This is what makes C# a managed language. Because of this, we do not have to manually and explicitly deal with pointers and memory allocation in C#.
- The compiler resolves a `using` statement to a `try-finally` code block. This allows us to abstract away the `Dispose` call we find in a `try-finally` block when using classes that implement `IDisposable`. Abstracting away the `Dispose` call decreases the chances of forgetting to correctly dispose of the object and, therefore, creating a possible memory leak.
- A `try-catch` code block can catch and handle exceptions. Whenever you have code that throws exceptions (expected or unexpected), consider wrapping it in

a `try-catch` block. When you wrap code in a `try-catch` block and catch exceptions, you are given a chance to elegantly handle the exception and log it, or gracefully shut down the application.

- The `finally` code block in a `try-catch-finally` or `try-finally` is always executed right before the code block is exited, even if an exception was caught. The `finally` block is an optional addition to the `try-catch` code block. This is useful if you need to perform teardown or cleanup operations (such as disposal of an object implementing `IDisposable`).

- C# supports method overloading. This means we can have methods with the same name but with different arguments. Method calls are routed at run time by the CLR to the appropriate method. This is useful when extending an existing class's functionality without changing the original method.

- A `static` constructor is always executed once before the first instantiation of an object. This can be used to set values to static properties before any logic execution that uses them.

- The `[FromBody]` attribute allows you to do parameter binding and deserialize a JSON body into a model. This is a big time saver when dealing with HTTP endpoints because you do not have to write your own JSON mapping logic.

- The Don't Repeat Yourself (DRY) principle tells us to not duplicate code. Instead, refactor the code into an extracted method and call that. Using the DRY principle promotes code maintainability.

Part 3

The database access layer

In part 2, we examined the existing code base of Flying Dutchman Airlines in depth. We came up with things we could change and talked about why these changes would be necessary. In this part, we'll take things one step further and start our rewrite of the service. You will learn how to create a new .NET 5 project, and how to connect to, query, and reverse-engineer a database with Entity Framework Core.

Setting up a project and database with Entity Framework Core

This chapter covers

- Refactoring a legacy codebase to be clean and secure
- Using Entity Framework Core to query a database
- Implementing the repository/service pattern
- Creating a new .NET 5 solution and project using the command line

The time has finally come. You are probably eager to fix some of the issues we saw in chapters 3 and 4, and now we'll get to do that. First things first, let's come up with a game plan on how to tackle this refactoring. We already know a couple of things that we need to do differently:

- In chapter 3 we were told to use .NET 5 instead of the .NET Framework for the new version of the Flying Dutchman Airlines service.
- We need to rewrite the endpoints to be clean code (in particular, adhering to the DRY principle).
- We need to fix the security vulnerability—a hardcoded connection string.

- The object names do not match the database column names. We should fix that to ensure a perfect isomorphic relationship between the codebase and the database.
- We need to adhere to the OpenAPI file discussed in chapter 3 and shown in appendix D.

Although not necessarily part of the requirements, we would like to include some additional deliverables to improve the quality of the job, thus ensuring a job well done:

- We want to use test-driven development to write unit tests that back the codebase.
- We want to use Entity Framework Core to revamp the database layer by reverse-engineering the deployed database.
- We want to autogenerate an updated OpenAPI file on the launch of the service to compare against the provided OpenAPI from FlyTomorrow.

Of course, we will do much more than just these improvements, but it is good to have some general broad strokes in mind. We are also in a very interesting position: we are stuck somewhere in the middle of having to keep the old codebase alive and working and greenfield development.

> **DEFINITION**   *Greenfield development* means that we are working on a project that isn't held back by any previous design decisions or old code. In practice, this usually means a brand-new project.

We have set requirements and an old codebase that we need to mimic (where appropriate and possible), but we also start with an empty project. In the real world, you will often encounter this scenario. You no doubt have had the experience of trying to create a new version of an existing product—a "next-gen" version, if you will. Figure 5.1 shows where we are in the scheme of the book.

Our first order of business is to create a new .NET 5 solution.

5.1   *Creating a .NET 5 solution and project*

In this section, we'll create a new .NET 5 solution and project. We'll also look at what predefined solution and project templates exist for .NET 5. You have the following two ways to create a new .NET 5 solution:

- You can use a command line, be it the Windows command line or a macOS/ Linux terminal.
- You can use an IDE like Visual Studio. Using Visual Studio automates the process somewhat. Most things you can do in a command line or terminal with C# you can also do in Visual Studio with a couple of clicks.[1]

---

[1] Installation instructions for Visual Studio can be found in appendix C. If you want to learn more about Visual Studio, see Bruce Johnson's *Professional Visual Studio 2017* (Wrox, 2017) and Johnson's *Essential Visual Studio 2019* (Apress, 2020). Disclaimer: The author was the technical reviewer for *Essential Visual Studio 2019: Boosting Development Productivity with Containers, Git, and Azure Tools.*

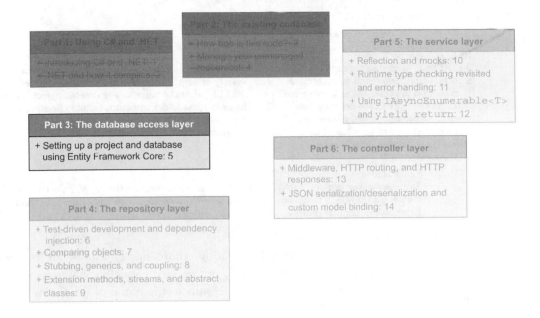

Figure 5.1 **In this chapter, we'll start the process of reimplementing the Flying Dutchman Airlines codebase. We'll start with the database access layer. In the following chapters, we'll look at the repository layer, service layer, and controller layer.**

The outcome of using either route is the same: you end up with a new .NET 5 solution. We'll be using the command line. Creating a new, empty .NET 5 solution or project is very simple, as shown here:

```
\> dotnet new [TEMPLATE] [FLAGS]
```

NOTE Before you attempt to create a .NET 5 project, please make sure you have installed the latest .NET 5 SDK and runtime. Installation instructions are in appendix C.

We can use a variety of templates. Some of the more common ones are web, webapp, mvc, and webapi. For our purposes, we use perhaps two of the most popular of all: sln and console. The dotnet new sln command creates a new solution, whereas dotnet new console creates a new project and a "hello, world" source file. As discussed in section 3.3.2, C# uses solutions and projects to organize its codebases. A solution is the top-level entity and contains multiple projects. We write our logic within the projects. Projects can be thought of as different modules, packages, or libraries, depending on our language of preference.

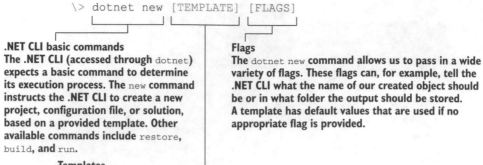

We also pass the -n flag along with the creation command. This allows us to specify a name for our solution and project. If we do not explicitly specify a name for our solution, the name of our project or solution defaults to the name of the folder in which we create the files.

To create our starting point, run the following command. Note that the command-line tool does not let you create a new solution folder when creating a new solution. If you want to do this, you can either use Visual Studio (which does allow for it) or create the folder first and then run the following command in the solution folder.

```
\> dotnet new sln -n "FlyingDutchmanAirlinesNextGen"
```

The command creates only one thing: a solution file called FlyingDutchmanAirlines-NextGen.sln, shown in figure 5.2. We could open this solution file in Visual Studio, but we cannot do much without a project.

```
C:\Windows\System32\cmd.exe                                           -  □  x
Microsoft Windows [Version 10.0.18362.720]
(c) 2019 Microsoft Corporation. All rights reserved.

C:\Users\Jort\Desktop\Code>dotnet new sln -n "FlyingDutchmanAirlinesNextGen"
The template "Solution File" was created successfully.
```

Figure 5.2   After running the command to create a new .NET solution, the command line lets us know that the operation was successful.

Now that we have a solution file, we should create a project called FlyingDutchman-Airlines. To create a new project, we use the console template, as shown next. This creates a .NET 5 console application, which we'll then change to be a web service.

```
\> dotnet new console -n "FlyingDutchmanAirlines"
```

After running the command, we are greeted by a message saying that "Restore succeeded." A restore is a process that the .NET CLI performs before the creation of a new project and before compiling after a "clean" operation ("clean" deletes all local executable files, including dependencies) or first compilation, to gather required dependencies. We can also run this command on its own by saying

```
\> dotnet restore
```

A restore can come in handy when dealing with dependency troubles. The restore command also creates a new folder next to our solution file called FlyingDutchman-Airlines (the same as the project name we passed in), as shown in figure 5.3. When we enter the folder, we see another folder called obj. The obj folder contains configuration files for NuGet and its packages. Back in the root folder for the project, we have a project file and a C# source file.

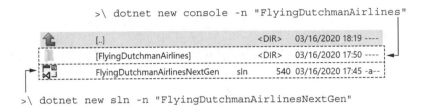

```
>\ dotnet new console -n "FlyingDutchmanAirlines"
```

[..]		<DIR>	03/16/2020 18:19 ----
[FlyingDutchmanAirlines]		<DIR>	03/16/2020 17:50 ----
FlyingDutchmanAirlinesNextGen	sln	540	03/16/2020 17:45 -a--

```
>\ dotnet new sln -n "FlyingDutchmanAirlinesNextGen"
```

Figure 5.3   The folder structure after running the command-line commands to create a solution and project. The FlyingDutchmanAirlines folder was created using the command to create a project, whereas the FlyingDutchmanAirlinesNextGen.sln file was created using the command to create a new solution.

Our project is created, but we still need to add it to the solution. When you create a project, dotnet does not scan any subdirectories looking for a contained solution. To add a project to a solution, use the "solution add" command as follows:

```
\> dotnet sln [SOLUTION PATH] add [PROJECT PATH]
```

The [SOLUTION PATH] points to the path of the solution file to which you want to add a project. The [PROJECT PATH], similarly, points to a csproj file to be added to the solution. You can add multiple projects at the same time by adding multiple [PROJECT PATH] arguments to the command.

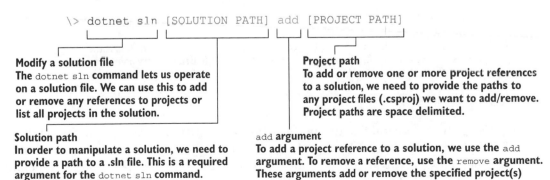

```
\> dotnet sln [SOLUTION PATH] add [PROJECT PATH]
```

Modify a solution file
The dotnet sln **command lets us operate on a solution file. We can use this to add or remove any references to projects or list all projects in the solution.**

Project path
To add or remove one or more project references to a solution, we need to provide the paths to any project files (.csproj) we want to add/remove. Project paths are space delimited.

Solution path
In order to manipulate a solution, we need to provide a path to a .sln file. This is a required argument for the dotnet sln **command.**

add **argument**
To add a project reference to a solution, we use the add **argument. To remove a reference, use the** remove **argument. These arguments add or remove the specified project(s) to/from the provided solution file.**

In our situation, running from the root FlyingDutchmanAirlinesNextGen folder, the command takes just the one csproj into account, as shown here:

```
\> dotnet sln FlyingDutchmanAirlinesNextGen.sln add
➡ .\FlyingDutchmanAirlines\FlyingDutchmanAirlines.csproj
```

The terminal lets us know with a message—Project `FlyingDutchmanAirlines\FlyingDutchmanAirlines.csproj` added to the solution.—that we were successful in our effort. If we open up the FlyingDutchmanAirlinesNextGen.sln file in a text editor, we see a reference to the FlyingDutchmanAirlines.csproj file as follows:

```
Project("{…}") =
➡ "FlyingDutchmanAirlines",
➡ "FlyingDutchmanAirlines\FlyingDutchmanAirlines.csproj", "{…}"
EndProject
```

This is the reference added by the `solution add` command. The reference tells an IDE and the compiler that there is a project with the name FlyingDutchmanAirlines as part of this solution.

5.2 Setting up and configuring a web service

In section 5.1 we created a new solution and project to use for the next-gen version of the Flying Dutchman Airlines service. In this section, we'll look at the source code generated as a result of the actions we took in section 5.1 and configure the console application to function as a web service.

The only source file in the solution (and project) at this point is Program.cs, shown in the next listing. This file is automatically generated through the `console` template we used in section 5.1 to create a new project. It contains the entry point for the program—a `static` method called `Main`—which returns nothing. Here, it also accepts a string array called `args`. This array contains any command-line arguments passed in on launch.

Listing 5.1   Program.cs with the `Main` method

```
using System;

namespace FlyingDutchmanAirlines {
  class Program {
    static void Main(string[] args) {        A static void Main is the
      Console.WriteLine("Hello World!");      default entry point for a
    }                                         C# console application.
  }
}
```

Using the command line to run the FlyingDutchmanAirlinesNextGen project, it outputs "Hello World!" to the console. Let's remove the `"Hello World!"` string from the code. This puts us in a good spot to change the console application to something more functional: a web service.

5.2.1 Configuring a .NET 5 web service

We need to configure our brand-new .NET 5 app to accept HTTP requests and route them to the endpoints we'll implement. To do this, we also need to set up Host, which is the underlying process that runs the web service and interacts with the CLR. Our application lives inside the Host, which in turn lives inside the CLR.

> **NOTE** We can draw similarities between web containers (such as IIS) and Tomcat. To put it in Java terms, .NET 5 is your JVM and Spring, whereas Host is your Tomcat.

We configure Host to launch a "host process" that is responsible for app startup and lifetime management. We also tell Host that we want to use WebHostDefaults. This allows us to use Host for a web service, as shown in figure 5.4. At a minimum, the host configures the server and request-processing pipeline.

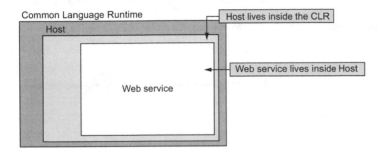

Figure 5.4 A web service runs inside the Host, which runs inside the CLR. This model allows the CLR to spin up a Host that can execute our web service.

My preferred way of configuring the Host in .NET 5. is to follow these three steps:

1. Use the CreateDefaultBuilder method on the static Host class (part of the Microsoft.Extensions.Hosting namespace) to create a builder.
2. Configure the Host builder by telling it we want to use WebHostDefaults and set a startup class and a startup URL with a port specified.
3. Build and run the built Host instance.

When we try to configure a startup class for our builder's returned Host instance, we have to use the UseStartup class. This comes as part of ASP.NET, which is not installed through .NET 5 by default. To access this functionality (and anything in ASP.NET), we need to add the ASP.NET package to the FlyingDutchmanAirlines project. We can do this through the NuGet package manager in Visual Studio or through our trusty command line when we are inside the project folder, as follows:

```
\> dotnet add package Microsoft.AspNetCore.App
```

After executing the command, the command line lets you know that the package was successfully added to the project.

NOTE The command also executes a `restore` action. For more details on restore, see section 5.1.

If we try to build the project now, we get a warning saying that we should be using a framework reference instead of a package reference. This is due to some shuffling that went on with .NET namespaces in the last couple of years. This warning doesn't prohibit us from using the code as it is now, but we can get rid of it pretty easily. In a text editor such as Notepad++ or (for the brave) Vim, open the FlyingDutchmanAirlines.csproj file. In that file, add the boldface code and remove the package reference to ASP.NET:

```xml
<Project Sdk="Microsoft.NET.Sdk">
  <PropertyGroup>
    <OutputType>Exe</OutputType>
    <TargetFramework>net5.0</TargetFramework>
  </PropertyGroup>

  <ItemGroup>
      <FrameworkReference Include="Microsoft.AspNetCore.App" />
  </ItemGroup>

  <ItemGroup>
     <PackageReference Include="Microsoft.AspNetCore.App" Version="2.2.8" />
     ...
  </ItemGroup>
</Project>
```

Now that the `Microsoft.AspNetCore` package is installed (as a framework reference), and we got rid of the compiler warning, we can use ASP.NET functionality. The first thing we want to do is tell the compiler we want to use the `AspNetCore.Hosting` namespace, as shown in the next listing. In this book, the namespace imports are often omitted from code listings. This is done because they take up precious space and can be autopopulated in most IDEs.

Listing 5.2 Program.cs with no "`Hello, World!`" output

```csharp
using System;
using Microsoft.AspNetCore.Hosting;        ◁——  We use the
                                                 Microsoft.AspNetCore.Hosting
                                                 namespace.
namespace FlyingDutchmanAirlines {
  class Program {
    static void Main(string[] args) {
                        ◁——  We no longer output
    }                        "Hello, World!" to
  }                          the console.
}
```

5.2.2 Creating and using HostBuilder

In this section, we'll

1. Create an instance of `HostBuilder`.
2. Say we want to use the `Host` as a web service.
3. Set the startup URL to be http://0.0.0.0:8080.
4. Build an instance of `Host` using `HostBuilder`.
5. Run the `Host`.

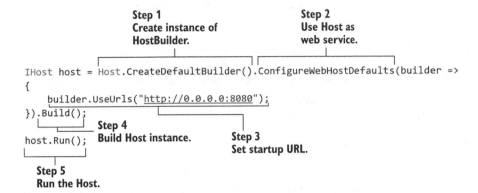

In the program's `Main` method, we add a call to `Host.CreateDefaultBuilder`. This call returns a `HostBuilder`, with some defaults already. We then tell the resulting builder we want to use a specific URL and port by calling `UseUrls`. Then we call `Build` to build and return the actual `Host`. We assign the output to a variable of type `IHost`. We assign our new `Host` to an explicitly typed variable of type `IHost`. Finally, the code starts the `Host` by calling `host.Run()`, as shown next:

```
using System;
using Microsoft.AspNetCore;
using Microsoft.AspNetCore.Hosting;

namespace FlyingDutchmanAirlines {
  class Program {
    static void Main(string[] args) {
      IHost host =
➡ Host.CreateDefaultBuilder().ConfigureWebHostDefaults(builder => {
        builder.UseUrls("http://0.0.0.0:8080");
      }).Build();

      host.Run();
    }
  }
}
```

If you try to compile and run the service in this state, the service launches but then terminates with an `InvalidOperationException`. This exception tells us we do not have a `Startup` class configured and tied to the `Host`. But before we create this `Startup` class, let's leave the `Program` class in the best shape possible. We have our `Host` creation and call to `Run` in the `Main` method, but should it really be in there?

In section 1.4, we discussed the importance of writing methods that read like a narrative. If I am a new developer, looking at a public method (in this case `Main`), I probably do not care about implementation details. Instead, I want to get an understanding of the broad strokes of what the method does. To that end, we can extract the initialization and assignment of host and the call to `host.Run` into a separate, private method as follows:

```
private static void InitalizeHost() {
  IHost host = Host.CreateDefaultBuilder()
     .ConfigureWebHostDefaults(builder =>
    {
      builder.UseUrls("http://0.0.0.0:8080");
    }).Build();

  host.Run();
}
```

Having extracted the `Host` creation logic into a separate method is a good step, but we can do just a bit more. We should consider two other things. First, we don't need to store the result of the `HostBuilder` in a variable, because we use it only to call `Run`. Why don't we just call `Run` directly after `Build` and avoid the unnecessary memory assignment, as shown next:

```
IHost host = Host.CreateDefaultBuilder()
     .ConfigureWebHostDefaults(builder =>
    {
      builder.UseUrls("http://0.0.0.0:8080");
    }).Build().Run();
```

 The second thing we should consider is changing the method to an "expression" method, as shown next. Similar to a lambda expression, an expression method uses => notation to indicate that the method will evaluate the expression to the right of the => and return its result. You can think of the => operator as a combination of assignment and evaluation algebraically (=) and a return statement (>). Lambda expressions may look a bit funny at first, but the more you see them, the more you want to use them.

```
private static void InitalizeHost() =>
  Host.CreateDefaultBuilder()
    .ConfigureWebHostDefaults(builder =>
    {
      builder.UseUrls("http://0.0.0.0:8080");
    }).Build().Run();
```

How does this impact our `Main` method? Not much. All we have to do is call the `InitializeHost` method as follows:

```
namespace FlyingDutchmanAirlines {
  class Program {
    static void Main(string[] args) {
      InitializeHost();
    }

    private static void InitalizeHost() =>
      Host.CreateDefaultBuilder()
        .ConfigureWebHostDefaults(builder =>
      {
        builder.UseUrls("http://0.0.0.0:8080");
      }).Build().Run();
  }
}
```

Our code is clean and readable, but we still have that runtime exception to deal with. Clean code is nice, but if it doesn't have the required functionality, it isn't good enough. The exception said that we need to register a `Startup` class with the `Host-Builder` before we build and run the resulting `IHost`. I guess we have no choice but to make that our next item of work.

5.2.3 *Implementing the Startup class*

We do not have a `Startup` class yet, but we can remedy that by creating a file called Startup.cs (in the project's root folder is fine for this purpose) as follows:

```
namespace FlyingDutchmanAirlines {
  class Startup { }
}
```

To configure our `Startup` class, create a `Configure` method in the `Startup` class. This method is called by the `HostBuilder` and contains a crucial configuration option, shown in the next listing, which allows us to use controllers and endpoints.

Listing 5.3 **Startup.cs** `Configure` **method**

```
public void Configure(IApplicationBuilder app) {
  app.UseRouting();
  app.UseEndpoints(endpoints => endpoints.MapControllers());
}
```

Uses routing and makes routing decisions for the service in this class

Uses an endpoint pattern for routing web requests. MapControllers scans and maps all the controllers in our service.

The small method in listing 5.3 is the core of our configuration code. When `Use-Routing` is called, we tell the runtime that certain routing decisions for the service are made in this class. If we did not have the call to `UseRouting`, we would not be able to hit any endpoint. `UseEndpoints` does what it says it does: it allows us to use and specify endpoints. It takes in an argument of a type we have not encountered before: `Action`. This is an instance of a delegate.

Delegates and anonymous methods

A delegate provides a way to reference a method. It is also type-safe, so it can point only to a method with a given signature. The delegate can be passed around to other methods and classes and then invoked when wanted. They are often used as callbacks.

You can create delegates in one of the following three ways:

- Using the `delegate` keyword
- Using an anonymous method
- Using a lambda expression

The oldest way of creating them is by explicitly declaring a type of `delegate` and creating a new instance of that delegate by assigning a method to the delegate as follows:

```
delegate int MyDelegate(int x);
public int BeanCounter(int beans) => beans++;

public void AnyMethod(){
  MyDelegate del = BeanCounter;
}
```

This code is readable but a bit clumsy. As C# matured, new ways were introduced to work with delegates.

The second option is to use an anonymous method. To create a delegate with an anonymous method, we specify the method return type and body inside a new delegate instantiation, as shown here:

```
delegate int MyDelegate(int x);
public void AnyMethod() {
  MyDelegate del = delegate(int beans) {
    return beans++;
  };
}
```

Notice the difference between the original and anonymous ways of creating a delegate. An anonymous method can clean up your code tremendously but comes with a big warning: you should use an anonymous method only if you are required to do so or if you are confident that you can adhere to the DRY principle. If you need to execute the same logic somewhere else in your codebase and you are not passing in the delegate to that location, use a normal method instead and call it from both places.

The third, and current, evolution of this process is a fairly easy step to reach from the anonymous method: lambda expressions, shown next:

```
delegate int MyDelegate(int x);
public void AnyMethod() {
  MyDelegate del = beans => beans++;
}
```

We simply determine what we want the input to be in our anonymous method (beans) and what logic we want to perform and return (beans++). Additionally, you can add and subtract methods from a delegate by using the addition (+) and subtraction (-) operators. If you have multiple methods tied to the same delegate, the delegate becomes a multicast delegate.

Finally, to use a delegate, call the Invoke method, shown next. This invokes the underlying Action, executing whatever code you have attached to it.

```
del.Invoke();
```

We pass in a lambda expression, which when executed will configure the app's endpoints by calling MapControllers. A handy method, MapControllers scans our codebase for any controllers and generates the appropriate routes to the endpoints in our controllers.

The only thing remaining to do before registering our Startup class with the Host is to create a ConfigureServices method and call AddControllers on the passed-in IServiceCollection, as shown in the next code sample. The IServiceCollection interface allows us to add functionalities to the service, such as support for controllers or dependency-injected types. These functionalities get added to an internal service collection.

```
public void ConfigureServices(IServiceCollection services) {
  services.AddControllers();
}
```

Why do we need to add controller support to the service collection? Didn't we just scan for the controllers and add routes to the RouteTable? At runtime, Host first calls ConfigureServices, giving us a chance to register any services we want to use in our app (in this case, our controllers). If we skipped this step, MapControllers would not find any controllers.

To use IServiceCollection, we need to use the Microsoft.Extensions .DependencyInjection namespace, shown in the next code snippet. Dependency injection is used by the runtime to provide the current, up-to-date ServiceCollection. You can find more information about dependency injection in section 6.2.9.

```
namespace FlyingDutchmanAirlines {
  class Startup {
    public void Configure(IApplicationBuilder app){
      app.UseRouting();
      app.UseEndpoints(endpoints => endpoints.MapControllers(); });
    }

    public void ConfigureServices (IServiceCollection services) {
      services.AddControllers();
    }
  }
}
```

We are done with the `Startup` class. Now, let's configure it to be used by the `Host-Builder`. We do this by going back to Program.cs and adding a call to `UseStartup<Startup>()` to the `HostBuilder`:

```
namespace FlyingDutchmanAirlines {
  class Program {
    static void Main(string[] args) {
      InitializeHost();
    }

    private static void InitalizeHost() =>
      Host.CreateDefaultBuilder()
        .ConfigureWebHostDefaults(builder =>
      {
        builder.UseStartup<Startup>();
        builder.UseUrls("http://0.0.0.0:8080");
      }).Build().Run();
  }
}
```

Now when we launch the application, we get a console window telling us that the service is running and listening on http://0.0.0.0:8080. This code looks slightly different from what the autogenerated template would give us. The functionality remains the same, and both are good jumping-off points.

Now that we have the prerequisites out of the way, we can start adding some logic to our service.

5.2.4   *Using the repository/service pattern for our web service architecture*

The architectural paradigm we plan to use for the Flying Dutchman Airlines next-gen service is the repository/service pattern. With this pattern, we use an upside-down development strategy, where we work from the bottom up: first implement the low-level database calls, then work our way up to creating the endpoints.

Our service architecture comprises the following four layers:

1 The database access layer
2 The repository layer
3 The service layer
4 The controller layer

The benefit we get by working from the bottom up is that the code complexity grows organically. Typically, that would be a very bad thing. But in this case, we have the tools to control this growth and keep it in check.

We can examine the data flow of our architecture (figure 5.5) by taking any endpoint and walking through the required steps to satisfy the requirements. For example, let's take `POST /Booking/{flightNumber}`. First, an HTTP request enters the `Booking` controller. That would have an instance of a `BookingService` (every entity

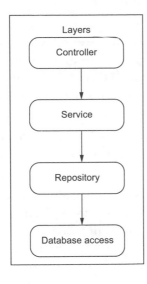

Figure 5.5   The repository pattern used in FlyingDutchmanAirlinesNextGen.sln. Data and user queries flow from the controller to the service to the repository to the database. This pattern allows us to easily separate concerns between layers and do incremental development.

will have its own service and repository), which would call the BookingRepository and any other services it needs for any entity it may need to interact with. Then the BookingRepository calls any appropriate database methods. At that point, the flow is reversed, and we go back up the chain to return the result value to the user.

As mentioned before and shown in figure 5.6, all entities have their own set of service and repository classes. If there is a need for an operation on another entity, the initial service makes the call to that entity's service to request the operation to be performed.

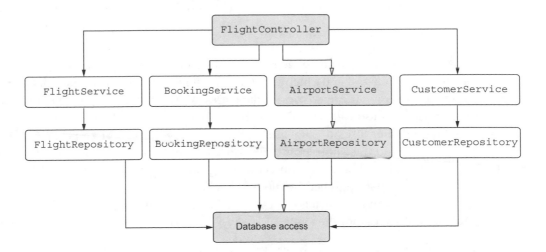

Figure 5.6   The repository pattern applied to the database entities. The FlightController holds instances of a service for every entity it needs to operate on. An entity's service holds (at least) an instance of the respective entities' repositories. Services can call other repositories, if necessary. This graphic traces the dependencies flow for Airport (the colored boxes).

5.3 Implementing the database access layer

If we look back at chapter 4, we are reminded of the curious way that database access was handled in the previous version of the application. The connection string was hardcoded into the class itself and no ORM was used. To refresh our minds: an object-relational mapping tool is used to map code against a database, ensuring a good match (or isomorphic relationship). Our two major goals in this section are to

1 Set up Entity Framework Core and "reverse-engineer" the deployed database.
2 Store the connection string securely through the use of an environment variable.

One of the most powerful features of Entity Framework Core is the ability to "reverse-engineer" a deployed database. Reverse-engineering means that Entity Framework Core autogenerates all the models in your codebase from a deployed database, saving you a lot of time. Reverse-engineering also guarantees that your models work with the database and are mapped correctly to the schema. In chapter 3, we discussed the need for a correct isomorphic relationship between model and schema, and using an ORM tool to reverse-engineer models is a way to achieve that.

5.3.1 Entity Framework Core and reverse-engineering

In this section, we'll learn how to use Entity Framework Core to reverse-engineer the deployed database and automatically create models to match the database's tables. Because we reverse-engineer the database, we can be assured that we are working with compatible code to query the database.

To reverse-engineer our database, we first need to install Entity Framework Core by running the `dotnet install` command, as shown next. Entity Framework Core (EF Core) does not come automatically installed with .NET 5 as it is a separate project.

```
\> dotnet tool install --global dotnet-ef
```

On success, the command line lets you know that you can invoke the tool by using the `dotnet-ef` command and which version you just installed. Entity Framework Core can connect to many different types of databases. Most databases (SQL, NoSQL, Redis) have packages (also called database drivers) that allow Entity Framework Core to connect to them. Because our database is a SQL Server, we install the respective driver. We also need to add the Entity Framework Core Design package. These packages contain the functionality we need to connect to a SQL Server database (the `SqlServer` namespace) and reverse-engineer the models (the `Design` namespace).

Make sure you run the following commands from your project's root folder (Flying-DutchmanAirlines, not the solution's root folder, FlyingDutchmanAirlinesNextGen):

```
\> dotnet add package Microsoft.EntityFrameworkCore.SqlServer
\> dotnet add package Microsoft.EntityFrameworkCore.Design
```

The commands install all required packages and dependencies for connecting to a SQL Server with the help of Entity Framework Core.

We can now reverse-engineer the database by using the next command:

```
\> dotnet ef dbcontext scaffold [CONNECTION STRING] [DATABASE DRIVER] [FLAGS]
```

The command contains two unfamiliar terms—dbcontext and scaffold:

- dbcontext refers to the creation of a class of type DbContext. A dbcontext is the main class we use to set up our database connection in the code.
- scaffold instructs Entity Framework Core to create models for all database entities in the database we are connected to. Much like real-life scaffolding, it creates a sort of wrap around the original item (a house or a building) that we can use to modify the said item. In our case, it puts a scaffold around the deployed SQL database.

We can use flags to specify the folder of the generated models and dbContext. We'll save these into a dedicated folder as follows, to avoid having a bunch of model files in our project root folder:

```
\> dotnet ef dbcontext scaffold
➥ "Server=tcp:codelikeacsharppro.database.windows.net,1433;Initial
➥ Catalog=FlyingDutchmanAirlines;Persist Security Info=False;User
➥ Id=dev;Password=FlyingDutchmanAirlines1972!;
➥ MultipleActiveResultSets=False;Encrypt=True;
➥ TrustServerCertificate=False;Connection Timeout=30;"
➥ Microsoft.EntityFrameworkCore.SqlServer --context-dir DatabaseLayer
➥ --output-dir DatabaseLayer/Models
```

If you run into issues running the command, please double-check all spaces, line breaks (there should be none), and flags. The command starts by building the current project. Then, it tries to connect to the database with the given connection string. Finally, it generates the dbContext class (FlyingDutchmanAirlinesContext.cs) and the appropriate models. Let's examine the created FlyingDutchmanAirlinesContext class. A generated DatabaseContext has the following four major pieces:

- Constructors
- Collections of type DbSet containing entities
- Configuration methods
- Model-creation options

But before we look at these items, there is something peculiar in the class declaration:

```
public partial class FlyingDutchmanAirlinesContext : DbContext
```

What is this partial business?

If you look at the generated class, you'll notice it has two different constructors. By default, in C#, if you do not provide a constructor, the compiler generates a parameterless constructor for you under the hood. This constructor is called the default constructor, or the implicit constructor. C# creates the default constructor whenever there is no explicit constructor so you can instantiate a new instance of the said class.

Partial classes

You can use the `partial` keyword to break up the definition of a class across multiple files. In general, it creates a bit of a readability mess but can be useful. Partial classes are especially useful for automatic code generators (like Entity Framework Core), because the generator can put code in partial classes, thus allowing the developer to enrich the class's implementation.

That said, we know we are not going to be providing more functionality to `Flying-DutchmanAirlinesContext` in a different file, so we can remove the `partial` keyword from the class. This is a good example of making sure that the code that is automatically generated is exactly how you want it. Just because a generator or template did it a certain way does not mean you cannot edit it.

```
public class FlyingDutchmanAirlinesContext : DbContext
```

Note that this change is optional.

As seen in listing 5.4, both constructors can create an instance of `FlyingDutchman-AirlinesContext`. In the case of `FlyingDutchmanAirlines`, you can create a new instance with or without passing in an instance of type `DbContextOptions`. If you do pass that instance into the constructor, it invokes the constructor of its base class (`DbContext` in this case).

Listing 5.4   `FlyingDutchmanAirlinesContext` constructors

```
public FlyingDutchmanAirlinesContext() { }           ◁——— An explicit default constructor

public FlyingDutchmanAirlinesContext(DbContextOptions
➡ <FlyingDutchmanAirlinesContext> options) : base(options) { }    ◁——

           An overloaded constructor with a parameter that calls the base constructor
```

For more information on method and constructor overloading, see chapter 4.

5.3.2   *DbSet and the Entity Framework Core workflow*

In this section, we'll discuss the `DbSet` type as well as the general workflow when using Entity Framework Core. Looking past the constructors, we see four collections of type `DbSet`, each holding one of our database models. The `DbSet` types are collections that we consider part of the internals of EF Core. Entity Framework Core uses the `DbSet<Entity>` collections to store and maintain an accurate copy of the database tables and their contents.

We also see a familiar concept: auto-properties. The collections are `public`, but they are also virtual, as shown next:

```
public virtual DbSet<Airport> Airport { get; set; }
public virtual DbSet<Booking> Booking { get; set; }
public virtual DbSet<Customer> Customer { get; set;}
public virtual DbSet<Flight> Flight { get; set; }
```

When you declare something `virtual`, you tell the compiler that you allow the property or method to be overridden in a derived class. If you do not declare something as `virtual`, you cannot override it.

Hiding parent properties and methods/sealing classes

In a world where you have a class that implements a base class containing properties or methods not declared as `virtual`, we cannot override the implementation of said properties and methods. What to do? Well, we have a workaround for this problem. We can "hide" the properties and methods of the parent by inserting the `new` keyword into the method or property signature, as shown in the next code. This keyword tells the compiler that, instead of providing a new implementation to the existing parent method, we just want to call this brand-new method that happens to have the same name. In practice, it allows you to "override" nonvirtual properties and methods.

```
public new void ThisMethodWasNotVirtual() {}
```

Be warned, however, that hiding is frowned on. In an ideal world, the developer of the original class has the know-how to predict which properties and methods to declare as `virtual`. If you need to do things outside of the system (using a workaround to perform unexpected and uncontrolled overrides), think twice before hitting that commit code button. The original developer did not expect you to do this, nor did they want you to override it in the first place (if they did, they would have provided you with a `virtual` property or method).

From the perspective of the developer of the base class, how can you prevent your nonvirtual methods and properties from being hidden in a derived class? Unfortunately, there is no atomic way of specifying this per property or method. We do have, however, a more nuclear option: the `sealed` keyword. You can declare a class sealed with the `sealed` keyword, as shown next. This is a good option to safeguard your classes because you cannot create a derived class based on a sealed class. Because inheritance is off the table, so is overriding or hiding anything.

```
public sealed class Pinniped(){}
```

Like many other ORM tools, Entity Framework Core often behaves unintuitively at first. All operations you would normally make directly against the database are done against an in-memory model before they are saved to the database. To do this, Entity Framework Core stores most available database records in the DbSet. This means that if you have added a `Flight` entity with a primary key of `192` in the database, you also have that particular entity loaded into memory during runtime. Having access to the database contents from memory at runtime allows you to easily manipulate objects and abstract away that you are using a database at all. The drawback is performance. Keeping lots of records in memory can become quite the resource hog, depending on how large your database is (or becomes). As shown in figure 5.7, the normal workflow for operating on an entity through Entity Framework Core follows:

1 Query the appropriate DbSet for the object you want to manipulate (not needed for INSERT/ADD operations).

2 Manipulate the object (not needed for READ operations).

3 Change the DbSet appropriately (not needed for READ operations).

Query the DbSet   Manipulate the object   Change the DbSet

Figure 5.7 The three general steps to make changes to a database through Entity Framework Core: query the DbSet, manipulate the object, and then change the DbSet.

It is good to keep in mind that just because changes have been made in a DbSet, they are not necessarily made in the database yet. Entity Framework Core still needs to commit these changes to the database, and we'll explore how to do that further in this chapter.

5.3.3 *Configuration methods and environment variables*

The third building block of the FlyingDutchmanAirlinesContext class comprises two configuration methods: OnConfiguring and OnModelCreating, shown in the next code. OnConfiguring is called on the configuration of the DbContext, which is done automatically at launch, whereas OnModelCreating is called during model creation (at runtime, during launch).

```
protected override void OnConfiguring(DbContextOptionsBuilder
    optionsBuilder) {
  if (!optionsBuilder.IsConfigured) {
    optionsBuilder.UseSqlServer(
  "Server=tcp:codelikeacsharppro.database.windows.net,1433;Initial
  Catalog=FlyingDutchmanAirlines;Persist Security Info=False;User
  ID=dev;Password=FlyingDutchmanAirlines1972!;
  MultipleActiveResultSets=False;
  Encrypt=True;TrustServerCertificate=False;Connection Timeout=30;");
  }
}
```

The OnConfiguring method takes in an argument of type DbContextOptionsBuilder. The OnConfiguring method is called by the runtime automatically on the configuration of the DbContext and uses dependency injection to provide the DbContextOptionsBuilder. Here, we should configure any settings related to how we connect to the database. Therefore, we need to provide a connection string.

But, unfortunately, the hardcoded connection string rears its ugly head once more. Surely there must be a better way to do this. I propose we use environment variables for this. An environment variable is a key-value pair, {*K, V*}, which we set at the operating system level. We can retrieve environment variables at run time, making them excellent for providing variables that either change per system or deployment or values that we do not want hardcoded in our codebase.

> **NOTE** Environment variables are often used for web services deployed through containerized orchestration systems such as Kubernetes. If you do not want to (or cannot) set an environment variable on the operating system level, you can instead use cloud solutions such as Azure Key Vault and Amazon AWS Key Management Service. For more information on Kubernetes, see Ashley David's *Bootstrapping Microservices with Docker, Kubernetes, and Terraform* (Manning, 2021) or Marko Lukša's *Kubernetes in Action* (2nd edition; Manning, 2021).

Every operating system does environment variables slightly differently—we'll discuss the practical differences between Windows and macOS in a moment. The way we retrieve an environment variable in C# does not change based on the operating system, however. In the `System.IO` namespace is a method called `GetEnvironmentVariable` that we can use for that exact purpose, as shown here:

```
Environment.GetEnvironmentVariable([ENVIRONMENT VARIABLE KEY]);
```

You just pass it in the key of the environment variable you want to retrieve (`ENVIRONMENT VARIABLE KEY`), and the method does so for you. If the environment variable does not exist, it returns a null value without throwing an exception, so you need to do some validation based on that null value. What would your environment variable look like? Because it is a key-value pair, and because environment variables cannot contain any spaces, you can do something like {`FlyingDutchmanAirlines_Database_Connection_String`, `[Connection String]`}.

> **TIP** Because environment variables are system wide, you cannot have environment variables with duplicate keys. Keep this in mind when choosing a value for the key.

5.3.4 *Setting an environment variable on Windows*

The process of setting environment variables differs slightly from operating system to operating system. In Windows, you set an environment variable through the Windows command line, using the `setx` command, followed by the desired key-value pair, as follows:

```
\> setx [KEY] [VALUE]
\> setx FlyingDutchmanAirlines_Database_Connection_String
➡ "Server=tcp:codelikeacsharppro.database.windows.net,1433;Initial
➡ Catalog=FlyingDutchmanAirlines;Persist Security Info=False;User
➡ ID=dev;Password=FlyingDutchmanAirlines1972!;
➡ MultipleActiveResultSets=False;Encrypt=True;
➡ TrustServerCertificate=False;Connection Timeout=30;"
```

If successful, the command line reports that the value was saved successfully (SUCCESS: Specified value was saved.). To verify that the environment variable was saved, launch a new command line (newly set environment variables do not show up in active command-line sessions), and run the echo command for the environment variable. If you do not see the environment variable show up, as shown next, you may have to reboot your machine:

```
\> echo %FlyingDutchmanAirlines_Database_Connection_String%
```

If everything went all right, the echo command should return the value of the environment variable (in this case, our connection string). We can now use this environment variable in our service!

5.3.5 Setting an environment variable on macOS

Like Windows, we use a command-line environment to set environment variables on macOS: the macOS terminal. Setting an environment variable is just as easy on macOS as it is on Windows, as shown here:

```
\> export [KEY] [VALUE]
\> export FlyingDutchmanAirlines_Database_Connection_String
➥ "Server=tcp:codelikeacsharppro.database.windows.net,1433;Initial
➥ Catalog=FlyingDutchmanAirlines;Persist Security Info=False;User
➥ ID=dev;Password=FlyingDutchmanAirlines1972!;
➥ MultipleActiveResultSets=False;Encrypt=True;
➥ TrustServerCertificate=False;Connection Timeout=30;"
```

And you can verify by using echo on macOS as well, like so:

```
\> echo $FlyingDutchmanAirlines_Database_Connection_String
```

On macOS, things are somewhat trickier when we run the service and try to grab the environment variables when debugging a codebase through Visual Studio. In macOS, environment variables defined through the command line do not automatically become available to GUI applications such as Visual Studio. The workaround is to launch Visual Studio through the macOS terminal or to add the environment variables in Visual Studio as part of the runtime configurations.

5.3.6 Retrieving environment variables at run time in your code

Having set the environment variable, we can now grab it in our code. We want to grab it in the OnConfigure method instead of hardcoding the connection string. We can use the Environment.GetEnvironmentVariable method for this. Because the Environment.GetEnvironmentVariable returns a null value if it cannot find the environment variable, we use the null coalescing operator (??) to set it to an empty string in that case, as follows:

```
protected override void OnConfiguring(DbContextOptionsBuilder
➥ optionsBuilder)  {
```

```
    if(!optionsBuilder.IsConfigured) {
      string connectionString = Environment.GetEnvironmentVariable(
➡   "FlyingDutchmanAirlines_Database_Connection_String")
➡   ?? string.Empty;
      optionsBuilder.UseSqlServer(connectionString);
    }
}
```

We could have handled the null case in a couple of different ways (most notably by using either a conditional or by inlining the GetEnvironmentVariable call along with the null coalescing operator into the UseSqlServer method), but this is my preferred way. It is readable yet succinct. By doing this little trick, we increased the security of our application tenfold, especially when you consider the problems caused by a hard-coded connection string committed to a source control management system.

The remaining code we have not touched on yet in the FlyingDutchmanAirlines-Context are the OnModelCreating methods, shown in the next listing.

Listing 5.5 FlyingDutchmanAirlinesContext OnModelCreating

```
protected override void OnModelCreating(ModelBuilder modelBuilder) {       ◁──┐   Overrides
  modelBuilder.Entity<Airport>(entity => {                                         the base's
    entity.Property(e => e.AirportId)                                              OnModelCreating
      .HasColumnName("AirportID")                                                  method
      .ValueGeneratedNever();

    entity.Property(e => e.City)                     Prepares the
      .IsRequired()                                  EF Core to use
      .HasMaxLength(50)                              the Airport
      .IsUnicode(false)                              model

    entity.Property(e => e.Iata)
      .IsRequired()
      .HasColumnName("IATA")
      .HasMaxLength(3)
      .IsUnicode(false)
    });

  modelBuilder.Entity<Booking>(entity =>  {
    entity.Property(e => e.BookingId).HasColumnName("BookingID");

    entity.Property(e => e.CustomerId).HasColumnName("CustomerID");

    entity.HasOne(d => d.Customer)                                Prepares the
      .WithMany(p => p.Booking)                                   EF Core to use
      .HasForeignKey(d => d.CustomerId)                           the Booking
      .HasConstraingName("FK__Booking__Custome_71D1E811");        model

    entity.HasOne(d => d.FlightNumberNavigation)
      .WithMany(p => p.Booking)
      .HasForeignKey(d => d.FlightNumber)
      .OnDelete(DeleteBehavior.ClientSetNull)
      .HasConstraintName("FK__Booking__FlightN__4F7CD00D");
    });
```

```
    modelBuilder.Entity<Customer>(entity => {
      entity.Property(e => e.CustomerId)
        .HasColumnName("CustomerID")                      Prepares the
                                                          EF Core to use
        entity.Property(e => e.Name)                      the Customer
        .IsRequired()                                     model
        .HasMaxLength(50)
        .IsUnicode(false)
    });

  modelBuilder.Entity<Flight>(entity => {
    entity.HasKey(e => e.FlightNumber);

    entity.Property(e => e.FlightNumber).ValueGeneratedNever();

    entity.HasOne(d => d.DestinationNavigation)
      .WithMany(p => p.FlightDestinationNavigation)       Prepares the
      .HasForeignKey(d => d.Destination)                  EF Core to use
      .OnDelete(DeleteBehavior.ClientSetNull)             the Flight
      .HasConstraintName("FK_Flight_AirportDestination"); model

    entity.HasOne(d => d.OriginNavigation)
      .WithMany(p => p.FlightOriginNavigation)
      .HasForeignKey(d => d.Origin)
      .OnDelete(DeleteBehavior.ClientSetNull);
  });

    OnModelCreatingPartial(modelBuilder);        ◁──── Calls the partial
}                                                      OnModelCreatingPartial method

partial void OnModelCreatingPartial(ModelBuilder modelBuilder);   ◁──
                                                      Defines the partial
                                                      OnModelCreatingPartial method
```

Note that the exact constraint names may differ on your system, because they are auto-generated. The OnModelCreating method sets up the entities internally for Entity Framework Core, along with the key constraints defined in the database schema. This allows us to operate on the entities without directly messing with the database (which is the whole idea of Entity Framework Core). A generated method (and a call to it) is also called OnModelCreatingPartial. The Entity Framework Core console toolset generated the OnModelCreatingPartial method, so you can execute additional logic as part of the model-creation process. We are not going to do that, so we can remove the OnModelCreatingPartial method and the call to it. Do be aware that if you have to rerun the reverse-engineering process (or any other code-generator tool), your changes will be overwritten again.

Exercises

EXERCISE 5.1
If we want to prevent somebody from deriving from a class, what keyword do we need to attach to the class?

a Virtual

b Sealed

c Protected

EXERCISE 5.2
If we want to allow somebody to override a property or method, what keyword do we attach?

a Virtual

b Sealed

c Protected

EXERCISE 5.3
Fill in the blanks: "A _____ is the underlying process that runs the web service. It, in turn, lives inside the _____.

a host

b Tomcat

c JVM

d CLR

EXERCISE 5.4
True or false? When using a Startup class, you need to register it with the Host.

EXERCISE 5.5
Try it yourself: Write an expression-body-style method that accepts two integers and returns their product. This should be a one-line solution. Hint: Think about lambda.

EXERCISE 5.6
Within the context of a repository/service pattern, how many controller, service, and repository layers should there be?

Summary

- We can create .NET 5 solutions and projects by using predefined templates in the command line such as console and mvc. Templates are ways to easily create common flavors of solutions and projects.
- A restore is an operation that gets all necessary dependencies for a project to compile.
- We can add a project to a solution by using the dotnet sln [SOLUTION] add [PROJECT] command.

- A Host is a process living inside the CLR that runs a web application, providing an interface between the CLR and the user.
- Methods that just return the value of an expression can be written succinctly using a syntax similar to lambda expressions. This is called an expression-bodied method and can make our code more readable.
- In a Startup class, we can set up routes and allow for the use of controllers and endpoints. This is important for MVC web applications because it allows us to call endpoints and use the concept of controllers.
- The repository/service pattern comprises multiple repositories, services, and controllers (one per entity). This easy-to-follow paradigm helps us control the flow of data.
- Entity Framework Core is a powerful object-relational mapping tool that can reverse-engineer deployed databases by scaffolding them. This saves the developer a lot of time and allows for a near-perfect isomorphic relationship between the database and the codebase.
- Use the partial keyword to define classes and methods that have their implementation spread across multiple fields. The partial keyword is often used by automatic code generators.
- When declaring something as virtual, you say that this property, field, or method can be overridden safely. This is useful when balancing the needs for the extensibility and the sanctity of your codebase.
- You can "hide" nonvirtual properties and methods by adding the new keyword to a method or property signature.
- When a class is sealed, you cannot inherit from it. In effect, sealing a class stops any class from deriving from it. Sealing classes becomes useful when you know for a fact that your class is the lowest level of inheritance there is and you want to prevent tampering with your code.
- Environment variables are key-value pairs that can be set in an operating system. They can store sensitive data such as connection strings or passwords.

Part 4

The repository layer

In part 3, we started our implementation of the next-gen Flying Dutchman Airlines service. We created a new .NET 5 project and wrote a database access layer. In this part, we'll implement the repository layer classes. In the following chapters, you'll learn about test-driven development, custom comparison classes, generics, extension methods, and much more.

Test-driven development and dependency injection

In chapters 3 and 4, we looked at the codebase we inherited and discussed potential improvements. To solve the issues we found, we started a new version of the Flying Dutchman Airlines service and implemented the database access layer with Entity Framework Core in chapter 5. In this chapter, we'll start implementing the business logic by moving into the repository layer and creating the Customer-Repository class. Figure 6.1 shows where we are in the scheme of the book.

The repository layer is the meat and potatoes of our service. In the repository layer we do the following two things:

1 Query and manipulate the database by communicating with the database access layer
2 Return the requested entities or information to the service layer

We want to create isolated, small, clean, and readable methods that follow the single-responsibility principle (SRP). Following the SRP makes it easier to test and maintain our code because we can quickly understand every method and fix any potential bugs.

111

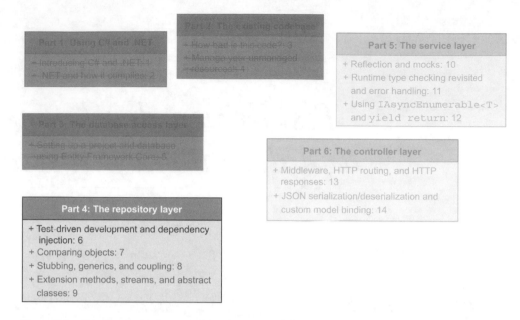

Figure 6.1   **After having implemented the database access layer in chapter 5, we'll move on to implementing the CustomerRepository in this chapter.**

The single-responsibility principle

One of the clean code tenets identified by Robert Martin, the single-responsibility principle (SRP) is the harmonica of clean code: easy to play, but mastery takes years of practice. The SRP builds on the concept of "separation of concerns" as evangelized (and coined) by Edsger Dijkstra in his paper "On the Role of Scientific Thought."[a] In practice, the SRP means that a method should do only one thing and do that well. This goes back to the monster methods we discussed earlier in the book. More formally, according to Martin in a blog post published in 2014 (https://blog.cleancoder .com/uncle-bob/2014/05/08/SingleReponsibilityPrinciple.html), the SRP states that "each software module should have one and only one reason to change."

Going back to practical terms, how do you know whether you violated the SRP? The easiest way I have found is to ask yourself if you are doing more than one thing in the method. If you need to use the word "and" in either your explanation of the method or in the method name, that usually means you are violating the SRP. The SRP is closely tied to the Liskov principle, which I discuss in chapter 8.

---

[a] Edsger Dijkstra wrote his papers with a fountain pen and numbered them "EWD [*N*]," where *N* is the number of the paper (EWD stands for his full name: Edsger Wybe Dijkstra). "On the Role of Scientific Thought" is EWD 447 and can be found in Dijkstra's *Selected Writings on Computing: A Personal Perspective* (Springer-Verlag, 1982).

When we consider the endpoints in the existing codebase we looked at in chapters 3 and 4, we see that a lot of the methods do multiple things. They call multiple database tables and perform multiple processing tasks. We want to separate those operations into individual methods, so we can reuse the code and be confident in our code quality.

6.1 Test-driven development

Using test-driven development (TDD) to implement your code sets you apart from a lot of developers. Your code will be more robust and better tested than that of your peers who don't use TDD. If you have never used TDD, I'll guide you through the process of actually using TDD practically. Test-driven development is, at its most fundamental level, the practice of writing unit tests before writing the code that implements what you are trying to test. You update your tests and code in tandem and build them up simultaneously, which promotes good design and solid code because the feedback loop is tight and you are acutely aware of any code that breaks your tests. In this section, we'll use TDD to write unit tests for the `CustomerRepository`.

> **NOTE** In this book, I practice what I like to call TDD-light. In theory, you should write a test before any actual logic. In practice, however, people typically tend not to do that. You will see this approach throughout the book. It is not "pure TDD," but it's a practical solution to balancing the workload of TDD and quick iteration.

To do TDD (or any kind of testing), we should create a test project in our solution. We do that by using a template as we did in chapter 5 and adding a new reference to the solution that points to the new csproj file as follows:

```
\> dotnet new mstest -n FlyingDutchmanAirlines_Tests
\> dotnet sln FlyingDutchmanAirlinesNextGen.sln add
➡ FlyingDutchmanAirlines_Tests\FlyingDutchmanAirlines_Tests.csproj
```

We now have a testing project running on the MSTest platform in our solution. A variety of supported testing frameworks for C# exists besides MSTest, such as xUnit and NUnit. We'll use MSTest in this book because MSTest comes supplied with .NET.

The new project also contains an autogenerated unit test file called UnitTest1.cs, shown next:

```
using Microsoft.VisualStudio.TestTools.UnitTesting;

namespace FlyingDutchmanAirlines_Tests {
  [TestClass]
  public class UnitTest1 {
    [TestMethod]
    public void TestMethod1() { }
  }
}
```

NOTE If your test class does not have an access modifier of `public`, the MSTest runner cannot find the class, and, therefore, the tests inside the class are not run.

Throughout this chapter, we'll use the UnitTest1.cs file and adapt it to suit our needs for the first repository: `CustomerRepository`. Why start with `CustomerRepository` as opposed to `FlightRepository` or `BookingRepository`? To refresh our memories, when we finish implementing them, we will have one repository per database model (Customer, Flight, Airport, and Booking). Within these repositories, we perform create, read, update, and delete (*CRUD*) operations that query or manipulate the database. The `Customer` entity does not have any outgoing foreign key constraints, so we are less likely to go down the rabbit hole of needing to create a repository for a different entity before we can finish the one we really want to work on. In my experience, it is easier working from the lowest (most nested/least foreign key constraints) entity up to the highest. By the time you reach the entity with the most constraints, you have all the dependencies already done. This is the same argument as to why we started (in chapter 5) with the database access layer and not the controller level for the implementation of our next-gen service.

Before we write our first unit test, let's create the repository class and the skeleton of our first method: `CreateCustomer`. The `CreateCustomer` method accepts an input of type `string` representing a customer's name, validates that input, and inserts a new entity into the database. `CustomerRepository` lives in a new folder called Repository-Layer in the FlyingDutchmanAirlines project, as shown next:

```
namespace FlyingDutchmanAirlines.RepositoryLayer {
  public class CustomerRepository {
    public void CreateCustomer(string name) { }
  }
}
```

The `CustomerRepository` doesn't look like much at this point—just a class declaration and one method, both with a `public` access modifier—but it is enough to get us started with our first unit test. In keeping with TDD tradition, we follow a binary strategy akin to a red-green traffic light pattern, as shown in figure 6.2.

With the TDD traffic light, we continually go from the "red" stage, where our tests don't compile or pass, to the "green" stage, where all is well and we can implement some more code. This workflow is the core strength of test-driven development.

Let's switch back to our test project. We need to add a reference to the `Flying-DutchmanAirlines` if we want to call any of the methods in there. We can run a command similar to how we added the FlyingDutchmanAirlines.csproj to the Flying-DutchmanAirlinesNextGen.sln in chapter 5 as follows:

```
\> dotnet add
⮕ FlyingDutchmanAirlines_Tests/FlyingDutchmanAirlines_Tests.csproj
⮕ reference FlyingDutchmanAirlines/FlyingDutchmanAirlines.csproj
```

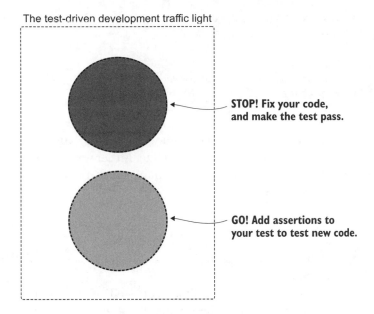

The test-driven development traffic light

STOP! Fix your code, and make the test pass.

GO! Add assertions to your test to test new code.

Figure 6.2 The test-driven-development traffic light. We go from red (compilation problems and test failures) to green (all tests pass and code compiles) back to red in a vicious cycle. This promotes an iterative development life cycle.

Then, we can rename UnitTest1.cs as CustomerRepositoryTests.cs and change the namespace and method name to something more appropriate. Now we can instantiate our CustomerRepository class and call our new CreateCustomer method, like so:

```
using FlyingDutchmanAirlines.RepositoryLayer;
using Microsoft.VisualStudio.TestTools.UnitTesting;

namespace FlyingDutchmanAirlines_Tests.RepositoryLayer {
  [TestClass]
  public class CustomerRepositoryTests {
    [TestMethod]
    public void CreateCustomer_Success() {
      CustomerRepository repository = new CustomerRepository();
    }
  }
}
```

This test actually tests nothing yet, so before we move on, let's add the simplest assertion of all: that repository should not be null. You may say that is just verifying a language feature and not our code because we are just calling the default constructor, and, yes, you are right. In my mind, however, testing a constructor can still be valuable, because you never know when somebody changes the implementation to an explicit constructor with no arguments or does something else unexpected.

To add an assertion with the MSTest framework, use the pattern `Assert`
`.[Assertion]([Arguments]).[TestMethod]` as follows:

```
public void CreateCustomer_Success() {
  CustomerRepository repository = new CustomerRepository();
  Assert.IsNotNull(repository);
}
```

To run our unit tests, we can either use Visual Studio's Unit Test Explorer or we can invoke the testing framework through the command line. Either way, we need to compile the code first and then execute the tests. To run all tests in a solution, use the next command in the command line:

```
\> dotnet test
```

If you ever have trouble running the tests in this book through Visual Studio (if you use Visual Studio), give dotnet test a try.

Once the test run finishes, we see that our first test passed, as shown in figure 6.3. Note, though, that unit tests are meant to be isolated from other tests and test only individual methods. Therefore, the order in which the MSTest runner executes tests is not guaranteed to be sequential or the same from session to session.

```
Microsoft (R) Test Execution Command Line Tool Version 16.3.0
Copyright (c) Microsoft Corporation.  All rights reserved.

Starting test execution, please wait...

A total of 1 test files matched the specified pattern.

Test Run Successful.
Total tests: 1
     Passed: 1
 Total time: 1.4535 Seconds
```

Figure 6.3   The MSTest framework runs our unit test, and it passes. Making sure our tests pass after every change helps catch bugs sooner rather than later.

Exercises

EXERCISE 6.1

What does the single-responsibility principle advocate?

    a All method names should be only one word long.

    b Don't perform the same logic in two separate places.

    c Make your methods only do one thing.

EXERCISE 6.2

True or false? With test-driven development, you write tests before and during implementation.

EXERCISE 6.3

True or false? A test runner can see your test classes as long as they have an access modifier of `internal`.

6.2 The CreateCustomer method

In this section, we'll implement the `CreateCustomer` method in the `CustomerRepository` class. We want to accept an argument of type `string` representing the customer's name and return a Boolean value indicating whether the customer was successfully added to the database.

In the existing codebase (discussed in chapters 3 and 4), a massive method called `FlightController.Post` adds a `Customer` instance to the database. The `Post` method was about 80 lines long and also executed logic to get details on airports. It also retrieved and booked a flight. Doing more than one thing in a method violates the single-responsibility principle. The `FlightController.Post` method does not just do one thing (as the principle prescribes); instead, it does many things. The actual code concerning creating a customer is only eight lines long, as shown in the next listing.

Listing 6.1 How the old codebase dealt with creating a customer in the database

We should write code that is clear enough without comments.

The connection variable is instantiated before this code snippet.

```
// Create new customer
cmd = new SqlCommand("SELECT COUNT(*) FROM Customer", connection);
var newCustomerID = 0;
using(var reader = cmd.ExecuteReader()) {
  while (reader.Read()) {
    newCustomerID = reader.GetInt32(0);
    break;
  }
}
```

A good use of the using statement, but uses an implicit type

Reads the return from the database into an ID variable

The code snippet in listing 6.1 is not the worst we have seen, but we can definitely make the following improvements:

- Our code should be self-documenting. Somebody unfamiliar with the logic should be able to read the code and understand, in broad strokes, what is going on. We should delete the comment.
- Using hardcoded SQL statements is a potential stumbling block for maintaining a service. If the database schema changes, we now need to change the SQL query as well. It is safer to use an ORM tool, like Entity Framework Core, to abstract away the SQL query.

With those improvements identified, let's start with our new implementation by creating the method signature of the new `CreateCustomer` method:

```
public bool CreateCustomer(string name) {}
```

Our `CreateCustomer` method doesn't have any actual logic implemented at this point, so let's change that. To create a customer entry in our database, we need to do the following four things:

1 Validate the input argument of `name`.
2 Instantiate a new `Customer` object.
3 Add the new `Customer` object to the Entity Framework Core's internal `DbSet<Customer>`.
4 Tell Entity Framework Core that we want to commit our change.

We follow this general pattern in all of our repository methods. Being consistent makes our codebase easier to read and maintain, because developers can come to rely on the expectation of seeing this pattern.

6.2.1 *Why you should always validate input arguments*

In an ideal world, people never pass `null` or invalid arguments into your methods. The unfortunate truth is that we don't live in an ideal world. To counteract unreliability in other people, the best thing we can do is to lead by example. If we consider a method to be nothing more than a mathematical function, we can treat it as a black box into which we can input any information and return an acceptable outcome. If we pass into this black box an invalid value and we assumed that another developer handled the validation upstream, we are in trouble and heading for the land of runtime exceptions.

Let's validate our input by considering what criteria our `string` representing a customer name must adhere to. First, I think it is safe to assume that we never want our name string to be null. In the case of null, we should return out of the method with a `false` Boolean, indicating that we could not successfully add a new `Customer` object to the database with the given input parameters, as shown next:

```
public bool CreateCustomer(string name) {
  if (string.IsNullOrEmpty(name)) {
    return false;
  }

  return true;
}
```

 ISNULLOREMPTY As part of the `string` class, .NET exposes the `IsNullOrEmpty` method. This method returns a Boolean indicating whether the given string is null or empty.

We added the second return statement to satisfy the method signature. If we do not have the `return true` statement, the compiler throws an error saying that not all code paths in the `CreateCustomer` method return a value of type `bool`. If returning a `bool` type value based on input validation was the only thing we did in the `CreateCustomer` method, we could have just returned the resulting Boolean value of `string.IsNullOrEmpty`. But, alas, we have other logic to include. Let's update our existing unit test, which is the success scenario, to call the `CreateCustomer` method and pass along a valid name string, then check whether the method returned a true value, as follows:

```
[TestMethod]
public void CreateCustomer_Success() {
    CustomerRepository repository = new CustomerRepository();
  Assert.IsNotNull(repository);

  bool result = repository.CreateCustomer("Donald Knuth");
  Assert.IsTrue(result);
}
```

Go ahead and run the test; it should pass. We introduced the following two new return branches for our method:

- The `name` argument is null.
- The `name` argument is an empty string.

We should add unit tests that cover these possibilities.

6.2.2 Using "arrange, act, assert" to write unit tests

In this section, we'll dive deeper into test-driven development by examining its core testing philosophy. We'll also continue writing the `CreateCustomer_Success` unit test by following the same pattern for tests we have followed in this book so far: instantiate an object, call it, and assert that the output is correct. This section examines the "three As" of testing: arrange, act, and assert, as shown in figure 6.4.

1. ARRANGE
Set up your tests' instances so they have all the information required to test the piece of code you are evaluating.

2. ACT
Using the instances set up in the arrange phase, run the method you want to test and store the output.

3. ASSERT
Using the data retrieved in the act phase, perform assertions to verify the output is correct.

Figure 6.4 "The three As of testing": arrange, act, and assert. Using them allows us to write tests in an organized and predictable manner.

```
[TestMethod]
public void CreateCustomer_Failure_NameIsNull() {
  CustomerRepository repository = new CustomerRepository();
  Assert.IsNotNull(repository);

  bool result = repository.CreateCustomer(null);
  Assert.IsFalse(result);
}

[TestMethod]
public void CreateCustomer_Failure_NameIsEmptyString() {
  CustomerRepository repository = new CustomerRepository();
  Assert.IsNotNull(repository);
```

```
    bool result = repository.CreateCustomer("");
    Assert.IsFalse(result);
}
```

 EMPTY STRINGS `""` and `string.Empty` are both valid ways to describe an empty string. In fact, `string.Empty` resolves to `""` under the hood. Use whichever one you want. I like to use `string.Empty` because it is more explicit. In this book, I use them both.

And just like that, we are up to three tests. Now, when we make any further changes to the method, we can run these tests and be confident that the existing code did not break.

6.2.3   *Validating against invalid characters*

The second item on our to-do list for validating the input is checking the actual content of the `name` string for invalid characters. We don't expect a name to contain special characters, such as the following:

- Exclamation point: !
- At sign: @
- Pound sign: #
- Dollar sign: $
- Percentage sign: %
- Ampersand: &
- Asterisk: *

We cannot possibly limit our allowed character set based on the characters we allow. The list of possible Unicode characters is gigantic, especially when you take into consideration the special notation of letters in a language such as Vietnamese and Armenian. So how do we check for special characters?

We could create a character array and loop over the string, then loop over the character array for every character in the string. That would both be many lines long and fairly inefficient.[1] We could also use a regular expression (regex) to match against a regex string, but that would be overkill for our problem. The easiest and cleanest way to determine whether a string contains a given character is to specify an array with forbidden characters and then use the LINQ `Any` method to iterate over the source string, passing in an `Action` that checks whether any of the elements in the collection contain an element from the forbidden characters collection. The `Any` method checks whether an expression (through an `Action`) is valid for any of the elements

---

[1] The runtime complexity of iterating over a set of N characters for every character in a given string is $O(n^2)$. This is calculated by taking the runtime of iterating over a set of N characters ($\{N\}$):$O(n)$ and multiplying that by the runtime iterating over every character in a string, also $\{N\}$. This gives us $O(n) * O(n)$, which we can further combine into $O(n * n)$, and once more into the final runtime of $O(n^2)$. To summarize: $O(n) * O(n) = O(n * n) = O(n^2)$. There is a chance that the regex implementation does its processing with the same concepts and runtime complexity.

in a collection. LINQ can be difficult to understand the first time you look at it, so let's unpack our LINQ code step-by-step next:

```
char[] forbiddenCharacters = {'!', '@', '#', '$', '%', '&', '*'};
bool containsInvalidCharacters = name.Any(x =>
➥   forbiddenCharacters.Contains(x));
```

Although the runtime complexity of using the `Any` LINQ method and character array approach is the same as the nested `for` loop described earlier (since we are basically throwing some syntactical sugar on top of it), it is more readable and more idiomatic C#. LINQ (Language-Integrated Query) is a sort of programming language inside of C# that allows us to perform (and chain) operations to query and change collections. Here, we call a method (`Any`) in the LINQ library using normal C# syntax.

First, we declare, initialize, and assign a variable of type array of `char` and call it `forbiddenCharacters`. This array contains the characters we do not allow. Second, we initialize a Boolean variable called `containsInvalidCharacters` and assign it to the result of our LINQ query. We can read the LINQ query as a narrative: "If any element in the string called `name` contains a character from the `forbiddenCharacters` collection, return `false`, else return `true`."

The call to `Any` evaluates to `true` if the passed-in expression results to `true` for any of the values in the collection (in this case for any of the characters in the `name` string). We pass in an expression to be evaluated through a lambda expression. We use the `Contains` method on `forbiddenCharacters` to evaluate whether the `forbidden-Characters` collection contains the passed-in value. Combined with the `Any` call, this means that if we evaluate the `Contains` call to be `true` (which it is for a character representing a forbidden character), it also means that the `Any` returns `true`, meaning that there was a forbidden character in the string.

We could just put the forbidden character code after our conditional to check whether the `name` string was null or empty, or even inline it into the conditional, but I vote for a different approach. If I tell you that those are implementation details, unnecessary for the casual reader to know intimately, where should we put the code? That's right, in a separate `private` method.

We should extract the `IsNullOrEmpty` conditional into its own method and add the invalid character code. We can call the method `IsInvalidCustomerName` and have it return a Boolean (note that we also have to import the `System.Linq` namespace to use LINQ queries), as shown in the next listing.

Listing 6.2 CustomerRepository.cs with extracted `IsInvalidCustomerName`

```
using System.Linq;

namespace FlyingDutchmanAirlines.RepositoryLayer {
  public class CustomerRepository {
    public bool CreateCustomer(string name) {
      if (IsInvalidCustomerName(name)) {
```

```
        return false;
    }

    return true;
    }
}

private bool IsInvalidCustomerName(string name) {
    char[] forbiddenCharacters = {'!', '@', '#', '$', '%', '&', '*'   };
    return string.IsNullOrEmpty(name) || name.Any(x =>
    forbiddenCharacters.Contains(x));
    }
}
```

As you can see in listing 6.2, we extracted the code into its own separate method. We also immediately return based on the resulting Boolean value of combining the conditional and LINQ query.

 SHORT-CIRCUITING AND LOGICAL OPERATORS   An alternative approach would be to use the "exclusive OR" operator (XOR, ^) instead of the conditional logical OR operator (||). The XOR operator evaluates to true if one, and only one, option is true. If both the IsNullOrEmpty and Any Contains checks are valid, something really strange is going on (a string cannot be both null or empty and contain an invalid character), so using an XOR operator could work for us. Because XOR is a "logical" operator, it evaluates both sides of the equation before returning a verdict on true or false. Logical operators can be less performant than conditional operators (such as ||) because logical operators do not evaluate the left-hand side of the equation if the right-hand side is false. This is also called "short-circuit evaluation."

Coming back to the forbiddenCharacters array, a memory-conscious reader may object and say, "You're allocating memory for the forbiddenCharacters array when there is a possibility that you never use it because of name potentially being null." To that objection I would reply by agreeing with your factual statement but also counter by saying that it is a small price to pay for readability.

We almost fulfilled the first of our goals: validate the input argument of name. The logic is in place, but we don't have any unit tests backing this new logic yet. That is not very TDD compliant of us. How do we go about writing a test for this new logic? Are we okay with testing only the new private method, or do we also want to test the remaining CreateCustomer method as it calls the private method?

We do not want to directly test any private methods. In an ideal world, all private methods are called by a public method (this could be directly or indirectly through another private method(s)) and are tested through that public method. Because we are already testing the success case with our general CreateCustomer success case test, we don't need to create another success case (or "happy path") test. We do need a test for the failure case, however.

6.2.4 In-lining test data with the [DataRow] attribute

We want to test for all invalid characters, which, if we had a unit test for every single character, would require us to write N tests, where N is the number of invalid characters. That would be a lot of work for little reward. Luckily, MSTest has the [DataRow] attribute that we can use with the MSTest platform. We can use [DataRow] to specify an input parameter for the test method, as shown in the next listing. This allows us to just add a bunch of [DataRow] attributes to one test.

> **Listing 6.3 CreateCustomer_Failure_NameContainsInvalidCharacters with [DataRow]**

```
[TestMethod]
[DataRow('#')]
[DataRow('$')]
[DataRow('%')]
[DataRow('&')]
[DataRow('*')]
public void CreateCustomer_Failure_NameContainsInvalidCharacters(char
➥ invalidCharacter) {
  CustomerRepository repository = new CustomerRepository();
  Assert.IsNotNull(repository);

  bool result = repository.CreateCustomer("Donald Knuth" +
➥ invalidCharacter);
  Assert.IsFalse(result);
}
```

The test in listing 6.3 passes in a string containing the full name "Donald Knuth" postfixed by one of the invalid characters (as dictated by the [DataRow] attribute), for example: "Donald Knuth%". Using "Donald Knuth%" as an input argument to the CreateCustomer method returns a false Boolean on which we assert. If we now run the test, we can see that everything passes and we are back to great coverage of our codebase.

When I talk about coverage in the context of testing, I do not mean the percentage of your code covered by a test. For more information on code coverage and unit testing, see Vladimir Khorikov's *Unit Testing Principles, Practices, and Patterns* (Manning, 2020)[2] and Roy Osherove's *The Art of Unit Testing* (3rd edition; Manning, 2020).

6.2.5 Object initializers and autogenerated code

Coming back to the CreateCustomer method in CustomerRepository, we are ready to tackle the next item on our list: "Instantiate a new Customer object," shown in the next code listing.

---

[2] The author was a tech reviewer for Vladimir Khorikov's *Unit Testing Principles, Practices, and Patterns* (Manning, 2020).

Listing 6.4   CustomerRepository.cs `CreateCustomer` **creates a new customer**

```
Customer newCustomer = new Customer();
newCustomer.Name = name;
```

We can clean up the code in listing 6.4 a little bit by using what we call an "object initializer." Using an object initializer allows you to directly set field values of an instance at creation as follows:

```
Customer newCustomer = new Customer() {
  Name = name
};
```

Object initializers are great for when you need to set values manually, but what happens if a new developer comes in and accidentally changes the code to not set that name value; or, perhaps, for whatever reason, somebody creates an instance of type `Customer` somewhere else in the code without knowing they should set that property to a valid value?

Perhaps it is better if we control how the object gets instantiated. We can define how `Customer` is instantiated by forcing the use of a constructor that takes in a parameter of type `string` for the name. But we first need to verify that we can add a new constructor with no issue by looking at the Customer.cs class, shown next:

```
using System;
using System.Collections.Generic;

namespace FlyingDutchmanAirlines.DatabaseLayer.Models {
  public partial class Customer {
    public Customer() {
      Booking = new HashSet<Booking>();
    }

    public int CustomerId { get; set; }
    public string Name { get; set; }

    public virtual ICollection<Booking> Booking { get; set; }
  }
}
```

The `Customer` class is completely autogenerated by Entity Framework Core. It maps to the Customer table in our database and holds a list of `Bookings`. Entity Framework Core created this list, having found the relative foreign key constraint in the database. In my ideal world, properties and fields come before constructors, so they are visible at first glance when browsing a class, but that is not the case in the Entity Framework Core autogenerated files. If you wish, you can reorganize your files to reflect that pattern. In this book, I rearranged all models to that style. We can see the result of the rearrangement in listing 6.5. We also remove the `partial` keyword from the model's respective class signature. We can do this because we are not going to use the `partial` feature, and it is safer to get into the habit of removing code you know you are not going to use. Removing unused code promotes cleanliness in your code, and somebody reading through your classes in the future will thank you. Many developers get into the trap of keeping code that "they may use/need later." This only promotes a cluttered codebase in my opinion.

Listing 6.5 Customer.cs (EF Core–generated and reorganized)

```
using System;
using System.Collections.Generic;

namespace FlyingDutchmanAirlines.DatabaseLayer.Models {
  public class Customer {
    public int CustomerId { get; set; }
    public string Name { get; set; }

    public virtual ICollection<Booking> Booking { get; set; }

    public Customer() {
      Booking = new HashSet<Booking>();
    }
  }
}
```

6.2.6 *Constructors, reflection, and asynchronous programming*

We already have a constructor for the `Customer` class. It doesn't take any arguments but assigns a new instance of a `HashSet` of `Booking` to the `Booking` property. We want to keep the assignment because a reference type does not default to a zero value (an empty collection in this case). Instead it defaults to null.

> **NOTE** You can assign the default value for any type explicitly by using the `default` keyword instead of a value. This can come in helpful when dealing with nonprimitive value types, where the default value can be unknown to you. Reference types always have a default value of null.

We don't want to pass in an argument of type `HashSet<Booking>`, however. We want to let Entity Framework Core deal with any key constraints. But we do want to have an argument of type `string` reflecting the customer's name. Additionally, we also should make sure that nobody can inherit from our `Customer` object and consequently use polymorphism to add that to the database. So, we also seal our class by using the `sealed` keyword. Sealing a class means we need to remove the `virtual` keyword from the `Booking` property, because you cannot have virtual members or properties in a sealed class. We should also seal the other models in our codebase, as follows:

```
using System;
using System.Collections.Generic;

namespace FlyingDutchmanAirlines.DatabaseLayer.Models {
  public sealed class Customer {
```

```
    public int CustomerId { get; set; }
    public string Name { get; set; }

    public ICollection<Booking> Booking { get; set; }

    public Customer(string name) {
      Booking = new HashSet<Booking>();
      Name = name;
    }
  }
}
```

When we attempt to compile the code, we get a compilation error because we are not passing in the required parameter when we instantiate our `Customer` object in the `CustomerRepository`. In fact, we are still using the object initializer. Let's fix that as follows:

```
Customer newCustomer = new Customer(name);
```

We can now compile, and our tests still pass. The third item on our list is to add the new `Customer` object to the Entity Framework Core's internal `DbSet<Customer>`. Why do we need to do this? As discussed earlier, Entity Framework Core operates under the assumption that any changes to the database are first made to the in-memory datasets. To add a new object of type `Customer` to the database, we first have to add it to the in-memory `DbSet<Customer>`. To access the `DbSet`, we need to create a new instance of the database context class.

We can use two methods on a `DbContext` to add models to a `DbSet`: `Add` and `[Entity].Add`. If we call the general `Add` method, C# uses reflection to determine the entity type and add it to the correct set. I prefer using the explicit `[Entity].Add` because it leaves no room for ambiguity and saves some overhead (reflection is very expensive!).

Reflection

Reflection is a powerful technique in C# used to access information at run time about assemblies, types, and modules. In practice, this means that you can find out what the type is of an object or change some of its properties while executing your code. You can use reflection for much more than that, however. The opportunities are surprising.

For example, you can use reflection to create custom method attributes, create new types, or invoke code in a file you don't know the name of yet, all at runtime. You can even access private fields from outside classes (but please do not do that; respect the developers' access guidance).

As you can imagine, reflection is not the cheapest thing to execute in terms of memory and CPU cycles. To perform some of its operations, it has to load in and keep track of a lot of metadata in memory. Imagine the amounts of processing needed to detect the type of an unknown object at run time. Libraries and frameworks often cannot make assumptions about the type of objects they operate on, so they use reflection to gather metadata and make decisions based on that data.

Before using reflection, reflect on your use case.

Because the DbContext class implements the IDisposable interface, we need to dispose of it correctly. The DbContext class needs to be disposable because it can hold connection objects for infinite amounts of time. Finally, to commit and save our reference changes to the database, we call the SaveChangesAsync method in the context, as shown here:

```
using (FlyingDutchmanAirlinesContext context = new
  FlyingDutchmanAirlinesContext()) {
  context.Customer.Add(newCustomer);
  context.SaveChangesAsync();
}
```

This little snippet is what Entity Framework Core is all about. If we did not have the abstraction of Entity Framework Core (or a different ORM tool), we would have to instantiate a SQL connection, open it, write actual SQL to insert the new customer, and then execute that query. The code to do that is more complex and longer than what we have written now.

There is one little snag with this code, however: we call an asynchronous method, yet execute the method synchronously. For this particular method, building the code does not throw a compile error because it saves the changes synchronously. To convert a synchronous method to an asynchronous method, we need to follow three steps:

1 Use the await keyword on method calls we execute asynchronously and wait for.
2 Return an object of type Task from the method.
3 Add the async keyword to the method signature.

To not wait for (in other words, asynchronously execute) a method, C# uses the await keyword. People often confuse asynchronous programming with multithreaded programming. There is a big difference: asynchronous programming allows us to perform multiple things at the same time, coming back to something once it is done executing. Multithreaded programming typically refers to running multiple sets of logic in parallel, taking advantage of extra threads to speed up our code.

6.2.7 *Locks, mutexes, and semaphores*

Locking resources and controlling thread access are the bane of many software engineers' existence. Code blows up in complexity once you deal with multiple threads because the number of places errors can crop up increases rapidly. To lessen the burden on developers, C# exposes one statement (lock) and two main types of synchronization primitives to save you: mutexes and semaphores.

What are their differences, and when would you use one over the other? The easiest to use is the standard `lock` statement. To lock a resource using the `lock` statement and allow only one thread at a time to operate on it, use the `lock([RESOURCE]){...}` syntax as follows:

```
decimal netWorth = 1000000;
lock(netWorth) {
   ...
}
```

The `netWorth` variable is locked for the duration of the lock code block (after the code leaves the code block, the lock is released) and can be accessed by only one thread at a time. It is also worth noting that the `lock` statement prohibits two threads to lock the same resource at the same moment. If two threads could instantiate a lock at the same time, a lock would not be able to fulfill its "one thread at a time" promise. This is what we call a *deadlock*: two threads holding onto the same resource, waiting for the other to release that resource. Belaboring the obvious, we try to avoid deadlocks in our code because they are notoriously hard to debug.

We can make an analogy to canal locks: to raise and lower boats across a canal's elevation changes, we use canal locks. When a ship is second in line for the canal lock, a different ship uses the canal lock. Therefore, the initial ship "owns" and locks the canal lock. Only when the initial ship leaves the canal lock (the resource) is the canal lock freed and back in an available state. The second ship can now enter and use the canal lock. Programmatic locks come in handy when modeling queuing systems dealing with critical systems such as canal locks.

The `lock` statement works very well for locking properties within a specific process (e.g., a running program). If you want to lock a resource across multiple processes (e.g., multiple instances of your program running and interacting with your instance), use a mutex. When you finish using a mutex, you have to explicitly release it. This extra bit of verbosity makes a mutex easier to develop with than a lock.

USING MUTEXES FOR CROSS-PROCESS THREAD CONTROL

Unlike with a lock, we don't need a keyword to use a mutex. Instead, we instantiate a static instance of the `Mutex` class. Why static? Mutexes are cross-process and cross-thread, so we want only one instance for the entire application. An important difference between locks and mutexes is that we don't place mutexes on a property. Instead, we place mutexes within methods and use them to gate the execution of said methods. When a thread encounters a method with a mutex, the mutex tells the thread it must wait for its turn by using the `WaitOne` method. To release a mutex, use the `ReleaseMutex` method, as shown next:

```
private static readonly Mutex _mutex = new Mutex();
public void ImportantMethod() {
  _mutex.WaitOne();
```

```
...
    _mutex.ReleaseMutex();
}
```

The first thread that calls the `ImportantMethod` has no problems entering and passing the mutex gate. When the mutex lets the thread in, the thread takes ownership of the `Mutex` instance object. If a second thread tries to enter `ImportantMethod` while the first thread owns the mutex, the second has to wait until the first thread releases the mutex and relinquishes ownership. There is only one mutex to go around after all, because it is static. When the first thread no longer owns the mutex, the second thread takes ownership, and the cycle repeats itself.

USING SEMAPHORES TO ALLOW ACCESS BY MULTIPLE CONCURRENT THREADS

So, we can lock a resource (by using a lock) or gate the execution of a method (by using a mutex). But what if we want to gate the execution of a method but not create a bottleneck of a queue where only one thread at a time can execute the method? This is what a semaphore is for. People sometimes explain semaphores as "generalized mutexes" because semaphores offer functionality similar to mutexes but with an added twist: they allow for a specified number of threads to be in a gated method at the same time. To use a semaphore, we instantiate a static instance of the `Semaphore` class. The constructor for the `Semaphore` class takes in two arguments: the initial count of threads inside the method (usually 0), and the maximum concurrent threads in the method, as shown next:

```
private static readonly Semaphore _semaphore = new Semaphore(0, 3);
public void VeryImportantMethod() {
  _semaphore.WaitOne();

    ...
    _semaphore.Release();
}
```

When a thread wishes to execute the `VeryImportantMethod` method, the semaphore checks its internal thread counter and decides whether or not to let the thread in. In this example, the semaphore allows up to three concurrent threads in the method. A potential fourth thread has to wait until the semaphore's internal thread counter returns to two. Releasing the semaphore decreases its internal counter.

6.2.8 *Synchronous to asynchronous execution . . . continued*

The second step to convert a synchronous method to an asynchronous method is to change the return type of the method to be of type `Task<[type]>`, where `[type]` is the type you want to return (you can use `Task<void>` if you want to return no specific type). A `Task` is a wrapper around a unit of operation that we can wait on. We use the `Task` class with asynchronous methods so we can verify that a task is performed and return information along with task metadata. In the `CreateCustomer` method's case, we returned bool when executing synchronously, so we should return Task<bool> when operating asynchronously. When returning a Task<T>, we only return the type we want to embed in the type. The compiler automatically converts the return to a Task<T>. For example, to return a Task<bool> from a method that has Task<T> as its return type, we just need to do the following:

```
return myBool;
```

When a Task completes its duties, the Common Language Runtime returns the Task to the caller method with its CompletedTask property (of type bool) set to true.

For the third step, we need to add the async keyword to the method signature, as shown in the next listing. The async keyword indicates that the method is asynchronous (and, therefore, should return a Task<T>). The compiler throws a warning if you have an asynchronous method with no await calls.

> **Listing 6.6   CustomerRepository.cs** CreateCustomer asynchronous

```
public async Task<bool> CreateCustomer(string name) {       ◁──┐  The CreateCustomer
  if (IsInvalidCustomerName(name))  {                              method signature
    return false;                                                  contains the async
  }                                                                keyword and returns a
                                                                   type of Task<bool>.
  Customer newCustomer = new Customer(name);
using (FlyingDutchmanAirlinesContext context = new
➥ FlyingDutchmanAirlinesContext())
  {
    context.Customer.Add(newCustomer);           The context.SaveChangesAsync call is
    await context.SaveChangesAsync();    ◁──      awaited, blocking the current thread
  }                                               until the changes have been saved.

  return true;      ◁──  The return of type bool is automatically
}                         converted to a type of Task<bool>.
```

One final note: when you try to run your tests, you will encounter compiler errors in each of them. This is because they now call an asynchronous method without an await or them being asynchronous themselves. We need to fix this.

Use your newfound knowledge and convert the failing tests from executing synchronously to asynchronously and await the call to CreateCustomer method. Keep in mind that unit test methods return void when executing synchronously. If you get stuck, you can find the solution in appendix A.

6.2.9   *Testing Entity Framework Core*

How would we go about testing that an object was added to the database? Sure, we can run the existing test, but that would interact with the database—a giant no-go for a unit test. But we want to verify that the tested method actually added an object to the database, and we do not have the code to route actual HTTP requests to the repository. Here is what I propose: we run the existing success case unit test once, check the database for the newly created entry, and then figure out a solution for the unit test's connectivity issue.

If we execute the CreateCustomer_Success unit test, we can query the actual deployed database for the created customer ("SELECT * FROM [dbo].[Customer]") outside of our code using a database management tool such as SQL Server Manager. The resulting customer entry is shown in figure 6.5.

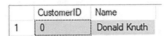

Figure 6.5 The result of the query to select all the customers in the database. Your mileage may vary on the number of customers in the database due to the database being deployed online.

But we do not want to create a new entry in the actual database every time we run our unit test. Entity Framework Core has the concept of an in-memory database, which allows us to spin up a database (with the same structure as our cloud or locally deployed database) in memory on our machine whenever we run a test. To facilitate this, we need to install the Microsoft.EntityFramework.Core.InMemory package in the FlyingDutchmanAirlines_Tests project. We also need to import the namespaces of Microsoft.EntityFrameworkCore and FlyingDutchmanAirlines.DatabaseLayer into the test class.

METHOD ATTRIBUTES FOR UNIT TESTING AND DEPENDENCY INJECTION

Besides creating an in-memory database, it would be useful if we could create a new context with the appropriate in-memory options for every test with the same code block. What if I told you there is a method attribute that allows us to create a method and run it before every single test?

As shown in table 6.1, the method attribute that accomplishes this is [Test-Initialize]. There are also method attributes to run a method *after* each test ([TestCleanup]), run a method before the test suite starts ([ClassInitialize]), and one for cleanup after the test suite is run ([ClassCleanup]). A test suite is all the tests in one class.

Table 6.1 Test method attributes and when the method runs

Method attribute	When does the method run?
[ClassInitialize]	Before any of the tests in a class
[TestInitialize]	Before every test in a class
[TestCleanup]	After every test in a class
[ClassCleanup]	After all the tests in a class

Let's add a TestInitialize method using the [TestInitialize] method attribute in the CustomerRepositoryTests class as follows:

```
private FlyingDutchmanAirlinesContext _context;

[TestInitialize]
public void TestInitialize() {
  DbContextOptions<FlyingDutchmanAirlinesContext> dbContextOptions = new
➥ DbContextOptionsBuilder<FlyingDutchmanAirlinesContext>()
➥ .UseInMemoryDatabase("FlyingDutchman").Options;
  _context = new FlyingDutchmanAirlinesContext(dbContextOptions);
}
```

We create a private field of type `FlyingDutchmanAirlinesContext` called `_context` to hold our database context so we can use it in our tests. Then we provide the initializer method (`TestInitialize`). In `TestInitialize` we first create an object of `DbContext-Options<FlyingDutchmanAirlinesContext>` that uses the Builder pattern to create a `DbContextBuilder`, specify that we want to use an in-memory database with the name `FlyingDutchman`, and return the options for setting up a context in memory.

Then, we pass those options into our `FlyingDutchmanAirlinesContext` constructor (autogenerated by Entity Framework Core). `FlyingDutchmanAirlinesContext` has two constructors: one constructor with no arguments (we have used this one before) and one that takes in an argument of type `DbContextOptions<FlyingDutchman-Airlines>` and allows us to create the in-memory context in this case.

By using this context, we can run the unit tests against an in-memory database, rather than a real database. Entity Framework Core creates a perfect copy of the database schema (with no existing data) and acts as if we were acting against the deployed database. This allows us to perform unit tests without messing with an actual database.

But wait a second! How do we actually use the context? We are not passing in the context to the repository layer. In fact, it creates a new context in `CustomerRepository`. This is where dependency injection shows up again.

6.2.10 *Controlling dependencies with dependency injection*

Dependency injection (DI) is a term coined by Martin Fowler in a 2004 article called "*Inversion of Control Containers and the Dependency Injection Pattern*," but it really is an evolution of the dependency injection technique as first written about by Robert Martin (of clean code fame) in a paper posted to the comp.lang.c++ Usenet group in 1994 called *OO Design Quality Metrics: An Analysis of Dependencies*.[3]

Dependency injection, in its most basic terms, is a technique to provide classes with all the dependencies they need rather than instantiating them in the class themselves. This means that we can resolve dependencies at run time rather than at compile time. When used with interfaces, dependency injection also becomes a powerful tool for testing because we can pass in mocks as dependencies whenever we want.

---

[3] The original post to the comp.lang.c++ usenet group can be found at https://groups.google.com/forum/#!msg/comp.lang.c++/KU-LQ3hINks/ouRSXPUpybkJ.

A traditional class without DI may have a dependency on an AWS (Amazon Web Services) client object (let's call it `AwsClient` and also have it implement an interface called `IAwsClient`). This object is to be the communicator between AWS and our codebase. We can create this classwide object and assign it to a new instance of the `AwsClient` class in the class's constructor as follows:

```
public class AwsConnector {
  private AwsClient _awsClient;
  public AwsConnector() {
    _awsClient = new AwsClient();
  }
}
```

Now imagine that we want to test this class. How do we test the `_awsClient` to control its returns? Because it is a private member, we cannot directly access it. We could use reflection to access the private member by doing some clever code magic, but that would be painful and computationally expensive as well as very unclean and complicated code. The alternative is to use dependency injection.

With dependency injection, instead of assigning the `_awsClient` to a new instance of `AwsClient` in the constructor, we pass in that new instance to the constructor. We need to ensure that the dependency is on an interface, in this case, `IAwsClient`, as shown in the next code example. That way, we can make new classes that inherit from `IAwSClient`, making testing much easier.

```
public class AwsConnector {
  private readonly IAWSClient awsClient;
  public AwsConnector(IAWSClient injectedClient) {
    awsClient = injectedClient;
  }
}
```

Every class that wants to instantiate a new copy of `AwsConnector` now has to pass in an instance of a class that inherits from `IAwsClient`. To prevent `_awsClient` from being changed anywhere else, it is read only and private. The power of dependency injection is that it inverts the control of the dependency. Instead of the class having control of the dependency and how it is instantiated, now the calling class has this control. This is what we mean by "inversion of control."

Let's change the `CustomerRepository` to use dependency injection for the `FlyingDutchmanAirlinesContext`. To do this, we need to do the following five things:

1 In `CustomerRepository`, add a `private readonly` member of type `FlyingDutchmanAirlinesContext`.
2 Create a nondefault constructor for the `CustomerRepository` constructor that requires an argument of type `FlyingDutchmanAirlinesContext`.

3 In the new constructor, assign the private FlyingDutchmanAirlinesContext to the injected instance.

4 Change the class to use the private member instead of creating a new Flying-DutchmanAirlinesContext in the CreateCustomer method.

5 Update our test to inject an instance of FlyingDutchmanAirlinesContext into the CustomerRepository.

We start by adding the private readonly member of type FlyingDutchmanAirlines-Context and the new CustomerRepository constructor. Currently, we only have the default (nonexplicit) constructor, so we have to create a new constructor that matches our needs, as shown in the following code snippet. This constructor takes the place of the default constructor, because we do not want to create an overloaded constructor without arguments. We want to force the use of our DI constructor.

```
private readonly FlyingDutchmanAirlinesContext _context;

public CustomerRepository(FlyingDutchmanAirlinesContext _context) {
  this._context = _context;
}
```

That takes care of the first three items on our list. This code does contain a keyword that I haven't used in this book before: the this keyword.

> ### Accessing a current instance's data using the "this" keyword
>
> Why did we have to use this? Imagine if we did not: we would have an assignment that assigns a variable called _context to another variable called _context.
>
> ```
> _context = _context;
> ```
>
> But what are we assigning to what? The class field is called _context (incorrect naming convention notwithstanding), but so is the passed-in argument. There are two ways to resolve this conundrum: either we rename one of them (the likely candidate would be the constructor argument), or we find a way to specify which one we mean at what time. The this keyword refers to the current instance of a class. So what we are really saying when we do this._context is "the variable called _context in the current instance of the class." And with that differentiator, we can safely assign the argument to the field. It is up to you to determine whether adding the this keyword is an acceptable alternative to renaming your variables, fields, or members.
>
> My litmus test boils down to this: if you have to change the name to something that makes it less clear what you are trying to convey, use the this keyword. Otherwise, rename it.

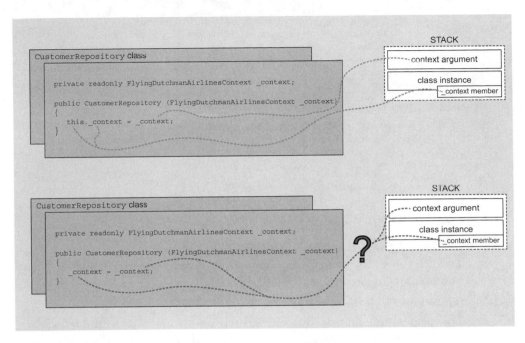

Now we have to make sure that the CreateCustomer method uses our newly initialized context instead of creating one within the method. To do this we strip the assignment of context to a new instance of FlyingDutchmanAirlines from the method and wrap the context member in the using statement as follows:

```
public async Task<bool> CreateCustomer(string name) {
  if (IsInvalidCustomerName(name)) {
    return false;
  }

  Customer newCustomer = new Customer(name);
  using (_context) {
    _context.Customer.Add(newCustomer);
    await _context.SaveChangesAsync();
  }

  return true;
}
```

You've now changed an existing method to use dependency injection. But what happens if the SaveChangesAsync method throws an error? Perhaps we cannot connect to the database anymore. Or there is something wrong with the deployed schema? We can wrap the database access code in a try-catch block, catching any exception so we can handle the exception (by returning false) instead of crashing the service, as shown next:

```
public async Task<bool> CreateCustomer(string name) {
  if (IsInvalidCustomerName(name)) {
    return false;
  }

  try {
    Customer newCustomer = new Customer(name);
    using (_context) {
      _context.Customer.Add(newCustomer);
      await _context.SaveChangesAsync();
    }
  } catch {
    return false;
  }

  return true;
}
```

The last thing that remains is to update our tests to injected dependency and create a unit test for the error case.

UNIT TESTING WITH TRY-CATCHES

To use dependency injection and asynchronous methods with our existing tests, we first have to make sure that all our test methods calling an asynchronous method (using `await`) return a type of `Task` and are asynchronous. Go ahead and update all tests. Then, we need to add the in-memory database context (`_context`) to the `Customer-Repository` instance creations, as shown here:

```
[TestMethod]
public async Task CreateCustomer_Success() {
  CustomerRepository repository = new CustomerRepository(_context);
  Assert.IsNotNull(repository);

  bool result = await repository.CreateCustomer("Donald Knuth");
  Assert.IsTrue(result);
}
```

All we did was add the `_context` instance to the new `CustomerRepository` constructor call. Do this for the other tests in the file, and you should be set on that front.

> **NOTE**   I like using the following template for my test names: {METHOD NAME} _{EXPECTED OUTCOME}. It uses snake casing to separate the method under test from the result: `CreateCustomer_Success`.

For the unit test, we can take two approaches to testing whether the method throws an `Exception` (by asserting that the method returned a Boolean with a value of false):

- Pass in `null` instead of the correctly instantiated `_context`.
- Stub `FlyingDutchmanAirlinesContext`, and have it throw an error based on a predefined condition.

For this test, we are going with the first approach: passing in `null` instead of `_context` to the `CustomerRepository` constructor. We'll discuss and use stubs in chapter 8. Passing in a `null` value for the dependency in the `CustomerRepository` constructor means that `CustomerRepository._context` is set to `null` and, therefore, causes a null pointer exception when trying to add a new `Customer`. This is sufficient for us to test the `try-catch` failure case as follows:

```
[TestMethod]
public async Task CreateCustomer_Failure_DatabaseAccessError() {
  CustomerRepository repository = new CustomerRepository(null);
  Assert.IsNotNull(repository);

  bool result = await repository.CreateCustomer("Donald Knuth");
  Assert.IsFalse(result);
}
```

If we run all the tests, we see that they pass. We are now testing with a completely in-memory database. Is there anything we can clean up before we move on? Well, yes, there is. If we look at our unit tests, we notice the following two repeating lines of code:

```
CustomerRepository repository = new CustomerRepository(_context);
Assert.IsNotNull(repository);
```

This is an excellent moment to apply the DRY principle. How about we extract the creation of the `CustomerRepository` into the `TestInitialize` method we created earlier, then expose it as a private member on the class for the tests to use, as shown next? It is updated before every test with a fresh instance of the `CustomerRepository`, so we are still guaranteed an isolated environment.

```
private FlyingDutchmanAirlinesContext _context;
private CustomerRepository _repository;

[TestInitialize]
public void TestInitialize() {
  DbContextOptions<FlyingDutchmanAirlinesContext> dbContextOptions = new
➥ DbContextOptionsBuilder<FlyingDutchmanAirlinesContext>()
➥ .UseInMemoryDatabase("FlyingDutchman").Options;
  _context = new FlyingDutchmanAirlinesContext(dbContextOptions);

  _repository = new CustomerRepository(_context);
  Assert.IsNotNull(_repository);
}
```

With the `CustomerRepository` creation now in the `TestInitialize` method, we can remove it for every test. For example, listing 6.7 shows how this impacts the `Create-Customer_Failure_NameIsNull` unit test. Note, however, that we do not want to do the same for `CreateCustomer_Failure_DatabaseAccessError`, because it relies on instantiating the repository with a `null` value as its input argument.

> **Listing 6.7   CustomerRepositoryTest updated** `CreateCustomer_Failure_`
> `NameIsNull`

```
[TestMethod]
public void CreateCustomer_Failure_NameIsNull() {
    CustomerRepository repository = new CustomerRepository(context);
    Assert.IsNotNull(repository);

    bool result = _repository.CreateCustomer(null);
    Assert.IsFalse(result);
}
```

So, to recap: we created a `CreateCustomer` method in `CustomerRepository` (along with the appropriate unit tests). The `CreateCustomer` method allows us to add new `Customer` objects to the database. But we also want to return the `Customer` objects when given a `CustomerID`. So, why don't we create a method that does that in the next chapter? By now you know the trick of TDD: we are going to create a unit test until we get stuck (that is, until we cannot compile or pass the test anymore), then we add the next piece of logic, then rinse and repeat.

Exercises

EXERCISE 6.4

Fill in the blanks: The three A's of testing are 1. _____, 2. _____, and 3. _____.

- a   affirm; assert; align
- b   affix; advance; await
- c   arrange; act; assert
- d   act; alter; answer

EXERCISE 6.5

True or false? With Language-Integrated Query, we can use query collections by passing in C++ code, which gets upgraded to C# and executed.

EXERCISE 6.6

How many checks does a conditional logical OR operator (||) make if the first condition evaluates to `false`?

- a   One
- b   Two
- c   Three
- d   It depends.

EXERCISE 6.7

How many checks does an exclusive OR operator (^) make if the first condition evaluates to `false`?

- a   One
- b   Two

    c Three

    d It depends.

EXERCISE 6.8

True or false? To convert a synchronous method to an asynchronous method, the method needs to return a type of `Task<[original return type]>` or `Task`, have the `async` keyword in the method signature, and `await` any asynchronous calls.

EXERCISE 6.9

Fill in the blanks: When unit testing, we perform operations against _____ database.

    a an in-memory

    b a deployed

    c a broken

EXERCISE 6.10

True or false? With dependency injection, we invert control over dependencies from the class to the caller.

Summary

- The single-responsibility principle tells us to do only one thing in a method and to do it well. If we heed this creed, we end up with code that is maintainable and extensible.
- Test-driven development has two stages: red (tests failing or not compiling) and green (tests are passing). Switching between the two stages (red and green) allows us to write tests in conjunction with features. In the red stage, the tests don't pass or the code does not compile. Our job in the red stage is to make the test pass and make the code compile. In the green stage, the code compiles and the tests pass. During the green stage, we write new code that implements the next step of our feature. This makes the tests fail, and, therefore, we are back in the red stage.
- Language-Integrated Query (LINQ) allows us to perform SQL-like queries against collections. We can use this to simplify our code tremendously when dealing with databases.
- We can use dependency injection (DI) with unit tests to provide more granular control on calls to dependencies. When using DI, the data flow is reversed, and the calling method needs to provide dependencies, as opposed to having them instantiated on the spot.

Comparing objects

This chapter covers

- Implementing the `GetCustomerByName` method
- Viewing methods through the lens of lambda calculus
- Using nullable types
- Using custom exceptions
- Operator overloading and custom equality comparisons

In the previous chapter, we implemented the `CustomerRepository` where we can add a customer to the database. We also learned how to use dependency injection to write testable code. This is a splendid start, but we are not done yet. We can add a `Customer` instance to the database, but how about retrieving one? See figure 7.1 for where we are in the scheme of the book.

In this chapter, we'll create the `GetCustomerByName` method that returns an appropriate `Customer` object when given a string containing the customer's name. Implementing this method allows us to touch on some technical concepts we may have missed otherwise. As before, we'll use test-driven development "light" to ensure

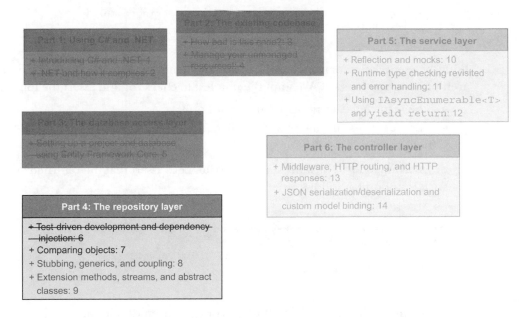

Figure 7.1 In this chapter, we'll continue the implementation of the `CustomerRepository` we started in chapter 6. This is the first step in implementing all the repositories for the Flying Dutchman Airlines service.

our code quality is adequate. Even though the API doesn't require an endpoint to get customers from the database, this method will prove useful for us when we implement our booking endpoint.

7.1 The GetCustomerByName method

To get started, let's create the following new unit test that does absolutely nothing besides an attempt to call our new (not yet created) method:

```
[TestMethod]
public async Task GetCustomerByName_Success() {
  Customer customer =
➥ await _repository.GetCustomerByName("Linus Torvalds");
}
```

After switching to the `CustomerRepository` class, let's add the `GetCustomerByName` method. Let's also add an argument of type `string` to the method signature, signifying the `CustomerName` we want passed in. We'll also add code to return a new instance of type `Customer`, to satisfy the return type of `Task<Customer>` in the method signature. We do not have any `await` calls in the method yet, so the compiler warns us of that (and we'll handle it in section 7.1.1). For now, we are okay with executing `Get-CustomerByName` synchronously as follows:

```
public async Task<Customer> GetCustomerByName(string name) {
  return new Customer(name);
}
```

With the compilation warning resolved, we can attempt another test run. Of course, we aren't testing anything yet. We want the unit test to check for and assert the following:

- The returned `Customer` instance is not null.
- The `Customer` instance has valid data for the `CustomerId`, `Name`, and `Booking` fields.

Those assertions should be fairly simple to write. Let's assert that the returned `Customer` instance is not null as follows:

```
[TestMethod]
public async Task GetCustomerByName_Success() {
  Customer customer =
➡ await _repository.GetCustomerByName("Linus Torvalds");
  Assert.IsNotNull(customer);
}
```

If we remember the red-green traffic light of test-driven development, we see that we have transitioned from the red stage (not compiling) to the green stage (compiling and our tests work). Now let's make the light red again. The red-green instant feedback loop provides small, gratifying wins throughout the procedure, making TDD very satisfying to use.

Now that we are in the red stage, we can add some new tests to assert based on code we have not written yet. So, what do we want to do in `GetCustomerByName`? As shown in figure 7.2:

1 Validate the input parameter (name, string).
2 Check the internal database set of Entity Framework Core for the appropriate customer.
3 Return the found customer or throw an exception saying we did not find the customer.

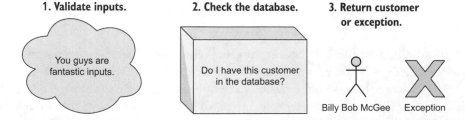

Figure 7.2 The three steps to implementing `GetCustomerByName` are (1) validate the input parameters, (2) check the database for an existing customer, and (3) return the found customer or an exception.

There's a lot to unpack, so let's start with the simplest (and first) item in the list: validating our input parameters. You may recall that we discussed input validation in section 6.2.1.

Before we move on, let me offer another argument about why we want to validate all our input parameters, regardless of whether they *should* have been validated and/or sanitized upstream. If we examine the abstract concept of a method through the lens of lambda calculus, we could say that any method (if visualized as a function), at its most basic level, is an isolated construct of an input, a function body, and an output. We can write this using some simple syntax where the lambda is wrapped (λ) in parentheses with the input followed by a period and the output, as shown in figure 7.3.

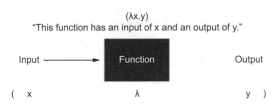

Figure 7.3 A method can be seen as a lambda function. It has an input, some logic that operates on that input, and a resulting output. Using lambda functions helps with adhering to the "code should read like a narrative" principle because you have room to do only one atomic operation.

We should treat this method as a so-called black box. We do not have any insight into the inner workings of the function, so how are we supposed to know whether a certain input is correct? The function should return a valid output for any input, regardless of how it processes the data. If we assume that a parameter is validated in an earlier method in the code and we pass in an invalid value to the method, we cause our (programmatic) method in code to hard crash. We do not comply with this lambda calculus black box thing we have going on. Note that because lambda calculus deals with mathematical functions, it's not the function itself that crashes but rather our flawed code implementation of the system.

7.1.1   *Question marks: Nullable types and their applications*

Now that we have a skeleton for the `CustomerRepositoryTests.GetCustomerByName _Success` unit test and the `CustomerRepository.GetCustomerByName` method, we can validate the input into `GetCustomerByName`. What are the rules for our input arguments to abide by? Well, we never want a null value, so that should be the first check.

Until C# 8, any reference type was nullable. This meant you could assign a null value to reference types and prevent the compiler from throwing an error when it found a null value. In practice, this often was the reason why we saw null-pointer exceptions being raised at runtime. Many times, you did not know a reference type would be null, yet you'd still try to use it somehow. To combat runtime null-pointer exceptions, C# 8 introduced explicit nullable reference types, which lets us make a reference type null by explicitly signaling that we want to do so. The overarching goal behind nullable reference types is to remove unexpected null-pointer exceptions in C#. If the only time a reference type can be null is when you explicitly allow it to be null, you are in control. Instead of guessing whether a reference type could be null when you try to use it (or digging through lots of code to find out), you can look at its underlying type. If it is nullable, assume that it can be null and perform null checks.

To enable nullable reference types, either add the `<Nullable>enable</Nullable>` flag to your project file (.csproj) or add the `#nullable enable` tag per source file, if you do not want to enable nullable reference types for the entire project. (You can also use `#nullable disable` to disable nullable for a particular source file when enabling nullable for the entire project.) In effect, when using C# 8 or higher with the nullable reference type support enabled, if you want a reference type to be null, you need to declare the type to be nullable by post-fixing a question mark to the type, for example, `int?` or `Customer?`. Nullable value types have been present in C# since C# 2.0 and follow the same pattern. The provided `name` always needs to be valid. A valid name means a non-null or empty string. Let's say `name` is an invalid value—what then? We could throw an exception or return a null value up to the controller. In general, a good frame of mind is to limit any null returns. Because it is a value people rarely expect to be returned (unless the return type is `Nullable<T>` or an explicit nullable reference type), we should not throw the receiving method a curveball. Let's go with a custom `Exception`. Alternately, you can use one of the exceptions that .NET provides us. Some suggested choices are `ArgumentNullException` or `InvalidOperationException` (also discussed in section 14.1.1).

7.1.2   *Custom exceptions, LINQ, and extension methods*

Every exception in C# inherits from the `Exception` class. Of course, intermediate layers of inheritance can exist, but in the end, it all boils down to the `Exception` class. For example, the `InvalidCastException` class inherits `SystemException`, which inherits the `Exception` class, as shown in figure 7.4.

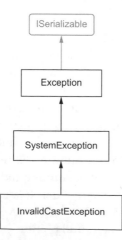

Figure 7.4   `InvalidCastException` **inherits from** `SystemException`, **which inherits from** `Exception`. `Exception` **inherits from and implements the** `ISerializable` **interface.**

The Exception inheritance tree means that if we create a class that inherits from Exception, we can use SystemException and InvalidCastException like they are any other instance of Exception. I propose we use inheritance from the Exception class to create a class called CustomerNotFoundException. Throughout the book, the exception-handling strategy used boils down to the following four major steps:

1 Check if an exception needs to be thrown.
2 Create an instance of a custom exception.
3 Raise the custom exception.
4 Catch the exception one layer above where it was thrown, and decide whether to handle there or rethrow it.

If customerName is an invalid name (we can use the IsInvalidName method we created in section 6.2.3), we "throw" our new exception. If we want to throw an exception (or "raise" it, as some languages would say), we use the throw keyword with the exception we want to throw. And because we want to be organized, we should also create a dedicated folder for custom exceptions (aptly named "Exceptions"), as shown next:

```
namespace FlyingDutchmanAirlines.Exceptions {
  public class CustomerNotFoundException : Exception { }
}
```

Because we do not need any functionality from CustomerNotFoundException besides what the Exception class already gives us, this code is the entire exception. After adding the appropriate import to the CustomerRepository class (using FlyingDutchmanAirlines.Exceptions), we can use our new exception and validate the input of name as follows:

```
public async Task<Customer> GetCustomerByName(string name) {
  if (IsInvalidCustomerName(name)) {
    throw new CustomerNotFoundException();
  }

  return new Customer(name);
}
```

We could have used an ArgumentException instead of our custom exception, but to me, it makes sense that a method that retrieves customer names from a database can return an exception called CustomerNotFoundException. By running our existing tests, we verify that the new code does not break any existing functionality. We can test for the invalid input by creating a new test in CustomerRepositoryTests that passes a negative integer to GetCustomerByName and then checks that the method threw an exception of type CustomerNotFoundException during execution. In section 4.1.2, we discussed how to check the type of an object through the typeof keyword. We use this knowledge in our failure case test. We can check for a thrown exception with MSTest in the following ways:

- Decorate the test method with a method attribute of type `[ExpectedException`
  `(typeof([your exception]))]`.
- Add a `try-catch` block in the code, and assert that the exception is the correct type.

For us, both approaches would work. There is a slight caveat with the first approach: the method attribute of type `ExpectedException(typeof([your exception])` does not allow us to access any of the properties of the thrown exception. So, if you attach some kind of message, custom data, or stack trace to your exception, you cannot access it unless you use the second approach. Not having access to a stack trace is not an issue for us, so let's use the first approach, as shown here:

```
[TestMethod]
[DataRow("")]
[DataRow(null)]
[DataRow("#")]
[DataRow("$")]
[DataRow("%")]
[DataRow("&")]
[DataRow("*")]
[ExpectedException(typeof(CustomerNotFoundException))]
public async Task GetCustomerByName_Failure_InvalidName(string name) {
  await _repository.GetCustomerByName(name);
}
```

Run the test; it should pass. If it does not, check whether your `ExpectedException` is of the right type (`CustomerNotFoundException`).

Switching back to the success case test, we can move on to the second item on our list of items to do in the `GetCustomerByName` method: check the internal database set of the Entity Framework Core for the appropriate customer. To test the logic, we must first have a `Customer` instance to check against. Before we can access a `Customer` instance, we need to add one to the in-memory database. Following that, we use the `GetCustomerByName` method to retrieve it. How about we add that in the `Test-Initialize` method so we have access to `Customer` in the database in every test?

We already wrote code to add a `Customer` instance to a database in the `Create-Customer` method, so let's use that (rather than calling the method itself in an initialization method). To add a `Customer` instance to the in-memory database, we need to add a new instance of `Customer` to the internal database set for `Customer` and save the changes through Entity Framework Core, as shown in the next listing. Because we should `await` the `SaveChangesAsync` call, we need to convert `TestInitialize` to an asynchronous method.

> ### Listing 7.1 **CustomerRepositoryTests.cs** `TestInitialize` **with in-memory database**

```
[TestInitialize]
public async Task TestInitialize() {
  DbContextOptions<FlyingDutchmanAirlinesContext> dbContextOptions = new
  DbContextOptionsBuilder<FlyingDutchmanAirlinesContext>().UseInMemoryDatabase
```

```
➡  ("FlyingDutchman").Options;
   _context = new FlyingDutchmanAirlinesContext(dbContextOptions);

   Customer testCustomer = new Customer("Linus Torvalds");
   _context.Customer.Add(testCustomer);
   await _context.SaveChangesAsync();

   _repository = new CustomerRepository(_context);
   Assert.IsNotNull(_repository);
}
```

Creates a new instance of Customer. The customer's name field is set to "Linus Torvalds".

Adds the testCustomer object to the DbSet<Customer> by calling the database context and accessing the DbSet<Customer>

Saves the changes to the in-memory database

As we can see by the bold code in listing 7.1, adding a new `Customer` object to the database is pretty straightforward. Let's hop back to the `GetCustomerByName_Success` test and see if we can get that `Customer` object back from the `GetCustomerByName` method. Remember, though, that what we inevitably get back from the method is not the same instance as what we stored in the database, but it is congruent to that instance (more on congruence in section 7.2). We know that the `Customer` object in the database has a `CustomerName` of `"Linus Torvalds"`, so we do not need to adjust that part of the existing test.

We want `GetCustomerByName` to search the database for an existing `Customer` object matching the input argument. We need to change this to grab the correct `Customer` object from the database. We grab the correct element from the database by accessing the database context's `DbSet<Customer>` and requesting the `Customer` instance with the given `CustomerName`. When querying a collection for an element, we can use the `DbSet<Customer>` and find our wanted `Customer` instance in two ways:

- We can loop over the collection with a `foreach`, `while`, or `for` loop.
- We can use LINQ.

We have seen examples of both in the book so far. Let's contrast these approaches. To use a loop to select our customer, we could end up with the following code:

```
foreach (Customer customer in _context.Customer) {
  if (customer.CustomerName == name) {
    return customer;
  }
}

throw new CustomerNotFoundException();
```

There is nothing wrong with that code. It is readable and to the point. Still, there is a better way to do it: with LINQ commands to query collections, as follows:

```
return _context.Customer.FirstOrDefault(c => c.Name == name)
➡  ?? throw new CustomerNotFoundException();
```

That is definitely shorter but also looks more intimidating. Let's unpack what this one-liner does. We access the `DbSet<Customer>` by using `context.Customer`—nothing we haven't seen before. But the next part is a bit odd: `FirstOrDefault(c => c.Name == name)`. The lambda expression finds matches between name properties, but we have not seen `FirstOrDefault` before. `FirstOrDefault` is an extension method defined in `System.Linq`.

Extension methods

Extension methods are static methods, and we call them on specific types. For example, we can call the `FirstOrDefault` LINQ extension method on any instance implementing the `IQueryable` interface. How do we know what type an extension method operates on and can be used with? Look at the method signature of an extension method: extension methods always have an argument that starts with the `this` keyword, followed by the specific type (or interface) they want to operate on. For example, `public static string MyExtensionMethod(this IDisposable arg)` signifies an extension method that any object implementing `IDisposable` can call that returns a string.

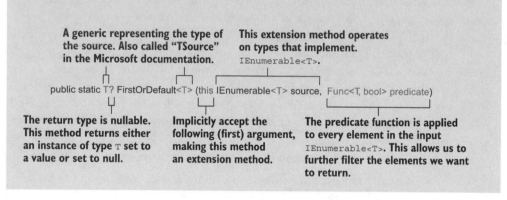

The `FirstOrDefault` LINQ extension method selects the first element in a collection that matches a provided predicate. If no matching elements are found, the `First-OrDefault` method returns the default value for the return type. What we want, in this code, is to find the first element in the `context.Customer` set that has a matching `Name` to our input argument of `name`. If no first matching `Customer` is found, `First-OrDefault` returns a null value (the default value for `Customer`).

That brings us to the second unfamiliar part of the return statement: `?? throw new CustomerNotFoundException();`. As you may recall from section 5.3.6, we call the `??` operator the "null-coalescing operator." A null-coalescing operator allows us to say, "If this thing is null, use this other value instead." So, in our case, "If the `FirstOrDefault` returns a null value (the default value for `Customer`), throw an exception of type `CustomerNotFoundException` instead." The asynchronous version of `FirstOrDefault` is `FirstOrDefaultAsync`, as shown next:

```
public async Task<Customer> GetCustomerByName(string name) {
  if (IsInvalidCustomerName(name)) {
```

```
    throw new CustomerNotFoundException();
  }


  return await _context.Customer.FirstOrDefaultAsync(c => c.Name == name)
⇒ ?? throw new CustomerNotFoundException();
}
```

We can now go back to our success case test and run it once more, verifying that all tests pass.

7.2 *Congruence: From the Middle Ages to C#*

According to myth and legend, local medieval legend Grutte Pier (a seven-foot-tall rebel leader with a massive sword, shown in figure 7.5) used a Frisian saying as a shibboleth to determine whether he faced an enemy (usually the Habsburgs and Saxons) or a true Frisian. Because Frisian is one of the closest linguistic relatives to Old English (modern-day English is still part of the Anglo-Frisian language group), see if you can pick out its meaning and give it a whirl:

> *"Bûter, brea, en griene tsiis; wa't dat net sizze kin is gjin oprjochte Fries"*

When translated to English, that strange-looking text means: "Butter, bread, and green cheese; who cannot say this is not a sincere Frisian." (The green cheese refers to a Frisian cheese embedded with cumin and cloves. The cheese's natural rind can take on a greenish hue.) So, what does a shibboleth have to do with C# or programming? Well, not a whole lot, but I can use it to show you the following example of equality and congruence:

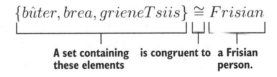

$$\{b\hat{u}ter, brea, grieneTsiis\} \cong Frisian$$

A set containing   is congruent to   a Frisian
these elements   person.

You see, Grutte Pier was testing whether somebody was a Frisian. Was Pier testing if person *A* was equal (in the sense of identical properties, not social equality) to person *B*? No. Person *A* may have blond hair, whereas person *B* may not. He tested for congruence between person *A* and the Frisian people. If you could say his shibboleth, he deemed you congruent to a Frisian and, therefore, you got to live. And you said congruence never saved somebody's life! If we use mathematical set notation and state that a set *A* is equal to $\{b\hat{u}ter, brea, grieneTsiis\}$ and set *B* equals $\{aachje \cdots zeppelin\}$ representing all Frisian words in somebody's vocabulary, we can say $\{x | x \in A \wedge x \in B\} \Leftrightarrow frisian$.

In section 7.1, we implemented and tested the `CustomerRepository.GetCustomer-ByName` method, which accepts an input parameter representing a customer's name and returns the appropriate `Customer` instance from the database. Before we call it a

Figure 7.5   A drawing of Grutte Pier by Pieter Feddes van Harlingen (1568–1623). The Latin inscription at the bottom of the painting roughly translates to "we assert to the great liberty of Pier." Pier is the keeper of liberty for the Frisian people.

day, however, I want to take a slight detour and see whether there is anything else we can do to improve the unit tests in the CustomerRepositoryTests class.

I'd say we have the following, more elegant ways to check for equality (or, rather, congruity) between the Customer instance in the database and the Customer instance we used to assert in the GetCustomerByName_Success unit test:

- Creating a custom comparer class using EqualityComparer<T> (section 7.2.1).
- Overriding object.Equals (section 7.2.2).
- Operator overloading (section 7.2.3).

In the following three sections, we combine these approaches into one unified way of testing for equality. If you are just looking for the simplest way of achieving this, over-riding object.Equals is the easiest (and a common) way of doing equality checks.

7.2.1   *Creating a "comparer" class using EqualityComparer<T>*

A "comparer" class allows us to define how to compare two instances of the same type and when they are "equal." We already discussed congruence, and, in this section, we apply the concept of congruence to equality comparisons.

In my opinion, the use of the term "equality" is unfortunate because we really say that something is congruent, not equal, to something else. But, alas, these are the cards .NET 5 and C# have dealt us. A "comparer" class derives from the Equality-Comparer<T> class. The EqualityComparer<T> class is an abstract class that contains the following two abstract methods that the compiler forces us to override and implement:

- `bool Equals(T argumentX, T argumentY)`
- `int GetHashCode(T obj)`

By overriding and implementing the Equals and GetHashCode methods, we adhere to the requirements of the EqualityComparer<T> base class. At first, you may think it strange we need to implement the GetHashCode method. After all, don't we just want to determine something is equal to something else? Yes, but GetHashCode (as well as Equals) is a method present on the Object class in .NET. Because *every* class in .NET derives ultimately from the Object class, the GetHashCode method is present in every class, be it explicitly or implicitly through inheritance up to the object class. Dictionaries use hash codes under the hood to perform element lookups and equality comparisons. This means that a dictionary is a conceptual hash table. (C# does have an explicit Hashtable implementation. The difference is that a dictionary is generic, whereas Hashtable is not.) By using hash codes, we get the benefit of very quick lookup, insert, and delete operations when compared to a regular list (which does not use hash codes).[1] Hash codes operate under the assumption that the same hash code is always generated for the same object. So, if two objects are identical, two identical hash codes are generated. If by chance two objects are not different but the same hash code is generated for both of them, we speak of a *hash collision*. This means we have to come up with some other way to insert the items into the array.[2]

Because GetHashCode is present on every object in .NET, we can come up with a somewhat dynamic way of generating a hash code by using another class's GetHash-Code implementation. To generate a hash code, we do need some seed information. The Customer object has only two fields we can use on which to base our hash code–generation logic. We can use a combination of the length property of Customer.Name, the Customer.CustomerID property, and a "randomly" generated integer, as shown in the next listing. Note that a lot of discussions arise around when and when not to use GetHashCode. I would refer you to the Microsoft documentation for the most up-to-date information on this (as well as for the plethora of warnings to keep in mind when using GetHashCode).

---

[1] The average time complexity of a hash table's insert, lookup, and search operations (and, by extension, a dictionary) is $O(1)$. The worst case for these operations is $O(n)$. A generic list in C#, (List<T>), acts as a dynamic array. For a dynamic array, the average and worst-case time complexity for search, insertion, and deletion is $O(n)$, where n is the number of elements in the dynamic array.

[2] A hash collision is an unwanted result but not a rare occurrence. Donald Knuth writes about the "Birthday Paradox" in *The Art of Computer Programming Volume 3: Sorting and Searching* (2nd edition; Addison-Wesley, 1998): given a hash function that generates hash codes based on a person's birthday and a room with at least 23 people (a map of n people to a table of size 365, one entry for each day of a non–leap year, where $n \geq 23$), the probability of at least two people sharing the same birthday (and generating the same hash code) is 0.4927.

Listing 7.2   CustomerEqualityComparer's `GetHashCode` implementation

**Overrides the abstract
GetHashCode method**

```
internal class CustomerEqualityComparer : EqualityComparer<Customer> {
    public override int GetHashCode(Customer obj) {
        int randomNumber = RandomNumberGenerator.GetInt32(int.MaxValue / 2);
        return (obj.CustomerId + obj.Name.Length + randomNumber).GetHashCode();
    }
}
```

**Generates a random
number up to half of the
maximum integer value**

**Concatenates variables and fields
and hashes the resulting value**

We can generate "random" numbers in C# using the following two general methods:

- Use the `Random` class.
- Use the `RandomNumberGenerator` class.

At first glance, they may seem similar, but if we dig a little deeper, we see differences. The `Random` class lives in the (root) `System` namespace, whereas the `RandomNumber-Generator` class lives in the `System.Security.Cryptography` namespace. The namespaces in which the respective classes live provide a major hint at why they both exist: the `Random` class is a low-overhead random-number picker that is very good at quickly spitting out a number based on a time seed number. The `RandomNumberGenerator` class excels at generating "random" numbers through a variety of cryptography concepts, making sure that numbers are fairly unique and somewhat equally distributed in a range over time.

In other words, if you were to use the `Random` class in a high throughput application and request two random numbers at the same time, chances are you would get the same number back from the "random" generator. Generating a pseudo-random number is fine for a lot of applications, but for a web service, where we cannot predict what load the system could be under, it is unsuitable. We may very well be in a situation where two people want to retrieve information for the same flight at the exact same moment. We now have two customers generating the same hash code and a security flaw on our hands. That is why we should use the `RandomNumberGenerator` class instead of the `Random` class.

As you explore the world of random numbers and cryptography in C#, you may come across people advocating the usage of the `RNGCryptoService-Provider` class. The `RandomNumberGenerator` class is a wrapper around the `RNGCryptoServiceProvider` class and much easier to use. A good resource for further cryptography information is David Wong's *Real-World Cryptography* (Manning, 2021).

We overrode and implemented the `GetHashCode` method, so now it is time to do the same for the `Equals` method.

"Random" is never random

Imagine you want to listen to some music through your favorite music-streaming application. You probably have a playlist with thousands of songs but don't want to start at the top every time you want to listen to music. You would tire of listening to the same songs in the same pattern very quickly. So, you press the "shuffle" button, assuming that your application shuffles your playlist randomly and plays the songs in a new order. Unfortunately, I am here to burst that bubble. Shuffling a playlist rarely gets you a true random representation of your music. Applications like Spotify use a shuffling algorithm that attempts to create an on-the-fly playlist shuffle experience where no songs from the same album or artist are played after each other. We have all had that experience, though. Why is it that shuffling a playlist is such a tricky problem? The issue is that randomness in computing is never completely random.

It all boils down to the fact that computers have to be told how to pick a random number. Random-number pickers use an algorithm that bases their starting point on a "seed" number, often the current timestamp. A seed number of X always returns the same return Y. If you use the current time as your seed number, running the same algorithm in parallel starting at the same moment, you get two identical (but "random") outputs. This makes picking a random number a potential security issue. If you know the seed number and algorithm used by the picker, you can predict the next output value.

Hackers use "random-number-generator attacks" to exploit this vulnerability. A historical example of problems around randomness in computing is failing to generate a correct random value for an elliptic curve digital signature algorithm in Sony's Playstation 3 video game console. By exploiting this error, hackers could tell the system that homebrew applications (and as a result, pirated video games) were valid applications and, therefore, to run them.

I leave you with this quote by computing pioneer John von Neumann, intended as a lighthearted warning against misunderstanding the limits of randomness in computing:

> *"Anyone who considers arithmetical methods of producing random digits is, of course, in a state of sin."*

7.2.2   *Testing equality by overriding the Equals method*

Before we override `Equals`, let's settle on what things need to be equal to say that `Customer` instance X is "equal" to `Customer` instance Y. The `Customer` class docs not have a lot of properties to check for: only `CustomerId` and `Name` are usable. The `Booking` field is a collection representing any foreign key constraints on the `Customer` model. But, for our congruence check, those properties are not relevant because we don't use them to establish congruence, so we don't use the collection in our check. If `Customer` X has the same `Name` and `CustomerId` property values as `Customer` Y, they are equal (and so, we return a `bool` set to `true` out of the `Equals` method, as shown in the next listing).

Listing 7.3   CustomerEqualityComparer's `Equals` method implementation

```
public override bool Equals(Customer x, Customer y) {
    return x.CustomerId == y.CustomerId        ⊲─┐   Verifies that both Customer
        && x.Name == y.Name;          ⊲─┐            instances have the same
}                                     │               CustomerId value
              Verifies that both Customer instances
                    have the same Name value
```

We want to call our `Equals` method every time we compare two instances of type `Customer`. We could expose an `Equals` method in the `Customer` class and call the `CustomerEqualityComparer.Equals` method. That would work very well, because `Equals` is part of `object` and, therefore, available to most derived types. It is probably what you want to do in real life, and I am assuming you can implement this on your own. However, this presents an excellent opportunity for me to talk about something else: if we are already going down a bit of a rabbit hole by implementing a "comparer" class, we may as well go all the way. Probably the most common technique of checking equality in two objects is by using the equality operator: `==`.

7.2.3 *Overloading the equality operator*

Most of the time, you never think twice about the functionality behind the equality operator. Sure, you probably mistype and accidentally put down the assignment operator (`=`) at times, but surely the actual functionality of the equality operator is somewhat set in stone. In general, you can rely on the equality operator doing reference-type equality checks, but that functionality doesn't work for us. Checking the reference pointers on two objects is not sufficient for comparing two `Customer` objects because the result would always be `false`. What to do? The solution is simple: if there is an implementation that does not meet your needs for a specific set of inputs, overload the implementation. In C#, we can overload operators.

Overloading an operator works much like overriding (more so than overloading) a method. In the world of operators, their programmatic names are their symbols (e.g., the plus sign, `+`, for the addition operator). One enormous difference between method and operator overloads, however, is that operator overloads are always static and public. It makes little sense to create an operator that is instance-level (static). Non-instance-level overridden operators create a confusing scenario where you have multiple versions of the same operator for the same type floating around with no clear boundaries to the casual observer. The syntax for using an operator does not allow for an `[instance].[operator]`, or `string.+` construct (this is allowed in languages such as Scala). As far as the `public` access modifier is concerned, when you use an operator on a specific type, you are not operating within that type's class file.

To overload an operator, use the following syntax: `public static [return type]` `operator [operator name] (T x, T y) { … }`, where `T` stands for the type you want to operate on. In our overload of the equality operator inside the `Customer` class, we want to call the `CustomerEqualityOperator`'s `Equals` method and return the result, as shown in the next code sample.

NOTE When overloading operators, if the operator has a matching operator (e.g., == and !=), you have to overload both operators.

```
public static bool operator == (Customer x, Customer y) {
  CustomerEqualityComparer comparer = new CustomerEqualityComparer();
  return comparer.Equals(x, y);
}

public static bool operator != (Customer x, Customer y) => !(x == y);
```

Right now, we create a new instance of the comparer every time we call the overloaded operator. In an actual production codebase, you should consider moving the instantiation to the instance level. This sidesteps incurring the overhead of instantiation on every call to the overloaded operator.

The overload of the != operator calls our overload of the equality operator and negates the result from that method's execution. Now comes the fun part: we get to use the overloaded operators in our CustomerRepositoryTests.GetCustomerByName _Success unit test instead of having to check for congruity by comparing object fields.

To check the instance in the database against the returned Customer from the GetCustomerByName method, we first need to grab the Customer from the in-memory database using the LINQ First method, as shown in the next listing.

Listing 7.4 Use LINQ's `First` method on a database's internal set (EF Core)

```
[TestMethod]
public async Task GetCustomerByName_Success() {
  Customer customer =
➥  await _repository.GetCustomerByName("Linus Torvalds");      │ Gets a Customer from
  Assert.IsNotNull(customer);                                   │ the in-memory database

  Customer dbCustomer = _context.Customer.First();       ◁─┐  Grabs the first
                                                             │  (and only) element
                                                             │  directly from the
  bool customersAreEqual = customer == dbCustomer;   ◁──┐   │  in-memory database
  Assert.IsTrue(customersAreEqual);   ◁─┐
}
           Verifies that both Customer           Uses the overloaded
           instances are "equal"                 equality operator
```

In listing 7.4, we used our overloaded equality operator to test for our definition of equivalence between two instances of Customer. Before we wrap up this chapter, I'm going to let you in on one other secret: we can condense the code in listing 7.4 even more and make it more idiomatic. The Assert.AreEqual method calls the object's Equal method, which in turn (depending on the provided implementation) uses the equality operator. Because we overloaded the equality operator for Customer, the CLR (indirectly) calls the overloaded equality operator when we use the Assert.AreEqual method on two instances of Customer! Let's give it a whirl:

```
[TestMethod]
public async Task GetCustomerByName_Success() {
    Customer customer =
➥    await _repository.GetCustomerByName("Linus Torvalds");
    Assert.IsNotNull(customer);

    Customer dbCustomer = _context.Customer.First();
    Assert.AreEqual(dbCustomer, customer);
}
```

How about we actually run the `GetCustomerByName_Success` test? Did it pass? Good. Now run all the other unit tests as well. Every unit test should pass, as shown in figure 7.6. If one doesn't, please go back to the respective section and see what went wrong before moving on.

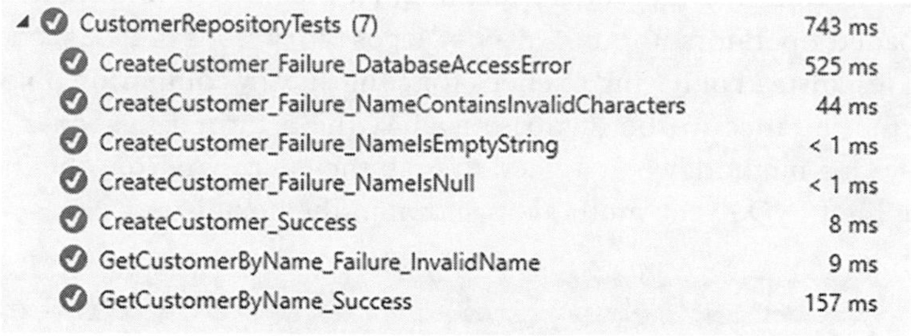

Figure 7.6   All our existing tests pass (as shown in the Visual Studio Test Explorer). The checkmarks represent tests that have passed. We also see the run time for the tests both individually and combined.

We can now add a new customer to the database and get it back when given an ID. That covers all the functionality we need from the `CustomerRepository`. We use the patterns used in the `CustomerRepository` in the remaining repositories. In section 6.2, we examined how the inherited codebase handled adding a new customer to the database.

Let's recap our findings there. We determined that the major design flaws of the existing codebases with adding a `Customer` object to the database were as follows:

- The code should be self-documenting.
- We should not use hardcoded SQL statements.
- We should use explicit types instead of implicit types (the `var` keyword).

I think we did very well in addressing those concerns. Our code is readable and clean. The code is self-documenting, and we use Entity Framework Core to abstract away any SQL queries. How did the existing code retrieve `Customer` objects from the database? Well, it did not retrieve any `Customer` objects from the database at all! That seems odd at first. If the existing codebase retrieved nothing from the `Customer` table, why does our service retrieve `Customer` entities? Keep in mind that to book a flight, we need access to an up-to-date `Customer` object. The old service created a new `Customer` object every time somebody booked a flight through its API, resulting in potentially duplicate entries in the database for the same `Customer`. We know better and do not have that issue, as long as we pass the correct information to our methods. In this chapter, you also learned how to use an equality "comparer" class and operator overloads to test for your definition of equivalency (or rather, congruity).

Exercises

EXERCISE 7.1
Currently, there is no unit test around a possible null condition when returning from `GetCustomerByName` when the given name does not match a `Customer` object in the database. How would we test for this?

EXERCISE 7.2
Which of the following is a valid nullable type?

   a `Customer!`

   b `Customer?`

   c `^Customer`

EXERCISE 7.3
Fill in the blank: A custom exception has to inherit from the _____ class so we can throw it where appropriate.

EXERCISE 7.4
What does the LINQ extension method `FirstOrDefault` return if it cannot find a matching item in the collection?

   a A null value

   b `-1`

   c The default value for the collection's type

EXERCISE 7.5
What does the equality operator test for in this code snippet, and what is its verdict?

```
int x = 0;
int y = 1;
x == y;
```

   a The equality operator tests for reference equality. It returns `false`.

   b The equality operator tests for reference equality. It returns `true`.

   c The equality operator tests for value equality. It returns `false`.

   d The equality operator tests for value equality. It returns `true`.

EXERCISE 7.6

What does the equality operator test for in this code snippet, and what is its verdict?

```
Scientist x = new Scientist("Alan Turing");
Scientist y = new Scientist("John von Neumann");
x == y;
```

    a The equality operator tests for reference equality. It returns `false`.
    b The equality operator tests for reference equality. It returns `true`.
    c The equality operator tests for value equality. It returns `false`.
    d The equality operator tests for value equality. It returns `true`.

EXERCISE 7.7

True or false? When we overload an equality comparison operator, we can determine congruence between two types and return our own definition of equality.

EXERCISE 7.8

When we overload the equality comparison operator, we also need to overload

    a `!=`
    b `^=`
    c `==`

EXERCISE 7.9

True or false? By using the `Random` class to generate a random number, we are guaranteed a perfect random number.

EXERCISE 7.10

True or false? By using the `RandomNumberGenerator` class to generate a random number, we are guaranteed a perfect random number.

EXERCISE 7.11

True or false? In many (pseudo) random-number-generation algorithms, using the same seed number twice results in the same random numbers.

Summary

- We can examine input validation through the lens of lambda calculus. If we treat any function as a black box, with just an input and an output, separated from all other functions, we have to do input validation or risk a bad outcome. We shouldn't rely on the validation of arguments elsewhere.
- Nullable reference types allow us to explicitly state which reference types may have a null value. Using nullable reference types helps to avoid unexpected null-pointer exceptions.
- To designate a type as nullable, you add the ? operator: `int? myNullableInt = 0;`.
- Every thrown exception (ultimately) derives from the `Exception` base class. This allows us to create our own (custom) exceptions and throw them like any other. Custom exceptions promote atomic error handling.

- You can check if a method throws a specific exception during a unit test run by adding the `[ExpectedException(typeof([your exception]))]` method attribute to your unit test. This allows you to unit-test failure scenarios of your code.

- Entity Framework Core can operate under an "in-memory" mode. This allows you to spin up a local, in-memory database identical to your real one. Because we don't want to unit-test against live data, this provides us with the "fake" database we need.

- You can use a custom `Comparer` class to create equivalency checks between two types if the standard reference equivalency check does not suffice. This allows you to reconcile two different instances of the same object, with the same values but different pointers.

- We can overload operators such as the equality operator to provide our own definition of equality and congruence. This is useful when wanting to compare two reference types for congruence instead of pure equality (the memory address matches).

Stubbing, generics, and coupling

This chapter covers

- Creating the `Booking` repository class using test-driven development
- Separation of concerns and coupling
- Programming with generics
- Unit testing with stubs

This chapter sees the continuation of our short-term mission to implement repositories for every entity in the database. If we look at the larger picture, we can remind ourselves why we implement these repositories in the first place: Aljen van der Meulen, the CEO of Flying Dutchman Airlines, wants us to bring their old codebase into the modern era. We received an OpenAPI specification to adhere to (the service needs to integrate with a flight search aggregator), and we settled on using the repository/service pattern in our new codebase. Figure 8.1 shows where we are in the scheme of the book.

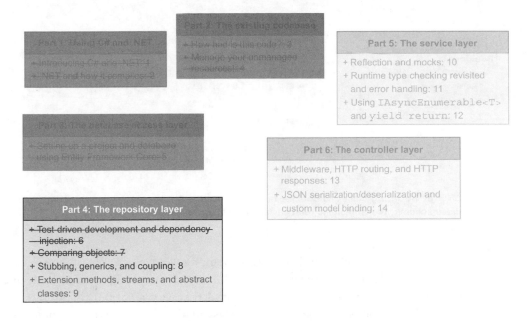

Figure 8.1 **In this chapter, we'll implement the** `BookingRepository` **class. In chapters 6 and 7, we implemented the** `CustomerRepository` **class. That just leaves the** `AirportRepository` **and** `FlightRepository` **classes for the repository section of our codebase. We'll implement those in the next chapter.**

In chapters 6 and 7, we implemented the repository class for the `Customer` entity. This time around, we'll focus on the `Booking` entity. After reading this chapter, I hope you are familiar with the following:

- The Liskov substitution principle
- Separation of concerns and coupling
- How to use generics
- How to write watertight input-validation code
- Using optional parameters

And, of course, much more.

8.1 *Implementing the Booking repository*

So far in our quest to refactor and implement a new version of the FlyingDutchman-Airlines codebase, we have set up Entity Framework Core and implemented a database access layer (chapter 5) as well as a `Customer` repository class (chapters 6 and 7). In this section, we'll start writing the `BookingRepository` class, shown in figure 8.2. Revisiting the `Booking` model, we see we have three fields: `BookingID` (the primary key), `FlightNumber`, and `CustomerID` (the foreign key to `Customer.CustomerID`). The integer is nullable because there may not be a foreign key. Of course, a booking without a customer is an oddity, so this should not happen.

```
public class Booking {
    public int BookingId { get; set; }

    public int FlightNumber { get; set; }

    public int? CustomerId { get; set; }


    public virtual Customer Customer { get; set; }

    public virtual Flight FlightNumberNavigation { get; set; }
}
```

Figure 8.2 The `Booking` **class and Booking table. Because the** `Booking` **class is reverse-engineered from the database schema, the isomorphic relationship between code and database is strong.**

We only have one endpoint dealing with Booking, POST /Booking, which creates a new booking in the database. Because we are doing only one thing, we need only one public method in our new BookingRepository: CreateBooking. But first things first—we should create the BookingRepository class in the RepositoryLayer folder and the respective test class in the FlyingDutchmanAirlines_Tests project (along with the skeleton for the success test case), as shown in the next code sample. At the risk of repeating myself, the plan is to create one repository per database entity (Customer, Booking, Airport, and Flight). A repository class contains small methods that interact with the database through the database access layer. A service layer class calls those repositories, gathering information to present back to a controller class. We discussed the repository/service pattern in section 5.2.4.

```
namespace FlyingDutchmanAirlines.RepositoryLayer {
  public class BookingRepository {
    private readonly FlyingDutchmanAirlinesContext _context;

    public BookingRepository(FlyingDutchmanAirlinesContext _context) {
      this._context = _context;
    }
  }
}
```

As in the previous chapters, we'll use test-driven development to ensure our code functions the way we want it to and to prevent future regressions when extending the code. In section 6.1, I introduced test-driven development (light) as a technique to increase the likelihood of our code being correct and testable. In test-driven development, we create unit tests before we write logic implementations. Because we build up both the tests and the actual logic at the same time, we keep verifying the code against our expectations during development, saving us the hassle of having to fix bugs that come up if we were to write unit tests after implementing all the code, as shown in the next listing.

> **Listing 8.1 A skeleton `BookingRepositoryTests` class**

```
namespace FlyingDutchmanAirlines_Tests.RepositoryLayer {
  [TestClass]
  public class BookingRepositoryTests {
    private FlyingDutchmanAirlinesContext _context;
    private BookingRepository _repository;

    [TestInitialize]
    public void TestInitialize() {
      DbContextOptions<FlyingDutchmanAirlinesContext>
      dbContextOptions =
      new DbContextOptionsBuilder<FlyingDutchmanAirlinesContext>()
      .UseInMemoryDatabase("FlyingDutchman").Options;
      _context = new FlyingDutchmanAirlinesContext(dbContextOptions);

      _repository = new BookingRepository(_context);
      Assert.IsNotNull(_repository);
    }

    [TestMethod]
    public void CreateBooking_Success() { }
  }
}
```

The TestInitialize method runs before every test.

Creates an in-memory SQL database

Creates an instance of BookingRepository, using DI to pass in the database context

Asserts that the BookingRepository instance was created successfully

Before we move on, let's revisit how the old code implemented the `Booking`-related code and the improvements we identified. The old code crammed all the code related to every entity into one class: `FlightController`. When you have implementation details inside of a controller, especially those that deal with a different entity than the controller does, you tightly couple the implementation details of the database to the controller. Ideally, we would have some abstraction layers (such as services, repositories, and database access layers) between the controller and the database. Let's imagine that, after developing the codebase, you want to change the database vendor from Microsoft Azure to Amazon AWS. If you tightly couple your controllers to the database, you have to change every controller you have when you switch vendors. If you abstracted the database logic by introducing a repository/service pattern with a database access layer, loosening the coupling between database and controller, you would have to make changes only in the database access layer. For us, within the context of a `BookingRepository`, we want to extract out the code that actually inserts a new `Booking` object into the database as follows:

```
cmd = new SqlCommand("INSERT INTO Booking (FlightNumber,
  CustomerID) VALUES (" + flight.FlightNumber + ", '" +
  customer.CustomerID + "') ", connection);
cmd.ExecuteNonQuery();
cmd.Dispose();
```

The rest of the original code also manually grabs some of the data tied to foreign key constraints. We'll look at how to deal with foreign keys in a service layer class in section 11.3.

8.2   *Input validation, separation of concerns, and coupling*

In this section, we'll mimic the approach we took when adding a customer to the database in chapter 6 and apply it to bookings as follows:

- Validate the inputs.
- Create a new instance of type `Booking`.
- Add the new instance to Entity Framework Core's `DbSet<Booking>` by calling it through the database context.

The `CreateBooking` method has two inputs: a `customerID` and a `flightNumber`. They are both of type `integer` and have the following identical validation rules:

- `customerID` and `flightNumber` must be positive integers.
- `customerID` and `flightNumber` necd to be valid when matched against existing flights and customers.

The proposed validation rules mean we need to check the `DbSet` collections for `Customer` and `Flight` to verify that they contain entries matching the input information. The issue is, however, that we do not want to deal with `DbSets` of entities other than `Booking` in the `BookingRepository` due to separation of concerns. Additionally, we do not want to deal with the foreign key constraints on the repository level but rather on the service level. For a repository/service architecture, a good rule of thumb is this: keep your repositories dumb and your services smart. This means that your repository methods should be methods with a stringent adherence to the single-responsibility principle (discussed in the introduction of chapter 6), whereas this adherence is a bit laxer on the service side.

Services can call whatever repository methods they need to fulfill their tasks. A repository method should not have to call a different repository to do their job. If you find yourself cross-calling between repositories, take a step back and reread section 5.2.4 on the repository/service pattern again. In the `BookingService` in chapters 10 and 11, we'll look at how to write a service that manages these concerns, but for now, it suffices to understand why we do not want to call `DbSet<Customer>` and `DbSet<Flight>` in `BookingRepository`. In the end, it all boils down to separation of concerns and coupling.

Separation of concerns and coupling

"Separation of concerns" is a term coined by Edsger Dijkstra in his paper "On the Role of Scientific Thought" (EWD 447, Springer-Verlag, 1982). At its most basic level, it means that a "concern" should do only one concrete thing. But what is a "concern"? A concern is a mental model of a programming module, which can take the form of things like methods or a class. When we take separation of concerns to the class level and apply it to `BookingRepository`, we might say that the `BookingRepository` should concern itself only with operations on the Booking database table. This means that retrieving information from the Customer table, for example, is not within the scope of the concern. If we apply it to a method, we could say that a method needs to do one singular thing and nothing else. This is a very important clean code tenet because it helps us to develop code that is readable and maintainable.

We discussed the concept of writing code that reads like a narrative using small methods before. This is that same concept. In his monumental work *Clean Code: A Handbook of Agile Software Craftsmanship* (Prentice-Hall, 2008), Robert C. Martin touches on this subject many times. One particular occasion is the section appropriately titled "Do One Thing." He tells us that "Functions should do one thing. They should do it well. They should do it only." If we hold this message in the back of our heads when we write code, we are one step ahead of the curve when it comes to writing amazing code. We discussed the single-responsibility principle, which concerns itself with writing clean methods that do only one thing, in chapter 6.

What is coupling, and how does it relate to the idea of separation of concerns? Coupling is a different angle with which to approach the problem of separation of concerns. Coupling is a metric that quantifies how integrated one class is with another. If classes are highly coupled, it means that they depend highly on each other. We call this tight coupling. We do not want tight coupling. Tight coupling often results in methods calling a lot of other methods at the wrong architectural level: think about the `BookingRepository` calling the `FlightRepository` to retrieve information about a flight.

Loose coupling is when two methods (or systems) are not very dependent on each other and can execute independently (and, therefore, be changed with minimal side effects). Larry Constantine coined the term *coupling*, which first appeared in the book *Structured Design: Fundamentals of a Discipline of Computer Program and Systems Design* (Prentice-Hall, 1979) by Constantine and Edward Yourdon. When trying to determine the amount of coupling between two things, one can ask the question that Constantine and Yourdon pose in their book: "How much of one module must be known to understand another module?"

How much of `CustomerRepository` and `FlightRepository` must be known to understand `BookingRepository`? How strong is the interconnection between the repositories? If we handle the coupling at the service level, the repositories should have very loose coupling and a high degree of separation of concerns.

Going back to input validation: although we do not have to check whether the foreign key constraints between the customer and flight database tables are valid, we do implicitly check them when we save the changes to the database. The database balks if a change is requested that violates a key constraint.

Remember when we discussed having methods that can take any input, even faulty ones, and still return an appropriate result? If we get a bad `customerID` or `flightNumber` input, the call to update the database will throw an exception and we'll catch it. By catching the exception, we can control the data and execution flow and throw a custom exception of our own to tell the user something went wrong, as shown in the next listing. Validating our inputs becomes easy: check whether the input is a positive integer, and we are set.

Listing 8.2   BookingRepository.CreateBooking method with basic input-validation logic

```
namespace FlyingDutchmanAirlines.RepositoryLayer {          CreateBooking requires a
  public class BookingRepository {                          customerID and flightNumber.
    public async Task CreateBooking(int customerID, int flightNumber) {
      if (customerID < 0 || flightNumber < 0) {
        throw new ArgumentException("Invalid arguments provided");
      }
    }                                         If the input arguments are invalid,
  }                                              throws an ArgumentException
}
                                        Validates the input arguments: customerID and
                                        flightNumber need to be positive integers.
```

C# provides an exception that we can use when arguments are invalid in a method: `ArgumentException`. We want to throw an exception of type `ArgumentException` when `customerID` or `flightNumber` is not a positive integer. To throw an `ArgumentException`, we pass in an error message (of type `string`) to the `ArgumentException` and use the `throw new` pattern to instantiate and throw a new instance of `ArgumentException`.

Within C#, certain types have classes that wrap the type and extend on them by providing additional functionality. An example of this is the `String` class and the `string` type. Note the casing on both the class and the type. It is C# convention that a class starts with an uppercase character, whereas a type often starts with a lowercase one. For most types and their wrapping classes, you can often use them interchangeably (until you need to use a method exposed by the class—for `String`, this could be `IsNullOrEmpty`). Do note that `String` and `string` typically resolve to the same underlying Intermediate Language code.

After the input-validation code throws the `ArgumentException`, a developer may see the message we passed in and wonder what went wrong. Developers would love to see what the actual arguments are, but we don't want to return the input arguments in an error message and expose those outside of the method (or potentially to the end user). Can you imagine using an application and getting back an error message containing the actual input argument values? Surely any UI engineer or UX designer would take issue with that. Of course, there are always exceptions to this (perhaps you also control the only client this service ever uses). We would do well to at least log these arguments to the console so that a developer stands a better chance at recovering these values. Some companies use technologies such as Splunk to automatically capture logs written to the console and store them in a searchable database. To write to the console, we use the `Console.WriteLine` method, as shown in the next listing. If you don't want to write to the console, ASP.NET has dedicated logging functionality you can use (see the MSDN ASP.NET documentation for more information). You could also use a third-party logging library such as Log4net or NLog. I prefer to use the simplest type of logging that gets the job done. In this case, logging to the console is good enough.

Listing 8.3 `BookingRepository.CreateBooking` **method with string interpolation**

```
public async Task CreateBooking(int customerID, int flightNumber) {
  if (customerID < 0 || flightNumber < 0) {
    Console.WriteLine($"Argument Exception in CreateBooking! CustomerID
➥ = {customerID}, flightNumber = {flightNumber}");
    throw new ArgumentException("Invalid arguments provided");
  }
}
```

Logs the invalid argument values to the
console by using string interpolation

The string we write to the console is an interpolated string. With string interpolation, we can interpolate (or inline) expressions and values in a string without having to explicitly concatenate multiple strings together (string concatenation still happens under the hood). We create interpolated strings by prefixing the string itself with the dollar character: $. Then, we insert values and expressions (even method calls) directly into the string by wrapping them in curly braces. The string {customerID} interpolates the value of customerID, as shown in figure 8.3.

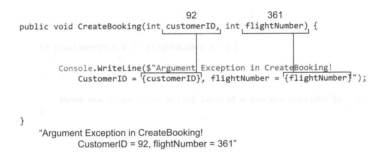

Figure 8.3 String interpolation allows us to inline variable values into strings. When using string interpolation, prefix the string with a dollar character ($) and wrap the variables you want to use in curly braces ({ [variable] }).

The compiler converts an interpolated string to a C# statement that concatenates a bunch of strings. The syntactical sugar provided by string interpolation is an excellent and idiomatic way of crafting readable strings. Because strings are immutable, using string interpolation does not remove the performance drawbacks of using string concatenation. String interpolation can actually perform worse than normal string concatenation because of the additional overhead involved, with strings being immutable. We also need to unit-test our input-validation logic. The unit test should make assertions based on invalid input arguments and verify that the input-validation logic throws an error of type ArgumentException when the input arguments are invalid (negative integers), as shown in the next listing.

Listing 8.4   Using the `DataRow` method attribute

```
[TestMethod]
[DataRow(-1, 0)]
[DataRow(0, -1)]
[DataRow(-1, -1)]
[ExpectedException(typeof(ArgumentException))]
public async Task CreateBooking_Failure_InvalidInputs(int customerID,
    int flightNumber) {
  await _repository.CreateBooking(customerID, flightNumber);
}
```

> The [DataRow] method attribute runs tests with the specified test data.

> This test expects an exception of type ArgumentException to be thrown.

> Calls the CreateBooking method and awaits it

The `CreateBooking_Failure_InvalidInputs` unit test combines a couple of different techniques we used before, described next:

- Using the `[DataRow]` method attribute, we provide the unit test with test data without having to write separate unit tests for all three test cases.
- Using the `[ExpectedException]` method attribute, we tell the MSTest runner that the method should throw an exception of type `ArgumentException` during test execution.
- Assigning the `_repository` field to a new instance of `BookingRepository` in the `TestInitialize` method.

When the `CreateBooking_Failure_InvalidInputs` unit test runs, and we use the `[DataRow]` method attribute, we check for three separate test cases, as shown in table 8.1.

Table 8.1   Three different test cases run in BookingRepositoryTests.cs `CreateBooking_Failure_InvalidInputs`

customerID	flightNumber
−1	0
0	−1
−1	−1

All test cases in table 8.1 are sets of input arguments to `CreateBooking` that fail the input-validation logic, causing the `CreateBooking` method to throw an `Argument-Exception`.

Exercises

EXERCISE 8.1

Fill in the blank: Within the context of separation of concerns, a concern refers to _____.

- a a worrisome thought
- b a business
- c a logical module

EXERCISE 8.2

True or false? If two classes heavily depend on each other, we speak of loose coupling.

EXERCISE 8.3

Fill in the blanks: In a repository/service architecture, actual database queries should be made on the _____ level, whereas calls to the methods doing the database queries should be made on the _____ level.

- a repository; service
- b service; repository
- c service; service
- d repository; repository

EXERCISE 8.4

What would this print to the console if `fruit` is "kiwi"? `Console.WriteLine($"I enjoy eating {fruit}");`

- a Nothing; it results in a compiler error.
- b "I enjoy eating {fruit}"
- c "I enjoy eating kiwi"
- d "$I enjoy eating kiwi"

EXERCISE 8.5

True or false? A string is mutable. This means it is a reference type where every change made to a string overwrites the same location in memory.

8.3 *Using object initializers*

In the previous section, we validated the input arguments to `CreateBooking` and learned about separation of concerns, coupling, and string interpolation. In this section, we'll take the method a step further by adding the logic to add a new booking to the database. To add a booking to the database, we need to perform the following four major steps:

1. Create a new instance of type `Booking` in the `CreateBooking` method.
2. Populate the new instance of `Booking` with the `customerID` and `flightNumber` arguments.
3. Add the new instance of `Booking` to Entity Framework Core's internal `DbSet <Booking>`.
4. Save the changes to the database asynchronously.

To start, we can easily take care of the first two steps: create a new instance of type `Booking` in the `CreateBooking` method, and populate it with the `customerID` and `flightNumber` arguments, as shown in the following listing.

**Listing 8.5   `BookingRepository.CreateBooking`: create and populate a `Booking`
instance**

**Validates
the input
arguments**

```
public async Task CreateBooking(int customerID, int flightNumber) {
    if (customerID < 0 || flightNumber < 0) {
        Console.WriteLine($"Argument Exception in CreateBooking! CustomerID
        = {customerID}, flightNumber = {flightNumber}");
        throw new ArgumentException("Invalid arguments provided");
    }

    Booking newBooking = new Booking();
    newBooking.CustomerId = customerID;
    newBooking.FlightNumber = flightNumber;
}
```

**Creates a new instance
of type Booking**

**Assigns the customerID input
argument to the appropriate
property in newBooking**

**Assigns the flightNumber input argument to
the appropriate property in newBooking**

There we go, just as ordered: one instance of type `Booking`. We also populated the
`CustomerId` and `FlightNumber` properties with our validated input arguments. Something irks me about the code in listing 8.5, though: it's possible for the population of
fields on a new instance to become very cumbersome if we have to keep typing
`[instance].[property] = [value]`. Remember our discussion of object initializers in
section 6.2.5? This minor change in syntax (another case of syntactic sugar), shown
here, can make a sizeable difference when initializing an object with large amounts of
properties you need to set:

```
Booking newBooking = new Booking {
    CustomerId = customerID,
    FlightNumber = flightNumber
};
```

It really is a "squashing" of the regular object property assignment code into one
block, as shown in figure 8.4. Object initializers also work when dealing with collections such as lists (they are called *collection initializers* when using them on collections;
of course, you could nest an object initializer inside a collection initializer).

All that is left for us to do is attempt to add `newBooking` to the database and save
the changes to the database asynchronously. We need to make sure that we have no issues
in adding the `Booking` instance to the database, so we wrap the logic to save the changes
in a `try-catch` statement, throwing a custom exception (`CouldNotAddBookingTo-
DatabaseException`, which inherits from `CouldNotAddEntityToDatabaseException`,
which inherits from `Exception`) when a database error occurs. When this exception is
thrown (as with any exception in the repository layer), we catch the exception again
back in the service layer. I leave it to you to create the custom exceptions.

To save the new booking to the database using `SaveChangesAsync`, we need to
`await` the `SaveChangesAsync` call. Awaiting the `CreateBooking` method means it has
to execute asynchronously. To accomplish this, we change the type of the method to
be `Task` and add the `async` keyword to the method signature, as shown in the following listing.

Old school

```
List<Animal> animals = new List<Animal>();
animals.Add(new MajesticGiraffe());
animals.Add(new AngryPenguin());
animals.Add(new DangerousCorgi());

ZooKeeper john = new ZooKeeper();
john.Subordinates = animals;
john.isQualified = false;
```

Object initializer

```
ZooKeeper john = new ZooKeeper {
    Subordinates = new List<Animal> {

            new MajesticGiraffe(),
            new AngryPenguin(),
            new DangerousCorgi()
        },
    isQualified = false
};
```

Figure 8.4 Contrasting approaches to object initialization: with and without using an object initializer. John is an unqualified zookeeper who looks after a majestic giraffe, an angry penguin, and a dangerous corgi.

Listing 8.6 BookingRepository.cs CreateBooking complete

```
public async Task CreateBooking(int customerID, int flightNumber) {
  if (customerID < 0 || flightNumber < 0) {
    Console.WriteLine($"Argument Exception in CreateBooking! CustomerID
= {customerID}, flightNumber = {flightNumber}");
    throw new ArgumentException("invalid arguments provided");
  }

  Booking newBooking = new Booking {
    CustomerId = customerID,
    FlightNumber = flightNumber
  };

  try {
    _context.Booking.Add(newBooking);
    await _context.SaveChangesAsync();
  } catch (Exception exception) {
    Console.WriteLine($"Exception during database query:
{exception.Message}");
    throw new CouldNotAddBookingToDatabaseException();
  }
}
```

Validates the input arguments

Creates and initializes a new instance of Booking using an object initializer

Adds the new booking to EF Core's internal DbSet<Booking>

Saves changes to the database asynchronously

Catches any exception that was thrown in the try-block

Writes developer information to the console

Throws an exception of type CouldNotAddBookingToDatabaseException

Instead of using hardcoded SQL statements and messing with disposing of objects and using statements, we used Entity Framework Core and simple code to achieve the same result.

So, what is next? I'm sure you know by now: we need to fix our success case unit test. That should be easy enough, though. All we need to do is send in valid input arguments. But what if we have a database error? We can have valid values for `customerID` and `flightNumber` and still error out because of a database exception.

8.4   *Unit testing with stubs*

In this section, I introduce you to the wonderful world of stubbing. Stubbing, within the context of unit testing, is the act of executing a stub class (a class that acts as a certain class but overrides implementations) instead of the original class. We left the previous section as we were about to test for the possibility of the `CreateBooking` method throwing a `CouldNotAddBookingToDatabase` exception because of a database error. To test for a thrown `Exception`, we need to set aside the success test case for a bit longer and focus on stubbing and a new test method: `CreateBooking_Failure_Database-Error`. I prefer using snake case for test unit tests, as shown in the next code sample, but opinions differ on this:

```
[TestMethod]
public async Task CreateBooking_Failure_DatabaseError() { }
```

A stub is a piece of code (potentially a whole class) that takes the place of a normal class at runtime. A stub redirects to itself method calls made to the original class and executes overridden versions of those methods. Method redirection and overriding are especially useful in unit testing because they allow us to mimic error conditions by redirecting method calls and throwing exceptions when we want them thrown.

Looking at the `CreateBooking` method, we want to verify that we can handle an error coming out of the database or the internals of Entity Framework Core correctly. But how do we handle a database exception? The easiest way is to expand on our redirection of the dependency injection `FlyingDutchmanAirlinesContext`. We still want to use an in-memory database, but we also want to make sure we throw an exception when a certain method is called. What if we create a class (a stub) that inherits from `FlyingDutchmanAirlinesContext` and then inject that into `CreateBooking`, as shown in figure 8.5?

Let's create a new folder in the FlyingDutchmanAirlines_Tests project called Stubs and a new class called `FlyingDutchmanAirlinesContext_Stub`, as shown in the next listing. This class inherits from `FlyingDutchmanAirlinesContext`.

Listing 8.7   A skeleton stub for `FlyingDutchmanAirlinesContext`

```
namespace FlyingDutchmanAirlines_Tests.Stubs {          The class inherits from the
  class FlyingDutchmanAirlinesContext_Stub :            original nonstubbed class,
➥  FlyingDutchmanAirlinesContext { }      ◁             allowing us to use it in its place.
}
```

Going back to `BookingRepositoryTests`, we swap in the stub for the context and see if our tests still pass, as shown in the following code sample.

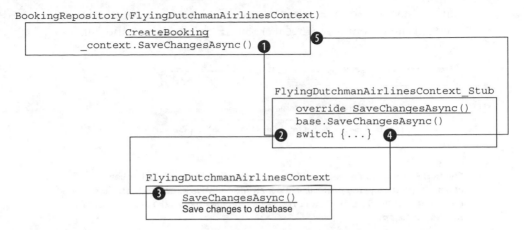

Figure 8.5 Redirecting `SaveChangesAsync` through `FlyingDutchmanAirlinesContext_Stub`. The repository calls the `SaveChangesAsync` method on the dependency injection `FlyingDutchman-AirlinesContext_Stub`. The stub calls the base class and determines what value to return in a `switch` statement.

Listing 8.8 `BookingRepositoryTests` initializing a stub instead of the original class

```
namespace FlyingDutchmanAirlines_Tests.RepositoryLayer {
  [TestClass]
  class BookingRepositoryTests {
    private FlyingDutchmanAirlinesContext _context;      ◁──  The backing
    private BookingRepository _repository;                     field's type is the
                                                              nonstubbed class.

    [TestInitialize]
    public void TestInitialize() {
      DbContextOptions<FlyingDutchmanAirlinesContext>
⇒     dbContextOptions = new
⇒     DbContextOptionsBuilder<FlyingDutchmanAirlinesContext>.UseInMemoryDatab
⇒     ase("FlyingDutchman").Options;                      ◁──  The DbContextBuilder
      _context = new                                            pattern uses the
⇒     FlyingDutchmanAirlinesContext_Stub(dbContextOptions);  ◁─  nonstubbed class
                                                              for a generic type.
      _repository = new BookingRepository(_context);      ◁──
      Assert.IsNotNull(_repository);                            We can assign the backing
    }                                                          field a new instance of the
  }                         The repository accepts               stub because of
}                            our stub in place of                polymorphism.
                            the nonstubbed class.
```

The code in listing 8.8 does not compile. Because we did not define an explicit constructor for the stub, the CLR creates an implicit default constructor when we create a new instance of `FlyingDutchmanAirlines_Stub`. But `FlyingDutchmanAirlinesContext` (the base/nonstubbed class) has a second constructor that takes in the `DbContext-Options<FlyingDutchmanAirlinesContext>` type that we need if we want to use an in-memory database. Because the stub inherits from the nonstub, we should be able to call `FlyingDutchmanAirlinesContext_Stub`'s parent's constructor, as depicted in figure 8.6. The parent is `FlyingDutchmanAirlinesContext`, after all.

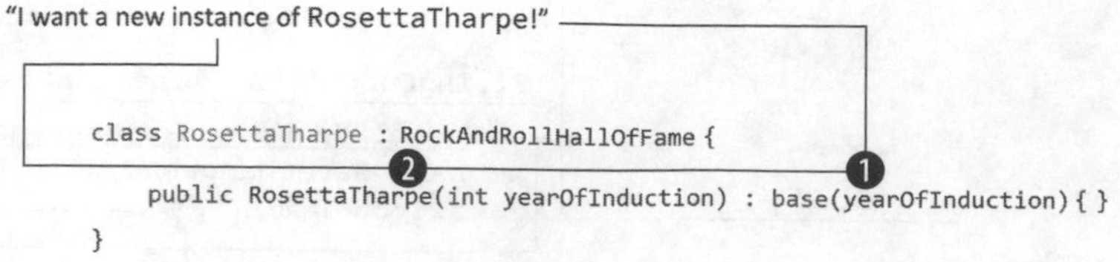

Figure 8.6   When a derived class's constructor includes a call to the base class's constructor, the base class's constructor always executes first. Here, the constructor of `RockAndRollHallOfFame` executes before the constructor of `RosettaTharpe`.

To make the code compile and be able to use the stub in place of the nonstubbed class, we need to create a constructor that can deliver an instance of the stub with all the hooks to the base class (the nonstub) intact. We have overridden no methods in the stub yet, so every call to the stub should automatically go to the nonstub. To redirect the method call to our stubbed logic, we need a constructor that calls the base class's constructor. Adding a constructor that calls the base class's constructor guarantees us an instance of the base class that we can use in our redirection story.

To call a base class's constructor, add `: base([arguments])` to a regular constructor, replacing `[arguments]` with whatever arguments you want to pass into the base's constructor, as shown in the next code snippet. This is similar to using the `super` keyword in Java or Python. Note that the CLR always calls a base's constructor before our own (a derived) constructor. So, if you want to do processing in your own constructor that has a base constructor call, be aware of that.

```
namespace FlyingDutchmanAirlines_Tests.Stubs {
  class FlyingDutchmanAirlinesContext_Stub :
    FlyingDutchmanAirlinesContext {
    public FlyingDutchmanAirlinesContext_Stub
    (DbContextOptions<FlyingDutchmanAirlinesContext> options)
    : base(options) { }
  }
}
```

Explicitly defining this constructor forces the code to always pass in a type of `DbContextOptions<FlyingDutchmanAirlinesContext>` to instantiate a new `FlyingDutchmanAirlines_Stub`. Now we can compile the code and run all the tests. Everything passes because, besides a redirect to the stub, nothing has changed. All method calls to the stub currently still go to the nonstubbed version of `FlyingDutchmanAirlinesContext` because of inheritance and the lack of overridden methods in the stub. We can use `FlyingDutchmanAirlinesContext_Stub` as if it were an instance of `FlyingDutchmanAirlinesContext`.

The Liskov substitution principle (polymorphism)

This type of polymorphism is most often attributed to Barbara Liskov, a computer scientist (and winner of both the John von Neumann Medal and the Turing Award) who, together with Jeannette Wing, published a paper that describes the Liskov substitution principle:

> "Let ø(x) be a property provable about objects x of type T. Then ø(y) should be true for objects y of type S where s is a subtype of T."[a]

You may have to read that twice to get the gist of it. What Liskov and Wing tell us is that when using the Liskov substitution principle flavor of polymorphism, if you have a type (Kit-Kat) that is a subtype of a different type (Candy), the type S (Kit-Kat) should be able to do everything that T (Candy) can do. One can apply the duck-typing test to such an object—"If it looks like a duck, swims like a duck, and quacks like a duck, then it's probably a duck"—to determine whether we can use type S as if it were type T. The Liskov substitution principle is often considered one of the major tenets of clean code and helps us write code that is reusable with an appropriate level of abstraction.

[a] Barbara H. Liskov and Jeannette M. Wing's *A Behavioral Notion of Subtyping* (ACM Transactions on Programming Languages and Systems (TOPLAS), 1994).

Before we implement any logic, according to the TDD gods, we need to add an assertion to our unit test and make it fail. (If we remember the stoplight phases of TDD, we are now in the green phase, going to red.) The code path we want to test (but have not yet implemented) results in a thrown exception of type CouldNotAddBookingToDatabaseException. In the try-catch block surrounding the code where we add the new booking to the database, we call and wait on the SaveChangesAsync method. What if we could make that method throw an exception based on a certain condition, such as if we set the customerID on the new Booking object to something else besides 1? We can achieve that goal by overriding the SaveChangesAsync method in our stub. The method signature for the overridden version of SaveChangesAsync in our stub is a bit gnarly (when overriding a method, one has to keep the same method signature), but we can get through it step by step, as shown here:

```
public async override Task<int> SaveChangesAsync(CancellationToken
    cancellationToken = default) {
  return await base.SaveChangesAsync(cancellationToken);
}
```

Besides override (which you should be familiar with), we see the following two unfamiliar concepts wrapped in overridden method:

- Generics (which we have seen in action before)
- Optional parameters

Settle in, because those are two exciting topics.

8.5   *Programming with generics*

In this section, I lift the veil on a topic we have seen quite a few times already in the book but have never explored beyond its funky syntax: generics. We have worked with generics right from the start. Anytime you see this pattern, you are working with generics: [type] < [differentType] >. Examples of generics syntax in action are List<string>, DbSet<Customer>, and EntityEntry<TEntity>. If you are familiar with Java generics or C++ templates, this section should feel familiar to you.

Generics is a concept that allows us to restrict classes, methods, and collections in terms of what types they can deal with. For example, a collection often has a generic version and a nongeneric version: A List is nongeneric, whereas a List of Tigers (List<Tiger>) is generic. The List<Tiger> collection works with any class that can be cast to Tiger (the Tiger class itself or a derived class). A HashSet is nongeneric, whereas a HashSet of Baklava (HashSet<Baklava>) is generic. An example of a method using a generic argument in the "wild" is the Heapsort method, used by the Sort method in Systems.Collections.Generic.ArraySortHelper class to perform the heap sort algorithm[1] on the input, as shown here:

```
private static void Heapsort(T[] keys, int lo, int hi,
    IComparer<T> comparer) {
  int n = hi - lo + 1;
  for (int i = n / 2; i >= 1; i = i - 1) {
    DownHeap(keys, i, n, lo, comparer);
  }

  for (int i = n; i > 1; i = i - 1) {
    Swap(keys, lo, lo + i - 1);
    DownHeap(keys, 1, i - 1, lo, comparer);
  }
}
```

The Heapsort method accepts a generic argument of T[], representing an array of keys to be sorted, and a generic argument of IComparer<T>, representing a comparison object.

Even though you typically encounter generics in collections, methods and classes are not immune to using them, either. So, what does a generic type look like? We know how to *use* them, but not yet how to *make* them. A generic class or method uses the "generic type" of <T>. Any letter is fine, however, as long as you are consistent within the scope of the class or method signature. You may want to restrict the types that can use your method or class. Constricting the use of generics to a specific type or subset of types is done by using generic constraints.

---

[1] For details on the heapsort algorithm, see A. K. Dewdney's *New Turing Omnibus*, chapter 40, "Heaps and Merges" (W.H. Freeman and Company, 1993) or Robert Sedgewick and Kevin Wayne's *Algorithms*, chapter 2.7, "Heapsort" (4th edition; Pearson Education, Inc., 2011).

To create a generic constraint, postfix a clause to the respective method or class signature saying "`where T : [type]`." For example, if we wanted to create a generic class that would accept only instances of type `Attribute` for `T`, we would do the following:

```
public class MyGenericClass where T : Attribute
```

Or, when we want to create a generic method that accepts only `List`s of 16-bit integers (signified as `Int16` or `short`) we can say

```
public void MyGenericMethod<T>(T shorts) where T : List<short>
```

Methods can also have input parameters of a generic type (be it `T`, `X`, `Y`, or whatever letter you fancy). Finally, we can have multiple generic types in one class or method and multiple generic constraints, as shown next:

```
public void MyGenericMethod<T, Y>(T key, Y encryption) where T :
    List<Int16> where Y : RSA
```

Here, `MyGenericMethod` has two generic types: `T`, which maps to `List<Int16>`, and `Y`, which is constrained to be of type `RSA`. The `RSA` type is the base class for all Rivest–Shamir–Adleman (RSA) encryption functionality in .NET. `Y` being constrained to `RSA` does not mean that classes using polymorphism to act as an `RSA` type are forbidden; you can use those without a problem. Constraints are rarely used, but it is good to be aware of them. In fact, to find a reasonably good example of constraints used in .NET itself, we have to dig quite deep. We can find it, however, in the `WindowsIdentity` class through the `GetTokenInformation` method, shown here:

```
private T GetTokenInformation<T>(TokenInformationClass
    tokenInformationClass) where T : struct {
  using (SafeLocalAllocHandle information =
    GetTokenInformation(m_safeTokenHandle, tokenInformationClass)) {
    return information.Read<T>(0);
  }
}
```

The `GetTokenInformation` method returns the requested field (determined by the passed-in `TokenInformationClass` instance) from the currently held Windows token. The type of the requested field can be anything, as long as it is a struct. This is signified by the constraint on the generic `T`.

8.6   *Providing default arguments by using optional parameters*

In the previous section, we started our dissection of the new concepts in the `Save-ChangesAsync` method signature by looking at generics. In this section, we'll finish that expedition and consider optional parameters.

Optional parameters are parameters in a method signature that have a default value assigned to them (inside the signature). The CLR uses the default assigned value as the argument value if you do not pass in an appropriate argument. Consider the following method signature:

```
public void BuildHouse(int width, int height, bool isPaid = true)
```

The `isPaid` parameter is assigned a value directly in the method signature. This is what we call an *optional parameter*.

```
BuildHouse(int width, int height, bool isPaid = true)
```

Optional parameter
**Optional parameters always come
last in the list of method parameters.
They are assigned a "fallback" value.
Here,** `isPaid` **is an optional parameter
of type** `bool` **with a default value of** `true`.

The CLR assigns an optional parameter to the default value specified in the method signature if we pass in no matching argument. The parameter is truly optional but is still available to the method with the set value. We can call the `BuildHouse` method in two ways, as shown in the next listing.

Listing 8.9   Calling a method on optional parameters

```
BuildHouse(10, 20);
BuildHouse(10, 20, false);
```

**The optional parameter
isPaid has the value
of true.**

**The optional parameter isPaid
has the value of false.**

In the first example, we use the optional parameter's (`isPaid`) default assigned value of `true`. In the second one, we assign a value of `false`. In both cases, the method's logic has access to an initialized version of `isPaid`.

METHOD OVERLOADING WITH OPTIONAL PARAMETERS   If you overload a method with only the addition of an optional parameter and do provide not an argument for the optional parameter, the CLR ignores the overload with the optional parameter and calls the original method. For example, if we have two methods called `BuildHouse(int width, int height)` and `Build-House(int width, int height, bool isPaid = true)` and we do not pass in an argument for `isPaid`, the CLR calls the `BuildHouse(int width, int height)` version.

A word of caution, however: we can never follow optional parameters with non-optional parameters. The compiler requires optional parameters to be the last in the line of arguments. The compiler requiring optional parameters to come last in the parameter list means that the following change of the `BuildHouse` method signature does not compile:

```
public void BuildHouse(int width, bool isPaid = true, int height)
```

Under the hood, an optional argument functions as a regular argument but has the additional `[opt]` keyword added to the generated Intermediate Language code. Because the argument of type `CancellationToken` is optional in the `SaveChangesAsync` method, it is up to us whether we want to pass it in. Keep in mind that we need to add it to our method signature because we want to override the base's `SaveChangesAsync` method, whose signature contains the optional `CancellationToken` parameter.

The CancellationToken class

You can cancel database queries in progress by using an instance of `Cancellation-Token` and calling the `CancellationToken.Cancel()` method. Cancellation tokens are also used to notify other parts of your code of a canceled request. We don't use these in our code because our requests are simple insertions and retrievals of single records with limited foreign key constraints.

If you were to kick off a stored procedure that could take minutes to execute, you may want to cancel it under some edge condition. In that case, use a cancellation token. If we do not pass in an instance of `CancellationToken`, the CLR assigns a new instance to the argument on its own.

Our stub's overridden `SaveChangesAsync` method currently has the following one statement inside it:

```
return base.SaveChangesAsync(cancellationToken);
```

The overridden `SaveChangesAsync` method returns a call to the base (nonstub) class's version of `AddAsync`. Returning a call to the base class's method does not work for us. In effect, we overrode the `SaveChangesAsync` method only to have it act like a non-overridden version of it. We need to replace the call to the nonstub base version of the `SaveChangesAsync` method with our implementation. We'll do this in the next section.

8.7 *Conditionals, Func, switches, and switch expressions*

Let's remember why we are going through this ordeal in the first place: we want to unit-test the database exception code path and make sure the code handles the exception gracefully. In this section, we'll take a step forward and implement the logic inside the stubbed `SaveChangesAsync` method. We'll discuss conditionals, the `Func` type, switches, and `switch` expressions.

To use the stubbed `SaveChangesAsync` method, we need some way to differentiate between success and failure paths. We definitely do not want to throw an exception every single time the `CreateBooking` method calls `SaveChangesAsync`. Because the value of `customerID` is within our control, why don't we base our stub logic around that? If we throw an exception when we set the `entity.CustomerID` to any positive integer but "1" (an arbitrary number—we just need a number to control the code flow with), we can test the database exception code branch without breaking existing tests.

We can use a variety of ways to check whether `entity.CustomerID` is a positive integer of value 1. We could write a simple conditional that checks whether the `CustomerID` is 1 and return the base class's `AddAsync` result, or else throw an exception, as shown in the next listing. We do, however, need to grab the `Booking` object we just added to the internal `DbSet<Booking>` through the `CreateBooking` method from the context because the `Booking` object is not passed into the `SaveChangesAsync` method.

Listing 8.10 Implementing a stubbed version of `SaveChangesAsync`

**Overrides the nonstub's
SaveChangesAsync method**

```
public async override Task<int> SaveChangesAsync(CancellationToken
    cancellationToken = default) {
  if (base.Booking.First().CustomerId != 1) {          ◁── Checks if the entity's
    throw new Exception("Database Error!");                  CustomerID is 1 or not
  }
  return await base.SaveChangesAsync(cancellationToken);  ◁──
}
```

**Throws an exception if
the CustomerID is not 1**

**Calls the base's SaveChangesAsync
if CustomerID is 1**

Because there is only one `Booking` in the base's `Booking` DbSet (we added it in `CreateBooking` before calling `SaveChangesAsync`), we can use the `First` LINQ method to select the booking.

8.7.1 The ternary conditional operator

To condense the code further, we can also combine the conditional into a simple return statement paired with the ternary conditional operator (`?:`), as shown in the following code listing.

Listing 8.11 Using a ternary conditional operator to condense a conditional return block

```
public async override Task<int> SaveChangesAsync(CancellationToken
    cancellationToken = default) {
  return base.Booking.First().CustomerId != 1          ◁── Is the Booking's
    ? throw new Exception("Database Error")                  CustomerID set to 1?
    : await base.SaveChangesAsync(cancellationToken);  ◁──
}
```

**False condition: Calls the
nonstub's SaveChangesAsync**

**True condition:
throws an
exception**

 TERNARY CONDITIONAL OPERATOR MNEMONIC If you ever get confused as to what the order of operations in a ternary conditional operator is, a good mnemonic is "expression ? true : false."

Both using an `if` statement and the ternary conditional operator approaches would work fine, but what if we ever want to expand on our conditional branches? Sure, we could create unlimited `else` clauses to tack onto the conditional, but that would become an annoyance when the number of conditional clauses grows larger and larger.

8.7.2 Branching using an array of functions

We could also do something more technical, such as creating an array of `Func<Task<int>>` objects that use a lambda delegate and calling them using the value of `CustomerID` as the index to the list, then invoking the delegate to execute the appropriate logic, as shown in the next code sample.

Listing 8.12 Using a `Func<Task<int>>` and invoking lambda delegates by index

Creates an array of Func's of Task of Integer (Func<T<Y>>)

```
public async override Task<int> SaveChangesAsync(CancellationToken
➥ cancellationToken = default) {
  Func<Task<int>>[] functions = {
    () => throw new Exception("Database Error!"),
      async () => await base.SaveChangesAsync(cancellationToken)
  };

  return await
➥ functions[(int)base.Booking.First().CustomerId].Invoke();
}
```

> This Task throws an exception.

> This Task returns the base call's SaveChangesAsync integer result.

Invokes a Task using Booking.CustomerID as the index to functions

Using a `Func<Task<int>>[]` is surely a bit excessive and works only for specific index values. If the `functions` array has only two elements, and the `CustomerID` is 2 (remember, in C# collections are zero-based), we would receive an out-of-range exception because the requested element's index is higher than the last element in the collection.

8.7.3 Switch statements and expressions

Instead of using a simple conditional, a conditional with a ternary conditional operator, or invoking a `Task` based on an index, I advocate for the use of the trusted old `switch` statement, shown next.

Listing 8.13 Using a regular `switch` statement to branch code

Switches logic branches based on the CustomerId value

```
public async override Task<int> SaveChangesAsync(CancellationToken
➥ cancellationToken = default) {
  switch(base.Booking.First().CustomerId) {
    case 1:
      return await base.SaveChangesAsync(cancellationToken);

    default:
      throw new Exception("Database Error!");
  }
}
```

> If CustomerId is 1, calls the nonstub SaveChangesAsync

> If no other cases match, executes the default: throws an exception

In the `switch` statement of listing 8.13, we execute the regular, nonoverridden `SaveChangesAsync` path for `CustomerIds` of 1. In a `switch` statement, if no cases match, it looks for a `default` case and executes that. If you do not provide a `default` case, and there are no case matches, the `switch` statement won't execute any case. Here, the default case is when `CustomerId` is anything but 1. Our `default` case throws an exception.

C# 8 introduced a new feature for `switch` statements called `switch` *expressions*. It allows us to write slightly more concise `switch` statements by using syntax similar to lambda expressions, as shown in the following listing.

Listing 8.14   Using `switch` expressions to branch code

```
public async override Task<int> SaveChangesAsync(CancellationToken
➥ cancellationToken = default) {
  return base.Booking.First().CustomerId switch {        ⊲─── Returns the result
    1 => await base.SaveChangesAsync(cancellationToken),  ⊲───  of the switch
    _ => throw new Exception("Database Error!"),    ⊲───      statement
  };
}                                          Calls the nonstub
                            The default case:   SaveChangesAsync
                            throws an exception  if CustomerID is 1
```

Using a `switch` expression can condense your long `switch` statements quite a bit. We should also see whether the code throws a `CouldNotAddBookingToDatabaseException`. To do this, the appropriate unit test must use the following `[ExpectedException]` method attribute:

```
[TestMethod]
[ExpectedException(typeof(CouldNotAddBookingToDatabaseException))]
public async Task CreateBooking_Failure_DatabaseError() {
  await _repository.CreateBooking(0, 1);
}
```

Let's run the test. Lo and behold, it passes! We are now ready to come back to, and wrap up, our final test for `BookingRepository`: `BookingRepository_Success`.

As things stand now, we have only a skeleton of a method, but all we have to do is pass in valid arguments to `CreateBooking`, as shown in the next listing. There is no output from the `CreateBooking` method, so any assertions we make need to be done on Entity Framework Core's internal `DbSet<Booking>`. We want to assert that a `Booking` was indeed created in the in-memory database and that it has a `CustomerID` of 1.

Listing 8.15   Completed `BookingRepository.CreateBooking_Success` unit test

```
[TestMethod]
public async Task CreateBooking_Success() {               Creates the booking in
  await _repository.CreateBooking(1, 0);                   the in-memory database
    Booking booking = _context.Booking.First();   ⊲─── Retrieves the booking from
                                                         the in-memory database
```

Verifies
that the
booking is
not null

```
Assert.IsNotNull(booking);
Assert.AreEqual(1, booking.CustomerId);
Assert.AreEqual(0, booking.FlightNumber);
}
```

Verifies that the
booking has the
correct CustomerID

Verifies that the booking has
the correct FlightNumber

Let's run the test and see what happens. Hang on! The `CreateBooking_Success` test fails. But why? It says the method threw an exception of type `CouldNotAddBooking-ToDatabaseException`. We fell into one of the most common pitfalls that Entity Framework Core offers: we did not save our changes to the `DbSet<Booking>` (and to the database) before accessing it.

8.7.4 Querying for pending changes in Entity Framework Core

If we look back at the `SaveChangesAsync` method in the stub, we see that we access `context.Booking` before calling `base.SaveChangesAsync`. Accessing the `Booking` `DbSet` before saving any changes we made to the internal `DbSets` to the database means that there is nothing in the booking collection yet, causing a `NullReferenceException`, which we catch in the `CreateBooking` method. The `CreateBooking` method then throws a `CouldNotAddBookingToDatabaseException`.

The solution is simple: call `base.SaveChangesAsync` before accessing `context.Booking`. Because we are using an in-memory database, we can commit a `Booking` object to the database during the failure path unit test because the `TestInitialize` method creates a new instance of the database context (and implicitly wipes the database) before the next test. The important part of the test is that the exception gets thrown. That means we do not need the `default` case in our `switch` statement anymore. That being said, let's change the executed logic on the non-`default` statement to return an integer of value 1. The `SaveChangesAsync` method returns (in a non-stubbed scenario) the number of entries written to the database. I see no reason to deviate from that pattern in the stub. We are mimicking its operations, after all.

The only purpose of the nondefault `switch` value (in this scenario) is to satisfy the required return type of `Task<int>`. By returning a value of `0`, we complete the method and do no harm. We still throw an exception in case `CustomerID` is anything but `1`, as shown in the next listing.

Listing 8.16 Stubbed `SaveChangesAsync` method with base `SaveChangesAsync` call

```
public override async Task<int> SaveChangesAsync(CancellationToken
➥ cancellationToken = default) {
    await base.SaveChangesAsync(cancellationToken);

    return base.Booking.First().CustomerId switch {
        1 => 1,
        _ => throw new Exception("Database Error!")
    };
}
```

Calls the nonstub
`SaveChangesAsync`

Switches
based on the
CustomerId

If the CustomerID is not 1,
throws an exception

If the CustomerID
is 1, returns a 0

If we run the test now, we see it passes. However, we have an additional problem to consider here. Currently, we're throwing an exception if the `CustomerId` is anything but 1, but our changes have already been saved to the database. We really should test the `CustomerID` before saving to the database. To do this, we need to be able to access the pending changes to the database. Entity Framework Core lets us do this by querying its internal `StateTracker` for entities with an `EntityState` of `Added` as follows:

```
IEnumerable<EntityEntry> pendingChanges =
    ChangeTracker.Entries().Where(e => e.State == EntityState.Added);
```

The resulting `IEnumerable` collection contains only our pending changes. What we really want, though, is the `Entity` objects on the pending changes. We can use a LINQ `Select` statement to grab only the `Entity` objects, as shown here:

```
IEnumerable<object> entities = pendingChanges.Select(e => e.Entity);
```

From here, we can cast the `EntityEntry` to our `Booking` type and grab the `CustomerId`. To cast (and select only) the entities mapped to a `Booking`, we can use the `OfType<T>` method on the `IEnumerable` as follows:

```
IEnumerable<Booking> bookings =
    pendingChanges.Select(e => e.Entity).OfType<Booking>();
```

We can use these instances of `Booking` to verify we don't have any pending changes with a `CustomerId` of 1, like so:

```
bookings.Any(c => (b => b.CustomerId != 1)
```

All we have to do is throw an exception in case we do have such a pending change. If we don't, then we can go ahead and save the changes to the database, as shown in the following code sample.

> **Listing 8.17   Checking for valid `CustomerID` in stub before saving to the database**

```
public override async Task<int>
    SaveChangesAsync(CancellationToken cancellationToken = default) {
  IEnumerable<EntityEntry> pendingChanges = ChangeTracker.Entries()
    .Where(e => e.State == EntityState.Added);
  IEnumerable<Booking> bookings = pendingChanges
    .Select(e => e.Entity).OfType<Booking>();
  if (bookings.Any(b => b.CustomerId != 1)) {
    throw new Exception("Database Error!");
  }

  await base.SaveChangesAsync(cancellationToken);
  return 1;
}
```

To make sure we didn't break anything, let's run all the unit tests in the solution. It seems that the `CreateBooking_Success` test case passes when run individually but not when run in tandem with the other tests. The test runner reports back that an exception of type `CouldNotAddBookingToDatabaseException` was thrown. Well, we went straight from an Entity Framework Core pitfall into an inheritance pitfall: when creating a new instance of a class, the base class does not get instantiated if it already exists. When we request a new instance of `FlyingDutchmanAirlinesContext_Stub`, the CLR does not instantiate an instance of its parent (`FlyingDutchman-AirlinesContext`) if one already exists. In practical terms, this means we are dealing with the same database context across unit tests, and, therefore, the contents of the in-memory database do not get wiped after every test. Therefore, when we execute the `CreateBooking_Success` test case, there is a chance that a lingering `Booking` instance remains in the database. Because we request the first booking's `CustomerID` from the context in our overridden `SaveChangesAsync` method, we could end up getting one with a wrong `CustomerID`. What can we do about this? Either of the following two approaches may work for us here:

- Manually clear the database's `DbSet<Booking>` in the `TestInitialize` method.
- Use Entity Framework Core's `EnsureDeleted` method, which checks whether a database is deleted. If the database is still alive, `EnsureDeleted` unceremoniously deletes the database anyway.

Both approaches work equally well, but to keep things interesting, let's try our hand at using the `EnsureDeleted` method. We could call the `EnsureDeleted` method in either the `TestInitialize` method or in the constructor of `FlyingDutchmanAirlines_Stub`. In my view, we are better off putting it in the stub's constructor, as shown in the next listing. Using the `EnsureDeleted` method is very much related to us using a stub, and I like to keep the `TestInitialize` methods as similar as possible between test classes.

> **Listing 8.18** Use `EnsureDeleted` to delete an in-memory database

```
public
  FlyingDutchmanAirlinesContext(DbContextOptions
  <FlyingDutchmanAirlinesContext> options) {
  base.Database.EnsureDeleted();        ◁──  Deletes the nonstub's
}                                              in-memory database
```

If we now run all our tests, we see that the `CreateBooking_Success` test case passes quite nicely.

And with that, we've completed the `BookingRepository`. You are now well versed in the worlds of generics, optional parameters, switch expressions, and the Liskov substitution principle.

Exercises

EXERCISE 8.6
True or false? When using a stub, you have to overload the base class's methods.

EXERCISE 8.7

Because of which principle were we able to use an instance of FlyingDutchman-
Context_Stub as if it were an instance of type FlyingDutchmanContext?

    a   The Liskov substitution principle

    b   The DRY principle

    c   The Phragmén–Lindelöf principle

EXERCISE 8.8

When programming with generics, can I add an instance of type float to a List<bool>?

    a   Yes

    b   No

    c   Let me Stack Overflow that for you.

EXERCISE 8.9

What is this an example of? where T : Queue<int>

    a   A generic collection

    b   A generic generalization

    c   A generic constraint

EXERCISE 8.10

True or false? We can use generics only with classes.

EXERCISE 8.11

True or false? Classes with generics can have only one generic constraint.

EXERCISE 8.12

True or false? You cannot have a generic type as a type of method parameter.

EXERCISE 8.13

True or false? The use of optional parameters is optional.

EXERCISE 8.14

In a method's parameter list, where do optional parameters go?

    a   At the start

    b   At the end

    c   Anywhere

EXERCISE 8.15

True or false? Like a default implicit constructor, if you do not declare a default case
in a switch statement, the compiler generates it for you and executes the first case
you specified.

Summary

- Separation of concerns means that we want to isolate modules of logic from
  each other. This ensures that our code is testable and atomic. Atomic code is
  more readable and extendable.

- Coupling refers to how integrated two "concerns" are. Tight coupling can mean that a certain class deeply depends on another class, whereas loose coupling between two classes means a class can be changed and expanded without causing an issue for the other class. Classes with tight coupling are more difficult to maintain, because you can easily introduce side effects when you don't know the full extent of the dependencies.

- You can inline values from variables into a string by using string interpolation. This makes it easy to construct complex strings without using the explicit concatenation operator.

- Strings are immutable. Any operator (concatenation, deletion, replacements) on a string causes the CLR to allocate a new area in memory for the new copy of the string. This means that if you do a lot of operations of a string, every step (concatenation, deletion) along the way results in new memory allocations. This is important to keep in mind when dealing with many concatenations or deletions.

- When assigning numerous properties to values after instantiating a new object, using the object initializer allows for condensed and more readable syntax. Object initializers are the idiomatic way to instantiate complex objects when no appropriate constructor is provided.

- The Liskov substitution principle states that a subtype of a type should be able to do everything the parent type can do. This means that we can use a subtype as if it were the parent type. The Liskov substitution principle explains why we can use polymorphism.

- A stub is a piece of code that uses the Liskov substitution principle to act as if it were its parent class (or functionality) while overriding and redirecting certain methods to guarantee certain functionality. Stubs are very useful for throwing exceptions and returning specific responses when unit testing.

- Generics allow us to constrict classes, methods, or types to work with a certain type. For example, a `Stack<MaineCoon>` or a `List<ISnack>` uses generics to constrain their functionality to a certain type or group of types. Constraining your code in this way is a useful technique to control your data types and ensuring that they stay within your expectations throughout your code.

- Optional parameters allow us to define nonrequired arguments for methods. An optional parameter takes on the value of the defined value if no matching argument is passed into the method. Optional parameters are useful when our code relies on multiple possible sets of parameter values, but we can continue processing if we do not pass in a specific parameter.

- The Entity Framework Core `EnsureDeleted` method checks whether a database is deleted. If it is not, it deletes it. This comes in handy when working with an in-memory database during testing to ensure no remnants of previous test data remain.

Extension methods, streams, and abstract classes

9

This chapter covers

- Using streams to redirect console output
- Using abstract classes to provide common functionality across derived classes
- Using the `AddRange` LINQ method to add many things to a collection at once
- Using the `SortedList` collection
- Using extension methods to extend existing types with new functionality
- Refactoring "magic numbers"

In sections 3.1 and 3.2, the CEO of Flying Dutchman Airlines tasked us with creating a new version of the existing FlyingDutchmanAirlines codebase. The existing codebase is old and riddled with design flaws, and does not play nice with the new API requirements put in place by a newly signed business deal with a search aggregator. In chapters 3 and 4, we considered the existing codebase and earmarked potential improvements. In chapter 5, we started our refactor and implemented a database access layer with Entity Framework Core. Following that, in chapters 5 through 8 we implemented (and tested) two repositories out of the following four required classes:

- `CustomerRepository`—We implemented this repository class in chapters 6 and 7.
- `BookingRepository`—We implemented this repository class in chapter 8.
- `AirportRepository`—We implement this repository class in this chapter.
- `FlightRepository`—We implement this repository class in this chapter.

See figure 9.1 for where we are in the scheme of the book.

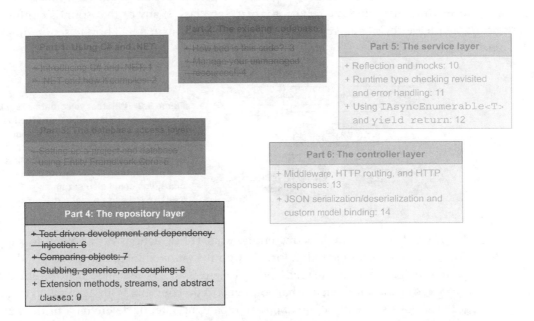

Figure 9.1 In this chapter, we'll implement both the `AirportRepository` and `FlightRepository` classes. These are the last two required repositories to finish the repository section of our refactor.

Having learned things such as test-driven development, the DRY principle, Liskov substitution principle, and LINQ, as well as being familiar with the overall structure and testing patterns of these repositories by now, we can pick up speed as we finish the repository layer in this chapter by implementing `AirportRepository` and `Flight-Repository`. We'll also learn about abstract classes (an alternative to interfaces that forces us to implement the same method in all derived classes) and revisit extension methods (section 9.6) so we can provide new functionality to existing types.

9.1 *Implementing the Airport repository*

In chapters 6 through 8, we followed a basic first step when starting an implementation: creating skeleton classes for both the repository and unit tests. I follow the same approach in this chapter.

The `AirportRepository` skeleton uses dependency injection, which injects an instance of type `FlyingDutchmanAirlinesContext` into `AirportRepository`'s explicit (nondefault) constructor, as shown in figure 9.2. The constructor assigns the injected `FlyingDutchmanAirlinesContext` to a private backing field. Additionally, the access modifier of the `AirportRepository` class is public. The `AirportRepositoryTest` class has a `TestInitialize` method that initializes the `FlyingDutchmanAirlinesContext` and assigns it to a private backing field, so we can use a fresh instance of the in-memory database in every unit test. The `TestInitialize` method also instantiates and assigns a new instance of `AirportRepository` to a private backing field. A `[TestClass]` attribute annotates the `AirportRepositoryTest` class. If any of that sounds confusing to you, please revisit chapters 6 and 7, where I show you in detail how to set up these skeleton classes.

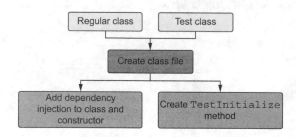

Figure 9.2 **Whether you create a regular class or a test class, the first step is to create the actual class file. If you are working on a regular class, proceed to add dependency injection to the class and constructor. If you created a test class, you could also set up an optional `TestInitialize` method.**

When we deal with the `Airport` entity, what HTTP actions do we need to support? Conventional wisdom says that for every entity, we need logic that corresponds to the commonly grouped create-read-update-delete (CRUD) actions. I beg to differ. I say, only expose and implement what you need to do your job. With `Airport`, it makes little sense for us to expose the ability to create, update, or delete data in the `Airport` table through the API. All we need is a read operation.

9.2   *Getting an Airport out of the database by its ID*

What does a read operation map do within the context of the `AirportRepository`? We need to "read" the `Airport` entity from the database, meaning we should return an `Airport` when given its ID. We did something similar in section 6.2, where we returned a `Customer` object from the database when given its ID. In this section, we'll start our implementation of the method needed to return an `Airport` from the database: `GetAirportByID`.

But, as always, first comes the red-light stage of test-driven development—the success case unit test for `GetAirportByID`, shown next:

```
[TestMethod]
public void GetAirportByID_Success() {
  Airport airport = await _repository.GetAirportByID(0);
  Assert.IsNotNull(airport);
}
```

When we attempt to compile this, not only do we get a compile error saying that the compiler cannot find `GetAirportByID` (which we expected because we have not implemented the method yet), but we also have another compile error, as follows:

`"The await operator can only be used within an async method."`

You will undoubtedly get this error many times throughout your C# career, because it is easy to forget to mark a method that is awaiting something as `async` and with the appropriate return value (`Task`).

> **NOTE** As discussed in section 6.2.8, asynchronous methods expect a return of type `Task`. If you want to return nothing (`void`), use the nongeneric version: `Task`. If you want to return an actual value, use the generic version `Task<T>`, where `T` is your return type. For example, to return a Boolean[1] value along with a `Task`, use `Task<bool>`. `Task` represents a single unit of work (a concern).

To refresh our memories, if we want to convert a method from executing synchronously to executing asynchronously, we need to use the `async` keyword and a return type of `Task` or `Task<T>` (if the `Task` returns some data) in the method signature as follows:

```
[TestMethod]
public async Task GetAirportByID_Success() {
  Airport airport = await _repository.GetAirportByID(0);
  Assert.IsNotNull(airport);
}
```

To compile the code and pass the success case unit test (the green stage of test-driven development), we need to create a `GetAirportByID` method that accepts an argument of type `integer` in `AirportRepository`, as shown here:

```
public async Task<Airport> GetAirportByID(int airportID) {
  return new Airport();
}
```

If we compile our code and run the `GetAirportByID_Success` test case now, we see that it passes. Obviously, the code in `GetAirportByID` is not really doing much for us. It simply returns a new instance of type `Airport` instead of a particular entry from the database. I want to try an experiment with you, my dear reader: for one minute, I want you to think about the four major steps necessary to retrieve an `Airport` object from the database. Ready? Go!

---

[1] Why is Boolean capitalized and `bool` is not? When we speak of Boolean values, we mean truth values (true and false) through the lens of Boolean algebra. Boolean algebra was invented by English mathematician George Bool and first showed up in his work *The Mathematical Analysis of Logic: Being an Essay towards a Calculus of Deductive Reasoning* (Bool, 1847). When we talk about a `bool`, we mean the type inside the C# programming language representing Boolean truth values and backed by `System.Boolean`.

A minute has passed? Are you sure? Okay, then, let's move on. In broad strokes, the four major steps we need to undertake follow and are shown in figure 9.3:

1 Validate the given `airportID`.
2 Retrieve the correct `Airport` from the database.
3 Handle any potential `Exception` from the database with a custom exception.
4 Return the found `Airport` instance.

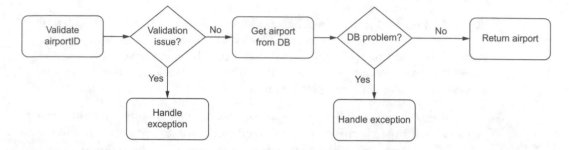

Figure 9.3   The steps involved with returning an `Airport` from the database. First, we check if the given input arguments are valid. If not, we throw and handle the exception. If the inputs are valid, we attempt to get the correct `Airport` from the database. If the database encounters a problem, we throw and handle the exception. If we encountered no errors, we return the found `Airport` instance.

If you feel adventurous, I invite you to implement the `GetAirportByID` method following those broad steps. Come back to the book after you have completed the implementation and compare my implementation with yours. If my implementation differs from yours, that is okay. If you have the tests to back up your functionality, and they pass, you can be assured your code is great. (Your code being clean is a different matter altogether and not measurable by tests. To check the cleanliness of your code, use the clean code checklist in appendix B.)

I offer you one last word of advice before embarking on this grand adventure: keep it simple. Early in my career, I thought I was being clever when using very obscure corners of a programming language and odd algorithms. This led to code that was unreadable for anybody (including me) and, by extension, unmaintainable. Be clever by keeping it simple (or just complicated enough, depending on your outlook on life).

9.3 *Validating the AirportID input parameter*

As discussed in section 9.2, the four steps to getting an `Airport` from the database follow:

1 Validate the given `airportID`.
2 Retrieve the correct `Airport` from the database.
3 Handle any potential `Exception` from the database with a custom exception.
4 Return the found `Airport` instance.

In this section, we'll tackle the first of the four: validate the user input. The Get-AirportByID method accepts one argument of type integer. The AirportID should be a positive integer (an integer greater than or equal to 0). To test that AirportID is a positive integer, we use a similar conditional to the one we wrote in the GetCustomer-ByID and CreateBooking methods: if the argument's value is invalid, write a log to the console and throw an ArgumentException exception, as shown in the next listing. The log written to the console uses string interpolation to inline the value of airportID.

Listing 9.1 Validating the `airportID` argument in `GetAirportByID`

Determines whether airportID has a valid value

```
public async Task<Airport> GetAirportByID(int airportID) {
  if (airportID < 0) {
    Console.WriteLine($"Argument Exception in GetAirportByID! AirportID
 = {airportID}");
    throw new ArgumentException("invalid argument provided");
  }

  return new Airport();
}
```

Throws an exception of type ArgumentException

Returns a new instance of Airport. We'll change this implementation in this chapter.

Logs the AirportID value to the console for developers

That looks good. But you know what is coming next, don't you? We need to add a failure case unit test that checks for invalid input values. We know we can use the [DataRow] method attribute to supply the failure case unit test with a multitude of test data, but what data should we supply? Well, we have only one invalid input data point we need to test: a negative integer.

Because we need to test only one data point, we don't need the [DataRow] method attribute. We can use the [DataRow] method attribute with a unit test that deals with only one piece of data, but that would be overkill. If we're testing only one data point, it is cleaner to do without the [DataRow] method attribute, as shown next:

```
[TestMethod]
public async Task GetAirportByID_Failure_InvalidInput() {
 await _repository.GetAirportByID(-1);
}
```

The GetAirportByID_Failure_InvalidInput unit test passes a negative (and, therefore, invalid) integer to the GetAirportByID method. We expect the GetAirportByID method to see we supplied it with an invalid AirportID argument. Following that, we expect the method to log a message to the console and throw an ArgumentException. How do we verify that the GetAirportByID method threw the expected exception of type ArgumentException? We need the [ExpectedException(typeof(Argument-Exception))] method attribute annotating the unit test as follows:

```
[TestMethod]
[ExpectedException(typeof(ArgumentException))]
public async Task GetAirportByID_Failure_InvalidInput() {
 await _repository.GetAirportByID(-1);
}
```

We run the tests, and everything passes. Is there anything else we can test for input validation? With GetCustomerByName, we were satisfied with asserting that the input validation code in GetCustomerByName threw an exception of type ArgumentException in case of invalid input. But the GetAirportByName method also logs a message to the console. We should probably check for that.

9.4   *Output streams and being specifically abstract*

To verify that we logged a message to the console, we need access to the console's contents. The trick to retrieving console output is to provide an alternative output and set the console to write to that output. In this section, we'll discuss how to circumvent console output to our own data stream.

> **WARNING**   The concept of a stream in C# differs from using the Streams API in Java. In Java, using the Streams API is almost akin to using LINQ in C#. This section explains the C# concept of streams.

The Console class is a wrapper around an input and an output stream of data. A stream represents a sequence of data, often in bytes. The Console class deals with the following three data streams, shown in figure 9.4:

- A System.IO.TextReader, which represents the input stream
- A System.IO.TextWriter, which represents the output stream
- A System.IO.TextWriter, which represents the error stream.

From keyboard input to console output

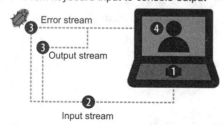

Figure 9.4   A possible life cycle from input to output. First, keyboard input (1) is sent to the input stream (2). Then, some processing is done inside the application (this can be anything you want). Following processing, if an exception was thrown, the error is written to the error stream (3). If there is no exception, information is written to the output stream (3). Finally, the error and output streams are displayed in the console (4).

Within the context of a Console application, the input stream handles any keyboard input. The output stream is where we write anything we want displayed in the output. The error stream is where exceptions are logged. We do not have access to the default TextReader and TextWriters, but we can specify our own by using the Console's SetOut, SetIn, and SetError methods.

By instantiating our instance of type `StringWriter` (a data stream dealing with strings) and hanging onto a reference to that variable while using it as the `Console`'s output stream, we can get the history data pretty easily. Instead of writing to some intangible output stream, the `Console.WriteLine` method writes to our `String-Writer`, as shown in figure 9.5. Take note that some programming languages such as Java distinguish between input and output streams on a type level. C# does not do this. You can use any `Stream`-derived class as an input or output stream.

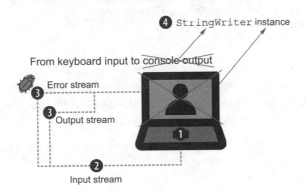

Figure 9.5 **When redirecting console output to a `StringWriter` instance, the output and error streams write to the `StringWriter` instance instead of to the regular console output. The life cycle from figure 9.4 changes: first, keyboard input (1) is sent to the input stream (2). Then, some processing is done inside the application (this can be anything you want). Following processing, if an exception was thrown, the error is written to the error stream (3). If we don't get an exception, information is written to the output stream (3). Finally, the error and output streams are written to our `StringWriter` instance (4).**

The `Stream` base class is the foundation for all data streams. `Stream` is an abstract class and the base class for many derived classes (such as `StringWriter`) that deal with a sequence of bytes. A `StringWriter` is a stream that deals with a sequence of bytes and exposes functionalities based on those bytes representing strings (and because, under the hood, a string is an array of characters—therefore, characters). Because all derived classes from `Stream` implement the `IDisposable` interface, we need to clean up the instantiated `Stream` once we are done with it, or we risk a memory leak.

Abstract classes

An abstract class is a class that cannot directly be instantiated or be static. You can instantiate a concrete subclass of an abstract class, which indirectly instantiates the abstract class. We can make a class abstract by using the `abstract` keyword in the class's signature. Abstract classes are a different way of supporting inheritance and, by extension, polymorphism. We often use abstract classes as "base" classes, sitting

(continued)

on top of an inheritance chain. As opposed to interfaces, abstract classes can provide method bodies (as long as the method itself is *not* abstract) and use access modifiers. This means that abstract classes are often used to spread a specific implementation of a method across derived classes. An abstract method must be overridden in a concrete implementation. Abstract methods are implicitly `virtual` and can be said to indicate an "incomplete" method because they cannot contain a method body. Abstract methods can live only in abstract classes. Derived classes must override abstract methods and extend functionality per their requirements or be marked as abstract themselves.

To use our `Console` output stream, we need to instantiate an instance of type `String-Writer`, wrap the stream in a `using` statement, and set it to the console's output stream. Then, once all processing is done, we retrieve the `StringWriter`'s contents and assert that the output matches our expectations, as shown next.

Listing 9.2   Define our console output stream

Sets our **StringWriter** instance as the Console's output

```
[TestMethod]
[ExpectedException(typeof(ArgumentException))]
public async Task GetAirportByID_Failure_InvalidInput() {
 using (StringWriter outputStream = new StringWriter()) {
   Console.SetOut(outputStream);
   await _repository.GetAirportByID(-1);

   Assert.IsTrue(outputStream.ToString().Contains("Argument Exception in
   GetAirportByID! AirportID = -1"));
 }
}
```

Creates a
StringWriter,
and promises to
dispose of it safely

GetAirportByID writes to the
StringWriter and throws an exception.

Asserts that the outputStream
contains the expected logged output

Run the test. You'll see it passes. But what if I told you that the test passing is a red herring? It's great that the test passes, but are we actually testing everything we want to test? I think not. Let's step through the code execution as follows:

1 The `TestInitialize` method executes.
2 The `GetAirportByID_Failure_InvalidInput` method starts.
3 The unit test creates a `StringWriter`, sets it as the console's output stream, and enters `GetAirportByID`.
4 We check if the passed-in `AirportID` is valid or not (it is not).
5 The code writes an error log to our `StringWriter` stream.
6 The method throws an `Exception` of type `ArgumentException`.
7 The method is aborted.
8 The test stops execution because an `Exception` was thrown and not caught.
9 The test determines that the expected `Exception` was thrown and marks the test as "passed."

Turns out, we did not assert based on the console's output stream at all. Because we did not catch the `ArgumentException` thrown in `GetAirportByID`, the unit test stopped executing before the code got to the `outputStream` assertion.

To fix this, we should catch the `ArgumentException`, execute the output stream assertion, and then throw another exception of type `ArgumentException` to satisfy the `ExpectedException` method attribute, all inside the `GetAirportByID_Failure_InvalidInput` unit test, as shown in the next listing.

Listing 9.3 Catching the thrown `ArgumentException` in a unit test

```
[TestMethod]
[ExpectedException(typeof(ArgumentException))]
public async Task GetAirportByID_Failure_InvalidInput() {
  try {
    using (StringWriter outputStream = new StringWriter()) {
      Console.SetOut(outputStream);
      await _repository.GetAirportByID(-1);          ← Catches the ArgumentException thrown in GetAirportByID
    }
  } catch (ArgumentException) {
    Assert.IsTrue(outputStream.ToString().Contains("Argument Exception in
    GetAirportByID! AirportID = -1");               ← Asserts that outputStream's content and the logged error are equal
    throw new ArgumentException();                   ← Throws a new ArgumentException for the ExpectedException attribute
  }
}
```

There is one catch, though. This code does not compile, because once the `GetAirportByID` throws `ArgumentException` and the unit test's `try-catch` block catches the exception, `outputStream` is out of scope, as shown in figure 9.6.

```
try {
    using (StringWriter outputStream = new StringWriter()){
        Console.SetOut(outputStream);
        await _repository.GetAirportByID(-1);   outputStream's scope
    }
}
catch (ArgumentException){
    Assert.IsTrue(outputStream.ToString().Contains("Argument
        Exception in GetAirportByID! AirportID = -1");
    throw new ArgumentException();
}
```

Figure 9.6 The `outputStream` variable is out of scope in the `catch` code block. The scope of `outputStream` reaches until the end of the `using` code block.

Because `outputStream` is out of scope, we cannot access it or its value anymore. If only we could extend the scope of `outputStream` but also correctly dispose of the instance. We could put the entire `try-catch` inside the `using` statement, but I prefer to have the `using` statement contain as little code as possible. Perhaps we can use the old-fashioned way of manually disposing of `outputStream` by adding a call to `output-Stream.Dispose` in a `finally` block. We would also need to instantiate the `String-Writer` outside of the `try-catch-finally`, then, as shown in the following code sample.

Listing 9.4   Correcting the scope issue for `outputStream`

```
[TestMethod]
[ExpectedException(typeof(ArgumentException))]
public async Task GetAirportByID_Failure_InvalidInput() {
  StringWriter outputStream = new StringWriter();        ◁─── Creates our outputStream
  try {
    Console.SetOut(outputStream);                        ◁─── Tells the console to use outputStream as the output stream
    await _repository.GetAirportByID(-1);                ◁─── Calls the GetAirportByID method
  } catch (ArgumentException) {
    Assert.IsTrue(outputStream.ToString().Contains("Argument Exception in
    GetAirportByID! AirportID = -1");                    ◁─── Asserts that outputStream's contents match the expected error log
    throw new ArgumentException();                       ◁─── Throws a new ArgumentException for the ExpectedException attribute
  } finally {
    outputStream.Dispose();                              ◁─── Disposes of outputStream
  }
}
```

Catches the ArgumentException
thrown in GetAirportByID

Now that the `outputStream` variable is within scope, when we assert that the `output-Stream` contents contain the error logged in `GetAirportByID`, we can compile the unit test and run it. It passes. We can now point to the `GetAirportByID_Failure_InvalidInput` and say that we know that our input validation code works.

Rethrowing exceptions and keeping your stack traces

The code in listing 9.4 has us catch an exception of type `ArgumentException` and then throw a new exception of the same type. This works fine for a lot of use cases, but what if you want to rethrow the same exception? You have two simple ways of doing this: you can use the `throw` keyword with or without a reference to the caught exception variable as follows:

```
catch (Exception exception) {
  throw;
}
```

```
catch (Exception exception) {
  throw exception;
}
```

Both ways of rethrowing exceptions work. There is one catch, however: rethrowing an exception can result in a loss of the stack trace information preserved along with an exception. To make sure you have access to the exception's stack trace after rethrowing the exception, we need to do things slightly differently and dive deep into a dark corner of .NET: the `ExceptionDispatchInfo` class.

The `ExceptionDispatchInfo` class allows us to save a specific state of an exception, including its stack frame. Doing this prevents the exception stack frame from being wiped out by a new stack frame when rethrowing. To save an exception's state, we need to pass in the exception's `InnerException` property (which contains the state that threw the original exception) to the `ExceptionDispatchInfo.Capture` method. After that, we can call the `Throw` method, as follows, and it is business as usual:

```
catch (Exception exception) {
  ExceptionDispatchInfo.Capture(exception.InnerException).Throw();
}
```

Rethrowing an `Exception` by capturing its current state through the `Exception-DispatchInfo` class safeguards your original exception's internal information, including the stack trace, from being overridden.

9.5 Querying the database for an Airport object

After section 9.4, we have the foundation for the `AirportRepository.GetAirport-ByID` method along with input validation of the `AirportID` argument. We know what an abstract class is and how to use a stream. In this section, we'll finish the implementation of `GetAirportByID`. To do so, we need to the following:

- Query Entity Framework Core's `DbSet<Airport>` for the matching `Airport` object.
- Make sure that, in case of a database problem, we throw the appropriate custom exception.
- Have unit tests that cover both success and failure code branches.

We asked Entity Framework Core to give us an entity when given an ID before (section 7.1.2), so I won't hold your hand too tightly through implementing the following code for that. In fact, if you feel like it, give it a whirl before moving on. For bonus points, use test-driven development to verify your code.

```
public async Task<Airport> GetAirportByID(int airportID) {
  if (airportID < 0) {
    Console.WriteLine($"Argument Exception in GetAirportByID! AirportID
➥ = {airportID}");
    throw new ArgumentException("invalid argument provided");
  }

  return await _context.Airport.FirstOrDefaultAsync(a => a.AirportId ==
➥ airportID) ?? throw new AirportNotFoundException();
}
```

Let's take a quick look now at the `return` statement, which is where the meat and potatoes of this section takes place:

```
return await _context.Airport.FirstOrDefaultAsync(a => a.AirportId ==
➥ airportID) ?? throw new AirportNotFoundException();
```

We can break down the return statement into the following four steps:

1 `await`—Execute the expression asynchronously and wait for completion.

2 `_context.Airport.FirstOrDefaultAsync`—Retrieve the first match (based on the expression in step 3) or the default value for the entity (null in the case of `Airport`) asynchronously.

3 `a => a.AirportId == airportID`—This is the predicate that is the matching expression for step 2. The predicate says to return the first element in the `Airport` collection that matches its `AirportId`.

4 `?? throw new AirportNotFoundException();`—Using the null-coalescing operator, if steps 2 and 3 returned the default value of `null`, we throw an `Airport-NotFoundException`.

In that brief `return` statement, we combined six separate techniques that make C# awesome: asynchronous programming is used to get the expression's completion and return values; Entity Framework Core lets us query its internal `DbSets` for entities, maintaining an isomorphic relationship between the database and running code; the `FirstOrDefaultAsync` LINQ method enumerates over a collection and returns a value based on a predicate; we use a lambda expression as the predicate to match `Airport` objects to `AirportID`'s; the null-coalescing operator checks for a returned null pointer and executes its expression; and a custom exception, using inheritance, is thrown.

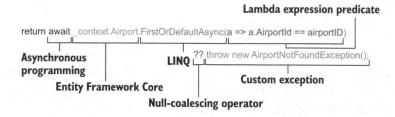

We kind of cheated on implementing `GetAirportByID` with test-driven development: we did not follow the red-green stoplight pattern to its minutest detail. That is okay. Like every technique (and like everything I tell you to do), we shouldn't be hamstrung by the rules, as long as we make sure we deliver everything correctly. For us, that means we need to finish the success case unit test for `GetAirportByID`.

What do we need to finish the `GetAirportByID_Success` test case (and with that, the `AirportRepository`)?

1 Add an `Airport` object to the in-memory database in the `TestInitialize` method.

2 Attempt to retrieve the newly added `Airport` object from the database by calling `GetAirportByID` along with the appropriate `airportID`.

3 Assert that the returned object is the same as the `Airport` object we stored in the database before calling `GetAirportByID`.

Listing 9.5 Basic `TestInitialize` method and a skeleton `GetAirportByID` unit test

```
[TestInitialize]
public async Task TestInitialize() {
  DbContextOptions<FlyingDutchmanAirlinesContext> dbContextOptions =
    ➥ new DbContextOptionsBuilder<FlyingDutchmanAirlinesContext>()
    ➥ .UseInMemoryDatabase("FlyingDutchman").Options;
  _context = new FlyingDutchmanAirlinesContext_Stub(dbContextOptions);

  Airport newAirport = new Airport {            Creates a new instance
    AirportId = 0,                              of Airport (Nuuk,
    City = "Nuuk",                              Greenland; GOH)
    Iata = " GOH"
  };

  _context.Airport.Add(newAirport);         ◁──      Adds the Airport
  await _context.SaveChangesAsync();        ◁──      instance to EF
                                                     Core's internal
  _repository = new AirportRepository(_context);     database set
  Assert.IsNotNull(_repository);
}                                             Saves the Airport object to
                                              the in-memory database

[TestMethod]
public async Task GetAirportByID_Success() {
  Airport airport = await _repository.GetAirportByID(0);

  Assert.IsNotNull(airport);
  Assert.AreEqual(0, airport.AirportId);        Asserts that the retrieved
  Assert.AreEqual("Nuuk", airport.City);        Airport matches the
  Assert.AreEqual("GOH", airport.Iata);         saved Airport
}
```

When we run the test, however, it does not pass. The compiler throws an exception because, as shown next, we use the `FlyingDutchmanAirlinesContext_Stub`, which overrides the `SaveChangesAsync` method and throws an exception when there are no `Booking` instances in the database with a `CustomerId` of 1:

```
public override async Task<int> SaveChangesAsync(CancellationToken
  ➥ cancellationToken = default) {
  IEnumerable<EntityEntry> pendingChanges =
  ➥ ChangeTracker.Entries().Where(e => e.State == EntityState.Added);
  if (pendingChanges.Any(c => ((Booking) c.Entity).CustomerId != 1)) {
    throw new Exception("Database Error!");
  }

  await base.SaveChangesAsync(cancellationToken);
  return 1;
}
```

This is what I like to call "controlled biting in the ass," and I'm sorry for leading you down the wrong path on purpose. If we had taken a moment to reflect on our implementation when we wrote the code, we could have seen this coming, but then a teaching moment would have been lost.

Because we did not add any bookings to the database in the `AirportRepository-Test`'s `TestInitialize` method, the `SaveChangesAsync` method throws an exception. To solve this, let's create a conditional in the stub's `SaveChangesAsync` method that checks whether we have an entity in the `Booking DbSet`. If no booking exists in the database, the code skips the `Booking` code block. Alternatively, you could create a different stub for this test. The thinking behind this is that a stub should only ever have the logic for one specific test. This is a valid approach, but for the sake of brevity and simplicity, we are sticking with the one stub. Similarly, we can check if there are any pending changes for an `Airport` model, as shown next.

Listing 9.6   **Overriding** `SaveChangesAsync` **in our stub**

```
public override async Task<int> SaveChangesAsync(CancellationToken
  cancellationToken = default) {
  await base.SaveChangesAsync(cancellationToken);
  cancellationToken = default) {
  IEnumerable<EntityEntry> pendingChanges = ChangeTracker.Entries()
  .Where(e => e.State == EntityState.Added);
  IEnumerable<Booking> bookings = pendingChanges
  .Select(e => e.Entity).OfType<Booking>();
  if (bookings.Any(b => b.CustomerId != 1)) {
    throw new Exception("Database Error!");
  }

  IEnumerable<Airport> airports = pendingChanges              // Retrieves all pending
  .Select(e => e.Entity).OfType<Airport>();                   // changes for Airport
  if (!airports.Any()) {                                      // Checks if pending
    throw new Exception("Database Error!");                   // changes for Airport
  }                                                           // are found
                                                              // If no pending changes for
  await base.SaveChangesAsync(cancellationToken);             // Airport are found, throws
  return 1;                                                   // an exception
}
```

By adding the extra logic in the stub, the test passes. As always, let's ask ourselves, what more can we test? Well, we covered our major code branches, but what if we want to make sure that we can get an airport from a database that contains more than one `Airport` object? So far, all the in-memory databases we used in our testing have contained only one record of the entity we were testing on. We can use the techniques we picked up before, as well as a new concept I shall introduce you to in just a second that adds multiple instances of `Airport` to the in-memory database and makes assertions on them.

Think about this for a minute: what is a suitable way to add multiple objects of the same type to a collection? What if I tell you that to do that, we need to operate on a collection? I hope you jumped out of your chair (or bed, if you use this book to fall asleep at night) and cried, "We can use a LINQ method!"

ADDRANGE AND SORTEDLIST<T>

The LINQ method `AddRange` lets you add multiple entries to a collection at once. "Range" refers to a range of objects, usually stored in a different collection. Because this is a LINQ method, it is not only available with Entity Framework Core, it's also available across the entire C# landscape. To use the `AddRange` functionality, we need the following two things:

1 A collection of objects we want to put into a different collection. We use a collection created and populated in the `TestInitialize` method for this.

2 A collection to store the objects in—in this case, EF Core's `DbSet<Airport>`.

First, we create a collection. The `System.Collections` and `System.Collections.Generics` namespaces contain many collections we can sample and use. There are the usual candidates such as `List<T>`, `ArrayList<T>`, `LinkedList<T>`, and `Dictionary<T, X>`, but we also have more esoteric collections such as `BitArray` or `Synchronized-ReadOnlyCollection<T>`. We can use the `AddRange` method on any of the collections (generic or not) that C# provides.

Why don't we have some fun, take the scenic route, and use a special collection called `SortedList<T>`? Alternatively, you could add all entries to a generic `List<T>` and call its `Sort` method. Because `SortedList<T>` is a generic collection, we find it in the `System.Collections.Generics` namespace. If we want to use the `System.Collections.Generics` namespace, that means we also have to import the namespace.

A `SortedList` allows for the collection to be sorted. To use a `SortedList`, we just have to add some data and, sometimes, specify how we want to sort the elements. A `SortedList` containing integers sorts elements by integer value, whereas a `SortedList` containing strings sorts elements alphabetically. If we want to sort an object (such as instances of type `Airport`), however, there is a catch: `SortedList`, when used with a nonprimitive type, turns into `SortedList<K, V>`, where `K` is a sortable primitive type and `V` is our object.

We want to sort objects of type `Airport`. Let's keep things interesting and sort them alphabetically by IATA code, rather than `AirportID`. This means we use the string primitive type as the first generic type in `SortedList<K, V>`.

We start by creating a `SortedList<string, Airport>` in the `TestInitialize` method and populate it with a handful of objects. Beginning with the airport we already added in the `TestInitialize` method (GOH—Nuuk, Greenland), we add `Airport` elements for PHX (Phoenix, AZ), DDH (Bennington, VT), and RDU (Raleigh-Durham, NC) as follows:

```
SortedList<string, Airport> airports = new SortedList<string, Airport> {
    {
      "GOH",
      new Airport
      {
```

```
        AirportId = 0,
        City = "Nuuk",
        Iata = "GOH"
      }
    },
    {
      "PHX",
      new Airport
      {
        AirportId = 1,
        City = "Phoenix",
        Iata = "PHX"
      }
    },
    {
      "DDH",
      new Airport
      {
        AirportId = 2,
        City = "Bennington",
        Iata = "DDH"
      }
    },
    {
      "RDU",
      new Airport
      {
        AirportId = 3,
        City = "Raleigh-Durham",
        Iata = "RDU"
      }
    }
  };
```

When inspecting the `SortedList<string, Airport>` after all those additions, we see an alphabetically sorted collection shown in figure 9.7: `"DDH"` -> `"GOH"` -> `"PHX"` -> `"RDU"`.

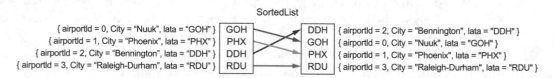

Figure 9.7 `SortedList` **takes in data and sorts that data based on a sorting type. In this example, we sort based on the string primitive type. This results in an alphabetically sorted collection.**

To add the values from the sorted list to the in-memory database, we use the `AddRange` LINQ method on the `context`'s `DbSet<Airport>` as follows:

```
_context.Airport.AddRange(airports.Values);
```

Adding all the values from the `SortedList<string, Airport>` to the `DbSet<Airport>` using `AddRange` is a piece of cake. Back when I asked you to think about what the best way to add a collection of elements to a different collection was, you may have thought we had to use a `foreach` loop and manually add all elements to the database. Under the hood, that is exactly what is happening when we use `AddRange`, but I for one am very thankful for the syntactical sugar that LINQ offers us. It saves a lot of typing, and using `AddRange` increases code clarity as well because the code is still very readable and condensed. That being said, we need to be sure we call the `SortedList<string, Airport>`'s `Value` property in the `AddRange` call, or else we would get the key-value pairs in the list instead of the `Airport` instances. Because `DbSet<Airport>` has a generic constraint around the `Airport` type, we cannot add instances of type `string` to the collection.

To be safe, let's run all existing tests and verify we broke nothing with this implementation. It looks like we are good. Now for the fun part: asserting that the entities entered into the database are there and that we can retrieve them. We can inline the `AirportIds` by using the familiar `[DataRow]` method attribute. Then, we call `GetAirportByID` and contrast the returned `Airport` instance to what we retrieve from the database directly from the context by using the `airportId` passed in by the MSTest runner, as shown in the next listing.

Listing 9.7 Using the `DataRow` attribute to test for `GetAirportByID` success

```
[TestMethod]
[DataRow(0)]
[DataRow(1)]          Uses the [DataRow] method
[DataRow(2)]          attribute to inline test data
[DataRow(3)]
public async Task GetAirportById_Success(int airportId) {       Retrieves the
  Airport airport = await _repository.GetAirportById(airportId);   matching
  Assert.IsNotNull(airport);                                       Airport (based
                                                                   on AirportId)
  Airport dbAirport =                                              from the
➡ _context.Airport.First(a => a.AirportId == airportId);  ◄──      database
  Assert.AreEqual(dbAirport.AirportId, airport.AirportId);  │  Asserts the retrieved
  Assert.AreEqual(dbAirport.City, airport.City);            │  Airport instance against
  Assert.AreEqual(dbAirport.Iata, airport.Iata);            │  the one in the database
}
```

We could also have created a hardcoded `Airport` instance, added that to the database in our test setup, and used it to check that the correct `Airport` was inserted. This approach is fine, but I prefer to query the in-memory database in every test. This is more explicit because you don't rely on some code done in a different spot to run the test you are looking at. All that is left for us to do before declaring the `AirportRepository` finished is to write a unit test for the database exception logic branch.

TESTING FOR A DATABASE EXCEPTION WITH A STUB

In this section, we'll test the logic branch where the database encounters an error during the call to `SaveChangesAsync`. To test the database exception logic path, we have to update FlyingDutchmanContext_Stub's overridden SaveChangesAsync method to perform a switch based on the airport's ID. If AirportID evaluates to anything other than 0, 1, 2, or 3 (because we used those values for AirportIds in the success test case), the stub throws an exception. How about we use an integer value of 10 for this, as shown in the next code sample? It's as good as any number.

Listing 9.8   Changing the stub's `SaveChangesAsync` to test `AirportRepository`

```
public override async Task<int> SaveChangesAsync(CancellationToken
➥ cancellationToken = default) {
  await base.SaveChangesAsync(cancellationToken);
➥ cancellationToken = default) {
  IEnumerable<EntityEntry> pendingChanges = ChangeTracker.Entries()
➥ .Where(e => e.State == EntityState.Added);
  IEnumerable<Booking> bookings = pendingChanges
➥ .Select(e => e.Entity).OfType<Booking>();
  if (bookings.Any(b => b.CustomerId != 1)) {
    throw new Exception("Database Error!");
  }

  IEnumerable<Airport> airports = pendingChanges          Switches expression
➥ .Select(e => e.Entity).OfType<Airport>();               based on AirportId
  if (!airports.Any(a => a.AirportId == 10)) {        ◄─    If AirportID is 10,
    throw new Exception("Database Error!");          ◄      throws an exception
  }
                                                          The default case: returns
  await base.SaveChangesAsync(cancellationToken);          out of the method
  return 1;
}
```

Now, for the unit test, let's create a new unit test method called GetAirportByID_ Failure_DatabaseException. Because the GetAirportByID method throws an exception of type AirportNotFoundException when a database error occurs, the unit test needs to expect this. We use our trusted [ExpectedException] method attribute for this as follows:

```
[TestMethod]
[ExpectedException(typeof(AirportNotFoundException))]
public async Task GetAirportByID_Failure_DatabaseException() {
  await repository.GetAirportByID(10);
}
```

The test should pass. And with that, we wrapped up AirportRepository. We have only one more to go before we implement the service layer.

9.6 *Implementing the Flight repository*

Although it may not seem like it, we are actually almost done with most of the heavy work required to implement the Flying Dutchman Airlines next-gen API for Fly-Tomorrow. Because we perform most of the logic in the repository layer classes, the services and controllers act more as pass-throughs and data combiners. The most complicated logic inside a codebase often finds itself inside the repository layer due to the inherent complexity of dealing with a database. In a repository/service pattern, after implementing all the repositories, you have the logic that manipulates the state of a model wrapped up. But we are not quite there yet: in this section, we'll implement the `FlightRepository` along with the appropriate unit tests.

Go ahead and create the skeleton classes of `FlightRepository` and `Flight-RepositoryTests`. As with `AirportRepository`, we need only one method in `Flight-Repository`: `GetFlightByFlightNumber`. Before continuing, please also create a barebones `GetFlightByFlightNumber` method in `FlightRepository`. If you get stuck, see chapters 6 and 7 for more detailed walk-throughs.

The `GetFlightByFlightNumber` method accepts the following three parameters of type `integer`:

- `flightNumber`
- `originAirportId`
- `destinationAirportId`

The `originAirportId` and `destinationAirportId` parameters signify the airports from which the flight departs (`originAirportId`) and arrives (`destinationAirportId`). The IDs of the airports are subject to a foreign key constraint in the database. This means that in a `Flight` instance, the `originAirportId` and `destinationAirportId` point to specific `Airport` instances in the database matched based on their IDs. All three input parameters need to be a non-negative integer. We could use only the flight number to identify the flight and not bother with the extra airport details. In order to teach you how to retrieve data by using foreign key constraints, we'll use and retrieve the airport IDs. Previously, in the `BookingRepository.CreateBooking` method, we defined a conditional code block that checked whether the input parameters of `customerID` and `flightNumber` were valid arguments matched against the same validation rule we have for `originAirportId` and `destinationAirportId` (they need to be positive integers) as follows:

```
public async Task CreateBooking (int customerID, int flightNumber) {
  if (customerID < 0 || flightNumber < 0) {
    Console.WriteLine($"Argument Exception in CreateBooking! CustomerID = {
  customerID}, flightNumber = { flightNumber}");
    throw new ArgumentException("invalid arguments provided");
  }
    ...
}
```

We can use this code for the input validation of the `originAirportId` and `destination-AirportId` parameters of `GetFlightByFlightNumber`. But we don't just want to copy and paste the code: that would be a violation of the DRY principle, and copying and pasting is just bad practice in general. Instead, we should extract the conditional into a method accessible to both the `BookingRepository` and the `FlightRepository`.

We could name the method IsPositive, have it take an integer as a parameter, check whether it is more than (or equal to) zero, and return that result. Then, we could instantiate a new instance of BookingRepository in FlightRepository and access the IsPositive method, as shown next:

```
public class BookingRepository  {
  ....

  internal bool IsPositive(int toTest) {
    return toTest >= 0;
  }
}


public class FlightRepository {
  public async Task<Flight> GetFlightByFlightNumber(int flightNumber, int
➥ originAirportId, int destinationAirportId) {
  BookingRepository bookingRepository = new BookingRepository(_context);
  if (!bookingRepository.IsPositive(originAirportId) ||
➥ !bookingRepository.IsPositive(destinationAirportId)) {
    ...
  }

  ...

}
```

This seems messy and is a good example of bad coupling. If FlightRepository makes a method call to BookingRepository, we banish them to a dependent and coexisting life. In that scenario, changing the BookingRepository may have unintended consequences in FlightRepository. Instead, we can create an extension method on the integer type that determines whether an integer is positive (more than or equal to 0).

9.6.1　*The IsPositive extension method and "magic numbers"*

First, we want to make sure we separate our extension method from other code. Let's create a new class called ExtensionMethods. We place this in the root of the Flying-DutchmanAirlines project, as shown in figure 9.8, because creating a special folder (also called ExtensionMethods) to contain a single class would be overkill (unless you expect multiple files in the respective folder in the future).

Our ExtensionMethods class can have an access modifier of internal because we are not writing a unit test specifically for the extension method. The internal access modifier is perfect for us in this case because we can scope the access to only the FlyingDutchmanAirlinesNextGen solution. The unit test coverage for the Extension-Methods class is implicit and done through unit tests that cover methods calling the respective extension method. The ExtensionMethods class should also be static because we want to use the same instance of the class across the codebase. There is no need to instantiate a new instance of ExtensionMethods every time we want to check if an integer is positive, nor does the extension method we write change any object

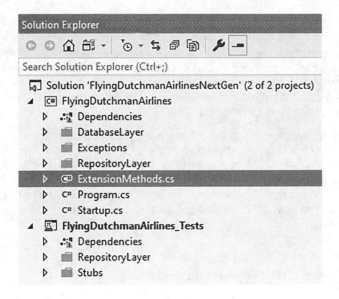

Figure 9.8 The `Extension-Methods` class is placed at the root of the FlyingDutchmanAirlines project. `ExtensionMethods` are not an architectural layer, nor will we have more than one of them, so leaving the class in the root is fine.

states. Previously, I held a diatribe about the pitfalls of using `static`. A class meant to wrap a collection of `ExtensionMethods` is supposed to be static, as shown here:

```
internal static class ExtensionMethods { }
```

To create an extension method, as discussed in section 6.3.2, we use the `this` keyword followed by the type we want to create an extension method for as part of the parameter list. You can create extension methods for any type (interfaces, classes, primitive types) as follows:

```
internal static bool IsPositive(this int input) { }
```

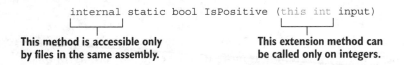

internal static bool IsPositive (this int input)

This method is accessible only by files in the same assembly.   **This extension method can be called only on integers.**

Within the scope of the `FlyingDutchmanAirlinesNextGen` project (because of `ExtensionMethods` and `IsPositive`'s internal access modifier), we can now call the `IsPositive` on *every* instance of type `integer`, as shown in figure 9.9.

Compiling extension methods

Extension methods sound great, but how are they executed? The call to the `IsPositive` extension method is resolved by the compiler at compile time. When the compiler encounters the `IsPositive` method call, it first checks if a method exists within the

(continued)

scope of the calling class. If not, which is the case we find ourselves in, the compiler checks for any public `static` methods in static classes with the same name. If a found `static` method also operates on the correct type (by using the `this` keyword in the method's parameter list), the compiler has found a match and generates the Intermediate Language code that calls the method.

Do note that, as with any method, if you have two extension methods with the same name and operating type but in different classes, the compiler cannot resolve which one to call. When this happens, the compiler throws an ambiguity compiler error: "CS0121 The call is ambiguous between the following methods or properties [*method/ property 1*] and [*method/property 2*]." To resolve an ambiguity error, you need to give the compiler enough information so it can determine which method to call.

Figure 9.9   The `IsPositive` extension method is available to all integers. For example, `airportID` can call the `IsPositive` method.

As far as the actual logic inside the `IsPositive` method goes, all we have to do is return whether the input argument is more than or equal to zero as follows:

```
internal static bool IsPositive(this int input) => input >= 0;
```

Nice and simple. You just wrote your first extension method!

We have a little cleanup to do before we move on. We need to remove the conditional code block that validates the input arguments to the `BookingRepository` `.CreateBooking` method, replacing it with a call to our brand-new `IsPositive` extension method. In the input validation code, we have to negate the call to `IsPositive`, as shown next, because we want to know when the input argument is *not* a positive integer.

```
public async Task CreateBooking(int customerID, int flightNumber) {

    if (customerID < 0 || flightNumber < 0)
    if (!customerID.IsPositive() || !flightNumber.IsPositive()) {
        Console.WriteLine($"Argument Exception in CreateBooking! CustomerID
        = { customerID}, flightNumber = { flightNumber}");
        throw new ArgumentException("invalid arguments provided");
    }
    ...
}
```

An identical conditional in `AirportRepository.GetAirportByID` remains that I leave for you to remove and replace. Not only do we now adhere to the DRY principle, but the calls to the `IsPositive` extension method are more readable than checking whether something is more than or equal to zero. A new developer would not intuitively know why we are checking whether something is more than zero. A random hardcoded number like that is what we call a "magic number." By writing code that is explicit and doesn't use a magic number, any developer can see that we are checking whether `customerID` and `flightNumber` are *not* positive integers.

Magic numbers

Suppose we are writing code to handle the steering of a car. Imagine what a method to move a car forward looks like. Have a look at the following code block. Is there anything wrong with it?

```
public double MoveCarForward(double direction) {
    if (direction == 0 || direction == 360) {
        GoStraight();
    }

    if (direction > 0 && direction <= 90) {
        GoEast();
    }

    if (direction >= 270 && direction < 360) {
        GoWest();
    }
}
```

The `MoveCarForward` method has the following two interesting aspects:

- First, we know we can use a switch or `switch` expressions to condense this code a bit, but we'll let that one go. We just want to clean up the code with minimal destruction of the existing pattern.
- Second, the code determines the direction the car moves in by comparing the direction input argument against predefined numbers. The numbers represent cardinal points in degrees as mapped out on a unit circle. That is not clear from the current code unless you have that knowledge. Numbers that appear randomly in code, hardcoded and without context, are what we call magic numbers.

(continued)

These numbers (0, 90, 270, and 360) are meaningless unless we know the context of what they should represent. We can do better than that.

When hardcoding numbers like that, you risk a developer unfamiliar with your intentions changing the number to "fix" something. If you had provided more context around what they represent, the code would be more readable, and the developer would likely not have touched their values. To do this, I suggest extracting the numbers into private constants. The value of a constant is defined at compile time and cannot change at run time. This ensures that the value never changes from what you defined it to be.

With `MoveCarForward`, we can isolate four potential constants: `DEGREES_NORTH_LOWER_BOUND`, `DEGREES_NORTH_UPPER_BOUND`, `DEGREES_WEST`, and `DEGREES_EAST`. It is my preference to always use snake casing (all letters are uppercase and punctuation, including spaces, are replaced by underscores) for constants, as shown next. This clarifies that a given variable has an immutable, predefined value.

```
private const int DEGREES_NORTH_LOWER_BOUND = 0;
private const int DEGREES_NORTH_UPPER_BOUND = 360;
private const int DEGREES_WEST = 270;
private const int DEGREES_EAST = 90

public double MoveCarForward(double direction) {
    if (direction == DEGREES_NORTH_UPPER_BOUND || direction ==
    DEGREES_NORTH_LOWER_BOUND){
        GoStraight();
    }

    if (direction > DEGREES_NORTH_LOWER_BOUND && direction <=
    DEGREES_EAST){
        GoEast();
    }

    if (direction >= DEGREES_WEST && direction <
    DEGREES_NORTH_UPPER_BOUND)){
        GoWest();
    }
}
```

This code is much more readable. We know now exactly what the magic numbers represent. In fact, there are no magic numbers anymore. Whenever you see a hardcoded numerical representation of anything, ask yourself, should I refactor this magic number to a constant or a local variable?

Of course, we need to run the unit tests for `BookingRepository` before we move on. I advise running every unit test in your test suite every time you make a change instead of limiting yourself to the tests in just the file you are messing with. Luckily, they pass. This is good because the only thing we did so far was extract existing logic into an extension method.

Let's use our new extension method to validate the originAirportId and destinationAirportId input arguments in FlightRepository.GetFlightByFlight-Number, as shown in the next listing. In case one of the input arguments is invalid, we throw an exception of type ArgumentException and log a message to the console.

Listing 9.9 GetFlightByFlightNumber **airport** Ids **input validation**

```
public class FlightRepository {
    public async Task<Flight> GetFlightByFlightNumber(int flightNumber,
    int originAirportId, int destinationAirportId) {
        if (!originAirportId.IsPositive() ||             Calls the extension
        !destinationAirportId.IsPositive())) {          method to validate
            Console.WriteLine($"Argument Exception in    the input arguments
        GetFlightByFlightNumber! originAirportId = {originAirportId} :
        destinationAirportId = {destinationAirportId}");    Logs the
            throw new ArgumentException("invalid arguments provided");  invalid
        }                                                               arguments
                          Returns a temporary         Throws an        to the
                          new instance of             ArgumentException console
        return new Flight();  Flight. We'll change     if the input is invalid
    }                     this implementation
}                         in section 9.6.2.
```

To prove our code works as expected, we create the next two unit tests:

- GetFlightByFlightnumber_Failure_InvalidOriginAirport
- GetFlightByFlightnumber_Failure_InvalidDestinationAirport

Both the unit tests should verify that the GetFlightByFlightNumber method throws an exception of type FlightNotFoundException during execution of the respective test as follows:

```
[TestMethod]
[ExpectedException(typeof(ArgumentException))]
public async Task GetFlightByFlightNumber_Failure_InvalidOriginAirportId(){
    await _repository.GetFlightByFlightNumber(0, -1, 0);
}

[TestMethod]
[ExpectedException(typeof(ArgumentException))]
public async Task
GetFlightByFlightNumber_Failure_InvalidDestinationAirportId(){
    await _repository.GetFlightByFlightNumber(0, 0, -1);
}
```

That takes care of the input validation for the originAirportId and destination-AirportId input arguments. But what about flightNumber? We can quickly add a conditional to check whether flightNumber is a positive integer. If flightNumber is not a positive integer, we want to log a message to the console and throw an error of our new exception type (I leave this for you to implement) called FlightNotFound-Exception as follows:

```
if (flightNumber < 0) {
  Console.WriteLine($"Could not find flight in GetFlightByFlightNumber!
  flightNumber = {flightNumber}");
  throw new FlightNotFoundException();
}
```

We also need a unit test to prove that the GetFlightByFlightnumber method throws an error of exception FlightNotFoundException when flightNumber is an invalid input argument, as shown here:

```
[TestMethod]
[ExpectedException(typeof(FlightNotFoundException))]
public async Task GetFlightByFlightNumber_Failure_InvalidFlightNumber() {
  await _repository.GetFlightByFlightNumber(-1, 0, 0);
}
```

9.6.2 *Getting a flight out of the database*

Let's recap what we have done so far with the FlightRepository and Flight-RepositoryTests classes. In the previous sections, we created and partially implemented a GetFlightByFlightNumber method in the FlightRepository class. The GetFlight-ByFlightNumber method currently performs input validation on the input if arguments (flightNumber, originAirportId, and destinationAirportID) and returns a placeholder Flight instance. We also created three unit tests in the FlightRepository-Tests class that check the input validations for their invalid input argument cases.

In this section, we implement the actual logic to retrieve a Flight instance from the database given its flight number. To do this, we take the same approach as we have done so many times before. We query the database's DbSet<Flight> for the matching flight. If the database throws an exception, we log the problem to the console with a developer-friendly message and throw a new exception. If all goes well, we return the found object of type Flight. But first, let's create the success case unit test and success setup code in TestInitialize shown next.

Listing 9.10 Testing GetFlight

```
[TestInitialize]
public async Task TestInitialize() {
  DbContextOptions<FlyingDutchmanAirlinesContext> dbContextOptions = new
  DbContextOptionsBuilder<FlyingDutchmanAirlinesContext>().UseInMemoryDat
  abase("FlyingDutchman").Options;
  _context = new FlyingDutchmanAirlinesContext_Stub(dbContextOptions);    ⟵

  Flight flight = new Flight {
  FlightNumber = 1,
    Origin = 1,
    Destination = 2
  };

  context.Flight.Add(flight);    ⟵
```

Creates and populates an instance of Flight

Adds the flight object to the EF Core's internal DbSet<Flight>

```
                                                                    Saves the flight to
    await _context.SaveChangesAsync();                              the in-memory
                                                                    database
    _repository = new FlightRepository(_context);
    Assert.IsNotNull(_repository);
}

                                                                            Executes
[TestMethod]                                                    GetFlightByFlightNumber
public async Task GetFlightByFlightNumber_Success() {
    Flight flight = await _repository.GetFlightByFlightNumber(1, 1, 2);   ⟵
    Assert.IsNotNull(flight);

    Flight dbFlight = _context.Flight.First(f => f.FlightNumber == 1);
    Assert.IsNotNull(dbFlight);
                                                                    Compares
                                                                    the flight from
    Assert.AreEqual(dbFlight.FlightNumber, flight.FlightNumber);     GetFlightByFlight-
    Assert.AreEqual(dbFlight.Origin, flight.Origin);                Number against
    Assert.AreEqual(dbFlight.Destination, flight.Destination);       the database's
}                                                                   flight
```

Gets the flight from the database

The `GetFlightByFlightNumber_Success` unit test fails because we are returning a temporary new (empty) instance of `Flight` in `GetFlightByFlightNumber`. We should change that to return the first match in the database when given the `flightNumber`. We can use the same pattern for returning a database entity we used in `Airport-Repository.GetAirportByID`: use a LINQ `FirstOrDefaultAsync` call to select an entity or return a default value (null in this case), followed by the null-coalescing operator, which throws an exception in case of null, as shown next:

```
public async Task<Flight> GetFlightByFlightNumber(int flightNumber,
⇥ int originAirportId, int destinationAirportId) {
    if (flightNumber < 0) {
    Console.WriteLine($"Could not find flight in GetFlightByFlightNumber!
⇥ flightNumber = {flightNumber}");
    throw new FlightNotFoundException();
}

    if (!originAirportId.IsPositive() ||
⇥ !destinationAirportId.IsPositive()) {
        Console.WriteLine($"Argument Exception in GetFlightByFlightNumber!
⇥ originAirportId = {originAirportId} : destinationAirportId =
⇥ {destinationAirportId}");
        throw new ArgumentException("invalid arguments provided");
    }

    return await _context.Flight.FirstOrDefaultAsync(f =>
⇥ f.FlightNumber == flightNumber) ?? throw new FlightNotFoundException();
}
```

This code either returns the correct instance of `Airport` as found in the database or throws an exception of type `AirportNotFoundException`. But who is to believe us without seeing the success case unit test pass and having a failure case unit test ready as well? Well, fear no more. With this code change, the `GetFlightByFlightNumber_Success` unit test passes.

All that is left for us to do before we wrap up both the `FlightRepository` and this chapter is to create a unit test that proves the `GetFlightByFlightNumber` method exception of type `FlightNotFoundException` if the input arguments of `flightNumber`, `originAirportId`, and `destinationAirportId` are correct but a database error threw an exception, as shown next. We have done this a couple of times by now, so if you want to give it a shot on your own before looking at the code: go ahead, I'll wait.

```
[TestMethod]
[ExpectedException(typeof(FlightNotFoundException))]
public async Task GetFlightByFlightNumber_Failure_DatabaseException() {
  await _repository.GetFlightByFlightNumber(2, 1, 2);
}
```

And voilà! There it is: one finished `FlightRepository`. We now have the following four repositories in our `FlyingDutchmanAirlinesNextGen` codebase:

- `AirportRepository`
- `BookingRepository`
- `CustomerRepository`
- `FlightRepository`

That means we wrapped up the repository portion of the refactor. In the next chapter, we'll go up one level in our architecture and implement the service layer. But here is the excellent news: we have completed the heavy lifting. Implementing the repository methods first guarantees usable and small methods that do only one thing (and do them well). This helps us in the service layer, where we can say "give me A, B, and C" and have methods that do each of those operations without side effects.

Exercises

EXERCISE 9.1
In test-driven development, the red stage means that

- a Your code compiles and the test passes.
- b Your code does not compile or/and the test does not pass.

EXERCISE 9.2
In test-driven development, the green stage means that

- a Your code compiles and the test passes.
- b Your code does not compile or/and the test does not pass.

EXERCISE 9.3
True or false? You cannot use the `[DataRow]` attribute if you have only one data point to test with.

EXERCISE 9.4

Data streams usually store their data as a sequence of what?

a Slow-moving water that ripples through the landscape

b Bytes

EXERCISE 9.5

True or false? Classes that do not have any derived classes are implicitly abstract.

EXERCISE 9.6

True or false? Every method in an abstract class also needs to be abstract.

EXERCISE 9.7

True or false? An abstract method can live in a nonabstract class.

EXERCISE 9.8

True or false? Abstract methods cannot contain a method body. They are supposed to be overridden by derived classes.

Summary

- The abstract class Stream is used as the base for many derived classes such as StringWriter and TextReader. We can use streams to deal with continuous streams of data such as strings or integers.

- We can redirect the console output to an instance of type StringWriter. This is helpful when testing console output because we can retrieve the contents of a StringWriter and check for the expected logged data.

- An abstract class is a class with the abstract keyword attached. Abstract classes cannot be instantiated or be static. Abstract classes support methods with bodies (given the methods are not abstract). They are often used as base classes to provide identical implementations of specific methods to all derived classes.

- The LINQ AddRange method allows us to add the contents of one collection (or "range" of objects) to another collection. This saves a lot of manual typing and iterating over collections.

- A SortedList<T> is a generic collection that automatically sorts the input data. SortedLists are useful for when you need to have a sorted collection and do not want to perform manual sorting.

- Extension methods are static methods that extend the functionality of the type they perform operations on. Extension methods are often used to execute commonly used functionality on primitive types. This means that extension methods are often useful in fixing DRY principle violations.

- Magic numbers are hardcoded values that have no additional context attached to them. You often find them in algorithms or conditionals. When seeing a hardcoded number with no explanation, it is often hard to figure out what it represents. Consider refactoring it out into a local variable of a class-level constant.

Part 5

The service layer

In part 4, we looked at the repository layer and implemented its classes. We touched on concepts like asynchronous programming, dependency injection, coupling, stubbing, streams, and more. In this part, we go up one architectural layer and implement the service layer classes. These chapters discuss (among other things) reflection, mocks, `yield return`, and error handling.

Reflection and mocks

This chapter covers

- A refresher on using the repository/service pattern and views
- Testing with mocks using the Moq library
- Detecting coupling in multilayered testing architectures
- Using preprocessor directives
- Using reflection to retrieve assembly information at run time

In chapters 6 through 9, we implemented the repository layer of our Flying-DutchmanAirlinesNextGen project. In this chapter, we'll refresh our knowledge of the repository/service pattern and implement (partially) two of the four following required service classes:

- CustomerService (implemented in this chapter)
- BookingService (implemented in this chapter and chapter 11)
- AirportService (implemented in chapter 12)
- FlightService (implemented in chapter 12)

Figure 10.1 shows where we are in the scheme of the book.

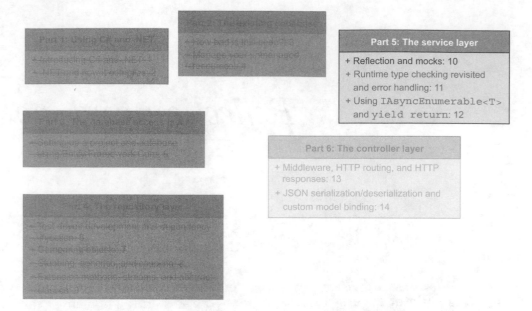

Part 5: The service layer

+ Reflection and mocks: 10
+ Runtime type checking revisited
  and error handling: 11
+ Using IAsyncEnumerable<T>
  and yield return: 12

Part 6: The controller layer

+ Middleware, HTTP routing, and HTTP
  responses: 13
+ JSON serialization/deserialization and
  custom model binding: 14

Figure 10.1 This chapter is the start of the service layer implementation. We'll implement CustomerService and BookingService in this chapter. In the following chapters, we'll implement AirportService and FlightService.

As you may have guessed, as with the repository classes, we want one service class per database entity. We'll discuss why in section 10.1, followed by the CustomerService implementation in section 10.2 and the start of the BookingService implementation in section 10.3.

Throughout the next couple of chapters, the speed of implementation increases once we get used to implementing a service class. Section by section, I take a more hands-off approach, leaving more and more implementation details for you to code. If you ever get stuck, you can always look back at the appropriate section for more details.

10.1 *The repository/service pattern revisited*

In section 5.2.4, we discussed the repository/service pattern. I showed you how, in a repository/service pattern, for every database entity (Customer, Booking, Airport, Flight) we have the following:

- Controller
- Service
- Repository

These controllers, services, and repositories sit atop a single database access layer, which we implemented in chapter 5. The request life cycle in our repository/service pattern, shown in figure 10.2, sees an HTTP request enter a controller. The controller

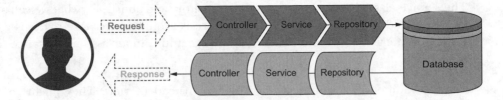

Figure 10.2   The controller-service-repository life cycle. When a request enters, it goes to the controller. The controller calls a service, which calls one or more repositories. Data flows down from the controller and back up from the repository.

calls its respective entity's service class. The entity's service class calls whichever repository classes it needs to deal with, organizing the information it needs to return to the user. The service class returns to the controller, who in turn returns all data to the user.

In chapters 5 through 9, we implemented the repositories required for our architecture. Now it's time to do the same for the services. Because a service is merely the middleman between the repository and controller, services are fairly light in complexity. Don't be mistaken, however: the service layer is perhaps the most important layer of all. Without it, we would have no abstraction layer dealing with how we want to represent data to the customer. A service class calls a collection of repository methods and returns a view of the data to the controller. A service class serves the controller with data.

10.1.1   *What is the use of a service class?*

In the United States, to buy a car you have to navigate a myriad of eager salespeople, followed by hours of paperwork. Experiences at car dealerships are often an example of bad service. When looking at software architecture, we can also see bad service in service classes. If a service class returns things to the controller the user did not ask for, we have an example of bad service on our hands.

For example, let's imagine we are developing an API for a car dealership. The dealership wants to display any car from their inventory to the user, withhold some of the more valuable information, such as the true value of the car (usually much less than the price they are asking). Whether withholding information for corporate gain is bad service depends on who you are. If you are the car dealership, this sounds very reasonable. If you are a buyer, you want as much information as possible. So how would you implement such an API?

An API to return car information consists of the following usual suspects:

- A controller accepting HTTP GET requests when given a specific car's ID
- A service layer that retrieves information from repositories and presents them to the controller
- A repository that collects car instances from the database

The service class calls methods from the repository and constructs what we call a view. We discussed views in section 3.3.2, but here is a quick refresher: a view is a "window" into a class. Views allow us to manipulate and spin a class's appearance to suit our needs.

> **NOTE** Sometimes people say ReturnView instead of view. They mean the same thing and you can use them interchangeably. This book tries to stick with view.

A view of a Car class may contain information such as the VIN, the make of the car, the year the car was built, and the model of the car, as shown in figure 10.3. But because it is just a "window" into the model, we can choose not to display the true value of the car or the total number of crashes it has seen in the last six months, in our view.

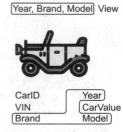

Year, Brand, Model View

CarID   Year
VIN   CarValue
Brand   Model

Figure 10.3   A view is a collection of elements taken from one or multiple models, presented in a way that makes sense for the user. In this example, we took the Year, Brand, and Model properties from the Car class.

A service class may also trace down foreign key constraints, retrieving information where needed to compile a full image of the required data. We see foreign key constraints in action throughout this book. We'll also take another, deeper dive into the world of unit testing. Yes, dear reader: this chapter sees us using test-driven development once again, but this time, we'll use TDD combined with a new testing concept: mocks.

Exercises

Exercise 10.1
In a repository/service pattern, what is the correct data flow for an incoming request?

  a Repository -> service -> controller
  b Controller -> service -> repository

Exercise 10.2
True or false? A service class (in a repository/service pattern) typically directly interacts with a database.

Exercise 10.3
True or false? When using a view, we can return a unified presentation of multiple different data sources.

EXERCISE 10.4

True or false? People often use view and ReturnView interchangeably to refer to the same concept.

10.2 Implementing the CustomerService

Are you ready to implement your first service? In this section, we'll implement the CustomerService class. This class allows us to funnel information to and from a controller and the CustomerRepository.

10.2.1 Setting up for success: Creating skeleton classes

What is the first thing we should do when starting work on a new class? Right, create an accompanying unit test class. I do not show you how to create a test class this time; just make sure you create one with a public access modifier and with a TestInitialize method (no need to add anything to the TestInitialize method for now). Also, to keep things somewhat organized, let's mimic the folder structure we followed with the repository test classes and create a ServiceLayer folder in the FlyingDutchman-Airlines_Tests project, as shown in figure 10.4.

Figure 10.4 The CustomerServiceTests file lives in the ServiceLayer folder inside the FlyingDutchmanAirlines_Tests project.

Before we can create a success case unit test, we need to figure out what methods we need in the CustomerService class. You may recall that in chapter 7 we implemented the following two methods in CustomerRepository:

- CreateCustomer
- GetCustomerByName

Should we mimic those method names in the CustomerService class? Well, yes, to an extent. If we maintain an isomorphic relationship between method names in the repository and the service, it makes our code more readable because we build up certain expectations. If a developer sees a method called GetCombineHarvester in both a service and repository class, the developer expects the service version of the Get-CombineHarvester method to call the repository version of the same method. Let's not let down the intuition of our fellow developers. Of course, a service method may call multiple repository methods, so pick the one that best reflects your intentions.

 NAMING SERVICE LAYER METHODS When deciding on a name for your service layer method, consider naming the method the same as the main repository layer method you call. This helps build intuition and makes your code more navigable.

That being said, no controller calls the `CreateCustomer` or `GetCustomerByName` methods directly. Instead, the only interaction we ever have with the `Customer` entity is through other services. How do we know a controller will not call a service directly? In figure 10.5, we see the following three required endpoints as laid out by the contract between Flying Dutchman Airlines and FlyTomorrow (discussed in sections 3.1 and 3.2):

- `GET /Flight`
- `GET /Flight/{FlightNumber}`
- `POST /Booking/{FlightNumber}`

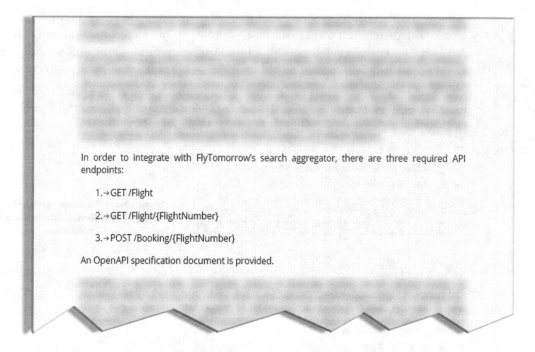

In order to integrate with FlyTomorrow's search aggregator, there are three required API endpoints:

1.→GET /Flight

2.→GET /Flight/{FlightNumber}

3.→POST /Booking/{FlightNumber}

An OpenAPI specification document is provided.

Figure 10.5   The three endpoints required by FlyTomorrow as discussed in chapter 3. There are two GET endpoints and one POST endpoint.

None of those endpoints interacts directly with the `Customer` entity. The word "customer" does not show up either in an endpoint path or as a path parameter. I am proposing something quite radical: if no controller ever calls a service, we do not need said service. In fact, we can go as far as saying that we do not need a controller for that entity, either. It would never get called anyway. In other words, we do not need a `CustomerService`, nor do we need a `CustomerController`. Well, that really opens up our day, doesn't it? I always appreciate less work.

10.2.2 *How to delete your own code*

At this point, I ask you to do something that may end up being the highlight of your day: deleting code. I'm quite serious about that. If deleting code makes you uneasy, this section is for you. I want you to view deleting code as a Zen-filled experience. Allowing yourself to delete your own code when you find an alternative approach (that works better) is a key skill for a developer and is harder than you think.

In section 10.2.1, we created the following two classes:

- `CustomerService`
- `CustomerServiceTests`

The `CustomerServiceTests` class contains an unimplemented `TestInitialize` method. We also determined that we don't need the `CustomerService` and `CustomerService-Tests` classes because they would never be called by a controller. In the real world, I am unequivocally in favor of deleting code that needs to go. Think about empty classes, commented-out code, and incorrect implementations. If you are worried about breaking existing code (and you should be), then I hope you have a full suite of tests you can rely on to verify the correctness of your refactoring. You should also use a source control system so you can revert to a previous state if the deletion of code has unexpected side effects (you should *always* use a source control system).

Deleting code

Deleting code is scary. A commonly used phrase for hesitation to delete your own work is "kill your darlings." Often, however, to deliver the best work possible, you have to swallow your pride and delete your own (usually beautiful and elegant) code. If you delete your code in favor of a better implementation, it is not defeat—quite the opposite, it is a win. Even if you did not write the new implementation yourself, you should consider this to be a positive change. The fresh approach is undoubtedly more readable and maintainable, saving yourself (and others) a lot of heartache down the road.

I want to draw your attention to a special case where you should be merciless in deleting code, both of your own design and of others: commented-out code. I'm going to say it, and I bet some of you disagree with me: commented-out code has no place in a production codebase. Period. You do *not* merge commented-out code into the main branch. Think about why the code is commented out in the first place. Is it something that is an alternative approach to a solution? Is it an old implementation? Is it a half-assed new implementation? Is it something that you might need in the future (unlikely)? In my humble opinion, those reasons are not good enough to warrant you spoiling my beautiful codebase with an ugly block of commented-out code. If you want commented-out code in the codebase, you can either make it work (and uncommented it), or you must not need it that badly.

For example, the following code block contains a method with an implementation but has a comment with a different implementation:

(continued)

```
// This code is too complicated! There is a better way.
// public bool ToggleLight() => _light = !_light;

public bit ToggleLight() => _light ^= 1;
```

Now, the comment in the code has a valid point. The IsToggleLight method running uses a bitwise XOR operator to flip the _light bit. The implementation in the comment may be easier to read, indeed. It also comes with some unknowns, however, because it changes the return type of the ToggleLight method and the underlying type of _light (both from bit to bool), but we could deal with that. Why was this code never uncommented or implemented, though? Did it not pass code review? Does it not work? Is this a passive-aggressive "for future reference" comment by a disgruntled senior engineer or a new developer trying to impress somebody? It doesn't matter.

So, grab your favorite destructive way to delete something (virtually; don't go using a jackhammer on your laptop—the publisher and I are not liable for your regrettable life choices). I am partial to the good old command-line remove command shown in figure 10.6: del /f [file] in Windows and rm -rf [file] in macOS.

```
Microsoft Windows [Version 10.0.18363.836]
(c) 2019 Microsoft Corporation. All rights reserved.

C:\Users\Jort\Documents\rodenburg\code\Chapter 10\FlyingDutchmanAirlines\ServiceLayer>
del /f CustomerService.cs
```

Figure 10.6   To delete a file in the Windows command line, use the del /f [FilePath] syntax. Feeling a surge of power and yelping "by the power of the gods!" is optional.

There, didn't that feel powerful? I sure got a boost out of it, but that might tell you more about me than necessary. Let's move on and do some actual work, shall we?

Exercises

EXERCISE 10.5

Why do we want to use the same name for a service class method name as the repository method it calls?

- a This establishes an isomorphic relationship between the two methods and helps create valid expectations for other developers.
- b We don't want to do that. The code would not compile if the service and repository classes contained methods with the same name.
- c We do want to do that, but only if there is a verb in the method name.

EXERCISE 10.6

You encounter a commented-out line of code that seems to indicate an alternative approach to the currently running code. What do you do?

- **a** Leave it be. It is not your problem.
- **b** Ask for clarification by adding questions to the original comment.
- **c** Figure out why it is there, and, in most cases, delete the commented-out code.

EXERCISE 10.7

What does the ^ operator represent?

- **a** A logical OR operation
- **b** A logical AND operation
- **c** A logical NAND operation
- **d** A logical XOR operation

EXERCISE 10.8

What is the effect of using the ^= operator on a Boolean value?

- **a** The Boolean value flips (`true` becomes `false`, `false` becomes `true`).
- **b** Nothing (`true` stays `true`, `false` stays `false`).
- **c** The Boolean value flips twice (`true` stays `true`, `false` stays `false`).

10.3 Implementing the BookingService

After the refresher of the repository/service pattern in section 10.1 and the false start to implementing an actual service class in section 10.2, we are finally at the point where we start work on an actual service class—no joke this time. In this section, we'll implement a service for the `Booking` entity.

When we discussed the need for service classes in section 10.2, we talked about not needing a dedicated service layer if no controller class is ever going to call the respective service. This is some good advice, even if I say so myself, so let's repeat that exercise for the `BookingService` class. Is there an API endpoint that needs to use the `Booking` entity directly? Well, let's look at the following three required endpoints per the FlyTomorrow contract again:

- `GET /Flight`
- `GET /Flight/{FlightNumber}`
- `POST /Booking/{FlightNumber}`

The `POST /Booking/{FlightNumber}` endpoint directly deals with the `Booking` entity, as is evident from the path. FlyTomorrow uses the `POST` endpoint to create a new booking in the database. And because we need to have a `BookingController` to accept the HTTP request, it stands to reason that we should call a `BookingService` from that controller. Remember that a service layer's goal is to collect and organize data from repositories. So, to create a booking, a controller calls a method in the `BookingService` class, which calls the needed repositories to perform its promised duty, as shown in figure 10.7.

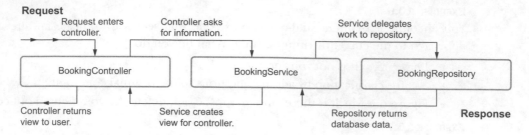

Figure 10.7   The life cycle of the `Booking` **entity. A request is handled through the** `BookingController` **(not yet written), which calls the** `BookingService`**, which calls the** `BookingRepository`**. Then, the path is walked back to the caller.**

By thinking about what functionality the `BookingService` should provide, we can come up with the method needed to create a new booking: an asynchronous `public` method that calls the `BookingRepository.CreateBooking` and returns the appropriate information to a controller. Here, the appropriate information could be a `Task<(bool, Exception)>` representing that the `CreateBooking` method has executed and completed. If the booking was unsuccessful, we get a false Boolean along with the exception that the `CreateBooking` method threw: `(false, thrownException)`. If the booking was successful, we return a `true` Boolean and a null pointer (if you enabled nullable reference types, you may have to make `Exception` a nullable type by postfixing a question mark character: `Exception?`). If you don't want to define a Boolean return, you could alternatively rely on `Task`'s internal `IsCompleted` bool.

We should also look at the database schema (figure 10.8). The `Booking` model has the following two foreign key constraints:

- An outgoing foreign key constraint to `Customer.CustomerID`
- An outgoing foreign key constraint to `Flight.FlightNumber`

As part of our input validation, we should check whether the passed-in values representing `CustomerID` and `FlightNumber` are valid. We validate the values passed in by calling the appropriate repository's methods (in this case, `CustomerRepository.Get-CustomerByID` and `FlightRepository.GetFlightByFlightNumber`). Validating the input arguments also begs the question: what do we do if the passed-in `CustomerID` or `FlightID` does not exist in the database? If the customer does not exist in the database, that means they have not booked a flight with Flying Dutchman Airlines before. We don't want to lose any customers (and, therefore, revenue), so we call the `Customer-Repository.CreateCustomer` method (implemented in chapter 11). If a flight does not exist, the booking is unsuccessful because we do not have the authority to add a new flight whenever we want.

We will call our method `CreateBooking`, because that is what we do in the method, and require two integers for input parameters (`customerID` and `flightNumber`). To call the `BookingRepository.CreateBooking` method, we first need to instantiate an

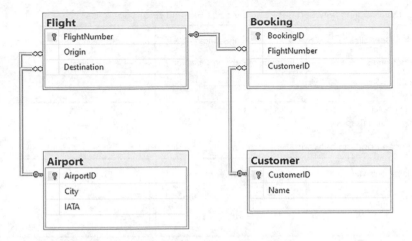

Figure 10.8 The Flying Dutchman Airlines database schema. The Booking model has two outgoing foreign key constraints: one to `Customer.CustomerID` **and one to** `Flight.FlightNumber`.

instance of type `BookingRepository`. If you remember, when we implemented `Booking-Repository` in chapter 8, we required an instance of `FlyingDutchmanAirlinesContext` in the repository's constructor. This was so we could "inject" the dependency and not worry about how it gets instantiated. Well, we have to worry about that now because we want to instantiate a `BookingRepository` and need to pass in the required `Flying-DutchmanAirlinesContext` dependency. Maybe we can kick the can a little further down the road instead. If we require the injection of an instance of `BookingRepository` into the constructor of `BookingService`, as shown in the next listing, our problem is solved . . . for now.

Listing 10.1 Injecting `BookingRepository` into `BookingService`

```
public class BookingService {
  private readonly BookingRepository _repository;          The backing field for
                                                           the injected instance

  public BookingService(BookingRepository repository) {    Injects an
    _repository = repository;          We can assign       instance of
  }                                     readonly fields only BookingRepository
}                                       in a constructor
```

So, where do we get this instance of `BookingRepository` from at runtime? We may not want the controller layer to mess with instantiating it because that would couple the repository layer to the controller layer. This sounds to me like unwanted tight coupling because the repository layer is already coupled to the service layer, and the service layer is coupled to the controller layer, as shown in figure 10.9.

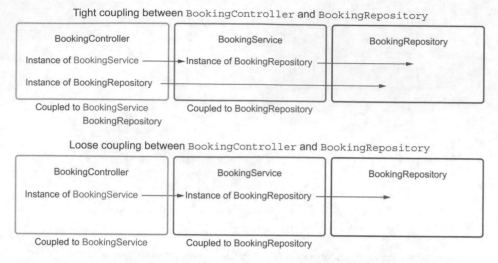

Figure 10.9   If we have an instance of `BookingRepository` **inside** `BookingController`, **we have a tight coupling between the two classes. If** `BookingController` **indirectly calls** `BookingRepository` **through** `BookingService`, **we have loose(r) coupling.**

How do we avoid having to create an instance of `BookingRepository` in the controller without losing the ability to create and use an instance of `BookingService`? The answer lies in plain sight: dependency injection. When we get to the controller layer, we inject an instance of `BookingService` into the `BookingController`. How this `BookingService` is instantiated is a mystery I leave for you to ponder (we'll discuss how to set up dependency injection at service launch in chapter 13). For now, it suffices to understand the basics of dependency injection and how we use it in conjunction with `BookingService`. The `BookingService` should also have an injected instance of type `CustomerRepository` so we can get customer details before booking them on a flight. I leave this for you to do. If you get stuck, follow the preceding paragraphs. Of course, you may want to rename the _repository variable to something along the lines of _bookingRepository before injecting the `CustomerRepository` type, but that is up to you. Think about what you would most like to see. What is most readable?

Before we continue with the actual implementation of the `BookingService.Create-Booking` method, we should create the backing unit test—we should at least attempt to adhere to test-driven development practices. If you have not done so already, create a skeleton test file (in a folder called ServiceLayer) called `BookingServiceTests` in the FlyingDutchmanAirlines_Tests project, as shown in figure 10.10.

To start our unit test, create a unit test method called `CreateBooking_Success` that instantiates a `BookingService` and calls the (still imaginary) `CreateBooking` method as shown next.

Figure 10.10 The BookingServiceTests file lives in the ServiceLayer folder inside the FlyingDutchmanAirlines_Tests project.

Listing 10.2 A skeleton `CreateBooking_Success` unit test

```
[TestClass]
public class BookingServiceTests {
  private FlyingDutchmanAirlinesContext _context;

  [TestInitialize]
  public void TestInitialize() {
  DbContextOptions<FlyingDutchmanAirlinesContext> dbContextOptions = new
  DbContextOptionsBuilder<FlyingDutchmanAirlinesContext>()
  .UseInMemoryDatabase("FlyingDutchman").Options;

  _context = new FlyingDutchmanAirlinesContext_Stub(dbContextOptions);
  }

  [TestMethod]
  public async Task CreateBooking_Success() {
  BookingRepository repository = new BookingRepository(_context);
  BookingService service = new BookingService(repository);
  (bool result, Exception exception) =
  await service.CreateBooking("Leo Tolstoy", 0);
  }
}
```

Sets up an in-memory database

Creates a BookingRepository instance, injecting the database context

Creates a BookingService instance, injecting the BookingRepository instance

On the surface, it seems we just have to deal with the inevitable compilation error saying that the compiler cannot find the CreateBooking method in BookingService. We expected that error and can deal with it: add a skeleton method called CreateBooking in the BookingService class. We'll have the CreateBooking method accept two parameters: an integer containing the customer name and an integer for the flight number, as follows:

```
public async Task<(bool, Exception)>
  CreateBooking(int customerName, int flightNumber)  {
  return (true, null);
}
```

There is another problem in listing 10.2: a snippet of code that is logically sound but won't *quite* do. I am talking about how we instantiate the BookingService in the assignment to the service variable as follows:

```
BookingService service = new BookingService(repository);
```

In the next section, we'll dissect the problem with this assignment further.

10.3.1 *Unit testing across architectural layers*

In this section, I'll introduce you to the concept of scoping your unit tests to only your immediate architectural layer. This section contains a somewhat unique element for a technical book: a Socratic dialogue.

Because the `BookingService` requires an injected instance `BookingRepository` (through its only available constructor), we simply created a new instance of `Booking-Repository` in listing 10.2. This is perfectly legitimate code in terms of syntax. But I want to convince you otherwise. Let's perform an experiment in (somewhat untrue to form and inspired by Alcibiades II) the following Socratic dialogue:

PERSONS OF THE DIALOGUE: Socrates and Phaidra

Setting: A cubicle somewhere deep in Mount Olympus

SOCRATES: Are you testing the `BookingService`, Phaidra?

PHAIDRA: Yes, Socrates, I am.

SOCRATES: You seem troubled and cast your eyes to the ground. Are you thinking of something?

PHAIDRA: Of what am I supposed to be thinking?

SOCRATES: Oh, of all kinds of things, I suppose. Perhaps how to correctly test a code base, or the airspeed velocity of an unladen swallow?

PHAIDRA: Certainly.

SOCRATES: Do you not imagine, then, that it is of the utmost importance that you determine what you are testing before you test it?

PHAIDRA: Certainly, Socrates. But you are speaking like a mad man; surely you do not offer that I do not know what I test?

SOCRATES: Well, then, let's discuss what it means to test something correctly. Does testing an ox cart mean you test the ox? Does testing the pluck of a lyre mean you test Apollo's skill like Marsyas, the Muses, and the Nysean nymphs?

PHAIDRA: Certainly not.

SOCRATES: Nor does the accurate representation of the scribe's hand reflect a test on the orator's vocals?

PHAIDRA: That is my opinion.

SOCRATES: Then does one need to test, and have an accurate representation of, a repository when dealing with a service?

PHAIDRA: Socrates, you are devious and cunning.

SOCRATES: So, we are agreed that if you test the BookingService class, do you need to also test the BookingRepository class?

PHAIDRA: We are agreed.

Even in ancient Greece, how to properly test code was a hot topic! Let us ask ourselves a question: what do we want to test in the BookingService unit tests? Should we verify that the BookingService returns the correct output when given an appropriate input? Yes, that sounds about right. Should we also test whether BookingRepository does the same? Well, yes, to a point.

If BookingRepository does not function correctly, it has unwanted consequences for BookingService. In testing BookingService, can we not assume that Booking-Repository works correctly because we already have unit tests in place for that class? Well, yes, that makes some sense. If we could somehow skip the BookingService code and have it return valid information when we want it, we could control all the code execution in the repository layer during the test. Additionally, if we instantiate a BookingRepository and inject that into BookingService, the tests would operate on the actual BookingRepository instance and, therefore, on the in-memory database as well, as shown in figure 10.11.

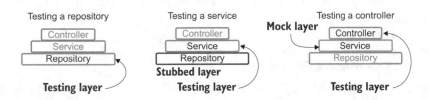

Figure 10.11   In a multilayered architecture, we test only the layer we are executing code in and mock or stub one layer down. As a result, we don't interact with layers further down.

When testing a multilayered architecture (such as the repository/service pattern we are using), you typically don't need to test the actual logic of a tier down from what you are working on. If you are testing the repository layer, you can stub or mock the database access layer (which is what we did with the FlyingDutchmanAirlinesContext_Stub class). If you are testing the service layer, you don't need to verify the logic of the repository layer.

10.3.2 *The difference between a stub and a mock*

Throughout the book, we used the FlyingDutchmanAirlinesContext_Stub to unit-test the repository layer of our FlyingDutchmanAirlines project. In this (and the following) section, I'll introduce you to another approach to controlling code execution during tests: mocks. We'll also look at the difference between a stub and a mock.

A stub is very helpful when we want to execute different code than what the original class does. For example, the `context.SaveChangesAsync` method saves the changes made to the internal `DbSets` of Entity Framework Core to the database. In section 8.4, we wanted to execute a different version of the method, so we made a stub (`Flying-DutchmanAirlinesContext_Stub`) and overrode the parent class's `SaveChangesAsync` method.

In a mock, we do not provide any new implementation for a method. When we use a mock, we tell the compiler to instantiate a type of `Mock<T>` that masquerades as `T`. Because of the Liskov substitution principle, we can use the mock as type `T`. Instead of an actual instance of class `T` being instantiated and injected into a constructor, we instantiate and inject the mock.

In our case, we want a `Mock<BookingRepository>`. When, during a test, the code in `BookingService` calls this mock's `CreateBooking`, we want to do one of two following things:

- Immediately return from the method (without actually creating the booking in the database) when we want to mimic a success condition.
- Throw an `Exception` when we want to mimic a failure condition.

Because we need to do only these two simple things, and we do not have to perform any logic that checks for entities within the in-memory database (like we do in the stub), it is easier to use a mock. You're not convinced? Well, hang on to your hats and read the next section.

10.3.3 *Mocking a class with the Moq library*

In section 10.3.2, we briefly discussed the difference between a mock and a stub. It's now time for me to show you how we can use a mock in practice and what we need to do to make that happen. First, neither C# nor .NET 5 has dedicated mocking functionality, so we need to use a third-party (open source) library to mock our classes: Moq. Of course, you can use plenty of other mocking libraries or frameworks (Telerik JustMock, FakeItEasy, and NSubstitute are examples). I chose Moq because it is widely used and easy to work with.

To install Moq, you can either use the NuGet package manager within Visual Studio or use the command line in the FlyingDutchmanAirlines_Tests folder as we did in section 5.2.1 and as shown next:

```
>\ dotnet add package Moq
```

This command adds the Moq package to the FlyingDutchmanAirlines_Test project. To verify the Moq package was added, you can either check Visual Studio for a Moq reference or open up the FlyingDutchmanAirlines_Test.csproj file and look for a Moq package reference, as shown in figure 10.12.

Before we can use Moq, we have to import its namespace into the `Booking-ServiceTests` class. To create a mock of type `BookingRepository` and return the

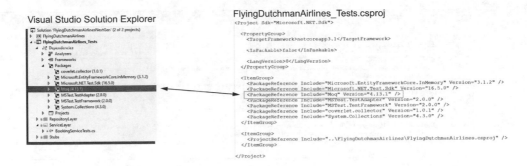

Figure 10.12   **A reference to a package is added to a project's .csproj file. Visual Studio scans this file and shows the added packages in the Solution Explorer panel. Edits made in the .csproj or Visual Studio automatically trickle down to both places.**

appropriate output from the CreateBooking method (a completed Task) we need to do the following:

- Instantiate a Mock<BookingRepository>.
- Set up the Mock<BookingRepository> to return a completed task when we call CreateBooking.

We know how to do the first item on the list—instantiate a Mock<BookingRepository>—because instantiating a mock is no different from instantiating any other class. Let's create our instance of the mock in the CreateBooking_Success unit test as follows:

```
Mock<BookingRepository> mockRepository = new Mock<BookingRepository>();
```

You can use the mock.Setup([lambda expression to call method]).[return] syntax to set up a mock where a method returns a specific value when called. Because we want to call (and mock) the CreateBooking method, the lambda expression we can use is repository => repository.CreateBooking(0, 0). We follow this by specifying what we want to return: Returns(Task.CompletedTask), as shown next.

Listing 10.3   **Setting up a mock of BookingRepository and calling CreateBooking**

We instantiate a new mock instance of BookingRepository.

```
Mock<BookingRepository> mockRepository = new Mock<BookingRepository>();
mockRepository.Setup(repository =>
   repository.CreateBooking(0, 0)).Returns(Task.CompletedTask);
```

If the mock calls CreateBooking with two parameters with zero values, returns a Task.CompletedTask

Unfortunately, the code in listing 10.3 won't run correctly. Moq throws a runtime exception, shown in figure 10.13, saying it cannot instantiate a mock from a class it cannot override.

```
CreateBooking_Success failed

Test method FlyingDutchmanAirlines_Tests.ServiceLayer.BookingServiceTests.CreateBooking_Success threw exception:
System.NotSupportedException: Unsupported expression: repository => repository.CreateBooking(0, 0)
Non-overridable members (here: BookingRepository.CreateBooking) may not be used in setup / verification expressions.
    at Moq.Guard.IsOverridable(MethodInfo method, Expression expression)
    at Moq.InvocationShape..ctor(LambdaExpression expression, MethodInfo method, IReadOnlyList`1 arguments, Boolean
       exactGenericTypeArguments)
    at Moq.ExpressionExtensions.<Split>g__Split|4_1(Expression e, Expression& r, InvocationShape& p)
    at Moq.ExpressionExtensions.Split(LambdaExpression expression)
    at Moq.Mock.SetupRecursive[TSetup](Mock mock, LambdaExpression expression, Func`3 setupLast)
    at Moq.Mock.Setup(Mock mock, LambdaExpression expression, Condition condition)
    at Moq.Mock`1.Setup[TResult](Expression`1 expression)
    at FlyingDutchmanAirlines_Tests.ServiceLayer.BookingServiceTests.CreateBooking_Success() in C:\Users\Jort\Documents\rodenburg\code
       \Chapter 10\FlyingDutchmanAirlines_Tests\ServiceLayer\BookingServiceTests.cs:line 29
    at Microsoft.VisualStudio.TestPlatform.MSTestAdapter.PlatformServices.ThreadOperations.ExecuteWithAbortSafety(Action action)
```

Figure 10.13   Moq throws a runtime exception because we tried to mock a class that is not overridable.

The BookingRepository.CreateBooking is not a virtual method, so Moq cannot override the method to implement a new version of it. Moq also needs to be able to call a parameterless constructor, which the BookingRepository does not have.

To remedy these two issues, we first make the BookingRepository.CreateBooking method virtual as follows:

```
public virtual async Task CreateBooking(int customerID, int flightNumber)
```

Then, we create a parameterless constructor for BookingRepository like so:

```
public BookingRepository() {}
```

But it would be a shame if all our work making sure developers instantiate an instance of BookingRepository through the constructor with the injected FlyingDutchman-AirlinesContext goes out the window. I really would like for the new constructor to have an access modifier of private, but then the unit tests wouldn't be able to access them (because the unit tests live in a different assembly than the repository layer). There are a couple of tricks that can help us here. The three most used follow:

- Use the [assembly: InternalsVisibleTo([assembly name])] attribute.
- Use the #warning preprocessor directive to generate a compiler warning.
- Verify that the executing assembly does not match the non–unit test assembly.

Let's unpack them one by one.

THE INTERNALSVISIBLETO METHOD ATTRIBUTE

First, the [assembly: InternalsVisibleTo([assembly name])] attribute, which you can apply only to assemblies, allows a different assembly (the FlyingDutchmanAirlines _Tests.ServiceLayer assembly, in our case) to access and manipulate methods, properties, and fields of the containing assembly (FlyingDutchmanAirlines) flagged with the internal access modifier. When the CLR sees the InternalsVisibleTo attribute, it notes the given assembly and designates it as a "friend" assembly to the one it is trying to access the internals of. In practical terms, the CLR treats a friend assembly as the same assembly as the containing assembly when it comes to compiling down to Intermediate Language.

The problem with using friend assemblies and the `InternalsVisibleTo` attribute approach is that the `InternalsVisibleTo` attribute is incredibly finicky. There are oodles of pages on Stack Overflow with questions about how to get the attribute working correctly. Besides the usability issue, we also aren't very keen on testing private methods. Ideally, we would test all private methods through the public methods that use them. Tests should not walk any paths that a normal user would not walk. Because a normal user does not interact with a class by calling its private methods, neither should a unit test. The `InternalsVisibleTo` method attribute is a good thing to know about, but not a practical thing to use. The real pro tip when it comes to `Internals-VisibleTo` is to save yourself the heartache of using it and just don't.

> **TIP** For more information on method and member accessibility, see the "bible" of the CLR: Jeffrey Richter's *CLR via C#* (4th edition; Microsoft Press, 2012). Be aware, however, that this book assumes a lot of the knowledge covered in this book.

PREPROCESSOR DIRECTIVES (#WARNING AND #ERROR)

Second, we can use preprocessor directives in our source code. Preprocessor directives are commands starting with the # character that are resolved before compilation. The compiler scans the codebase for preprocessor directives and executes them before compilation. To deal with compilation warnings and errors, we can use the `#warning` and `#error` preprocessor directives. `#warning` throws a compiler warning, and `#error` throws a compiler error when warnings and errors are encountered. To add a compiler warning through the `#warning` directive in our public parameterless constructor, add the directive along with a message to the constructor. It is good to note that we always insert preprocessor directives into the source code with no indentation (be they spaces or tabs), as follows:

```
  public BookingRepository() {
#warning Use this constructor only in testing
  }
```

Using the `#warning` preprocessor directive works decently well, but if we have a lot of `#warning` directives, our compilation process would cause a lot of warnings, diminishing the value of them collectively and making it easy to overlook other warnings. The other downside is that just because there is a warning doesn't mean that a developer pays attention to it. See figure 10.14 for an example.

MATCHING EXECUTING AND CALLING ASSEMBLY NAMES

Third, I propose the possibility of doing a bit of a programmatic hack: by using reflection, we can access the name of the executing or calling assemblies (for a discussion on what assemblies are, see section 2.3.1). When we call the parameterless constructor

Code	Description
⚠ CS1030	#warning: 'Use this constructor only for testing'

Figure 10.14   The #warning preprocessor directive generates a compiler warning with the given string. Here we see the compiler warning as shown in Visual Studio 2019.

of `BookingRepository.CreateBooking` from a class inside the `FlyingDutchmanAirlines` assembly, the calling assembly is `FlyingDutchmanAirlines`. If we call the same constructor from a different assembly, let's say, the `FlyingDutchmanAirlines_Tests` assembly, the CLR does not have the required info to provide us with the executing assembly name because it often can retrieve information only on the executing assembly.

We can take advantage of this by checking whether the calling assembly is equal to the currently *executing* assembly. If it is, somebody is being sneaky and instantiating `BookingRepository` in the wrong way. Of course, checking assembly names against each other is not foolproof. Somebody could create a new assembly and use the incorrect constructor, but the amount of effort to do that makes it unlikely. We access the names of the calling and executing assemblies by using the `Assembly` class, as shown in the next listing.

Listing 10.4   Comparing executing and calling assembly names

```
public BookingRepository() {
  if(Assembly.GetExecutingAssembly().FullName ==
  Assembly.GetCallingAssembly().FullName) {
  throw new Exception("This constructor should only be used for
  testing");
  }
}
```

Compares the executing assembly against the calling assembly names

Throws an exception if the constructor is accessed incorrectly

With the code in listing 10.4, if a developer tries to instantiate an instance of `Booking-Repository` from within the `FlyingDutchmanAirlines` assembly and does not use the appropriate constructor, the code throws an `Exception` at runtime because the names of the executing assembly and calling assembly match.

There is one caveat with using reflection to get the name of a calling assembly: the CLR uses the last executed stack frame to get the calling assembly name, but if some of the code was inlined by the compiler, there is a chance that this stack frame does not contain the correct information.

Compiler method inlining

During compilation, when a compiler encounters a call to a method in a different class, it is often beneficial for performance to replace the method call with the body of the called method. This decreases the amount of cross-file computation and, in general, improves performance. There is a point of diminishing returns, however. When the called method is very large and contains calls to other large methods, the compiler can get stuck in a rabbit hole. The compiler then copies the bodies of deeply nested methods into the original calling class, and before you know it, your class blows up in size and complexity. Modern compilers are very good at detecting this sort of thing, so in general, it is not something you need to worry about.

Additionally, compilers generally do not attempt to inline recursive methods because it would result in the compiler being stuck in an infinite loop where it tries to copy the body of the same method into itself into perpetuity. For more information on compiler inlining (and compilers in general), see Alfred V. Aho, Monica S. Lam, Ravi Sethi, and Jeffrey D. Ullman's *Compilers: Principles, Techniques & Tools* (2nd edition; Pearson Education, 2007).

Luckily, we can tell the compiler to not inline the code in a specific method by using the method implementation (`MethodImpl`) method attribute. The `MethodImpl` method attribute allows us to specify how the compiler should treat our method, and lo and behold, one option is to stop the compiler from inlining a given method. Let's add the `MethodImpl` method attribute to the constructor and ask the compiler not to inline the method, as shown here:

```
[MethodImpl(MethodImplOptions.NoInlining)]
public BookingRepository() {
  if (Assembly.GetExecutingAssembly().FullName ==
➥ Assembly.GetCallingAssembly().FullName) {
  throw new Exception("This constructor should only be used for
➥ testing");
  }
}
```

Coming back to the `CreateBooking_Success` unit test, we now have a `Mock<BookingRepository>` instance that we can inject into the `BookingService`. Injecting an instance of mock into the `BookingService` allows us to test the `BookingService` without worrying about the implementation details of the `BookingRepository` class. To inject a `Mock<T>`, we need to use the mock's underlying object, which is the actual mocked object: `Object`. If we do not use the `Object` property of a mock, we pass in the actual instance of type `Mock<T>`, which does not match the required dependency. To use a mock's `Object` property, you call the `[mock].Object` property, as shown in the following listing.

Listing 10.5 Injection a mocked instance into `RepositoryService`

```
[TestMethod]
public async Task CreateBooking_Success() {
  Mock<BookingRepository> mockBookingRepository = new
➥ Mock<BookingRepository>();
```

Creates a mock of BookingRepository

```
  mockBookingRepository.Setup(repository =>
➥ repository.CreateBooking(0, 0)).Returns(Task.CompletedTask);


  BookingService service = new
➥ BookingService(mockBookingRepository.Object);
  (bool result, Exception exception) =
➥ await service.CreateBooking("Leo Tolstoy", 0);

  Assert.IsTrue(result);
  Assert.IsNull(exception);
}
```

Sets up the correct return of the mock's CreateBooking method

The CreateBooking method returns a named tuple.

Injects the mock into the BookingService

We also need a mock of the `CustomerRepository` that returns a new `Customer` object when we call `GetCustomerByName`. We know what to do now. Go ahead and add the `virtual` keyword to the `GetCustomerByName` method, and make sure that we can mock the `CustomerRepository` (add a constructor similar to what we did for the `Booking-Repository`), shown next:

```
[TestMethod]
public async Task CreateBooking_Success() {
  Mock<BookingRepository> mockBookingRepository = new
➥ Mock<BookingRepository>();
  Mock<CustomerRepository> mockCustomerRepository = new
➥ Mock<CustomerRepository>();

  mockBookingRepository.Setup(repository =>
➥ repository.CreateBooking(0, 0)).Returns(Task.CompletedTask);
  mockCustomerRepository.Setup(repository =>
➥ repository.GetCustomerByName("Leo
➥ Tolstoy")).Returns(Task.FromResult(new Customer("Leo Tolstoy")));

  BookingService service = new
➥ BookingService(mockBookingRepository.Object,
➥ mockCustomerRepository.Object);
  (bool result, Exception exception) =
➥ await service.CreateBooking("Leo Tolstoy", 0);

  Assert.IsTrue(result);
  Assert.IsNull(exception);
}
```

In terms of test-driven development, we are currently in the green stage and attempting to go to the red stage. Before we go on, we should do some quick cleanups. Because we are using a mock, we do not need to use the stub of `FlyingDutchman-AirlinesContext` or the `dbContextOptions` in this test class. We should remove the instantiation of the stub, the corresponding backing field, and `dbContextOptions` from the `TestInitialize` method now. I leave this for you to do.

If we run our tests now, we see that they pass. Unfortunately, they pass for the wrong reasons. In section 10.3, we added a skeleton body to `BookingService.CreateBooking` along with a hardcoded return value. This is what makes the `CreateBooking_Success` unit test pass. An important lesson to keep in mind with unit testing is to always make sure your tests pass for the right reasons. It is easy to "fake" a successful test result by providing hardcoded return values or by asserting on incorrect data. How do we make sure the CreateBooking_Success unit test passes for the correct reasons? We have to continue implementing the CreateBooking method, which we'll do in section 10.3.4.

10.3.4 *Calling a repository from a service*

We came out of section 10.3.3 with a skeleton implementation of BookingService .CreateBooking and a finished unit test for the success case through Booking-ServiceTests.CreateBooking_Success. In this section, we'll look at further implementing the CreateBooking method so it calls the appropriate repository method and returns the correct information.

To finish the CreateBooking method, we need to implement the following two things:

- An asynchronous call to the BookingRepository.GetCustomerByName method inside a try-catch block
- The appropriate set of tuple values for returning out of the method

Calling repository methods inside a try-catch block allows us to do error handling. When an exception is raised inside the called repository method, the try-catch block catches the exception, as shown here:

```
public async Task<(bool, Exception)>
➡ CreateBooking(string name, int flightNumber) {
  try {
    …
  } catch (Exception exception) {
    …
  }

  return (true, null);
}
```

Inside the try part of the try-catch code block, we want to use the class-level private properties containing references to the injected CustomerRepository and Booking-Repository instances: _customerRepository and _bookingRepository (during the execution of our unit tests, this holds a reference to the mocked version of Booking-Repository, as explained in section 10.3.3). We use the _customerRepository instance to call its GetCustomerByName method. The GetCustomerByName method retrieves the appropriate Customer instance or throws a CustomerNotFoundException, which lets us know the customer was not found. If it does not exist, we call the Create-Customer method and have it created. After that, we call the CreateBooking method again, returning its return value. Calling into the same method in which you are located is also called *recursion*. Because the GetCustomerByName method throws an exception that we actually want to utilize, we wrap the call to `GetCustomerByName` inside its own `try-catch` block, as shown in the next code sample.

DEFINITION   Recursion happens when a method calls itself. When this happens, the CLR pauses the currently executing method to enter the new call of the method. Recursion often comes with a heavy performance and complexity penalty. Here it is used as a teaching device, but in production environments, it is often not the best (most performant) way to solve a particular problem.

Listing 10.6   Recursive call into `CreateBooking`

```
public async Task<(bool, Exception)>
➥ CreateBooking(string name, int flightNumber) {
  try {
    Customer customer;                    Checks if the customer exists in the
    try {                                database and gets its details if so
      customer =
➥ await _customerRepository.GetCustomerByName(name);   ◁──  The customer does
    } catch (CustomerNotFoundException) {              ◁──  not exist in the
      await _customerRepository.CreateCustomer(name);    ◁──  database.
      return await CreateBooking(name, flightNumber);  ◁──  Adds the
    }                                                        customer to
    ...                                                      the database
}                          Recursively calls this method now that
                           the customer is in the database
```

We can now use the `_bookingRepository` variable to call the `CreateBooking` method in the `BookingRepository`. Because the `BookingRepository.CreateBooking` method should execute asynchronously, we also `await` the call.

When the `Task` is completed, because the `try-catch` code block caught no exceptions, and the code returns the `BookingRepository.CreateBooking` method, we return a set of tuples representing a `true` Boolean state for the `success` variable and a `null` reference for the `exception` variable. If the `try-catch` block caught an `Exception` during the execution of the `BookingRepository.CreateBooking` method, we would return a set of named tuples with the `success` variable set to a `false` state along with a reference to the caught `Exception` instead. By terminating all code paths inside the `try-catch` statement, we do not need the placeholder return of `(true, null)` anymore, as shown next.

Listing 10.7   The `BookingService.CreateBooking` method

```
public async Task<(bool, Exception)>
➥ CreateBooking(string name, int flightNumber){
  try {
    Customer customer;
    try {
      customer = await _customerRepository.GetCustomerByName(name);
    } catch (CustomerNotFoundException) {
      await _customerRepository.CreateCustomer(name);
```

```
        return await CreateBooking(name, flightNumber);
    }

    await _bookingRepository.CreateBooking(customer.CustomerId,
➡ flightNumber);
    return (true, null);
} catch(Exception exception) {
    return (false, exception);
}
}
```

We only have the following things left to do before we can officially wrap up the Booking-Service class:

- Add input validation for the customerName and flightNumber input arguments.
- Verify that the requested Flight exists in the database. If it does not, we need to gracefully exit out of the method.
- Add unit tests for input validation, Customer verification and creation, and Flight verification.

We'll do these three things in the next chapter and finish implementing Booking-Service. In this chapter, we started implementing BookingService, learned about using mocks (with the Moq package), and refreshed our knowledge of the repository/service pattern.

Exercises

EXERCISE 10.9
True or false? When unit testing a multitiered architecture, we can replace the tier immediately below our testing concern with a mock or a stub.

EXERCISE 10.10
Imagine you are unit testing a class in the controller layer of a repository/service architecture. Which of these approaches is the correct approach?

- a Mock the controller layer, stub the service, and use the repository layer.
- b Stub the controller layer, do not use the service layer, and mock the repository layer.
- c Use the controller layer, mock the service layer, and do not use the repository layer.

EXERCISE 10.11
True or false? By using a service layer to control access to the various repositories in a repository/service pattern, the coupling between a controller and a repository is decreased because the controller calls the repository indirectly through the service.

EXERCISE 10.12

True or false? Mocks are used to provide alternative implementations to existing methods. To use a mock, you provide a new method body and write alternative logic for the methods you override.

EXERCISE 10.13

True or false? The `InternalsVisibleTo` method attribute can be used to block other assemblies from viewing the internals of the assembly the attribute is applied in.

EXERCISE 10.14

What preprocessor directive can you use to generate a compiler warning?

  a `#error`
  b `^&generate`
  c `#warning`
  d `^&compiler::warning`

EXERCISE 10.15

True or false? You can ask the CLR for the executing and calling assemblies' names at runtime by using reflection and methods inside the assembly namespace.

EXERCISE 10.16

When a compiler inlines a method, what happens to the code that calls the method?

  a Nothing—inlining means we immediately execute the called method. The code does not change.
  b The compiler replaces the method call with the called method's body
  c The compiler replaces the method call with the contents of the method's containing class.

EXERCISE 10.17

If we add the attribute `[MethodImpl(MethodImplOptions.NoInlining)]` to a property, what happens?

  a We get a compilation error because you cannot use the `MethodImpl` attribute on a property.
  b The property calls are inlined.
  c The property calls are inlined only if there is a significant performance gain to be made.

Summary

- The repository/service pattern divides an application into three layers: a controller, service, and repository. This helps us control the flow of data and separate concerns.
- In a repository/service world, the controller holds an instance of the service, and the service holds an instance of the repository. This is to ensure coupling is as loose as possible between the individual classes. If the controller were to hold

an instance of both the service and repository, we would have very tight coupling to the repository.

- A view is a "window" into one or more models that are returned to a user. We use views to collect and present information to the user.

- When testing a solution that follows the repository/service pattern (or any other multilayered architecture), you need to test the logic only at the level you want to test. For example, if you are testing a controller class, you may mock or stub the service layer, but the test does not need to execute the actual logic in the service layer. Consequently, the repository layer is not called at all in this scenario. This helps us test only atomic operations, as opposed to entire stacks. If we want to test across layers, we need an integration test.

- A mock is a class that returns a specific return when a method or property is called. It is used instead of the original class. This helps us focus on the layer we want to test.

- The `InternalsVisibleTo` method attribute is used to designate "friend" assemblies that can access internal methods, fields, and properties. This is helpful in unit testing, where usually the tests live in a separate assembly than the code we want to test.

- Preprocessor directives can generate compiler warnings (`#warning`) and compiler errors (`#error`). We can also use preprocessor directives to control our data flow when access modifiers and encapsulation are not enough. Putting in a compiler warning lets developers know that there is a potential pitfall at a specific location.

- Compiler inlining means that a compiler replaces a method call with the body of the called method. This is useful for performance because it reduces cross-file calls.

- By using the method implementation (`MethodImpl`) method attribute, we can control the compiler's inlining preferences. We can force the compiler not to inline a method by adding `[MethodImpl(MethodImplOptions.NoInlining)]` as a method attribute. This is useful to retain stack traces when rethrowing exceptions.

Runtime type checking revisited and error handling

11

This chapter covers

- Using the `Assert.IsInstanceOfType` test assertion
- Calling multiple repositories from a service class
- Using the discard operator
- Using multiple `catch` blocks
- Checking types at runtime with the `is` and `as` operators

After having implemented the database access layer in chapter 5 and the repository layer in chapters 6 through 9, we started to implement the `BookingService` in chapter 10. I also introduced you to using mocks in unit testing, and we discussed the repository/service pattern. In this chapter, we'll use those concepts and draw on our knowledge of service layers to wrap up the `BookingService` implementation. Figure 11.1 shows where we are in the scheme of the book.

While we finish implementing the `BookingService`, this chapter also discusses using the `Assert.IsInstanceOfType` test assertion to verify an object is of a certain

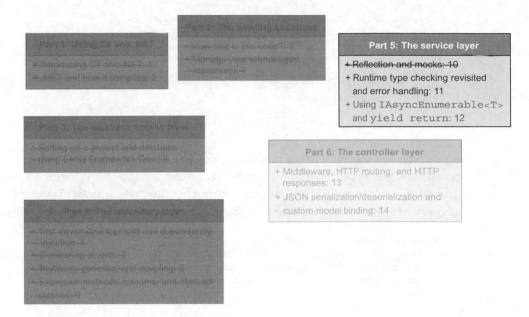

Figure 11.1 **In this chapter we finish implementing the** `BookingService` **class. In the next chapter, we wrap up the Services layer by implementing the** `AirportService` **and** `FlightService` **classes.**

type (or derived of a certain type), the discard (_) operator and its effect on Intermediate Language, and using multiple `catch` blocks in a `try-catch` code block.

To wrap up the `BookingService` implementation, we need to do the following:

- Validate the input parameters of the `BookingService.CreateBooking` method (section 11.1),
- Verify that the flight we want to book exists in the database (section 11.3).

11.1 *Validating input parameters of a service layer method*

Many times, a service layer class acts as a pipe between a controller class and a repository class. Even though not a lot of logic is involved, the service layer still provides an important abstraction layer to combat tight coupling. For a discussion on coupling, see section 8.2.

Before we move on, we should recap where we left off in the `BookingService`
`.CreateBooking` method:

```
public async Task<(bool, Exception)>
➥ CreateBooking(string name, int flightNumber) {
  try {
    Customer customer;
    try {
      customer = await _customerRepository.GetCustomerByName(name);
    } catch (FlightNotFoundException) {
      await _customerRepository.CreateCustomer(name);
```

```
        return await CreateBooking(name, flightNumber);
    }

    await _bookingRepository.CreateBooking(customer.CustomerId, flightNumber);
    return (true, null);
  } catch (Exception exception) {
    return (false, exception);
  }
}
```

To perform the required input validation, we can use the IsPositiveInteger extension method we implemented in section 9.6 and the string.IsNullOrEmpty method.
If the customer's name is a null or empty string, or the flight number is not a positive
integer, we return a set of variables indicating (*false,ArgumentException*), as follows:

```
public async Task<(bool, Exception)>
➡ CreateBooking(string name, int flightNumber) {
  if (string.IsNullOrEmpty(name) || !flightNumber.IsPositiveInteger()) {
    return (false, new ArgumentException());
  }

  try {
    Customer customer;
    try {
      customer = await _customerRepository.GetCustomerByName(name);
    } catch (FlightNotFoundException) {
      await _customerRepository.CreateCustomer(name);
      return await CreateBooking(name, flightNumber);
    }

  await _bookingRepository.CreateBooking(customer.CustomerId,
➡ flightNumber);
    return (true, null);
  } catch (Exception exception) {
    return (false, exception);
  }
}
```

Now, we should add a unit test, shown next, complete with the [DataRow] method
attribute to inline test data that checks that a return value of (*false,ArgumentException*)
comes out of the BookingService.CreateBooking method when given invalid input
arguments. For this unit test, we do not need to set up the mock of BookingRepository
with a return value, because it would never get executed.

> **Listing 11.1   Testing** BookingService.CreateCustomer**'s input validation**

```
[TestMethod]
[DataRow("", 0)]
[DataRow(null, -1)]                    Inline test
[DataRow("Galileo Galilei", -1)]       data
```

```
public async Task CreateBooking_Failure_InvalidInputArguments(string name,
   int flightNumber) {
  Mock<BookingRepository> mockBookingRepository =
   new Mock<BookingRepository>();
  Mock<CustomerRepository> mockCustomerRepository =
   new Mock<CustomerRepository>();
  BookingService service =
   new BookingService(mockBookingRepository.Object,
   mockCustomerRepository.Object);
  (bool result, Exception exception) = await
   service.CreateBooking(name, flightNumber);

   Assert.IsFalse(result);
   Assert.IsNotNull(exception);
}
```

Sets up mocks

Calls the CreateBooking method

The result should be (false, Exception).

That should do it for the invalid input arguments case. But what if the repository layer throws an exception? We hope the `try-catch` block in the `BookingService.Create-Customer` method catches the exception, but until we test for that, we do not know for sure. I don't like relying on my interpretation of what I think the code should do. Instead, it's best to "prove" our assumptions and create a unit test. We can create a unit test called `CreateBooking_Failure_RepositoryException` and set up a mock of `BookingRepository` that returns an `Exception` when `BookingRepository.Create-Booking` is called.

What type of `Exception` should we return? The repository returns either an `ArgumentException` (on invalid input) or a `CouldNotAddBookingToDatabaseException` exception. We could either check that those specific exceptions were thrown or check for a general `Exception`.

If a developer changes the type of exception thrown when a database error occurs from `CouldNotAddBookingToDatabaseException` to `AirportNotFoundException`, and we only test for the base `Exception` class to be thrown, we won't catch the `Airport-NotFoundException` exception at the earliest possible moment. This causes the test to incorrectly pass. It is for that reason that I propose we set up the following two mock return instances:

- If we pass in the parameter set of {0, 1} to the `BookingService.CreateBooking` method, throw an `ArgumentException` exception.
- If we pass in the parameter set of {1, 2} to the `BookingService.CreateBooking` method, throw a `CouldNotAddBookingToDatabaseException` exception.

To set up more than one return value on a mock, we can modify the mock logic to cover all the different cases we want to test. There is no practical limit on the amount of returned mocks we can add to a method, as long as they are all individually distinguishable for the compiler (as with any overridden method).

To verify that a thrown `Exception` is of a certain type, we can use the `Assert.IsInstanceOfType` assertion along with the `typeof` operator (discussed in section 4.1.2), shown in the next code.

Listing 11.2   CreateBooking_Failure_RepositoryException

```
[TestMethod]
public async Task CreateBooking_Failure_RepositoryException() {
  Mock<BookingRepository> mockBookingRepository =
  new Mock<BookingRepository>();
  Mock<CustomerRepository> mockCustomerRepository =
  new Mock<CustomerRepository>();

  mockBookingRepository.Setup(repository =>
  repository.CreateBooking(0, 1)).Throws(new ArgumentException());
  mockBookingRepository.Setup(repository =>
  repository.CreateBooking(1, 2))
  .Throws(new CouldNotAddBookingToDatabaseException());

  mockCustomerRepository.Setup(repository =>
  repository.GetCustomerByName("Galileo Galilei"))
  .Returns(Task.FromResult(
  new Customer("Galileo Galilei") { CustomerId = 0 }));
  mockCustomerRepository.Setup(repository =>
  repository.GetCustomerByName("Eise Eisinga"))
  .Returns(Task.FromResult(new Customer("Eise Eisinga") { CustomerId = 1
  }));

  BookingService service = new BookingService(mockBookingRepository.Object,
  mockCustomerRepository.Object);
  (bool result, Exception exception) =
  await service.CreateBooking("Galileo Galilei", 1);

  Assert.IsFalse(result);
  Assert.IsNotNull(exception);
  Assert.IsInstanceOfType(exception, typeof(ArgumentException));

  (result, exception) = await service.CreateBooking("Eise Eisinga", 2);

  Assert.IsFalse(result);
  Assert.IsNotNull(exception);
  Assert.IsInstanceOfType(exception,
  typeof(CouldNotAddBookingToDatabaseException));
}
```

Sets up a logic path to throw an ArgumentException exception

Sets up a logic path to throw a CouldNotAddBookingToDatabase Exception exception

Calls the CreateBooking method with ("Galileo Galilei", 1)

Calls the CreateBooking method with ("Eise Eisinga", 2)

Asserts that the returned exception is of type CouldNotAddBookingToDatabaseException

Assert.IsInstanceOfType is an invaluable assertion to have in your toolbox. Instead of asserting the type of an object through regular code (using the typeof operator), you can use this assertion in your tests. Alternatively, you could mimic the functionality of the Assert.IsInstanceType by adding the is syntax (as discussed in the next section) to the Assert.IsTrue check.

11.1.1 Runtime type checks with the is and as operators

`Assert.IsInstanceOfType` throws an `Exception` when it fails. This works very well in unit tests, where an assertion failure means a test failure. In production code, things can be different. Sometimes, we don't want to throw an `Exception` when we encounter an object of unexpected type. We already know about the `typeof` operator. If we *need* an object to be a specific type in production code, we can take the following two other approaches:

- Check if we can cast type `T` to type `Y` by using the `is` operator.
- Convert type `T` to type `Y` by using the `as` operator and handling a potential `null` return value.

Both the `is` and `as` operators are ways to use the Liskov principle to do type checking at run time. Whereas the `typeof` operator only works at compile time, we can use the `is` and `as` operators to dynamically determine what type something is at run time.

In table 11.1 we see a comparison of the `is` and `as` operators, along with their use cases and an example of their syntax.

Table 11.1 The `is` and `as` operators compared

Operator	Use case	Syntax
is	Check whether type `T` is of type `Y`	`apple is Fruit`
as	Determine whether type `T` can be cast to type `Y`	`Peugeot as Car`

Let's take the table one step further and examine both operators a little more in depth.

11.1.2 Type checking with the is operator

First up: the `is` operator. We often use `is` when we want to do a runtime type check in the vein of `GetType` (discussed in section 4.1.2). Let's say we are writing a (very naïve) implementation of an intercontinental internet package-switching system. We may have a tree of nodes (switches) containing a root node (an intercontinental switch), a continent or region switch, and dedicated country switches. I show such a setup in figure 11.2.

Let's also assume that two types derive from a base `Packet` class: `ExternalPacket` and `LocalPacket`, where `ExternalPacket` means any packet that needs to go to a different continent given a specific destination. For example, a packet going from leaf 3 (Panama) to leaf 4 (Brazil) is of type `LocalPacket` because it needs to travel only through the South/Middle America switch. A packet leaving from leaf 6 (Kenya) and going to leaf 1 (Luxembourg) is an `ExternalPacket`, because it needs to go through the Intercontinental switch.

How would we write code that directs these packets to the correct switch? One possible implementation assumes that we have a `PacketTransfer` class that attempts to handle the routing for us. In a `PacketTransfer`, we might have a method called

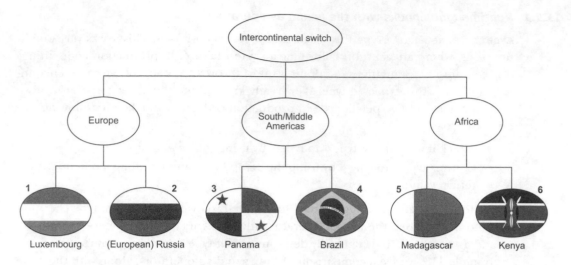

Figure 11.2   A possible and simplified network switch tree. The tree contains a root node acting as an intercontinental switch, three child nodes acting as continental switches, and six country-specific switches.

`DetermineNextDestination`, which returns an object of type `InternetSwitch`. The `InternetSwitch` class could have two derived types as well: `ContinentalSwitch` and `GlobalSwitch`.

To know where to route the packet, we need to figure out whether the packet is an `ExternalPacket` or `LocalPacket`. In listing 11.3 you see a potential implementation of logic to route external packets.

Listing 11.3   Using the `is` operator for packet routing

Checks if the packet object can be coerced into the ExternalPacket type

Checks if the packet destination object can be coerced into the ContinentalSwitch type

```
public InternetSwitch DetermineNextDestination(Packet packet) {
    if (packet is ExternalPacket) {
        if (packet.CurrentLocation is ContinentalSwitch) {
            return packet.CurrentLocation == PacketIsInDestinationRegion()
                ? packet.Destination : GetGlobalSwitch();
        }

        return GetContinentalSwitch(packet.Destination);
    }
    ...
}
```

Goes to the packet destination or global switch, depending on the current location

If the packet is an ExternalPacket and not at a ContinentalSwitch, sends it to one

By using polymorphism and the `is` operator, we can easily deduct whether the packet being routed is of type `ExternalPacket`. So, that is the `is` operator, but what about the `as` operator?

11.1.3 Type checking with the as operator

Let's imagine we routed a packet to its destination. Now the destination switch wants to accept the packet, but this particular switch accepts only local packets (not going through the GlobalSwitch object). We could try to use the received packet as a LocalPacket, as shown next, and see what happens.

Listing 11.4 Using the as operator for packet acceptance

```
public void AcceptPacket(Packet packet) {
  LocalPacket receivedPacket = packet as LocalPacket;      ◁── Tries to use the
  if (receivedPacket != null) {              ◁──               packet variable
    ProcessPacket(receivedPacket);      ◁──                    as a LocalPacket
  } else {                                                     instance
    RejectPacket(packet);      ◁──
  }
}
```

Tries to use the packet variable as a LocalPacket instance

Verifies the as operator did not return a null pointer

Processes the LocalPacket instance

Rejects the not LocalPacket instance

When using the as operator, if the variable cannot be cast to the requested type, the CLR assigns a null pointer to the variable. Using the as operator is a powerful tool and can be useful when dealing with incoming unknowns.

And now, for the grand finale: we combine both approaches by using pattern matching in the next code sample.

Listing 11.5 Using pattern matching for packet acceptance

```
public void AcceptPacket(Packet packet) {
  if (packet is LocalPacket receivedPacket) {
    ProcessPacket(receivedPacket);
  } else {
    RejectPacket(packet);
  }
}
```

If a packet can be used as a LocalPacket, it is assigned to receivedPacket and processed.

If the packet cannot be used as a LocalPacket, calls the RejectPacket method

11.1.4 What did we do in section 11.1?

In the CreateBooking_Failure_RepositoryException unit test, we tested and verified that we can handle exceptions thrown in the repository layer gracefully and as expected. We also instantiated the Mock<BookingRepository> in the same way as we did in the CreateBooking_Success and CreateBooking_Failure_InvalidInputs unit tests. Perhaps we can extract the initialization of the mock into a TestInitialize method and split up the CreateBooking_Failure_RepositoryExceptions into two tests. We also learned about using the is and as operators for runtime type checking.

11.2   Cleaning up the BookingServiceTests class

In wrapping up section 11.1, we identified the following two cleanup areas for the
BookingServiceTests class:

- Extract the initialization of Mock<BookingRepository> to a TestInitialize
  method. The current implementation sees us instantiate a mock of Booking-
  Repository in every test, violating the DRY principle.
- Split the CreateBooking_Failure_RepositoryException into two unit tests:
  one for the ArgumentException and one for the CouldNotAddBookingToDatabaseException exception.

Let's start by extracting the initialization of Mock<BookingRepository> to the Test-
Initialize method, shown next. We also want to add a private backing field for us to
store the reference to Mock<BookingRepository>.

```
[TestClass]
public class BookingServiceTests {
  private Mock<BookingRepository> _mockBookingRepository;

  [TestInitialize]
  public void TestInitialize() {
    _mockBookingRepository = new Mock<BookingRepository>();
  }

  …

}
```

All we have to do is change the existing unit tests to use the _mockBookingRepository
field instead of instantiating their own mock. For example:

```
[TestMethod]
public async Task CreateBooking_Success()  {
  Mock<BookingRepository> mockRepository = new Mock<BookingRepository>();
  _mockBookingRepository.Setup(repository =>
➡ repository.CreateBooking(0, 0)).Returns(Task.CompletedTask);

  BookingService service =
➡ new BookingService(mockBookingRepository .Object);

  (bool result, Exception exception) = await service.CreateBooking(0, 0);

  Assert.IsTrue(result);
  Assert.IsNull(exception);
}
```

We still want to set up any mocked returns because any existing mock instances are
reset every time we run a new test. Initializing no mocks in the TestInitialize
method allows us to set up different returned mock instances on a per-test basis.

The second improvement we identified was to split the CreateBooking_Failure_RepositoryException unit test into the following separate unit tests:

- CreateBooking_Failure_RepositoryException_ArgumentException
- CreateBooking_Failure_RepositoryException_CouldNotAddBookingToDatabase

The two new unit tests each test a logic branch that throws their respective Exception. In listing 11.6, you see the CreateBooking_Failure_RepositoryException_Argument-Exception unit test. I leave the CreateBooking_Failure_CouldNotAddBooking-ToDatabase for you to implement. If you get stuck, you can mimic the pattern in listing 11.6. My versions of both unit tests are provided in the source files for this book.

Listing 11.6 CreateBooking_Failure_RepositoryException_ArgumentException
unit test

```
[TestMethod]
public async Task
➥ CreateBooking_Failure_RepositoryException_ArgumentException() {
_mockBookingRepository.Setup(repository =>
➥ repository.CreateBooking(0, 1)).Throws(new ArgumentException());

  _mockCustomerRepository.Setup(repository =>
➥ repository.GetCustomerByName("Galileo Galilei"))
➥ .Returns(Task.FromResult(
➥ new Customer("Galileo Galilei") { CustomerId = 0 }));

  BookingService service =
➥ new BookingService(_mockBookingRepository.Object,
➥ _mockFlightRepository.Object, _mockCustomerRepository.Object);
  (bool result, Exception exception) =
➥ await service.CreateBooking("Galileo Galilei", 1);

  Assert.IsFalse(result);
  Assert.IsNotNull(exception);
  Assert.IsInstanceOfType(exception,
➥ typeof(CouldNotAddBookingToDatabaseException));
}
```

What have we accomplished in this section? We implemented the BookingService and have the following three unit tests to back up the functionality in our service class:

- CreateBooking_Success—This unit test verifies our "happy path" scenario and calls a mocked BookingRepository to mimic database operations.
- CreateBooking_Failure_RepositoryException_ArgumentException—This unit test tells the BookingRepository mock to throw an ArgumentException. We verify whether our service method can appropriately handle the thrown Argument-Exception.
- CreateBooking_Failure_CouldNotAddBookingToDatabase—This unit test tells the BookingRepository mock to throw a CouldNotAddBookingToDatabase-Exception exception. We verify whether our service method can appropriately handle the thrown CouldNotAddBookingToDatabaseException exception.

11.3   Foreign key constraints in service classes

In section 10.3, we determined that the `BookingService` has to deal with the following two outgoing foreign key constraints (also shown in figure 11.3):

- An outgoing foreign key constraint to `Customer.CustomerID`
- An outgoing foreign key constraint to `Flight.FlightNumber`

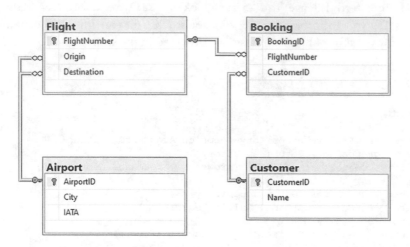

Figure 11.3   The Flying Dutchman Airlines database schema. The Booking model has two outgoing foreign key constraints: one to `Customer.CustomerID` **and one to** `Flight.FlightNumber`.

How do we "handle" these foreign key constraints? We also determined in section 10.3 that we want to use the `CustomerRepository.GetCustomerByName` method to verify a customer exists in the database with the passed-in `Name` value. The method returns a `Customer` object if it is found, which contains the appropriate `CustomerID` value. If it does not find a `Customer` object, we want to create it using the `CustomerRepository` `.CreateCustomer` method. For the `flightNumber` parameter: if there is no matching flight in the database, we should return out of the service method without creating the booking (or a new flight) in the database.

This is where the power of a service layer starts to show. Because we allow service layers (and only service layers!) to make calls to repositories not directly related to their immediate model, we can gather a collection of information to return a `View` to the controller, as shown in figure 11.4. In the case of the `BookingService`, its immediate model is the `Booking` entity. However, to correctly create a new booking in the database, we need to use the `Customer` and `Flight`'s repository layer classes.

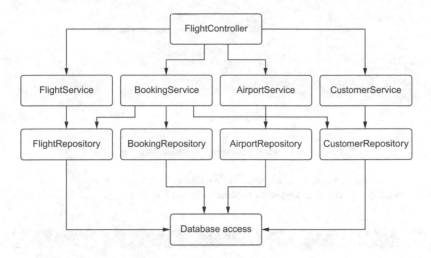

Figure 11.4 The BookingService **calls across the repository layer. It calls the**
BookingRepository **(its immediate concern), the** FlightRepository, **and**
the CustomerRepository.

11.3.1 *Calling the Flight repository from a service class*

Because the business logic on the Flight model is stricter than on the Customer model,
the first check we should do (after input validation) is making sure that the requested
Flight instance lives in the database. Let's see how far we get without getting stuck:

```
public async Task<(bool, Exception)>
➥ CreateBooking(string name, int flightNumber) {
  ...

  FlightRepository flightRepository = new FlightRepository();

  ...
}
```

Well, that's not very far at all. The FlightRepository constructor requires us to pass
(or inject) in an instance of FlyingDutchmanAirlinesContext. We do not have access
to that instance in the service layer. We could instantiate an instance of FlyingDutchman-
AirlinesContext, but we could also take the same approach we did for the Booking-
Repository: use dependency injection to provide the BookingService class with a
ready-to-go instance of FlightRepository.

To add an injected instance to the consuming class, we need to do the following, as
shown in figure 11.5 and listing 11.7:

1 Add a backing field of type T, where T is the injected type.
2 Add a parameter to the constructor of the consuming class of type T.
3 Inside the constructor, assign the injected instance of type T to the private backing field created in step 1.

1. Add backing field.

2. Add a parameter to the constructor.

```
public class BookingService
{
    private readonly BookingRepository _bookingRepository;
    private readonly FlightRepository _flightRepository;

    public BookingService(BookingRepository bookingRepository,
        FlightRepository flightRepository)
    {
        _bookingRepository = bookingRepository;
        _flightRepository = flightRepository;
    }
}
```

3. Assign the injected parameter to the backing field.

Figure 11.5   To use dependency injection, first add a backing field. Then inject the wanted type. Finally, assign the injected parameter to the backing field.

Listing 11.7   `BookingService` injects an instance of `FlightRepository`

```
public class BookingService {
    private readonly BookingRepository _bookingRepository;
    private readonly FlightRepository _flightRepository;
    private readonly CustomerRepository _customerRepository;

    public BookingService(BookingRepository bookingRepository,
        FlightRepository flightRepository, CustomerRepository
        customerRepository) {
        _bookingRepository = bookingRepository;
        _flightRepository = flightRepository;
        _customerRepository = customerRepository;
    }
}
```

Now we have an injected instance of `FlightRepository`, assigned to a backing field, that we can use in our `CreateBooking` method. There's one problem: the code in listing 11.7 does not compile. The compiler throws an exception, shown in figure 11.6, saying that there are not enough arguments in the calls to the `BookingService`'s constructor during our unit tests.

❌ CS7036   There is no argument given that corresponds to the required formal parameter 'customerRepository' of 'BookingService.BookingService (BookingRepository, FlightRepository, CustomerRepository)'

Figure 11.6   The compiler throws an exception if you do not have enough parameters to call a given method. In this case, we did not provide enough parameters to call the constructor of `BookingService` (we are missing the `customerRepository` parameter).

To solve the compiler error, we need to add a `Mock<FlightRepository>` instance to our existing unit tests in the `BookingServiceTests` class. Go ahead and add the mock instance to the unit tests. If you mimic the pattern used to instantiate the `Mock<BookingRepository>` object, you should be fine. If you get stuck, the provided source code contains the answers. You don't need to set up any return calls for the mocked `FlightRepository` class. One final tip: you have to create a parameterless constructor for `FlightRepository`. If you want more information on why you need to create a parameterless virtual constructor, see section 10.3.3.

Our code now compiles, and our existing unit tests pass. We can move on to verifying the flight exists in the database. Our first step, as always, is to add a unit test.

In `BookingServiceTests`, add a unit test called `CreateBooking_Failure_Flight-NotInDatabase`. The success case is covered in the `CreateBooking_Success` unit test, as long as we add a mock setup call to the `FlightRepository.GetFlightByFlight-Number` method as follows:

```
_mockFlightRepository.Setup(repository =>
➡ repository.GetFlightByFlightNumber(0))
➡ .Returns(Task.FromResult(new Flight()));
```

Now, for the failure path, we implement the `CreateBooking_Failure_FlightNotIn-Database` unit test, as shown here:

```
[TestMethod]
public async Task CreateBooking_Failure_FlightNotInDatabase() {
  BookingService service =
➡ new BookingService(_mockBookingRepository.Object,
➡ _mockFlightRepository.Object, _mockCustomerRepository.Object);
  (bool result, Exception exception) =
➡ await service.CreateBooking("Maurits Escher", 19);

  Assert.IsFalse(result);
  Assert.IsNotNull(exception);
  Assert.IsInstanceOfType(exception,
➡ typeof(CouldNotAddBookingToDatabaseException));
}
```

The `CreateBooking_Failure_FlightNotInDatabase` unit test compiles but does not pass. However, that is exactly what we want at this stage. Remember, in test-driven development, we go from not being able to compile or pass a test to implementing just enough to make the test pass.

In `BookingService.CreateBooking`, we want to make sure that we do not book a customer on a flight that does not exist. Taking a look at `FlightRepository.Get-FlightByFlightID`, we notice that the method accepts the following three parameters:

- `flightNumber`
- `originAirportId`
- `desinationAirporId`

Unfortunately, that doesn't work for us anymore. Luckily, we shouldn't be afraid to change (or delete) our own code. I'd like to give you an assignment: make the `Flight-Repository.GetFlightByFlightID` accept only the `flightNumber` argument and return the correct flight. This allows us to use the method in our service layer and forces you to get your hands dirty. If you get stuck, see this chapter's source code. An example implementation is shown in listing 11.8. Also, make sure you update the unit tests.

Now that the `FlightRepository.GetFlightByFlightNumber` method accepts only a `flightNumber`, we can actually use it. Listing 11.8 shows my implementation. You can see that the method offers only two possible return values: either the method returns a `Flight` instance, or it throws a `FlightNotFoundException`.

Listing 11.8 `FlightRepository.GetFlightByFlightNumber`

```
public async Task<Flight> GetFlightByFlightNumber(int flightNumber) {
  if (!flightNumber.IsPositiveInteger()) {
    Console.WriteLine($"Could not find flight in
➥ GetFlightByFlightNumber! flightNumber = {flightNumber}");
    throw new FlightNotFoundException();
  }

  return await _context.Flight.FirstOrDefaultAsync(f =>
➥ f.FlightNumber == flightNumber) ?? throw new FlightNotFoundException();
}
```

A possible implementation of the flight-verification logic would consist of a call to `GetFlightByFlightNumber`, as shown next. If no exception was caught by the `try-catch` in `BookingService.CreateBooking`, things must be all right and we can move on.

```
await _flightRepository.GetFlightByFlightNumber(flightNumber);
```

This code would work perfectly fine until somebody decides to change the implementation of `FlightRepository.GetFlightByFlightNumber`. What if it suddenly returns a null pointer instead of throwing an exception when the method cannot find the matching flight in the database? The code would execute as if nothing happened and allow a customer to be booked on a nonexisting flight.

Instead, let's do a little due diligence here and check the output of `GetFlightByFlightNumber`, as shown in the following code sample. If it is `null`, we also throw an `Exception`.

Listing 11.9 A better implementation of the flight verification code

```
public async Task<(bool, Exception)>
➥ CreateBooking(string name, int flightNumber) {
  if (string.IsNullOrEmpty(name) || !flightNumber.IsPositiveInteger()) {
    return (false, new ArgumentException());
  }

  try {
    __ = await _flightRepository.GetFlightByFlightNumber(flightNumber)
➥ ?? throw new Exception();
```

```
      ...
    }

      ...
}
```

Listing 11.9 handles the null case from `GetFlightByFlightNumber` proactively by throwing an `Exception`. The code also uses the discard operator (_). You can use the discard operator to "throw away" a returned value but still use operators relying on value assignment (such as the null-coalescing operator).

The discard operator and intermediate language

The discard operator (_) is an interesting case to think about. Does using the discard operator mean we aren't assigning the return value from a method to anything? Are we just throwing away the assignment variable immediately? We can find an answer by examining how a discard operator is compiled to Intermediate Language.

Let's take the method call to `FlightRepository.GetFlightByFlightNumber`, as shown in listing 11.9, and remove the null-coalescing operator so we can focus on just the discard operator:

```
_ = await _flightRepository.GetFlightByFlightNumber(flightNumber);
```

This compiles to a lengthy list of MSIL opcodes, but the assignment portion ends with the following:

```
stloc.3
```

The `stloc.3` command stores information to location number 3 on the stack. It seems that using the discard operator still results in some memory allocation. Of course, the allocated spot in memory is collected by the garbage collector as soon as possible because there are no calls to it.

So, to answer our initial question: yes, the discard operator allocates memory. But, because we cannot directly point at a discard operator and use it like any other variable, we still have performance benefits.

Another benefit of using the discard operator is clean code. It is often very confusing to assign values to unused variables. By using the discard operator, you explicitly say, "I am not going to use the return value from this method,"

The code in listing 11.9 is an improvement over what we see in listing 11.8, but we can take it one step further. In section 4.2, we talked about code reading like a narrative. The code in listing 11.9 seems like an excellent opportunity to put that into practice by extracting the flight-verification logic into its own separate private method. We can call the method `FlightExistsInDatabase` and have it return a Boolean value based on whether or not the return value from `FlightRepository.GetFlightByFlightNumber` is `null`, as shown next.

Listing 11.10   Using `FlightExistsInDatabase` in `CreateBooking`

```
public async Task<(bool, Exception)>
⇒ CreateBooking(string name, int flightNumber) {
  if (string.IsNullOrEmpty(name) || !flightNumber.IsPositiveInteger()) {
    return (false, new ArgumentException());
  }

  try {
    if (!await FlightExistsInDatabase(flightNumber))          If the given flight
      throw new CouldNotAddBookingToDatabaseException(); ◁─── does not exist in
    }                                                          the database,
                                                               throws an
    ...                                                        exception
  }

  ...
}

private async Task<bool> FlightExistsInDatabase(int flightNumber) {     If GetFlight-
  try {                                                                 ByFlightNumber
    return await                                                        returns a null
⇒ _flightRepository.GetFlightByFlightNumber(flightNumber) != null;      value, returns
  } catch (FlightNotFoundException) {                                   false; else,
    return false;                                                       returns true
  }                              If GetFlightByFlightNumber
}                                throws a FlightNotFound-
                                 Exception, returns false
```

That should do it for the actual implementation of the flight-verification code. We still need to update our unit tests, however, because we are not prepared to return a correct value when the mocked `FlightRepository`'s `GetFlightByFlightNumber` method is called.

You should be familiar with how to set up a mocked return value by now, so I'm going to show you how to set up the return value for the `CreateBooking_Failure_FlightNotInDatabase` and `CreateBooking_Success` unit tests, and you can try fixing the other unit tests. If you get stuck, the provided source code has the answers.

To tell the `Mock<FlightRepository>` that we want to throw an `Exception` of type `FlightNotFound` (which is the real code's logic) when we see a `flightNumber` of -1, we use the same syntax as described in section 10.3.3 and shown in the next listing:
[MOCK].Setup([*predicate to call method with arguments*]).Throws(new [*Type of Exception*]).

NOTE   As discussed in section 10.3.3, to mock a specific method call we need to make the original method `virtual`. Making a method `virtual` allows the Moq library to override the method. For a discussion on virtual methods, see section 5.3.2.

Listing 11.11 Setting up `Mock<FlightRepository>` exception return value

```
[TestMethod]
public async Task CreateBooking_Failure_FlightNotInDatabase() {
  _mockFlightRepository.Setup(repository =>
  repository.GetFlightByFlightNumber(-1))
  .Throws(new FlightNotFoundException());

  BookingService service = new
  BookingService(_mockBookingRepository.Object,
   mockFlightRepository.Object, _mockCustomerRepository.Object);
  (bool result, Exception exception) =
  await service.CreateBooking("Maurits Escher", 1);

  Assert.IsFalse(result);
  Assert.IsNotNull(exception);
  Assert.IsInstanceOfType(exception,
  typeof(CouldNotAddBookingToDatabaseException));
}
```

With the setup as shown in listing 11.11, when the mock's `GetFlightByFlightNumber` method is called and a value of `-1` is passed in as an input argument, the method throws an `Exception` of type `FlightNotFoundException` (mimicking the existing code). The `BookingService.FlightExistsInDatabase` method (which called the `GetFlightByFlightNumber` method) checks whether or not the return value from the method was `null` (it was `null` in this case because an exception was thrown) and returns the value of that expression. Based on that result, the `BookingService` throws an `Exception` of type `CouldNotAddBookingToDatabaseException`.

To fix the `CreateBooking_Success` unit test, we need to set up our mock of `FlightRepository` to return an instance of `Flight` when the `GetFlightByFlightNumber` method is called.

To add a mocked return of type `Task<Flight>` to the `GetFlightByFlightNumber` method, we need to use the asynchronous version of the `[MOCK].Setup` syntax, as shown in the next code snippet. If we used the synchronous version, the mock would try to return a `Flight` instance instead of a `Task<Flight>` instance, causing a compiler error, shown in figure 11.7.

> ❌ CS1503   Argument 1: cannot convert from 'FlyingDutchmanAirlines.DatabaseLayer.Models.Flight' to 'System.Threading.Tasks.Task<FlyingDutchmanAirlines.DatabaseLayer.Models.Flight>'

Figure 11.7   When trying to return a type not wrapped in a `Task` type, the compiler throws an error saying it cannot convert `T` to `Task<T>`.

```
[TestMethod]
public async Task CreateBooking_Success() {
  _mockBookingRepository.Setup(repository => repository.CreateBooking(0,
  0)).Returns(Task.CompletedTask);
```

```
_mockFlightRepository.Setup(repository =>
    repository.GetFlightByFlightNumber(0)).ReturnsAsync(new Flight());

BookingService service =
    new BookingService(_mockBookingRepository.Object,
    _mockFlightRepository.Object, _mockCustomerRepository.Object);

(bool result, Exception exception) = await service.CreateBooking(0, 0);

Assert.IsTrue(result);
Assert.IsNull(exception);
}
```

CALLING THE CUSTOMER REPOSITORY

The second input we need to validate is the name parameter. To validate the name parameter, the BookingService has to call the CustomerRepository's GetCustomer-ByName and (if the customer does not exist in the database) CreateCustomer methods. In section 10.3.4, we implemented a version of this logic. It's been a while since we looked at those methods (we implemented them in chapter 7), so let's refresh our memories with the next code sample:

```
public virtual async Task<Customer> GetCustomerByName(string name) {
    if (IsInvalidCustomerName(name)) {
        throw new CustomerNotFoundException();
    }

    return await _context.Customer.FirstOrDefaultAsync(c => c.Name == name)
    ?? throw new CustomerNotFoundException();
}
public async Task<bool> CreateCustomer(string name) {
    if (IsInvalidCustomerName(name)) {
        return false;
    }

    try {
        Customer newCustomer = new Customer(name);
        using (_context) {
            _context.Customer.Add(newCustomer);
            await _context.SaveChangesAsync();
        }
    } catch {
        return false;
    }

    return true;
}
```

Our unit tests are now in good shape . . . so, let's break them again! Remember, when everything goes well, the next stage in test-driven development is to break the tests again. In this case, let's add a new unit test that tests the logic when a customer is not in the database: CreateBooking_Success_CustomerNotInDatabase. Why is this unit test a success case? Did the customer validation not fail? Yes, but that just means the customer is not preexisting. In that case, we simply add the customer to the database and proceed as usual, as shown in figure 11.8. To call any method in the `Customer-Repository` from the `BookingService`, we use the injected instance of `Customer-Repository` as follows:

```
private readonly BookingRepository _bookingRepository;
private readonly FlightRepository _flightRepository;
private readonly CustomerRepository _customerRepository;

public BookingService(BookingRepository bookingRepository, FlightRepository
    flightRepository, CustomerRepository customerRepository {
  _bookingRepository = bookingRepository;
  _flightRepository = flightRepository;
  _customerRepository = customerRepository;
}
```

The addition of a `CustomerRepository` parameter to the `CustomerRepository`'s constructor breaks the existing unit tests. You know what to do: add a `Mock<Customer-Repository>` to the constructor call in the unit tests. I leave this for you to do. If you get stuck, see the provided source code for this chapter. You will have to set up the `CustomerRepository` test with a parameterless constructor and make the appropriate methods virtual so Moq instantiates and uses `Mock<CustomerRepository>`.

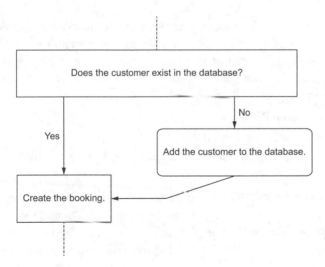

Figure 11.8 If the customer does not exist in the database, we add the customer to the database. In both scenarios, we create a booking.

Using the injected `CustomerRepository` instance, we start by creating two private methods that check whether a customer exists in the database and add it to the database if not. The `CustomerRepository.GetCustomerByName` method returns an `Exception` of type `CustomerNotFoundException`. We can catch this specific error in a `catch` code block and create the customer anyway, as shown in the next listing. If a different type of `Exception` is thrown, then we know something is wrong, so we rethrow the exception (the `CreateBooking` method catches and handles the exception). In section 9.4, we discussed how to rethrow exceptions while preserving the stack trace of the original problem.

Listing 11.12 `GetCustomerFromDatabase` and `AddCustomerToDatabase` methods

If a CustomerNotFoundException is thrown, the customer does not exist in the database.

```
private async Task<Customer> GetCustomerFromDatabase(string name) {
  try {
    return await _customerRepository.GetCustomerByName(name);
  } catch (CustomerNotFoundException) {
    return null;
  } catch (Exception exception){
    ExceptionDispatchInfo.Capture(exception.InnerException
 ?? new Exception()).Throw();
    return null;
  }
}

private async Task<Customer> AddCustomerToDatabase(string name) {
  await _customerRepository.CreateCustomer(name);
  return await _customerRepository.GetCustomerByName(name);
}
```

> **Attempts to retrieve the customer from the database**

> **If a different exception was thrown, something went wrong. Rethrow the exception.**

> **Adds a customer to the database**

The `GetCustomerFromDatabase` and `AddCustomerToDatabase` methods are not called anywhere yet, which gives us a good chance to think about how we can test their functionality. We know we are going to call at least `GetCustomerFromDatabase` in every execution of `CreateBooking`, so let's start with that. `GetCustomerFromDatabase` can determine the following three potential states:

1 The customer exists in the database.
2 The customer does not exist in the database.
3 An `Exception` other than `CustomerNotFoundException` was thrown in `Customer-Repository.GetCustomerByName`.

As far as success cases are concerned, paths 1 and 2 are relevant. If the customer is not found in the database, we add them by way of the `AddCustomerToDatabase` method. There is some more logic involved with that path, so, let's stick to the happy path (1) for now. We'll handle path number 3 (the total failure case) after dealing with the happy paths.

Before we can test any of the states, however, we need to add the customer database logic to the `CreateBooking` method as follows:

```
public async Task<(bool, Exception)> CreateBooking(string name,
 int flightNumber) {
  if (string.IsNullOrEmpty(name) || !flightNumber.IsPositiveInteger()) {
```

```
    return (false, new ArgumentException());
  }

  try {
    Customer customer = await GetCustomerFromDatabase(name)
    ?? await AddCustomerToDatabase(name);

    if (!await FlightExistsInDatabase(flightNumber)) {
      return (false, new CouldNotAddBookingToDatabaseException());
    }

    await
    _bookingRepository.CreateBooking(customer.CustomerId, flightNumber);
    return (true, null);
  } catch (Exception exception) {
    return (false, exception);
  }
}
```

To test the logic path where a customer does not exist in the database, we need to set up the Mock<CustomerRepository> to throw an exception of type CustomerNotFound-Exception when the GetCustomerByName method is called, as shown here:

```
[TestMethod]
public async Task CreateBooking_Success_CustomerNotInDatabase() {
  _mockBookingRepository.Setup(repository =>
  repository.CreateBooking(0, 0)).Returns(Task.CompletedTask);
  _mockCustomerRepository.Setup(repository =>
  repository.GetCustomerByName("Konrad Zuse"))
  .Throws(new CustomerNotFoundException());

  BookingService service =
  new BookingService(_mockBookingRepository.Object,
  _mockFlightRepository.Object, _mockCustomerRepository.Object);

  (bool result, Exception exception) =
  await service.CreateBooking("Konrad Zuse", 0);

  Assert.IsFalse(result);
  Assert.IsNotNull(exception);
  Assert.IsInstanceOfType(exception,
  typeof(CouldNotAddBookingToDatabaseException ));
}
```

That leaves just the following two code paths we need to provide tests for before we wrap up the BookingService implementation:

- The GetCustomerByName threw an exception other than CustomerNotFound-Exception.
- The CreateCustomer method returned a false Boolean.

Luckily, both are easy unit tests to add. What if BookingRepository.CreateBooking threw an Exception? The BookingService.CreateBooking code *should* return {false,

CouldNotAddBookingToDatabaseException}, but does it? There's only one way to find out:

```
[TestMethod]
public async Task
➥ CreateBooking_Failure_CustomerNotInDatabase_RepositoryFailure() {
  _mockBookingRepository.Setup(repository =>
➥ repository.CreateBooking(0, 0))
➥ .Throws(new CouldNotAddBookingToDatabaseException());
  _mockFlightRepository.Setup(repository =>
➥ repository.GetFlightByFlightNumber(0))
➥ .ReturnsAsync(new Flight());
  _mockCustomerRepository.Setup(repository =>
➥ repository.GetCustomerByName("Bill Gates"))
➥ .Returns(Task.FromResult(new Customer("Bill Gates")));

  BookingService service =
➥ new BookingService(_mockBookingRepository.Object,
➥ _mockFlightRepository.Object, _mockCustomerRepository.Object);

  (bool result, Exception exception) =
➥ await service.CreateBooking("Bill Gates", 0);

  Assert.IsFalse(result);
  Assert.IsNotNull(exception);
  Assert.IsInstanceOfType(exception,
➥ typeof(CouldNotAddBookingToDatabaseException));
}
```

It turns out that all is well. And with that, we can wrap up the implementation of BookingService and BookingServiceTests. In this section, we learned more about using mocks in unit tests and how to implement a service layer class that calls across the repository layer with dependency injection.

Exercises

EXERCISE 11.1

True or false? Repositories act as pass-throughs between controllers and services.

EXERCISE 11.2

Fill in the blanks: To add an injected dependency to a class, you have to add a class scoped private _____, which is assigned to a value in a _____ that requires an injected _____.

- a   method; constructor; property
- b   class; abstract method; variable
- c   field; constructor; parameter

EXERCISE 11.3

Let's say I have two models in a dataset schema called Apple and Banana. The Apple.ID column has an outgoing foreign key relationship to the Banana.TastyWith column. Which service is allowed to call what repository?

a The `Apple` service is allowed to call the `Banana` repository.

b The `Banana` repository is allowed to call the `Apple` repository.

c The `Kiwi` repository is injected in both the `Apple` and `Banana` services and will take it from there.

EXERCISE 11.4

True or false? A service class is allowed to call an unlimited number of repositories, as long as it has a valid reason to call every one of them.

EXERCISE 11.5

If you try to instantiate a type without providing the parameters required by any of its constructors, what do you get?

a A participation trophy

b A compilation error

c A runtime error

EXERCISE 11.6

True or false? The discard operator ensures you never allocate any memory to store an expression's return value.

EXERCISE 11.7

You have two `catch` blocks in a try-catch code block. The first is a `catch` on the `Exception` class; the second is a `catch` on the `ItemSoldOutException` class. If an `ItemSoldOutException` is thrown in the try part of the try-catch code block, which catch block is entered?

a `catch(Exception exception) {…}`

b `catch(ItemSoldOutException exception) {…}`

EXERCISE 11.8

You have two `catch` blocks in a `try-catch` code block. The first is a `catch` on the `ItemSoldOutException` class; the second is a `catch` on the `Exception` class. If an `ItemSoldOutException` is thrown in the try part of the try-catch code block, which catch block is entered?

a `catch(ItemSoldOutException exception) {…}`

b `catch(Exception exception) {…}`

Summary

- You can use the `Assert.IsInstanceOfType` to perform a test assertion on an object to check whether it is of a certain type (or can be coerced to that type using polymorphism). Checking types in unit tests can come in handy if you need to be sure a specific type was returned; for example, checking the type of `Exception` that was returned from a method.

- You can perform runtime type checks by using the `is` and `as` operators. This is helpful when dealing with objects that you may not know the exact type of.

- Service classes are allowed to call repository classes where appropriate. You use service classes to organize multiple data streams into one view. Calling repository classes from a service also allows you to track down foreign key constraints.

- The discard operator (`_`) allows you to explicitly indicate that a method's return value is a throwaway value. Sometimes using the discard operator can improve code readability.

- The discard operator does allocate blocks of memory, but the garbage collector can collect on them as soon as possible because there are no pointers to said block of memory. This helps speed up performance.

- You can have multiple `catch` blocks in a `try-catch` code block. Only the first matching `catch` block is entered. This is useful when dealing with more than one derived class of `Exception`, and your logic differs based on particular classes.

Using IAsyncEnumerable<T> and yield return

12

This chapter covers

- Using the generic `Queue` data structure
- Using `yield return` and `IAsyncEnumerable<T>`
- Creating views
- Using private getters and setters with auto-properties
- How structs differ from classes
- Using `checked` and `unchecked` keywords

In the previous chapters, we examined the codebase we inherited and noted where we could make improvements. Then, we partially implemented our version of the codebase, adhering to FlyTomorrow's OpenAPI specification. In chapters 10 and 11, we implemented the `BookingService` class and decided that there was no need for a `CustomerService` class. Figure 12.1 shows where we are in the scheme of the book.

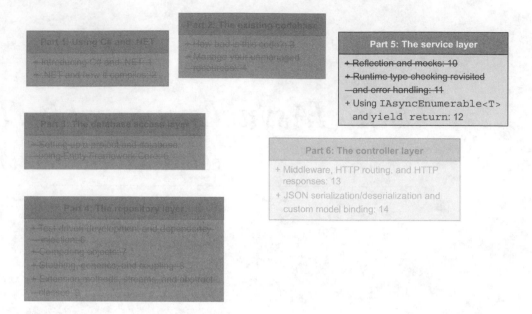

Figure 12.1   In this chapter, we wrap up the services layer by implementing the `AirportService` and `FlightService` classes. By implementing those classes, we finish the service layer rewrite of the Flying Dutchman Airlines service.

If we look at which classes we need to implement to complete our service layer, an encouraging picture follows:

- `CustomerService` (chapter 10)
- `BookingService` (chapters 10 and 11)
- `AirportService` (this chapter)
- `FlightService` (this chapter)

We are halfway done with the service layer classes. In this chapter, we'll wrap up the service layer implementation by writing code for the `AirportService` and `Flight-Service` classes. After this chapter, we are in an excellent spot to move on to our last architectural layer: the controller layer.

12.1   *Do we need an AirportService class?*

In section 10.2, we determined that if a service class would never get called by a controller class, we do not need to implement the service class. We also saw that you can determine whether you need a particular controller by checking the controller's model name against the OpenAPI specification. If there is no need for a controller, there is no need for a service class. As humans, being creatures of habit, let's repeat that process for the `AirportService` class.

The OpenAPI specification (as shown in figure 12.2) tells us we need to implement the following three endpoints:

- `GET /Flight`
- `GET /Flight/{FlightNumber}`
- `POST /Booking/{FlightNumber}`

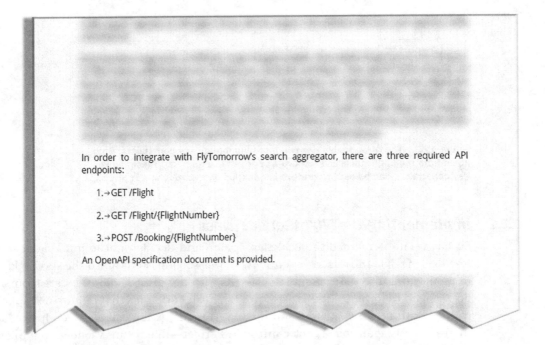

In order to integrate with FlyTomorrow's search aggregator, there are three required API endpoints:

1.→GET /Flight

2.→GET /Flight/{FlightNumber}

3.→POST /Booking/{FlightNumber}

An OpenAPI specification document is provided.

Figure 12.2   The OpenAPI specification from FlyTomorrow. We need to implement three endpoints: two GETs and one POST.

Do any of those endpoints have a controller related to the `Airport` model in their path? As shown in figure 12.3, I see two `Flight` controllers and one `Booking` controller, but no endpoints requiring an `Airport` controller. Well, that settles it then: we do not need to implement an `AirportService` class.

On the other hand, we do have a use case to keep the `AirportRepository` class. If we look at the database schema of our deployed database, we see that the Airport table has the following two incoming foreign key constraints:

- `Flight.Origin` to `Airport.AirportID`
- `Flight.Destination` to `Airport.AirportID`

In section 12.2, we'll dive deeper into those foreign key constraints and implement them. From our experiences in chapter 11, we know that we need to use the receiving table's repository to trace down these foreign key constraints.

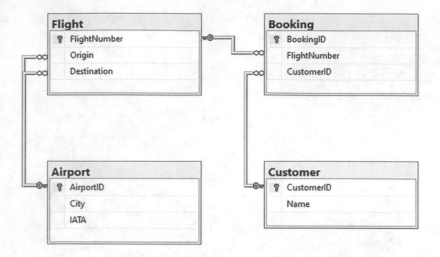

Figure 12.3   The Airport table has two incoming foreign key constraints. Both come from the Flight table and retrieve `Airport.AirportID`. These foreign key constraints can be used to retrieve information on a particular `Airport`.

12.2   *Implementing the FlightService class*

So far, we implemented the `BookingService` and decided not to implement services for the `Airport` and `Customer` entities. In this section, we'll finish the service layer by implementing the `FlightService` class. As with the prior sections, let's ask ourselves, do we need to implement this class? We have two endpoints that require a `Flight` controller. Both the `GET /Flight` and the `GET /Flight/{FlightNumber}` endpoints make their requests against a `Flight` controller. Perfect—that means we need to implement a `FlightService` class. Both endpoints return data that already exists in the database and are fairly simple in their complexity. Let's begin with the first: `GET /Flight`.

12.2.1   *Getting information on a specific flight from the FlightRepository*

In this section, we'll implement the `GET /Flight` endpoint as discussed in section 12.1. FlyTomorrow uses the `GET /Flight` endpoint to query our service for all available flights. We don't need to take into account (or validate) any special input parameters, but we have some foreign key restrictions to track down. We'll also create a `View` class for `Flight` so we can return a combination of data stemming from the `Flight` and `Airport` tables.

But first, the starting point of all our endeavors: we need to create skeleton classes for both the `FlightService` and `FlightServiceTests` classes, as shown in figure 12.4. You know what to do.

Now that we have the required classes in our projects, we can think about the things we need our method to do. Our method—let's call it `GetFlights`—has to return data on every flight in the database. To do this, we should use an injected instance of

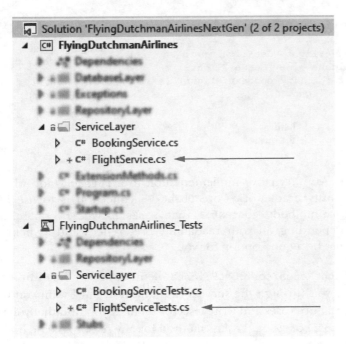

Figure 12.4 To start the implementation of the **FlightService**, **create two skeleton classes:** **FlightService** and **FlightServiceTests.** **These classes form the basis of our** **FlightService** and **FlightServiceTests** **implementations.**

the `FlightRepository` class. The `FlightRepository` class does not have a method to return all flights from the database, however, so we need to add that.

In `FlightRepository`, let's add a virtual method called `GetFlights`. We don't need to make the method asynchronous, because we do not query the actual database for the required information. Even though we want to get all the data from a specific table in the database, remember that Entity Framework Core stores a lot of metadata in memory. This brings us to one of the drawbacks of using an ORM; performance at scale. If you have a database that contains millions of records, Entity Framework Core still stores a lot of data locally. On the flip side, it means that we can query Entity Framework Core's internal `DbSet<Flight>` and see all flights currently in the database.

The `GetFlights` method should return a collection of `Flight`, but which collection to use? We don't need to access elements by some kind of key or index, so an `Array`, `Dictionary`, or `List` is unnecessary. Perhaps a simple `Queue<Flight>` would suffice.

A queue is a "first-in, first-out" (often abbreviated to FIFO) data structure. The first element to enter the queue is the first to come out, as shown in as shown in listing 12.1. Having a FIFO structure is helpful in our case because we can ensure we have an isomorphic relationship between how we represent the flights in our data structure and how they are represented in the database.

Listing 12.1   `FlightRepository.GetFlights`

```
public virtual Queue<Flight> GetFlights() {          Creates a queue
  Queue<Flight> flights = new Queue<Flight>();        to store flights
  foreach (Flight flight in _context.Flight) {
    flights.Enqueue(flight);                          Adds every flight to
  }                                                   the queue (in order)

  return flights;          Returns
}                          the queue
```

EF CORE FOREACH   An alternative implementation to a `foreach` loop when dealing with an Entity Framework Core `DbSet<T>` collection is to use EF Core's `ForEachAsync` method: `_context.Flight.ForEachAsync(f => flights .Enqueue(f));`. Depending on your readability preferences and asynchronous needs, this may be a good option for you.

That's all for the `FlightRepository.GetFlights` method, but we need unit tests to back this up. I'll walk you through the success case unit test, but I want you to think about some potential failure cases and write tests for them. If you find that you want to change the `FlightRepository.GetFlights` method for any reason, please do so!

If we look at the existing `FlightRepositoryTest` class's `TestInitialize` method, we see that only one flight is added to the in-memory database before each test. In an ideal world, we would like to have at least two flights in the in-memory database so we can assert against the order in the returned `Queue<Flight>` as follows:

```
[TestInitialize]
public async Task TestInitialize() {
  DbContextOptions<FlyingDutchmanAirlinesContext> dbContextOptions =
    new DbContextOptionsBuilder<FlyingDutchmanAirlinesContext>()
    .UseInMemoryDatabase("FlyingDutchman").Options;
  _context = new FlyingDutchmanAirlinesContext_Stub(dbContextOptions);

  Flight flight = new Flight {
    FlightNumber = 1,
    Origin = 1,
    Destination = 2
  };

  Flight flight2 = new Flight {
    FlightNumber = 10,
    Origin = 3,
    Destination = 4
  };

  _context.Flight.Add(flight);
  _context.Flight.Add(flight2);
  await _context.SaveChangesAsync();
```

```
_repository = new FlightRepository(_context);
Assert.IsNotNull(_repository);
}
```

 YIELD RETURN KEYWORDS   If you are okay with using a generic class instead of a concrete collection type such as Queue, List, or Dictionary, a neat concept to use is the yield return keywords.

When dealing with collections that implement the IEnumerable<T> interface, we can return the IEnumerable<T> type and not have to declare an actual collection inside a method. That may sound a bit confusing, so let me show you in the next code sample what the code in listing 12.1 looks like if we were to use this approach.

> **Listing 12.2   Using `yield return` and `IEnumerable<Flight>`**

```
public virtual IEnumerable<Flight> GetFlights() {
  foreach (Flight flight in _context.Flight) {
    yield return flight;
  }
}
```

The code in listing 12.2 does not explicitly declare a collection in which to store the Flight objects. Instead, by using the yield return keywords, we abstract away the collection initialization and let the compiler do its magic. (This is a simple example, and the code in listing 12.2 could also simply return the existing _context.Flight collection in this case.) This compiler magic consists of the compiler generating a class implementing the IEnumerable interface under the hood and returning that. The syntax suggests we are using the IEnumerable interface directly, but in fact, you are using the compiler-generated wrapper class.

You will also sometimes hear about the yield return keyword within the context of lazy evaluation. Lazy evaluation means that we delay all processing/iterating until it is absolutely necessary. The opposite of this is greedy evaluation, which does all processing up front and then lets us iterate over the results once it has all the information. By using the yield return keyword, we can come up with lazy logic that doesn't operate on the returned results until they are returned. This is explained further in the discussion on IAsyncEnumerable<T> later in this section.

Now that we can get a queue of all the flights in the database by calling the FlightRepository.GetFlights method, we can start to assemble the view we want to return to the controller. By default, the Flight object has three properties: FlightNumber, OriginID, and DestinationID. This information is crucial to the customer, so we want to return it. However, simply returning IDs for the origin and destination airports is not very useful. If we look at the database schema, we see that we can use foreign keys to get more information about the origin and destination airports.

The `Flight` table has the following two outgoing foreign key constraints, as shown in figure 12.5:

- `Flight.Origin` to `Airport.AirportID`
- `Flight.Destination` to `Airport.AirportID`

Figure 12.5   **The Flight table has two outgoing foreign key constraints. This figure does not show any other foreign key constraints (inbound or outbound). We'll use these foreign key constraints to create a view in section 12.2.2.**

If we were to trace down those foreign key constraints, we could get `Airport` information based on their IDs. The `AirportRepository` class has the following method that can help us here: `GetAirportByID`. The `GetAirportByID` method accepts an airport ID and returns the appropriate airport (if found in the database). We know that the `Airport` model has a property for its city name, so we can return the origin and destination city names along with the flight number to the controller. This amalgamation of two data sources forms the thinking behind our yet-to-be-created `FlightView` class.

12.2.2   *Combining two data streams into a view*

In section 10.1.1, we discussed views. We talked about how a view can give us a window into a model and combine data from various data sources. In this section, we'll create the `FlightView` class and populate it with data from both the `Flight` model and the `Airport` model.

We can easily create the `FlightView` class. It is a public class with the following three public properties:

- `FlightNumber` of type `string`
- An `Airport` object containing `OriginCity` (type `string`) and `Code` (type `string`)
- An `Airport` object containing `DestinationCity` (type `string`) and `Code` (type `string`)

The data for `FlightNumber` comes from the `Flight` model, whereas the data for the `Airport` object and the `OriginCity` and `DestinationCity` properties comes from the `Airport` model, as shown in figure 12.6. This information (for every flight in the database) is the data we ultimately return to FlyTomorrow when they query the `GET` `/Flight` endpoint.

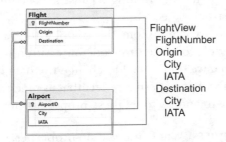

Figure 12.6 The `FlightView` class combines the `FlightNumber` data from the Flight table with the city and code data from the Airport table. This allows us to present exactly the information we want from multiple sources to the end user.

To keep things organized, let's create a new folder for the `FlightView` class called Views. The folder lives in the `FlyingDutchmanAirlines` project. Even though we don't expect a lot of views in this project, it is always good to be somewhat organized.

STRUCTS How do we deal with this `Airport` object we want to add inside the `FlightView`? Sure, we could add instances of `Airport` and ignore some fields, but that seems heavy handed to me. This is a prime chance to use the struct type. Many languages support either structs or classes, but C# does both. We can think of structs (within the context of C#) as light-weight classes that store simple information. Structs have less overhead than a full-fledged class, so when you just want to store a little information, use a struct.

Let's add a struct called `AirportInfo` inside the FlightView.cs file (Note: Not inside the `FlightView` class.), as shown in the next code sample. The `AirportInfo` type should store information about the `City` and `Code` of a destination. We could use `IATA` instead of `Code` and reflect the database. However, because this is a view, we can change the name of things if we feel they better represent the data. IATA is correct, but `Code` is easier to understand for people unfamiliar with aviation terms.

```
public struct AirportInfo {
  public string City { get; set; }
  public string Code { get; set; }

  public AirportInfo((string city, string code) airport) {
    City = airport.city;
    Code = airport.code;
  }
}
```

The `AirportInfo` constructor accepts a tuple containing two fields: `city` and `code`. This brings us to the second cool thing about using a struct: when adding a constructor to a struct, you need to assign every property a value. In a class, you do not need to assign a value to all properties, but this does not fly with a struct! If we were to have an `AirportInfo` constructor that assigns a value only to the `City` property, the compiler would cry foul. By adding a constructor to a struct, you guarantee a complete setup of the respective struct. We can use this for future-proofing against a (well-intended) developer not completely initializing a struct as needed.

Coming back to the `FlightView` class, we can do something cool with the properties there as well. We can use private setters to make sure code only within the struct itself can change the value. We know that we don't need to change the data once we retrieve it from the database, so let's make the properties reflect that as much as possible. We don't want just anybody to come in and try to set these properties, anyway.

ACCESS MODIFIERS AND AUTO-PROPERTIES   When using auto-properties, we can have different access modifiers for setting and getting a property.

Let's see what the `FlightView` class looks like with a split `get` and `set` system, as shown here:

```
public class FlightView {
  public string FlightNumber { get; private set; }
  public AirportInfo Origin { get; private set; }
  public AirportInfo Destination { get; private set; }
}
```

In this situation, only code that can access the properties through their private access modifiers can set new values, yet the `get` is still public. So where do we set these values? How about in a constructor? An alternative approach to using a private setter would be to make the properties `readonly`, because you can only set `readonly` properties in a constructor.

Let's create a constructor that accesses the properties' private setters and accepts arguments to set them to as follows:

```
public FlightView(string flightNumber, (string city, string code) origin,
    (string city, string code) destination) {
  FlightNumber = flightNumber;

  Origin = new AirportInfo(origin);
  Destination = new AirportInfo(destination);
}
```

We should also do some input validation on the passed-in parameters. We can use the `String.IsNullOrEmpty` method to see whether any of the input arguments are a null pointer or an empty string. Alternatively, you can use the `String.IsNullOrWhitespace`, which checks whether the string is null, empty, or just consists of whitespace. If they are, we set them to appropriate values. We also use the ternary conditional operator, as shown next:

```
public class FlightView {
  public string FlightNumber { get; private set; }
  public AirportInfo Origin { get; private set; }
  public AirportInfo Destination { get; private set; }

  public FlightView(string flightNumber,
➥ (string city, string code) origin,
➥ (string city, string code) destination) {
    FlightNumber = string.IsNullOrEmpty(flightNumber) ?
    ➥ "No flight number found" : flightNumber;

    Origin = new AirportInfo(origin);
    Destination = new AirportInfo(destination);
  }
}

public struct AirportInfo {
  public string City { get; private set; }
  public string Code { get; private set; }

  public AirportInfo ((string city, string code) airport) {
    City = string.IsNullOrEmpty(airport.city) ?
➥ "No city found" : airport.city;
    Code = string.IsNullOrEmpty(airport.code) ?
➥ "No code found" : airport.code;
  }
}
```

> **NOTE** Technically, we could make the FlightNumber, Origin, Destination, City, and Code properties to be "get" only and remove the private setter altogether. The compiler is smart enough to realize that we want to privately set the properties in the constructor. I like the verbosity of having the private setter, however. Your mileage may vary.

Of course, we should also create a test class and some unit tests to verify the Flight-View constructor logic. Figure 12.7 shows the newly created files.

There are different trains of thought on testing constructors. Some people say that testing a constructor is simply testing the instantiation of a new object and, therefore, testing a language feature. Others say testing a constructor is useful because you never know what happens with the code. I fall into the latter camp. Especially when testing a constructor represents a minimal effort, having a test suite, such as the following code, to back up your code is the way to go:

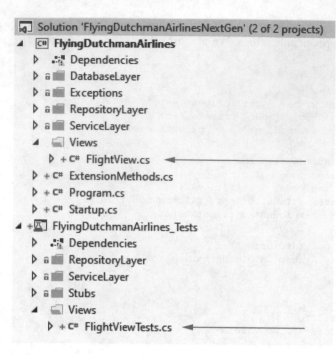

Figure 12.7 **Two new files are created: FlightView in FlyingDutchmanAirlines/Views, and FlightViewTests in FlyingDutchmanAirlines_Tests /Views. Storing the classes in a separate Views folder helps us with organizing our codebase.**

```
[TestClass]
public class FlightViewTests {
  [TestMethod]
  public void Constructor_FlightView_Success() {
    string flightNumber = "0";
    string originCity = "Amsterdam";
    string originCityCode = "AMS";
    string destinationCity = "Moscow";
    string destinationCityCode = "SVO";

    FlightView view =
    new FlightView(flightNumber, (originCity, originCityCode),
    (destinationCity, destinationCityCode));
    Assert.IsNotNull(view);

    Assert.AreEqual(view.FlightNumber, flightNumber);
    Assert.AreEqual(view.Origin.City, originCity);
    Assert.AreEqual(view.Origin.Code, originCityCode);
    Assert.AreEqual(view.Destination.City, destinationCity);
    Assert.AreEqual(view.Destination.Code, destinationCityCode);
  }

  [TestMethod]
  public void Constructor_FlightView_Success_FlightNumber_Null() {
    string originCity = "Athens";
    string originCityCode = "ATH";
    string destinationCity = "Dubai";
```

```
    string destinationCityCode = "DXB";
    FlightView view =
new FlightView(null, (originCity, originCityCode),
(destinationCity, destinationCityCode));
    Assert.IsNotNull(view);

    Assert.AreEqual(view.FlightNumber, "No flight number found");
    Assert.AreEqual(view.Origin.City, originCity);
    Assert.AreEqual(view.Destination.City, destinationCity);
}

[TestMethod]
public void Constructor_AirportInfo_Success_City_EmptyString() {
    string destinationCity = string.Empty;
    string destinationCityCode = "SYD";

    AirportInfo airportInfo =
new AirportInfo((destinationCity, destinationCityCode));
    Assert.IsNotNull(airportInfo);

    Assert.AreEqual(airportInfo.City, "No city found");
    Assert.AreEqual(airportInfo.Code, destinationCityCode);
}

[TestMethod]
public void Constructor_AirportInfo_Success_Code_EmptyString() {
    string destinationCity = "Ushuaia";
    string destinationCityCode = string.Empty;

    AirportInfo airportInfo =
new AirportInfo((destinationCity, destinationCityCode));
    Assert.IsNotNull(airportInfo);

    Assert.AreEqual(airportInfo.City, destinationCity);
    Assert.AreEqual(airportInfo.Code, "No code found");
}
}
```

We can now rest easy knowing that whatever may happen to the code in the FlightView class and the AirportInfo struct, we have tests to catch any changes that break existing functionality. We can now move on to populating the FlightView for every flight we get back from the FlightRepository. Of the five pieces of data we need for the FlightView (the flight number, the destination city, the destination code, the origin city, and the origin code), we know how to get the flight number. We just need to call the FlightRepository.GetFlights method. Of course, we need a GetFlights method in the FlightService first.

The GetFlights method returns an instance of FlightView wrapped in an IAsyncEnumerable. We discussed IEnumerable and how we can use the yield return keywords with it earlier in this section. The IAsyncEnumerable return type allows us to return an asynchronous collection implementing the IEnumerable interface. Because it is already asynchronous, we do not need to wrap it in a Task.

To start, let's call the `FlightRepository.GetFlights` method and construct a `FlightView` for every flight returned from the database, as shown in the next listing. To do this, we also need to inject an instance of `FlightRepository` into the `Flight-Service` class. I leave that to you. You know what to do there. If you get stuck, see the provided source code. Note that the code in listing 12.3 does not compile, as explained after the listing.

Listing 12.3   `FlightService.GetFlights` asks for all flights in the database

```
public async Task<IAsyncEnumerable<FlightView>> GetFlights() {          Asks for all flights
  Queue<Flight> flights = _flightRepository.GetFlights();      <—        in the database
  foreach (Flight flight in flights) {                          <——      Loops over the
    FlightView view =                                                    returned flights
    new FlightView(flight.FlightNumber.ToString(), ,);         <——
  }                                                                      Creates a FlightView
}                                                                        instance for every flight
```

Take a minute to read through listing 12.3 and see if you can spot why this code does not compile (besides not returning the correct type). Did you see it? The compiler throws an error because we did not provide enough arguments when instantiating the `FlightView` object for every flight. We don't even have the correct information to give the view, though. The view wants us to pass in values for the flight number, origin city, and destination city. We passed in the flight number but neither of the cities. The closest thing we have to city names are the `originAirportID` and `destinationAirportID` properties on the returned `Flight` objects. We know how to take those and get the airport city names and codes: we call the `AirportRepository.GetAirportByID` method and take the `Airport.City` property (we also need an injected `AirportRepository` instance), as shown here:

```
public async IAsyncEnumerable<FlightView> GetFlights() {
    Queue<Flight> flights = _flightRepository.GetFlights();
  foreach (Flight flight in flights) {
  Airport originAirport =
    await _airportRepository.GetAirportByID(flight.Origin),
  Airport destinationAirport =
    await _airportRepository.GetAirportByID(flight.Destination);

  FlightView view =
    new FlightView(flight.FlightNumber.ToString(),
      (originAirport.City, originAirport.Code),
      (destinationAirport.City, destinationAirport.Code));
  }
}
```

Now, here is where the real magic happens. Because we return a type of `IAsync-Enumerable<FlightView>`, we can use the `yield return` keywords to automatically add the created `FlightView` instances to a compiler-generated list as follows:

```
public async IAsyncEnumerable<FlightView> GetFlights() {
    Queue<Flight> flights = _flightRepository.GetFlights();
  foreach (Flight flight in flights) {
  Airport originAirport =
➥ await _airportRepository.GetAirportByID(flight.Origin);
  Airport destinationAirport =
➥ await _airportRepository.GetAirportByID(flight.Destination);

  yield return new FlightView(flight.FlightNumber.ToString(),
➥ (originAirport.City, originAirport.Code),
➥ (destinationAirport.City, destinationAirport.Code));
  }
}
```

We should also add a unit test in `FlightServiceTests` to verify we did a good job. Remember, we do not have to test the repository layers when testing service layer methods. Instead, we can use instances of `Mock<FlightRepository>` and `Mock<Airport-Repository>` as the injected dependencies to the `FlightService` class. To mock the `AirportRepository` class, make the appropriate methods virtual and add a parameterless constructor, as shown in the next listing. We've done this a couple of times now, so I leave that to you.

> ### Listing 12.4　Unit testing a method returning `IAsyncEnumerable<T>`

```
[TestMethod]
public async Task GetFlights_Success() {
  Flight flightInDatabase = new Flight {
    FlightNumber = 148,
    Origin = 31,
    Destination = 92
  };

  Queue<Flight> mockReturn = new Queue<Flight>(1);
  mockReturn.Enqueue(flightInDatabase);

  _mockFlightRepository.Setup(repository =>
➥ repository.GetFlights()).Returns(mockReturn);

  _mockAirportRepository.Setup(repository =>
➥ repository.GetAirportByID(31)).ReturnsAsync(new Airport
    {
      AirportId = 31,
      City = "Mexico City",
      Iata = "MEX"
    });

  _mockAirportRepository.Setup(repository =>
➥ repository.GetAirportByID(92)).ReturnsAsync(new Airport
    {
      AirportId = 92,
      City = "Ulaanbaataar",
      Iata = "UBN"
    });
```

Sets up the FlightRepository .GetAllFlights mocked return

Sets up the AirportRepository .GetAirportByID mocked returns

```
FlightService service = new FlightService(_mockFlightRepository.Object,
   _mockAirportRepository.Object);

await foreach (FlightView flightView in service.GetFlights()) {
    Assert.IsNotNull(flightView);
    Assert.AreEqual(flightView.FlightNumber, "148");
    Assert.AreEqual(flightView.Origin.City, "Mexico City");
    Assert.AreEqual(flightView.Origin.Code, "MEX");
    Assert.AreEqual(flightView.Destination.City, "Ulaanbaatar");
    Assert.AreEqual(flightView.Destination.Code, "UBN");
    }
}
```

Makes sure we received the correct flightView back

Receives flightViews as we construct them in the GetFlights method (one in this case)

Injects the mocked dependencies, and creates a new instance of FlightService

In listing 12.4, we get our first peek at how to use the returned IAsyncEnumerable type and can put together the puzzle of why it is such an outstanding feature. Instead of calling the FlightService.GetFlights method once, waiting for all the data to come back, and then operating on it, the IAsyncEnumerable type allows us to await on a foreach loop and operate on the returned data as it comes in.

12.2.3 *Using the yield return keywords with try-catch code blocks*

In section 12.2.2, we implemented the FlightService.GetFlights method. We did not, however, handle any exceptions coming out of the AirportRepository.Get-AirportByID method. Unfortunately, we cannot simply add a try-catch code block and wrap the entire method in it because we cannot use the yield return keywords in such a code block. Not allowing yield statements in try-catch blocks has been a point of discussion within the C# language community for a while. Because adding yield statements to just try code blocks (without the catch) is allowed, and the only blocker for adding yield statement support to try-catch code blocks is added compiler complexity due to garbage collection difficulties, we may see this feature added in the future. The workaround is to add the calls to the AirportRepository.Get-AirportByID method only in a try-catch block, so we can catch any outgoing exceptions, and then proceed as usual, as shown next:

```
public async IAsyncEnumerable<FlightView> GetFlights() {
    Queue<Flight> flights = _flightRepository.GetFlights();
  foreach (Flight flight in flights) {
    Airport originAirport;
    Airport destinationAirport;

    try {
      originAirport =
  await _airportRepository.GetAirportByID(flight.Origin);
        destinationAirport =
  await _airportRepository.GetAirportByID(flight.Destination);
    } catch (FlightNotFoundException) {
```

```
      throw new FlightNotFoundException();
    } catch (Exception) {
      throw new ArgumentException();
    }

    yield return new FlightView(flight.FlightNumber.ToString(),
⇒ (originAirport.City, originAirport.Code),
⇒ (destinationAirport.City, destinationAirport.Code));
  }
}
```

NOTE We have seen both IAsyncEnumerable and Task<IEnumerable> as return types. IAsyncEnumerable does not need to be wrapped in a Task<T> when returning from an asynchronous method, because IAsyncEnumerable is already asynchronous. Using a type with the generic Task<T> allows us to return a synchronous type from an asynchronous method.

This code allows us to catch any exception coming from the AirportRepository .GetAirportByID method. If the service class finds the repository method threw an exception of type FlightNotFoundException, it throws a new instance of FlightNot-FoundException. If the code throws a different type of exception, the second catch block is entered and the code throws an ArgumentException. The controller calling the service layer handles this exception.

The last piece of our service layer implementations is to write a unit test that verifies our handling of the exception code we just wrote. Let's look at that unit test shown next. It should be pretty straightforward.

Listing 12.5 Testing for exceptions in the FlightService

```
[TestMethod]
[ExpectedException(typeof(FlightNotFoundException))]
public async Task GetFlights_Failure_RepositoryException() {
  Flight flightInDatabase = new Flight {
    FlightNumber = 148,
    Origin = 31,
    Destination = 92
  };

  Queue<Flight> mockReturn = new Queue<Flight>(1);
  mockReturn.Enqueue(flightInDatabase);

  _mockFlightRepository.Setup(repository =>
⇒ repository.GetFlights()).Returns(mockReturn);

  _mockAirportRepository.Setup(repository =>
⇒ repository.GetAirportByID(31))
⇒ .ThrowsAsync(new FlightNotFoundException());

  FlightService service = new FlightService(_mockFlightRepository.Object,
⇒ _mockAirportRepository.Object);
```

Annotations:
- Expects the executed logic in this test to throw an exception
- Starts at the FlightRepository .GetAllFlights mocked return (same as listing 12.4)
- Sets up the AirportRepository.GetAirportByID mocked returns (same as listing 12.4)
- Creates a new instance of FlightService (same as listing 12.4)

```
  await foreach (FlightView _ in service.GetFlights()) {
    ;
  }
}

[TestMethod]
[ExpectedException(typeof(ArgumentException))]
public async Task GetFlights_Failure_RegularException() {
  Flight flightInDatabase = new Flight {
    FlightNumber = 148,
    Origin = 31,
    Destination = 92
  };

  Queue<Flight> mockReturn = new Queue<Flight>(1);
  mockReturn.Enqueue(flightInDatabase);

  _mockFlightRepository.Setup(repository =>
  repository.GetFlights()).Returns(mockReturn);

  _mockAirportRepository.Setup(repository =>
  repository.GetAirportByID(31))
  .ThrowsAsync(new NullReferenceException());

  FlightService service = new FlightService(_mockFlightRepository.Object,
  _mockAirportRepository.Object);

  await foreach (FlightView _ in service.GetFlights()) {
    ;
  }
}
```

Calls the GetFlights method, using the discard operator for the return assignment

Expects the executed logic in this test to throw an exception

Empty statement

Starts at the FlightRepository.GetAllFlights mocked return (same as listing 12.4)

Sets up the AirportRepository.GetAirportByID mocked returns (same as listing 12.4)

Creates a new instance of FlightService (same as listing 12.4)

Calls the GetFlights method, using the discard operator for the return assignment

Overall, the code in listing 12.5 should pose no challenges. It is good to point out that by using the discard operator in the foreach, we tell other developers that we do not need to use the returned values. In the same vein, inside the foreach loop, we added an empty statement (;). This does absolutely nothing but provide more readable code. By adding the empty statement, we say that having no logic inside the foreach loop was not a mistake.

We can do some further cleaning up: I am sure you noticed we have identical setup code for the Mock<Flight> and Mock<Airport> instances in both unit tests. Because this violates the DRY principle, we should refactor both unit tests and do this initialization in the TestInitialize method. This shortens our test methods considerably, as shown here:

```
[TestClass]
public class FlightServiceTests {
  private Mock<FlightRepository> _mockFlightRepository;
  private Mock<AirportRepository> _mockAirportRepository;

  [TestInitialize]
  public void Initialize() {
```

```
   _mockFlightRepository = new Mock<FlightRepository>();
   _mockAirportRepository = new Mock<AirportRepository>();

   Flight flightInDatabase = new Flight {
     FlightNumber = 148,
     Origin = 31,
     Destination = 92
   };

   Queue<Flight> mockReturn = new Queue<Flight>(1);
   mockReturn.Enqueue(flightInDatabase);

   _mockFlightRepository.Setup(repository =>
➥ repository.GetFlights()).Returns(mockReturn);
 }


 [TestMethod]
 public async Task GetFlights_Success() {
   _mockAirportRepository.Setup(repository =>
➥ repository.GetAirportByID(31)).ReturnsAsync(new Airport
   {
     AirportId = 31,
     City = "Mexico City",
     Iata = "MEX"
   });

   _mockAirportRepository.Setup(repository =>
➥ repository.GetAirportByID(92)).ReturnsAsync(new Airport
   {
     AirportId = 92,
     City = "Ulaanbaatar",
     Iata = "UBN"
   });

   FlightService service =
➥ new FlightService(_mockFlightRepository.Object,
➥ _mockAirportRepository.Object);

   await foreach (FlightView flightView in service.GetFlights()) {
     Assert.IsNotNull(flightView);
     Assert.AreEqual(flightView.FlightNumber, "148");
     Assert.AreEqual(flightView.Origin.City, "Mexico City");
     Assert.AreEqual(flightView.Origin.Code, "MEX");
     Assert.AreEqual(flightView.Destination.City, "Ulaanbaatar");
     Assert.AreEqual(flightView.Destination.Code, "UBN");
   }
 }

 [TestMethod]
 [ExpectedException(typeof(FlightNotFoundException))]
 public async Task GetFlights_Failure_RepositoryException() {
   _mockAirportRepository.Setup(repository =>
➥ repository.GetAirportByID(31)).ThrowsAsync(new Exception());
```

```
    FlightService service =
➡ new FlightService(_mockFlightRepository.Object,
➡ _mockAirportRepository.Object);
    await foreach (FlightView _ in service.GetFlights()) {
      ;
    }
  }
}
```

And that does it for the `GetFlights` method!

12.2.4 *Implementing GetFlightByFlightNumber*

All that is left is to add a similar method that retrieves only a single flight's information when given a flight number. The patterns should be very familiar to you by now, as shown next:

```
public virtual async Task<FlightView>
➡ GetFlightByFlightNumber(int flightNumber) {
  try {
    Flight flight = await
➡ _flightRepository.GetFlightByFlightNumber(flightNumber);
    Airport originAirport = await
➡ _airportRepository.GetAirportByID(flight.Origin);
    Airport destinationAirport = await
➡ _airportRepository.GetAirportByID(flight.Destination);

    return new FlightView(flight.FlightNumber.ToString(),
      ➡ (originAirport.City, originAirport.Iata),
      ➡ (destinationAirport.City, destinationAirport.Iata));
  } catch (FlightNotFoundException) {
    throw new FlightNotFoundException();
  } catch (Exception) {
    throw new ArgumentException();
  }
}
```

We should also add some unit tests to verify we can get the correct flight from the database and handle the `FlightNotFoundException` and `Exception` error paths. To do this, we first have to add a new setup call to the `TestInitialize` method. Our mock currently does not return any data when we call `FlightRepository.GetFlightByFlightNumber`. Let's fix that as follows:

```
[TestInitialize]
public void Initialize()  {
  …

  _mockFlightRepository.Setup(repository =>
➡ repository.GetFlights()).Returns(mockReturn);
  _mockFlightRepository.Setup(repository =>
➡ repository.GetFlightByFlightNumber(148))
➡ .Returns(Task.FromResult(flightInDatabase));
}
```

When the mock's `GetFlightByFlightNumber` returns data, we return the previously created flight instance. With that, we can add the `GetFlightByFlightNumber_Success` test case as follows:

```
[TestMethod]
public async Task GetFlightByFlightNumber_Success() {
  _mockAirportRepository.Setup(repository =>
➥ repository.GetAirportByID(31)).ReturnsAsync(new Airport
    {
      AirportId = 31,
      City - "Mexico City",
      Iata = "MEX"
    });

  _mockAirportRepository.Setup(repository =>
➥ repository.GetAirportByID(92)).ReturnsAsync(new Airport
    {
      AirportId = 92,
      City = "Ulaanbaatar",
      Iata = "UBN"
    });

  FlightService service = new FlightService(_mockFlightRepository.Object,
➥ _mockAirportRepository.Object);
  FlightView flightView = await service.GetFlightByFlightNumber(148);

  Assert.IsNotNull(flightView);
  Assert.AreEqual(flightView.FlightNumber, "148");
  Assert.AreEqual(flightView.Origin.City, "Mexico City");
  Assert.AreEqual(flightView.Origin.Code, "MEX");
  Assert.AreEqual(flightView.Destination.City, "Ulaanbaatar");
  Assert.AreEqual(flightView.Destination.Code, "UBN");
}
```

The unit test is pretty simple. We mimicked (read: copied and pasted) the airport setup code, so we added a flight to use in the in-memory database. Then we called `FlightService.GetFlightByFlightNumber` to check our service layer logic. Finally, we verified the return data. Now, when you saw the airport setup from the `Get-Flights_Success` unit test in the code that we copied and pasted, alarm bells should have started to ring in your mind. Obviously, this repetition is a giant violation of the DRY principle, and we should refactor the test class to do this database setup in the `TestInitialize` method as follows:

```
[TestInitialize]
public void Initialize() {
  _mockFlightRepository = new Mock<FlightRepository>();
  _mockAirportRepository = new Mock<AirportRepository>();

  _mockAirportRepository.Setup(repository =>
➥ repository.GetAirportByID(31)).ReturnsAsync(new Airport
    {
      AirportId = 31,
```

```
        City = "Mexico City",
        Iata = "MEX"
    });

    _mockAirportRepository.Setup(repository =>
⇒   repository.GetAirportByID(92)).ReturnsAsync(new Airport
        {
        AirportId = 92,
        City = "Ulaanbaatar",
        Iata = "UBN"
    });

    ...
}
```

This shortens the `GetFlights_Success` and the `GetFlightByFlightNumber_Success`
unit tests by a fair amount, as shown here:

```
[TestMethod]
public async Task GetFlights_Success() {
    _mockAirportRepository.Setup(repository =>
⇒   repository.GetAirportByID(31)).ReturnsAsync(new Airport
        {
        AirportId = 31,
        City = "Mexico City",
        Iata = "MEX"
    });

    _mockAirportRepository.Setup(repository =>
⇒   repository.GetAirportByID(92)).ReturnsAsync(new Airport
        {
        AirportId = 92,
        City = "Ulaanbaatar",
        Iata = "UBN"
    });

    FlightService service = new FlightService(_mockFlightRepository.Object,
⇒   _mockAirportRepository.Object);

    await foreach (FlightView flightView in service.GetFlights()) {
        Assert.IsNotNull(flightView);
        Assert.AreEqual(flightView.FlightNumber, "148");
        Assert.AreEqual(flightView.Origin.City, "Mexico City");
        Assert.AreEqual(flightView.Origin.Code, "MEX");
        Assert.AreEqual(flightView.Destination.City, "Ulaanbaatar");
        Assert.AreEqual(flightView.Destination.Code, "UBN");
    }
}

[TestMethod]
public async Task GetFlightByFlightNumber_Success() {
    _mockAirportRepository.Setup(repository =>
⇒   repository.GetAirportByID(31)).ReturnsAsync(new Airport
        {
```

```
        AirportId = 31,
        City = "Mexico City",
        Iata = "MEX"
    }};

_mockAirportRepository.Setup(repository =>
    repository.GetAirportByID(92)).ReturnsAsync(new Airport
    {
        AirportId = 92,
        City = "Ulaanbaatar",
        Iata = "UBN"
    }};

    FlightService service = new FlightService(_mockFlightRepository.Object,
        _mockAirportRepository.Object);
    FlightView flightView = await service.GetFlightByFlightNumber(148);

    Assert.IsNotNull(flightView);
    Assert.AreEqual(flightView.FlightNumber, "148");
    Assert.AreEqual(flightView.Origin.City, "Mexico City");
    Assert.AreEqual(flightView.Origin.Code, "MEX");
    Assert.AreEqual(flightView.Destination.City, "Ulaanbaatar");
    Assert.AreEqual(flightView.Destination.Code, "UBN");
}
```

Of course, all unit tests still pass. This gives us the confidence to know we broke nothing. Let's add some failure case unit tests for the GetFlightByFlightNumber method and then we can call it a day.

Starting with the failure path where the service layer throws an exception of type FlightNotFoundException, we expect the service layer to throw another such exception, as shown next:

```
[TestMethod]
[ExpectedException(typeof(FlightNotFoundException))]
public async Task
    GetFlightByFlightNumber_Failure_RepositoryException
    _FlightNotFoundException() {
    _mockFlightRepository.Setup(repository =>
    repository.GetFlightByFlightNumber(-1))
    .Throws(new FlightNotFoundException());
    FlightService service = new FlightService(_mockFlightRepository.Object,
    _mockAirportRepository.Object);

    await service.GetFlightByFlightNumber(-1);
}
```

The GetFlightByFlightNumber_Failure_RepositoryException_Exception unit test sees our old friend the ExpectedException method attribute again. We are well aware of its usefulness by now and also use it in the unit test to check for the next (and last) exception path: the repository layer throws an exception of any type besides Flight-NotFoundException. The FlightService.GetFlightByFlightNumber method catches the thrown exception and throws a new `ArgumentException`. Or so it says. Let's see if it actually does:

```
[TestMethod]
[ExpectedException(typeof(ArgumentException))]
public async Task
➥ GetFlightByFlightNumber_Failure_RepositoryException_Exception() {
  _mockFlightRepository.Setup(repository =>
➥ repository.GetFlightByFlightNumber(-1))
➥ .Throws(new OverflowException());
  FlightService service = new FlightService(_mockFlightRepository.Object,
➥ _mockAirportRepository.Object);

  await service.GetFlightByFlightNumber(-1);
}
```

The `GetFlightByFlightNumber_Failure_RepositoryException_Exception` unit test tells the `Mock<FlightRepository>` to throw an exception of type `OverflowException` when we call the `FlightRepository.GetFlightByFlightNumber` and pass in an input argument of `-1`. We could have used any exception class here because they are all derived from the base `Exception` class, and that is what the `catch` block in the method looks for. This is also the reason why the test is not more specific in its name regarding the exception type. We are testing the logic that happens if any type of `Exception` is thrown, not a specific one. Because `Exception` is the base class for all exceptions, we can test it with just that.

> ### Overflows and underflows (checked and unchecked)
>
> What do you get when you add two integers together? Let's say 2147483647 and 1? You get a negative number. Similarly, what do you get when you subtract 1 from −2147483647? A positive number. This is what we call over- and underflow. When you go over the maximum value of a primitive type, or under the minimum value of a primitive type, you are greeted by a "wrapped around" value. Why is this, and how can we protect against this?
>
> When there are not enough binary bits available in a type to represent your requested value, the type wraps around and flips (if it is an unsigned integer). This, depending on the context, is overflow and underflow. For example (albeit a simplistic one): an integer is a four-byte data type. This means we have 32 bits to play with (one byte contains eight bits, and 8 × 4 = 32). So, if we declare one variable that sets all 32 (31 if signed) bits to their "on" value, we have the maximum value we can represent in a 32-bit (or four-byte) type (in C#, we can use decimal, hexadecimal, or binary representations directly in our code; this is binary):
>
> ```
> int maxVal = 0b11111111_11111111_11111111_1111111;
> int oneVal = 0b00000000_00000000_00000000_0000001;
>
> int overflow = maxVal + oneVal;
> ```

In C#, when using direct binary representation, you have to prefix your value with either 0b or 0B (with hexadecimal, use 0x or 0X). You can opt, as in the code snippet, to include underscores in the binary representation for readability. We prefix these values so the compiler knows how to treat the value. In this code snippet, we do the equivalent of adding 1 to the max 2147483647. So, what does the overflow variable resolve to? It resolves to –2147483648. And if we were to subtract a value of 1 from that, we would end up with a positive value: 2147483647. Often, when you know you are dealing with values over a particular type's capacity, you use a different one. For example, you may use a `long` instead of an integer, or a `BigInteger` instead of a `long`. But what if you are, for whatever reason, restricted to a specific type, yet can see overflows and underflows as a realistic scenario?

 BIGINTEGER is an immutable, nonprimitive "type" that grows with your data and is effectively capped only by your memory. A `BigInteger` acts as an integer but is actually a cleverly designed struct. Java developers may be familiar with `BigInteger`.

C# provides us with a keyword and compilation mode that can somewhat prevent unexpected overflows and underflows: `checked`. By default, C# compiles in `unchecked` mode. This means that the CLR does not throw any exceptions on arithmetic overflow and underflow. This is fine for most use cases, because we have some additional overhead with checking for this possibility, and it is not a common occurrence in a lot of programs. But, if we use `checked` mode, the CLR throws an exception when it detects under- or overflow. To use `checked` mode, we can either compile the entire codebase with these checks in place, by adding the `-checked` compiler option to the build instructions, or we can use the `checked` keyword.

To have the CLR throw an exception when it sees under- or overflow in a specific code block, we can wrap code in a `checked` block as follows:

```
checked {
    int maxVal = 0b_11111111_11111111_11111111_1111111;
    int oneVal = 0b_00000000_00000000_00000000_0000001;

    int overflow = maxVal + oneVal;
}
```

Now, when we add the `maxVal` and `oneVal` variables, the CLR throws an `Overflow-Exception`! Consequently, if you compiled the entire codebase in `checked` mode, you can use the `unchecked` code block to tell the CLR *not* to throw any `Overflow-Exceptions` for that block's scope.

And that does it for the service layer classes. I hope you learned some valuable things, and if not, the end of the book is in sight. In chapter 13, we'll look at implementing the controller layer and integration testing.

Exercises

EXERCISE 12.1

True or false? For the endpoint GET /Band/Song, we need to implement the Band-Service class.

EXERCISE 12.2

True or false? For the endpoint POST /Inventory/SKU, we need to implement the SKUService class.

EXERCISE 12.3

What best describes the interactions with a Queue<T> data structure?

a First-in, last-out (FILO)

b First-in, first-out (FIFO)

c Last-in, first-out (LIFO)

d Last-in, last-out (LILO)

EXERCISE 12.4

If we use the yield return keywords inside a foreach loop embedded in a method with a return type of IEnumerable<T>, what could we expect to get back as a value from the method?

a A collection implementing the IEnumerable interface containing all the data from the foreach loop.

b A collection implementing the IEnumerable interface containing only the first piece of data to be processed in the foreach loop.

c A collection not implementing the IEnumerable interface returning a reference to the original collection.

EXERCISE 12.5

Imagine a class called Food with a Boolean property IsFruit. This property has a public getter and a protected setter. Can the class Dragonfruit, which derives from the Food class, set the IsFruit value?

EXERCISE 12.6

What does this evaluate to? string.IsNullOrEmpty(string.empty);

EXERCISE 12.7

What does this evaluate to? string.IsNullOrWhitespace("   ");

EXERCISE 12.8

True or false? If you add a constructor to a struct, you can set only one property. The other properties must go unset.

Summary

- To determine whether we need to implement a particular service, we can look at the required API endpoints. If there is no need for a particular model's controller, we don't need a service for that model, either. This saves us from implementing unnecessary code.

- A `Queue<T>` is a "first-in, first-out" (FIFO) data structure. Queues are very helpful when we want to preserve order and deal with information as if we are dealing with a queue of people. The first one there is the first one processed, or, "the early bird gets the worm."

- We can use the `yield return` keywords to asynchronously return an `IEnumerable<T>` implementation if we iterate over some data. This can make our code more readable and concise.

- A struct can be thought of as a "lightweight" class. We often use them to store small amounts of information and typically do not do any processing of data in a struct. Structs are a great way to signify to our fellow developers that this piece of code acts as a data storage device.

- When adding a constructor to a struct, the compiler requires us to assign every property in the struct to a value. This is to prevent structs that are only partly initialized and stops us from accidentally forgetting to set values.

- We can have different access modifiers for getters and setters in an auto-property. This allows us to make a property that can be publicly accessed but only set inside its respective class (private). Any combination of access modifiers is allowed. Because encapsulation is often our goal, by using these access modifiers, we can better control the encapsulation story.

- We can only set `readonly` values at their declaration or in a constructor. Because we can set a `readonly` value only once, and declaring a field means the compiler automatically assigns a default value to its spot in memory, we need to set it at the earliest possible moment. A `readonly` field can greatly reduce the amount of data manipulation others can do on our code.

- By using an `IAsyncEnumerable<T>` along with the `yield return` keywords, we can create code that asynchronously awaits on data and processes it as it receives the data. This is very helpful when dealing with external interactions such as database queries.

- Overflows and underflows happened when we try to represent a value that needs more bits than a specific type has access to. When this happens, your variable values suddenly become incorrect, which can have unexpected side effects.

- By default, C# code is compiled using `unchecked` mode. This means the CLR does not throw an `OverflowException` if it encounters an overflow or underflow. Similarly, `checked` mode means the CLR *does* throw such an exception.

- We can use `checked` and `unchecked` code blocks to change the compilation mode on a per-code-block basis. This is helpful when wanting to control the `Exception` story.
- In C#, we can represent integer values with decimal, hexadecimal, or binary representation. When using hexadecimal, we need to prefix our values with either 0x or 0X. With binary representation, use 0b or 0B. These different representations allow us to pick and choose what makes the most sense for our code's readability.

Part 6

The controller layer

In part 5, we created the service layer classes. These classes are the glue between the repository and controller architectural layers. We also looked at runtime type checking and using `IAsyncEnumerable<T>`. In this part, we'll finish our rewrite of the Flying Dutchman Airlines service by implementing the controller layer classes. Other topics considered include ASP.NET middleware, custom model binding, and JSON serialization/deserialization.

Middleware, HTTP routing, and HTTP responses

This chapter covers

- Routing HTTP requests to controllers and endpoints
- Declaring HTTP routes with `HttpAttribute` method attributes
- Injecting dependencies with middleware
- Using the `IActionResult` interface to return HTTP responses

We are almost at the end of our journey. In chapters gone by, we implemented the database access layer, the repository layer, and the service layer. Our service is almost implemented but not yet usable by FlyTomorrow (our client). To interact with our service, we need to provide controllers that accept HTTP requests and kick off the necessary processing.

In section 13.1, we'll discuss the controller's place within our repository/service architecture. Following that, in section 13.2, we'll determine which controllers we need to implement. In the following sections, we'll start to implement the `Flight-Controller` (section 13.3) and explore how to route HTTP requests to our endpoints (section 13.4).

Figure 13.1 shows where are in the scheme of the book.

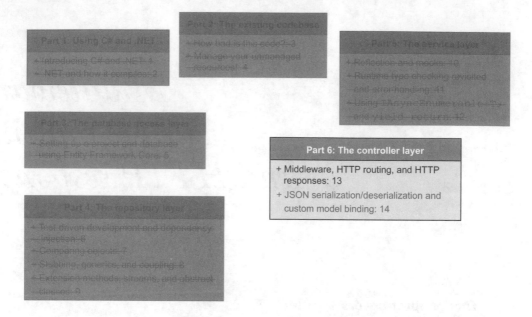

Part 1: Using C# and .NET
+ Introducing C# and .NET: 1
+ .NET and how it compiles: 2

Part 2: The existing codebase
+ How bad is this code?: 3
+ Manage your unmanaged resources!: 4

Part 5: The service layer
+ Reflection and mocks: 10
+ Runtime type checking revisited and error handling: 11
+ Using IAsyncEnumerable<T> and yield return: 12

Part 3: The database access layer
+ Setting up a project and database using Entity Framework Core: 5

Part 6: The controller layer
+ Middleware, HTTP routing, and HTTP responses: 13
+ JSON serialization/deserialization and custom model binding: 14

Part 4: The repository layer
+ Test-driven development and dependency injection: 6
+ Comparing objects: 7
+ Stubbing, generics, and coupling: 8
+ Extension methods, streams, and abstract classes: 9

Figure 13.1   In the previous chapters, we implemented the database access, repository, and service layers. In this chapter, we'll start to implement all controllers needed for our service.

After this chapter, we are only one more chapter away from having a fully implemented service that adheres to the API specification given to us by FlyTomorrow. In the next chapter, we'll finish up by wrapping up our controllers and diving into acceptance testing with Swagger so we can prove we did our work correctly.

13.1   *The controller class within the repository/service pattern*

In section 5.2.4, I introduced you to the repository/service pattern. We have used this pattern throughout the book to implement the new FlyingDutchmanAirlines service with much success. But now that we are at the controller layer, you may ask, how does the controller fit into this pattern? After all, it is the repository/service pattern, not the controller/service/repository pattern.

Sometimes a name can be misleading. One of my biggest pet peeves is when something (a method name or an architecture) is named incorrectly or incompletely. Unfortunately, I did not name this pattern, but if I had, it would be the "controller/repository/service pattern." Heck, perhaps even the controller/repository/service /database layer pattern, but that is even more of a mouthful. So where does the controller layer fit into the repository/service pattern?

The quick answer is this: a controller is typically the public-facing, topmost layer in the repository/service pattern. This is not surprising: the controller is normally the topmost layer for a service because it is typically the only point exposed to clients, as shown in figure 13.2. Examples of external systems include the FlyTomorrow website, a microservice requesting information for further processing, or a desktop application trying to load database information. Any consumer outside of your codebase is an external system. There is a caveat here: this assumes we live in a world where our service acts as a "server" for an external system calling our service. If you need to call any external HTTP services as part of the work in this service, you may end up doing this in the service or repository layer.

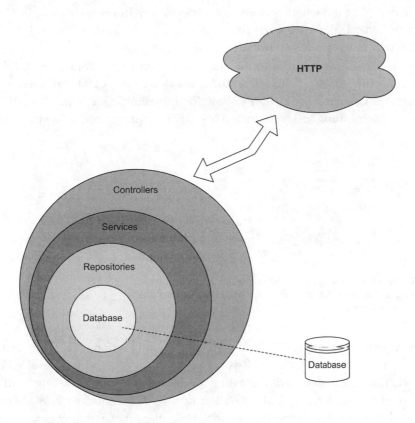

Figure 13.2   A controller is the outermost layer of our architecture and interacts with any potential external systems. If the service acts as a server. With this model in mind, we can easily model our repositories, services, and controllers.

So far, we have implemented the inner circles of our service. Right now, however, if FlyTomorrow were to send a request for information about all the flights in the database, we would have no way to accept that request. Consequently, without fully implemented controllers, nobody would use our service. You can have the cleanest, most performant, secure service, but if nobody uses (or can use) your product, it isn't good enough.

A controller exposes methods we call *endpoint methods*. These methods accept HTTP requests and return HTTP responses. An HTTP response usually comprises the following three key items, as shown in figure 13.3:

- *An HTTP status code like 200 (OK), 404 (Not Found), or 500 (Internal Server Error)*—The controller determines this status code based on the state of the service after processing the request.
- *Headers*—This is a collection of key-value pairs that often include the type of returned data and whether there are any cross-origin resource sharing (CORS) instructions. Unless you need to pass along an odd header, the ASP.NET can often take care of this step for you automatically.
- *A body*—Where appropriate, you can return data to the consumer. Often this data is returned as a JSON value and goes along with a 200 (OK) status code. Some HTTP status codes don't allow for returning data (e.g., the 201 status code, which means "no content"). This data is returned in the "body" section.

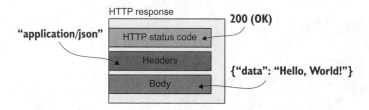

Figure 13.3   An HTTP response typically comprises an HTTP status code, headers, and a body. We use these fields to return appropriate information to the caller.

For more information on HTTP and web service interaction, see Barry Pollard's *HTTP/2 in Action* (Manning, 2019). If you want to learn more about developing the architecture that goes along with creating multiple services interacting with each other as external services, see Chris Richardson's *Microservices Patterns* (Manning, 2018), Sam Newman's *Building Microservices: Designing Fine-Grained Systems* (O'Reilly Media, 2015), or Christian Harsdal Gammelgaard's *Microservices in .NET Core* (2nd edition; Manning, 2020).

13.2   *Determining what controllers to implement*

As we implemented the service layer classes, we talked about how to determine whether a service layer class was necessary. We realized that we need to figure out whether we need a controller that calls said service layer. So, we can repeat that exercise once again and quickly figure out what controllers we need to implement.

Once again, we look at the endpoints specified in the contract between FlyTomorrow and Flying Dutchman Airlines (first introduced in section 3.1 and 3.2, and shown in figure 13.4):

- `GET /Flight`
- `CET /Flight/{FlightNumber}`
- `POST /Booking/{FlightNumber}`

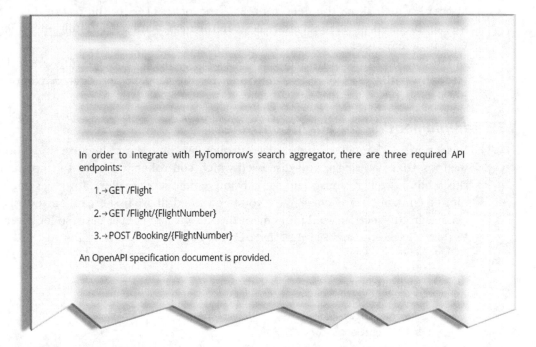

In order to integrate with FlyTomorrow's search aggregator, there are three required API endpoints:

1.→ GET /Flight

2.→ GET /Flight/{FlightNumber}

3.→ POST /Booking/{FlightNumber}

An OpenAPI specification document is provided.

Figure 13.4 The endpoints required by the contract with FlyTomorrow. We need to implement our controllers to reflect these endpoints.

These endpoints form the basis of all we have done so far. In the database access, repository, and service layers, we did not have to do much with the actual endpoints, but that changes when we talk about controllers.

To determine what controllers we need to implement, we ask ourselves, what entities can we see in the required endpoints, as shown in figure 13.5? Remember, when we talk about entities, we're talking about database entities (reflected in the codebase by model classes). Take a couple of seconds to look over the endpoints and see what you come up with. We have done this exercise before, so it shouldn't be too challenging.

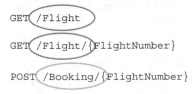

Figure 13.5 The required endpoints with the potential controllers identified. We can determine what controllers we need to implement by looking at what entities appear in the required endpoints.

If we look at the first endpoint (GET /Flight), we see the Flight entity in the path. This is a clear-cut sign that we should implement a FlightController class. Similarly, when we look at the GET /Flight/{FlightNumber} endpoint, we realize we need a FlightController class for that one as well. That leaves the POST /Booking/{Flight-Number}, which shows the need for a BookingController. In the rest of this chapter, we'll implement the FlightController. In the next chapter, we'll fully implement the BookingController.

But what about controllers for the Airport and Customer entities? Because no endpoint paths need to go to a controller for the Airport and Customer entities, we do not need them.

13.3 *Implementing the FlightController*

In section 13.1 we talked about the controller layer in our architecture. In section 13.2 we took that knowledge and discussed which controllers we need to implement. In this section, we'll go ahead and actually implement a controller. How does one implement a controller layer class? Well, you know the drill: we first create our two skeleton classes. In this section, we'll implement the FlightController class, so let's create the FlightController and FlightControllerTests classes, shown in figure 13.6.

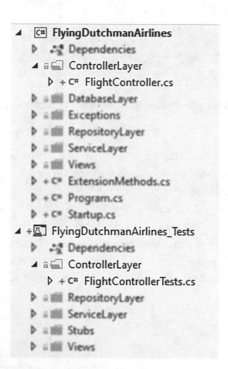

Figure 13.6 We add two skeleton classes: FlightController and FlightControllerTests. These form the basis of our FlightController implementation.

With the skeleton classes in place, we have to do only one additional thing before we can talk about how to create controller methods that are accessible from external systems: the `FlightController` needs to derive from the `Controller` class. This base class, shown in the next code sample, provides us with standard methods that we can use to return HTTP data to the consumer and allows us to set up routing to our endpoints:

```
public class FlightController : Controller
```

Now, we need to implement the following three pieces so we can hit our endpoint by an external system at run time.

- The `IActionResult` interface (section 13.3.1)
- Dependency injection in middleware (section 13.3.2)
- Routing endpoints (section 13.4)

After this chapter, we will have implemented the `FlightController`, along with the appropriate unit tests, and will be able to hit the endpoints through an external system simulator such as Postman or cURL.

13.3.1 *Returning HTTP responses with the IActionResult interface (GetFlights)*

In section 13.2, we discussed the composition of a typical HTTP response. Most of the time, an HTTP response contains an HTTP status code, headers, and a body containing some data. Think about how we would return something like that from a method. No primitive data types hold this information. We could use the lowest common denominator of any type in C#—`object`—but that would be a lazy workaround and somewhat tricky to deal with because it is still not in an acceptable form for the HTTP transport.

The solution is ASP.NET's `IActionResult` interface. The `IActionResult` interface is implemented by classes such as `ActionResult` and `ContentResult`, but in practice, we can leave the determination of which specific class to use to ASP.NET. This is another example of polymorphism and something we call "coding to interfaces."

Coding to interfaces

In section 8.4, we talked about using polymorphism and the Liskov substitution principle. These allow us to write code that is generic instead of constrained to one particular implementation. To drive this point home, let me show you an example.

Let's imagine you are writing a service for a book publisher in the mid-2000s. The era of e-books is on the rise, but your code did not account for this possibility. As a result, your code is tightly coupled to the `Book` class. In the following snippet, the author finished writing the book, and we want to send it to the printer:[a]

```
public void BookToPrinter(Book book) {
  if (book.IsApproved()) {
    BookPrinter printer =
➥ ExternalCompanyManager.SelectPrintingCompany(book);
    printer.Print();
  }
}
```

(continued)

This code works fine when dealing only with regular, paper books. But what happens if we want to "print" an e-book? Well, the method does not accept a type of `EBook` as an input parameter. If we wrote the `BookToPrinter` method using an interface for the parameter's type instead of a concrete type, our work would have been easier, as shown here:

```
public void BookToPrinter(IWork book) {
  if (book.IsApproved()) {
    BookPrinter printer =
  ExternalCompanyManager.SelectPrintingCompany(book);
    printer.Print();
  }
}
```

Now, printing an e-book does not make much sense. We may want to take things one step further and generalize the actual "printing" of the book, regardless of its medium type, as shown next:

```
public void ProduceWork(IWork work) {
  if (work.IsApproved()) {
    work.Produce();
  }
}
```

This way, we abstract away the implementation details to the derived classes of the `IWork` interface. The `ProduceWork` method does not care whether the book's medium is paper or e-book. Implementing logic to change the state of an object inside the actual object is an important tenet of object-oriented design and makes code more readable and maintainable. For an excellent discussion on this and how it ties into the Open/Closed Principle, see Robert C. Martin and Micah Martin's *Agile Principles, Patterns, and Practices in C#* (Prentice Hall, 2006).

---

[a]   At the time of writing, this joyous occasion seems still very far out for this book.

Let's get cracking with our first endpoint: /`GET Flight`. We know our return type (`IActionResult`), but what should the access modifier, name, and arguments be? Because ASP.NET uses reflection to use the method, the access modifier should be public. As for the name, a good way to name endpoint methods is to take the HTTP action (`GET` in this case) and append the entity (`Flight` for us), making the term plural where necessary: `GetFlights`. That leaves us with the input parameter. This is a `GET` action, so we do not need an input parameter, as shown in the next code snippet. `GET` actions are not allowed to pass in any data to specific methods per the HTTP specification, so that makes our lives a bit easier at this point.

```
public IActionResult GetFlights() { ... }
```

What do we need to do to return some JSON data? As mentioned in section 13.1, in most situations we do not need to explicitly specify any header information, so that leaves the status code and any body data. The ASP.NET library gives us an easy-to-use static class that we can return and use as an IActionResult: StatusCode. This class lives in the Controller base class that FlightController derives from. At first glance (and judging by its name), you would think the StatusCode allows us to return only a status code and no body, but nothing is further from the truth! To illustrate, let's return an HTTP status code of 200 (OK) and a string "Hello, World!" from the Get-Flights method as follows:

```
public IActionResult GetFlights() {
  return StatusCode(200, "Hello, World!");
}
```

That code compiles and returns exactly what we want. There is an additional tip here that bears understanding: instead of using the magic (hardcoded) number of 200 for the status code, we should use the HttpStatusCode enum and cast its value to an integer. It is a little bit more code, but it removes the magic number, as shown in the following example. For more information on magic numbers and why they are bad, see section 9.6.1.

```
public IActionResult GetFlights() {
  return StatusCode((int) HttpStatusCode.OK, "Hello, World!");
}
```

Unfortunately, this code doesn't satisfy our requirements. We need to return a collection of information on all the flights in the database from this endpoint method. We already implemented the service layer method to support this effort and created the FlightView class. In the FlightController.GetFlights method, we want to call that service layer method and return the collection along with a status code of 200 (OK). If something goes awry and the service layer throws an Exception, we want to return a status code of 500 (Internal Server Error) with no further data.

Before we move on, let's add a unit test, shown in the next listing, that verifies our expectations.

Listing 13.1 GetFlights_Success unit test, iteration 1

```
[TestMethod]
public void GetFlights_Success() {
  FlightController controller = new FlightController();
  ObjectResult response =
  controller.GetFlights() as ObjectResult;

  Assert.IsNotNull(response);
  Assert.AreEqual((int) HttpStatusCode.OK, response.StatusCode);
```

Instantiates an instance of FlightController

Mimics an HTTP GET call to /Flight, and casts a return to ObjectResult

Makes sure the HTTP response is not null

Verifies the HTTP response has a status code of 200

```
    Assert.AreEqual("Hello, World!", response.Value);
}
```
**Verifies the expected body
exists in the HTTP response**

Because the `FlightController.GetFlights` method returns a type of `IActionResult`, and we cannot access the status code and body values directly from the interface, we cast the response to an `ObjectResult` type. The `ObjectResult` class implements the `IActionResult` interface, so we can downcast the return to the derived class. When we *downcast* something, we use the polymorphic relationship between two classes and use the parent as the derived class. It is the inverse of the Liskov substitution principle.

To adjust the logic in the `GetFlights` method so we can use the `FlightService` class to get information on all the flights in the database, we need to have access to an instance of `FlightService`. It should come as no surprise that we use dependency injection once again!

13.3.2 *Injecting dependencies into a controller using middleware*

In the previous chapters, we used dependency injection to kick the can of instantiating new instances of said dependency down the road. For the repository layer, we used dependency injection to not worry about instantiating an instance of type `Flying-DutchmanAirlinesContext`. Similarly, in the service layer, we injected instances of repository layer classes. Finally, in the controller we are implementing in this chapter, we need to use an injected instance of `FlightService`. But where do these instances come from?

We are finally at the point where we have to actually set up these dependencies. We do this by adding some logic to what we call middleware. *Middleware* is any code that can help process an HTTP request. You can think of middleware as a collection of individual middleware pieces, strung together in a chain, as shown in figure 13.7.

Figure 13.7   An example of multiple middleware components and how they are executed. Middleware components are executed linearly and are often chained together to create the required processing story.

Before an HTTP request enters a controller (and proceeds down the architectural layers), the CLR executes any provided middleware, as shown in figure 13.8. Examples of middleware components are routing (which we'll see more of in section 13.4), authentication, and dependency injection.

Typically, we find middleware code in the `Startup` class for ASP.NET services. In section 5.2 (and as shown in listing 13.2), we added code to the `Startup` class that

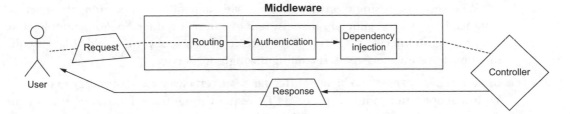

Figure 13.8 Middleware takes place after receiving an HTTP request but before executing the controller (and subsequent service and repository) code. Examples of middleware components are routing, authentication, and dependency injection.

allowed us to use controllers and routing with endpoints. These are examples of middleware code.

Listing 13.2 The `Startup` class

```
class Startup {
  public void Configure(IApplicationBuilder app,
    IWebHostEnvironment env) {
    app.UseRouting();
    app.UseEndpoints(endpoints => endpoints.MapControllers());
  }

  public void ConfigureServices(IServiceCollection services) {
    services.AddControllers();
  }
}
```

NOTE Injecting dependencies by writing middleware is not the only way to achieve DI in C#. Plenty of third-party (open source) DI frameworks for C# are out there, such as Autofac, Castle Windsor, and Ninject. For more information on some of these external frameworks, see Mark Seemann's *Dependency Injection in .NET* (Manning, 2011).

We can add dependencies to be injected in the `ConfigureServices` method in the following three ways:

- *Singleton*—One instance across the entire lifetime of the service
- *Scoped*—One instance across the lifetime of a request
- *Transient*—A new instance every time a dependency is used

USING A SINGLETON DEPENDENCY TO GUARANTEE THE SAME INSTANCE EVERY TIME
Adding an injected dependency with the singleton option mimics a singleton design pattern. In a singleton design pattern, you have only one instance per application. The CLR reuses this instance repeatedly for as long as your application runs. The instance may start as a null pointer, but at first use, the code instantiates it.

When we use a singleton dependency with dependency injection, the injected instance is always the same, no matter when or where it is injected. For example, if we were to add an injected singleton of type BookingRepository, we would always use the same instance for every request coming through our service.[1]

USING A SCOPED DEPENDENCY TO GUARANTEE THE SAME INSTANCE ON A PER-REQUEST BASIS

With a scoped dependency, every HTTP request instantiates its own version of the dependency that needs injecting. ASP.NET uses this instance for the entire request life cycle but instantiates a new instance for every new request that enters the hallowed halls of the service.

For example, if we were to instantiate a FlightRepository instance and we inject the FlightRepository type in two service layer classes, both service layer classes would receive (and operate on) the same instance of FlightRepository, as long as we are dealing with the same HTTP request.

USING A TRANSIENT DEPENDENCY (DI) TO ALWAYS GET A NEW INSTANCE

Transient dependencies in DI are perhaps the most common way of dealing with dependency injection. When we add a transient dependency, every time that dependency needs to be injected, ASP.NET instantiates a new instance. This guarantees that we work on a fresh copy of the injected class.

Because transient dependencies are the most common, and easiest to use, types of dependency injection, we shall fall in line. To add a transient dependency to the ConfigureServices method in the Startup class, use the services.[dependencyType]([Requested Type], [Injected Type]) syntax.

Let's see how we do this for the FlightService dependency for the FlightController class:

```
public void ConfigureServices(IServiceCollection services) {
  services.AddControllers();
  services.AddTransient(typeof(FlightService), typeof(FlightService));
}
```

We add the type of FlightService as both parameters to the AddTransient call. This tells us we want to have a type of FlightService added to the internal collection of instances whenever we request a type of FlightService to be injected. It's a bit round-about, but it is what we have to do. This is all you need to do to make sure the CLR can provide injected instances when you need them. Of course, we also want to add the dependencies that the FlightService class itself expects—FlightRepository and AirportRepository—as shown next:

---

[1] For more information on the singleton pattern, see Robert C. Martin and Micah Martin's *Agile Principles, Patterns, and Practices in C#*, chapter 24, "Singleton and Monostate" (Prentice Hall, 2006); or for a resource that also covers dependency injection in great detail, see Steven van Deursen and Mark Seemann's *Dependency Injection: Principles, Practices, and Patterns* (Manning, 2019).

```
public void ConfigureServices(IServiceCollection services) {
  services.AddControllers();

  services.AddTransient(typeof(FlightService), typeof(FlightService));
  services.AddTransient(typeof(FlightRepository),
➡ typeof(FlightRepository));
  services.AddTransient(typeof(AirportRepository),
➡ typeof(AirportRepository));
}
```

Following that, what dependencies do we need to provide for the FlightRepository and AirportRepository classes? Both require the same dependency—an instance of the FlyingDutchmanAirlinesContext class, shown here:

```
public void ConfigureServices(IServiceCollection services) {
  services.AddControllers();

  services.AddTransient(typeof(FlightService), typeof(FlightService));
  services.AddTransient(typeof(FlightRepository),
➡ typeof(FlightRepository));
  services.AddTransient(typeof(AirportRepository),
➡ typeof(AirportRepository));
  services.AddTransient(typeof(FlyingDutchmanAirlinesContext),
➡ typeof(FlyingDutchmanAirlinesContext));
}
```

We can now add the injected dependency to the FlightController and call the FlightService as follows:

```
public class FlightController : Controller {
  private readonly FlightService _service;

  public FlightController(FlightService service) {
    _service = service;
  }

  ...
}
```

What are we trying to accomplish with the GetFlights method? We want to return to the caller a JSON response that contains information on all the flights, right? Let's double-check with the OpenAPI specification we got from FlyTomorrow, as shown in figure 13.9. There, we see that we have the following three return paths for the GET /Flight endpoint:

- The success case that returns an HTTP code of 200 along with information on all the flights in the database
- A status code of 404 if no flights were found
- A status code of 500 for all other errors

GET /flight

Get all available flights

Returns all available flights

REQUEST

No request parameters

RESPONSE

STATUS CODE - 200:

RESPONSE MODEL - application/json

NAME	TYPE	DESCRIPTION
ARRAY OF OBJECT WITH BELOW STRUCTURE		
flightNumber	integer	
origin	object	
city	string	
code	string	
destination	object	
city	string	
code	string	

STATUS CODE - 404: No flights found

STATUS CODE - 500: Internal error

Figure 13.9   The required response from the GET /Flight endpoint. This is a screenshot from a generated OpenAPI specification.

Let's work on the success case first, as shown in the following listing, and use the injected `FlightService` to iterate over the returned data from the `FlightService.GetFlights` method, wrapped in a `try-catch` block so we can catch any potential thrown errors.

Listing 13.3   `GetFlights` calling the `FlightService`

```
public async Task<IActionResult> GetFlights() {
  try {
    Queue<FlightView> flights = new Queue<FlightView>();
    await foreach (FlightView flight in _service.GetFlights()) {
      flights.Enqueue(flight);
    }
    ...
  }
  catch(FlightNotFoundException exception) {
    ...
  } catch (Exception exception) {
    ...
  }
}
```

Adds flights to the queue

Processes each FlightView as they come in from the service class

Creates a Queue<FlightView> to hold returned FlightView instances

Because the `FlightService.GetFlights` method returns an `IAsyncEnumerable<FlightView>` and uses the `yield return` keywords, we don't have to wait for all the processing to be done before being able to see the fruits of our labor. As the database returns flights and the service layer populates `FlightViews`, the controller layer receives the instances and adds them to a `Queue` data structure.

How do we structure this queue of `FlightView` instances so we can return its contents along with an HTTP code of 200 to the user? The magic of ASP.NET, C#, and .NET makes this incredibly easy. Remember how we returned an HTTP code of 200 along with a body that read "`Hello, World!`" simply by adding those two as argument values to the `StatusCode` constructor in section 13.3.1? We can repeat this exercise, swapping out the "`Hello, World!`" string for our queue as follows:

```
public async Task<IActionResult> GetFlights() {
  try {
    Queue<FlightView> flights = new Queue<FlightView>();       ◁──┐
    await foreach (FlightView flight in _service.GetFlights()) {  ◁──
      flights.Enqueue(flight);       ◁──┐
    }

    return StatusCode((int)HttpStatusCode.OK, flights);
  } catch(FlightNotFoundException) {
    ...
  } catch (Exception) {
    ...
  }
}
```

Creates a Queue<FlightView> to hold returned FlightView instances

Adds flights to the queue

Processes each FlightView as it comes in from the service class

But are you going to take my word that this works? Of course not. We should update our unit test to verify that assumption. To do this, we temporarily need to add some returns so that the `GetFlights` method compiles. I'll leave this to you because it is not important what you return, as long as it meets the return type requirements based on the method signature.

To add a unit test that verifies the `FlightController.GetFlights` method, we need to mock the `FlightService` class (and as a result, we also need to set up a parameterless constructor for `FlightService` and make sure the `FlightService.GetFlights` method returns a correct response). First off, we need to make the `FlightService.GetFlights` virtual so the Moq framework can override it. But how do we return an instance of type `IAsyncEnumerable<FlightView>`? We can't simply instantiate that type, because you cannot instantiate types based on an interface alone. The trick here is to create a test helper method inside the test class that returns an `IAsyncEnumerable<FlightView>` with some mock data, as shown next.

> **Listing 13.4** Finished `GetFlights_Success` unit test

```
[TestClass]
public class FlightControllerTests {
```

```
[TestMethod]                                    Creates an instance of a mock of FlightService
public async Task GetFlights_Success() {
  Mock<FlightService> service = new Mock<FlightService>();

  List<FlightView> returnFlightViews = new List<FlightView>(2) {
        new FlightView("1932",
 ("Groningen", "GRQ"), ("Phoenix", "PHX")),                    Defines the
        new FlightView("841",                                 FlightViews
 ("New York City", "JFK"), ("London", "LHR"))                 used in the
  };                                                          mock

  service.Setup(s =>
 s.GetFlights()).Returns(FlightViewAsyncGenerator(returnFlightViews));

  FlightController controller = new FlightController(service.Object);
  ObjectResult response =
 await controller.GetFlights() as ObjectResult;     Sets up the mock to return
                                                        the list of FlightViews
  Assert.IsNotNull(response);
  Assert.AreEqual((int)HttpStatusCode.OK, response.StatusCode);

  Queue<FlightView> content = response.Value as Queue<FlightView>;
  Assert.IsNotNull(content);

  Assert.IsTrue(returnFlightViews.All(flight =>      For all entries in the FlightView
 content.Contains(flight)));                         list, checks if the returned data
  }                                                  contains the entry (LINQ)

  private async IAsyncEnumerable<FlightView>
 FlightViewAsyncGenerator(IEnumerable<FlightView> views) {   Returns an
    foreach (FlightView flightView in views) {               IAsyncEnumerable
      yield return flightView;                               <FlightView>
    }                                                        with the passed-in
  }                                                          FlightView objects
}
```

**Safely casts the returned data to a Queue<FlightView>,
and checks for null if it was a bad cast**

Great, that test passes. All we have left to do before wrapping up this method is to handle the exception cases. Earlier in this section, we identified (and added) two error conditions: the service layer throws an exception of type FlightNotFoundException, and the service layer throws an exception. Looking at the FlyTomorrow OpenAPI specification (shown in figure 13.10), we see that we should return an HTTP status code of 404 (Not Found) when the flights are not found and an HTTP status code of 500 (Internal Server Error) on all other errors.

Let's start with the 404, and add a unit test to check for this as follows:

```
[TestMethod]
public async Task GetFlights_Failure_FlightNotFoundException_404() {
  Mock<FlightService> service = new Mock<FlightService>();
  service.Setup(s => s.GetFlights())
 .Throws(new FlightNotFoundException());
```

```
FlightController controller = new FlightController(service.Object);
ObjectResult response = await controller.GetFlights() as ObjectResult;

Assert.IsNotNull(response);
Assert.AreEqual((int)HttpStatusCode.NotFound, response.StatusCode);
Assert.AreEqual("No flights were found in the database",
  response.Value);
}
```

The `GetFlights_Failure_FlightNotFoundException_404` unit test does not pass right now. Remember, when using test-driven development, we often want to create a unit test before implementing the actual method logic. This gives us a chance to think about how we want our code to be called, further decoupling the new functionality from other pieces of the codebase. In our case, we need to add some logic, shown in the next code sample, that returns the correct `StatusCode` object when the controller catches a `FlightNotFoundException` instance:

```
public async Task<IActionResult> GetFlights() {
  try {
    Queue<FlightView> flights = new Queue<FlightView>();
    await foreach (FlightView flight in _service.GetFlights()) {
      flights.Enqueue(flight);
    }

    return StatusCode((int)HttpStatusCode.OK, flights);
  } catch(FlightNotFoundException) {
    return StatusCode((int) HttpStatusCode.NotFound,
  "No flights were found in the database");
  } catch (Exception) {
    …
  }
}
```

Our `GetFlights_Failure_FlightNotFoundException_404` unit test now passes. I'm sure you can imagine what comes next: the 500 error case. We mimic the approach we took for the 404 and add a unit test as follows:

```
[TestMethod]
public async Task GetFlights_Failure_ArgumentException_500() {
  Mock<FlightService> service = new Mock<FlightService>();
  service.Setup(s => s.GetFlights())
  .Throws(new ArgumentException());

  FlightController controller = new FlightController(service.Object);
  ObjectResult response = await controller.GetFlights() as ObjectResult;

  Assert.IsNotNull(response);
  Assert.AreEqual((int)HttpStatusCode.InternalServerError,
  response.StatusCode);
  Assert.AreEqual("An error occurred", response.Value);
}
```

And to make the GetFlights_Failure_ArgumentException_500 unit test pass, we add the appropriate return in the GetFlights try-catch as follows:

```
public async Task<IActionResult> GetFlights() {
  try {
    Queue<FlightView> flights = new Queue<FlightView>();
    await foreach (FlightView flight in _service.GetFlights()) {
      flights.Enqueue(flight);
    }

    return StatusCode((int)HttpStatusCode.OK, flights);
  } catch(FlightNotFoundException) {
    return StatusCode((int) HttpStatusCode.NotFound,
 "No flights were found in the database");
  } catch (Exception) {
    return StatusCode((int) HttpStatusCode.InternalServerError,
 "An error occurred");
  }
}
```

And that makes the unit test pass, plus it wraps up implementing the logic for the GET /Flight endpoint. Of course, we cannot call this endpoint yet from an external system, but we'll look at setting up this routing in section 13.3.5.

13.3.3 *Implementing the GET /Flight/{FlightNumber} endpoint*

So far in this chapter, you learned about using middleware to do dependency injection and how to call the service layer from the controller layer while handling errors and providing unit tests. In section 13.3.2, we implemented the GET /Flight endpoint. Now we come to the GET /Flight/{FlightNumber} endpoint.

This endpoint should return information on an individual flight when given a flight number. To accomplish this, we need to do the following four things:

1 Get the provided flight number from the path parameter.
2 Call the service layer to request information on the flight.
3 Handle any potential exceptions thrown from the service layer.
4 Return the correct information to the caller.

To get the value of a path parameter, we need to do some routing magic and add the FlightNumber URL path parameter as a method parameter. In section 13.4, we'll look at the routing part, but for now, it suffices for us to create a new method in the FlightController called GetFlightByFlightNumber that requires a parameter representing a flight number, as follows:

```
public async Task<IActionResult> GetFlightByFlightNumber(int flightNumber){
  return StatusCode((int)HttpStatusCode.OK,"Hello from
 GetFlightByFlightNumber");
}
```

This sets us up to call the `FlightService`'s `GetFlightByFlightByNumber` method and pass along the `flightNumber` parameter. Before we move on, let's backtrack a bit and get back into the good graces of the test-driven development gods (more specifically, Kent Beck) by adding a unit test that we can build on, as shown here:

```
[TestMethod]
public async Task GetFlightByFlightNumber_Success() {
  Mock<FlightService> service = new Mock<FlightService>();
  FlightController controller = new FlightController(service.Object);

  await controller.GetFlightByFlightNumber(0);
}
```

The `GetFlightByFlightNumber_Success` unit test passes just fine in its current state. After all, the unit test only checks to see whether it can call a method called `GetFlightByFlightNumber` on the `FlightController` class with an input parameter of type `integer`.

To further implement our method, let's add the following expected behavior to the unit test:

```
public async Task GetFlightByFlightNumber_Success() {
  Mock<FlightService> service = new Mock<FlightService>();

  FlightView returnedFlightView = new FlightView("0", ("Lagos", "LOS"),
  ("Marrakesh", "RAK"));
  service.Setup(s =>
  s.GetFlightByFlightNumber(0))
  .Returns(Task.FromResult(returnedFlightView));

  FlightController controller = new FlightController(service.Object);

  ObjectResult response =
  await controller.GetFlightByFlightNumber(0) as ObjectResult;
  Assert.IsNotNull(response);
  Assert.AreEqual((int)HttpStatusCode.OK, response.StatusCode);

  FlightView content = response.Value as FlightView;
  Assert.IsNotNull(content);

  Assert.AreEqual(returnedFlightView, content);
}
```

As expected, the `GetFlightByFlightNumber_Success` unit test does not pass now. The returned data from the `FlightController.GetFlightByFlightNumber` method call is incorrect. But we can fix that. For the actual method implementation, we can use the same `try-catch` pattern we used for the `GetFlights` method and swap out the asynchronous `foreach` loop that calls the `IAsyncEnumerable` returned by `FlightService.GetFlights` for a call to the service's `GetFlightByFlightNumber` method (which returns a `FlightView` instance), as shown in the next code sample:

```
public async Task<IActionResult> GetFlightByFlightNumber(int flightNumber){
  try {
    FlightView flight = await
 _service.GetFlightByFlightNumber(flightNumber);
    return StatusCode((int)HttpStatusCode.OK, flight);
  } catch (FlightNotFoundException) {
      return StatusCode((int)HttpStatusCode.NotFound,
 "The flight was not found in the database");
  } catch (Exception) {
    return StatusCode((int)HttpStatusCode.InternalServerError,
 "An error occurred");
  }
}
```

If we now run the GetFlightByFlightNumber_Success unit test again, we see it passes.
That was pretty quick! In about a page and a half, we created a brand-new endpoint
and have a success path unit test to back up the expected functionality. We are on a
roll, so let's add the two failure cases as well. Once again, they should be very similar to
what we did with the GetFlights unit tests, as shown here:

```
[TestMethod]
public async Task
 GetFlightByFlightNumber_Failure_FlightNotFoundException_404() {
  Mock<FlightService> service = new Mock<FlightService>();
  service.Setup(s => s.GetFlightByFlightNumber(1))
 .Throws(new FlightNotFoundException());

  FlightController controller = new FlightController(service.Object);
  ObjectResult response =
 await controller.GetFlightByFlightNumber(1) as ObjectResult;

  Assert.IsNotNull(response);
  Assert.AreEqual((int)HttpStatusCode.NotFound, response.StatusCode);
  Assert.AreEqual("The flight was not found in the database",
 response.Value);
}


[TestMethod]
public async Task GetFlightByFlightNumber_Failure_ArgumentException_500() {
  Mock<FlightService> service = new Mock<FlightService>();
  service.Setup(s => s.GetFlightByFlightNumber(1))
 .Throws(new ArgumentException());

  FlightController controller = new FlightController(service.Object);
  ObjectResult response =
 await controller.GetFlightByFlightNumber(1) as ObjectResult;

  Assert.IsNotNull(response);
  Assert.AreEqual((int)HttpStatusCode.InternalServerError,
 response.StatusCode);
  Assert.AreEqual("An error occurred", response.Value);
}
```

Go ahead and run all the tests; they should pass. So, what else do we need to do for this endpoint? Let's have a quick look at the OpenAPI specification, shown in figure 3.10, and verify we have done all we need to do.

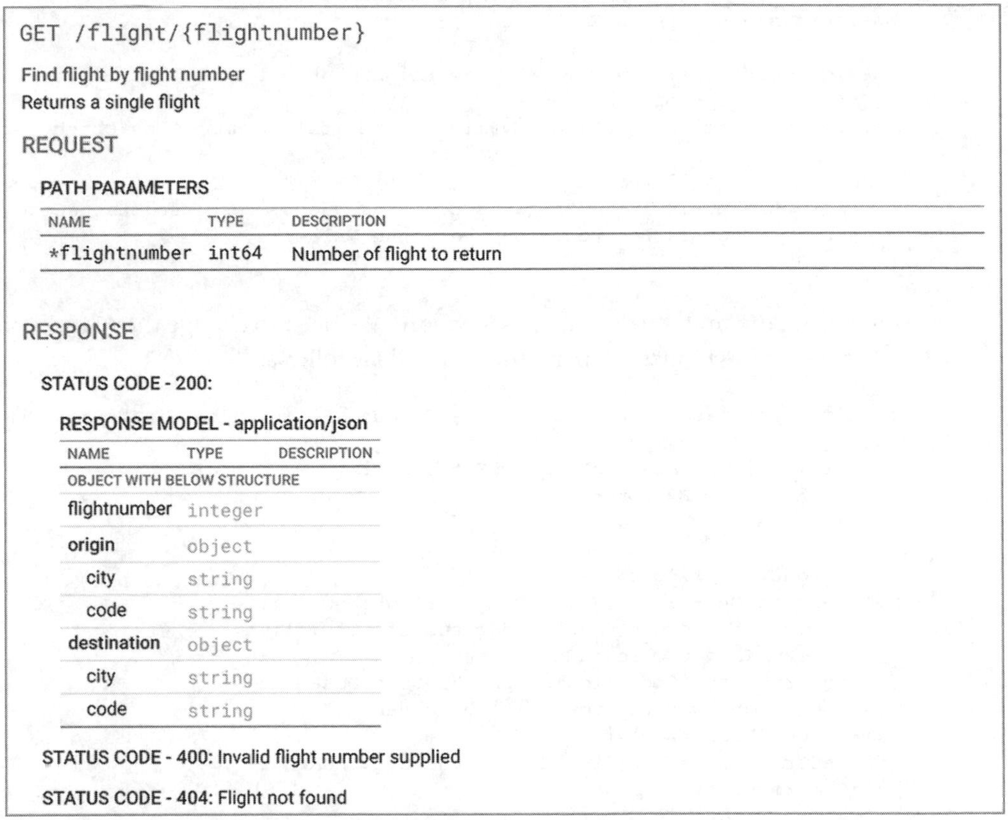

```
GET /flight/{flightnumber}
```
Find flight by flight number
Returns a single flight

REQUEST

PATH PARAMETERS

NAME	TYPE	DESCRIPTION
*flightnumber	int64	Number of flight to return

RESPONSE

STATUS CODE - 200:

RESPONSE MODEL - application/json

NAME	TYPE	DESCRIPTION
OBJECT WITH BELOW STRUCTURE		
flightnumber	integer	
origin	object	
city	string	
code	string	
destination	object	
city	string	
code	string	

STATUS CODE - 400: Invalid flight number supplied

STATUS CODE - 404: Flight not found

Figure 13.10 The OpenAPI specification for the `GET /flight/{flightNumber}` endpoint. This is a screenshot from a generated OpenAPI specification.

By looking at the OpenAPI specification, we see that we need to accept a parameter called flightNumber: check! We also have three returns: a 200 with the FlightView we constructed, a 404 when a flight cannot be found, and a 400 if an invalid flight number was supplied.

Well, we have two out of three correct. We just need to change our 500 internal error to a 400 status code (Bad Request) and verify that the passed-in flightNumber is a valid number. A valid flightNumber is (for our purposes) any positive integer.

Let's first hop into our unit test and make these changes as follows:

```
[TestMethod]
[DataRow(-1)]
```

```
[DataRow(1)]
public async Task
➥ GetFlightByFlightNumber_Failure_ArgumentException_400(int
➥ flightNumber){
  Mock<FlightService> service = new Mock<FlightService>();
  service.Setup(s => s.GetFlightByFlightNumber(1))
➥ .Throws(new ArgumentException());

  FlightController controller = new FlightController(service.Object);
  ObjectResult response =
➥ await controller.GetFlightByFlightNumber(flightNumber) as ObjectResult;

  Assert.IsNotNull(response);
  Assert.AreEqual((int)HttpStatusCode.BadRequest, response.StatusCode);
  Assert.AreEqual("Bad request", response.Value);
}
```

Of course, the unit test doesn't pass anymore. We need to change the FlightController
.GetFlightByFlightNumber method as well, as follows:

```
public async Task<IActionResult> GetFlightByFlightNumber(int flightNumber){
  try {
    if (!flightNumber.IsPositiveInteger()) {
      throw new Exception();
    }

    FlightView flight = await
➥ _service.GetFlightByFlightNumber(flightNumber);
    return StatusCode((int)HttpStatusCode.OK, flight);
  } catch (FlightNotFoundException) {
    return StatusCode((int)HttpStatusCode.NotFound,
➥ "The flight was not found in the database");
  } catch (Exception) {
    return StatusCode((int)HttpStatusCode.BadRequest,
➥ "Bad request");
  }
}
```

And what have we learned? To always double-check our code and tests against the
specification we are given.

So now that we have the GetFlights and GetFlightByFlightNumber methods in our
FlightController, it's time to expose them to external systems. After all, the code is
currently not usable, so it's somewhat worthless. To do this, we need to have a way for
our service to accept an incoming HTTP request and route that request to the appropriate controller and method. In the next section, we'll explore exactly how to do that.

13.4   *Routing HTTP requests to controllers and methods*

Now you have a bunch of repositories, services, and controllers. They are all filled to the
brim with amazing methods that can do anything you ever wanted. But how do you use
this stuff? Unlike a desktop application where you provide a GUI alongside the business

logic, we are dealing with a web service that lives somewhere in a deployed environment. How do we ask or tell the server to do anything? We use HTTP requests.

How does our service accept such a request? Well, right now the FlyingDutchman-Airlines service acts somewhat as a brick wall. If you were to send an HTTP request to it, the service would not know what to do with it. But if we introduce the concept of routing, shown in figure 13.11, the story changes.

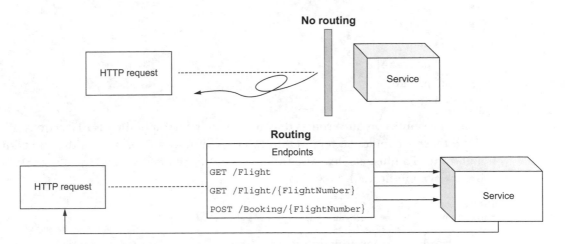

Figure 13.11 **HTTP requests entering a service with and without routing. When we do not have any routing set up, HTTP requests bounce from the service unresolved. If we route to endpoints, the service can execute the appropriate logic.**

Routing allows us to map URLs to specific controllers and endpoints. The mapping between requests and controller endpoints makes the GET /Flight method in the FlightController execute when you send an HTTP GET request to the [*Service-Address*]/flight URL. What do we need to do to add routing support? In section 12.3.2, we talked about middleware. Routing is just another piece of middleware we can add to our service. In fact, most of what we need to do is already there.

In section 5.2, we built the internal routing table containing a list of endpoints the service can route to. All we need to do to start the routing is tell the CLR where to route the requests. We do this by giving "routes" to endpoint methods and controllers in a two-step process. First, we add a [Route] attribute to the FlightController class as follows:

```
[Route("{controller}")]
public class FlightController : Controller { … }
```

The [Route] attribute accepts either a hardcoded route or a template. Here, I opted for the "{controller}" template.

CONTROLLER NAMES IN ROUTES   When using the "{controller}" template in the route attribute, the route is resolved to be the name of your controller class, minus the actual word *controller*. So, in our case, our class is called FlightController, so the route is /Flight.

The next step is to define method-specific routing. To do this, we use the following collection of attributes that map to HTTP actions:

- [HttpGet]
- [HttpPost]
- [HttpPut]
- [HttpDelete]
- [HttpHead]
- [HttpPatch]

All these attributes produce routes that map to their corresponding HTTP actions. We can use these attributes on methods in two ways: as they are, or by providing an additional route. To illustrate, let's use the [HttpGet] attribute on the FlightController .GetFlights method as follows:

```
[HttpGet]
public async Task<IActionResult> GetFlights() { … }
```

The method routes get added to the controller route. Using the [HttpGet] attribute on the GetFlights method produces a route of GET /Flight for this method, which is in line with what the FlyTomorrow OpenAPI specification would have us do. To test our endpoint, we can use either the cURL command-line tool (included in Windows, macOS, and Linux) or a dedicated HTTP tool such as Postman. I won't take a stand on which one is better: they each have their pros and cons. For most commands in the book, I use cURL on Windows. The usage of cuRL should be the same (or very similar) across platforms.

To reach our endpoint, we first need to launch it. Usually, we launch services locally on port 8080 (and this is the case with the provided source code). This works fine for most use cases, but sometimes you'll have a conflict on that port and need to use a different one. If you find that you cannot access the service, and you are serving on port 8080, change the port to something else in Startup.cs. In this example, I used port 8081. To launch our service, open a command-line window, point it to the FlyingDutchmanAirlines folder, and enter the following:

```
>\ dotnet run
```

Once the service is up and running (the command line tells us if it is), we can use cURL to "curl" our endpoint. To curl an endpoint, in a separate command-line window, use the [curl] -v [address] syntax (the -v flag tells cURL to give us some more details or verbosity), as shown next:

```
\> curl -v http://localhost:8081/flight
```

If your service is running, you will receive a response containing all the flights in the database, as shown in figure 13.12.

```
C:\Users\Jort\Documents\rodenburg\code\Chapter 13>curl -v http://localhost:8081/flight
*   Trying ::1...
* TCP_NODELAY set
*   Trying 127.0.0.1...
* TCP_NODELAY set
* Connected to localhost (127.0.0.1) port 8081 (#0)
> GET /flight HTTP/1.1
> Host: localhost:8081
> User-Agent: curl/7.55.1
> Accept: */*
>
< HTTP/1.1 200 OK
< Date: Sat, 06 Jun 2020 19:40:47 GMT
< Content-Type: application/json; charset=utf-8
< Server: Kestrel
< Transfer-Encoding: chunked
<
[{"flightNumber":"0","origin":{"city":"Groningen","code":"GRQ"},"destination":{"city":"London","code":"LHR"}},{"flightNumber":
"1","origin":{"city":"London","code":"LHR"},"destination":{"city":"Groningen","code":"GRQ"}},{"flightNumber":"2","origin":{"ci
ty":"Groningen","code":"GRQ"},"destination":{"city":"Prague","code":"PRG"}},{"flightNumber":"3","origin":{"city":"Prague","cod
e":"PRG"},"destination":{"city":"Groningen","code":"GRQ"}},{"flightNumber":"4","origin":{"city":"Groningen","code":"GRQ"},"des
tination":{"city":"Basel","code":"MLH"}},{"flightNumber":"5","origin":{"city":"Basel","code":"MLH"},"destination":{"city":"Gro
ningen","code":"GRQ"}},{"flightNumber":"6","origin":{"city":"Groningen","code":"GRQ"},"destination":{"city":"Paris","code":"CD
G"}},{"flightNumber":"7","origin":{"city":"Paris","code":"CDG"},"destination":{"city":"Groningen","code":"GRQ"}},{"flightNumbe
r":"8","origin":{"city":"Groningen","code":"GRQ"},"destination":{"city":"Cardiff","code":"CWL"}},{"flightNumber":"9","origin":
{"city":"Cardiff","code":"CWL"},"destination":{"city":"Groningen","code":"GRQ"}},{"flightNumber":"10","origin":{"city":"Gronin
gen","code":"GRQ"},"destination":{"city":"Edinburgh","code":"EDI"}},{"flightNumber":"11","origin":{"city":"Edinburgh","code":"
EDI"},"destination":{"city":"Groningen","code":"GRQ"}},{"flightNumber":"12","origin":{"city":"Groningen","code":"GRQ"},"destin
ation":{"city":"Cork","code":"ORK"}},{"flightNumber":"13","origin":{"city":"Cork","code":"ORK"},"destination":{"city":"Groning
en","code":"GRQ"}},{"flightNumber":"14","origin":{"city":"Groningen","code":"GRQ"},"destination":{"city":"Oslo","code":"OSL"}}
,{"flightNumber":"15","origin":{"city":"Oslo","code":"OSL"},"destination":{"city":"Groningen","code":"GRQ"}},{"flightNumber":"
16","origin":{"city":"Groningen","code":"GRQ"},"destination":{"city":"Berlin","code":"BER"}},{"flightNumber":"17","origin":{"c
ity":"Berlin","code":"BER"},"destination":{"city":"Groningen","code":"GRQ"}},{"flightNumber":"18","origin":{"city":"Groningen"
,"code":"GRQ"},"destination":{"city":"Lyon","code":"LYS"}},{"flightNumber":"19","origin":{"city":"Lyon","code":"LYS"},"destina
tion":{"city":"Groningen","code":"GRQ"}},{"flightNumber":"20","origin":{"city":"Groningen","code":"GRQ"},"destination":{"city"
:"Luxembourg","code":"LUX"}},{"flightNumber":"21","origin":{"city":"Luxembourg","code":"LUX"},"destination":{"city":"Groningen
","code":"GRQ"}},{"flightNumber":"22","origin":{"city":"Groningen","code":"GRQ"},"destination":{"city":"Salzburg","code":"SLZ"
}},{"flightNumber":"23","origin":{"city":"Salzburg","code":"SLZ"},"destination":{"city":"Groningen","code":"GRQ"}},{"flightNum
ber":"24","origin":{"city":"Groningen","code":"GRQ"},"destination":{"city":"Milan","code":"MXP"}},{"flightNumber":"25","origin
":{"city":"Milan","code":"MXP"},"destination":{"city":"Groningen","code":"GRQ"}},{"flightNumber":"26","origin":{"city":"Gronin
gen","code":"GRQ"},"destination":{"city":"Copenhagen","code":"CPH"}},{"flightNumber":"27","origin":{"city":"Copenhagen","code"
:"CPH"},"destination":{"city":"Groningen","code":"GRQ"}},{"flightNumber":"28","origin":{"city":"Groningen","code":"GRQ"},"dest
ination":{"city":"Belfast","code":"BFS"}},{"flightNumber":"29","origin":{"city":"Belfast","code":"BFS"},"destination":{"city":
"Groningen","code":"GRQ"}},{"flightNumber":"30","origin":{"city":"Groningen","code":"GRQ"},"destination":{"city":"Sorvag","cod
e":"FAE"}},{"flightNumber":"31","origin":{"city":"Sorvag","code":"FAE"},"destination":{"city":"Groningen","code":"GRQ"}},{"fli
ghtNumber":"32","origin":{"city":"Groningen","code":"GRQ"},"destination":{"city":"Norwich","code":"NWI"}},{"flightNumber":"33"
,"origin":{"city":"Norwich","code":"NWI"},"destination":{"city":"Groningen","code":"GRQ"}},{"flightNumber":"34","origin":{"cit
y":"Groningen","code":"GRQ"},"destination":{"city":"Liverpool","code":"LPL"}},{"flightNumber":"35","origin":{"city":"Liverpool
","code":"LPL"},"destination":{"city":"Groningen","code":"GRQ"}},{"flightNumber":"36","origin":{"city":"Groningen","code":"GRQ
"},"destination":{"city":"Toulouse","code":"TLS"}},{"flightNumber":"37","origin":{"city":"Toulouse","code":"TLS"},"destination
":{"city":"Groningen","code":"GRQ"}},{"flightNumber":"38","origin":{"city":"Groningen","code":"GRQ"},"destination":{"city":"Ca
en","code":"CFR"}},{"flightNumber":"39","origin":{"city":"Caen","code":"CFR"},"destination":{"city":"Groningen","code":"GRQ"}}
]* Connection #0 to host localhost left intact
```

Figure 13.12 The response from our service to a `GET HTTP /Flight` request: a massive JSON array containing all flights in the database. FlyTomorrow can use this data to represent all flights by Flying Dutchman Airlines to customers.

As you can see in figure 13.12, the cURL tool does not format the returned JSON information. It displays the data unformatted, making it hard to read. In figure 13.13, you can see part of the formatted response as shown in Postman, which formats the returned JSON. The wonderful news is that our endpoint worked! We did a full round trip from our HTTP request to the database and back to our command line. All the hard work we did in the previous chapters is finally paying off.

How do we reach our other endpoint: `/GET /Flight/{FlightNumber}`? After all, we are using a path parameter containing the flight number. When using an `Http-Attribute` method attribute (like `[HttpGet]`), we can provide additional routing instructions, as shown in the next code snippet. This is useful for when we want to provide

```
[
    {
        "flightNumber": "0",
        "origin": {
            "city": "Groningen",
            "code": "GRQ"
        },
        "destination": {
            "city": "London",
            "code": "LHR"
        }
    },
    {
        "flightNumber": "1",
        "origin": {
            "city": "London",
            "code": "LHR"
        },
        "destination": {
            "city": "Groningen",
            "code": "GRQ"
        }
    },
```

Figure 13.13   Part of the same JSON response data as shown in figure 13.12 but formatted. Formatted JSON is much more readable, and we can easily spot any issues.

some more route nesting (e.g., have an endpoint that goes to /Flight/Amazing-Flights/) or for receiving a path parameter such as {flightNumber}).

```
[HttpGet("{flightNumber}")]
public async Task<IActionResult> GetFlightByFlightNumber(int flightNumber){
    ...
}
```

With the GetFlightByFlightNumber method, the template specified as part of the [HttpGet] points the path parameter of {flightNumber} to the method's input parameter of flightNumber. We can now use the path parameter and request information on a specific flight. For example, we can easily retrieve information on flight 23 from Salzburg to Groningen by using cURL as follows:

```
\> curl -v http://localhost:8081/flight/23
```

The endpoint returns a serialized (a data structure converted to a binary or JSON format) version of the FlightView class for flight 23. Figure 13.14 shows the response data. We can also see in figure 13.15 what happens if we pass in an invalid flight number, such as -1 (not a positive integer) or 93018 (flight does not exist in the database).

So, to summarize: we now have a fully implemented FlightController along with unit tests. We can hit the GET /Flight and GET /Flight/{FlightNumber} endpoints

```
C:\Users\Jort\Documents\rodenburg\code\Chapter 13>curl -v http://localhost:8081/flight/23
*    Trying ::1...
* TCP_NODELAY set
*    Trying 127.0.0.1...
* TCP_NODELAY set
* Connected to localhost (127.0.0.1) port 8081 (#0)
> GET /flight/23 HTTP/1.1
> Host: localhost:8081
> User-Agent: curl/7.55.1
> Accept: */*
>
< HTTP/1.1 200 OK
< Date: Sat, 06 Jun 2020 19:59:02 GMT
< Content-Type: application/json; charset=utf-8
< Server: Kestrel
< Transfer-Encoding: chunked
<
{"flightNumber":"23","origin":{"city":"Salzburg","code":"SLZ"},"destination":{"city":"Groningen","code":"GRQ"}]
```

Figure 13.14   The data returned by the service when calling the GET /Flight/23 endpoint. By passing in an appropriate flight parameter value, we can query the service for flight 23 by using the GET /Flight/{FlightNumber} endpoint.

```
C:\Users\Jort\Documents\rodenburg\code\Chapter 13>curl -v http://localhost:8081/flight/-1
*    Trying ::1...
* TCP_NODELAY set
*    Trying 127.0.0.1...
* TCP_NODELAY set
* Connected to localhost (127.0.0.1) port 8081 (#0)
> GET /flight/-1 HTTP/1.1
> Host: localhost:8081
> User-Agent: curl/7.55.1
> Accept: */*
>                                                    ── HTTP 400 (Bad Request)
< HTTP/1.1 400 Bad Request ◄
< Date: Sat, 06 Jun 2020 20:10:44 GMT
< Content-Type: text/plain; charset=utf-8
< Server: Kestrel
< Transfer-Encoding: chunked
<
Bad request* Connection #0 to host localhost left intact
```

```
C:\Users\Jort\Documents\rodenburg\code\Chapter 13>curl -v http://localhost:8081/flight/93018
*    Trying ::1...
* TCP_NODELAY set
*    Trying 127.0.0.1...
* TCP_NODELAY set
* Connected to localhost (127.0.0.1) port 8081 (#0)
> GET /flight/93018 HTTP/1.1
> Host: localhost:8081
> User-Agent: curl/7.55.1
> Accept: */*
>                                                    ── HTTP 404 (Not Found)
< HTTP/1.1 404 Not Found ◄
< Date: Sat, 06 Jun 2020 20:10:52 GMT
< Content-Type: text/plain; charset=utf-8
< Server: Kestrel
< Transfer-Encoding: chunked
<
The flight was not found in the database* Connection #0 to host localhost left intact
```

Figure 13.15   We receive HTTP 400 and HTTP 404 back in our error conditions for the /GET /Flight/{FlightNumber} endpoint. These errors are useful to determine if the problem is on the client or server side.

and retrieve data from the database successfully. In the next chapter, we'll finish our refactoring journey and implement the last controller and endpoint: the Booking-Controller and the POST /Booking endpoint.

Exercises

EXERCISE 13.1
True or false? A controller is the only layer that should accept an HTTP request from an external system in a repository/service pattern architecture.

EXERCISE 13.2
A typical HTTP response comprises the following three attributes:

   a   Sender information, routing information, IP destination
   b   Name of sender, what programming language was used in the service, country of origin
   c   Status code, headers, body

EXERCISE 13.3
Which controller should you implement for this route: GET /Books/Fantasy?

   a   `BookController`
   b   `FantasyController`
   c   `BookShopController`

EXERCISE 13.4
True or false? Middleware is executed before any endpoint method logic.

EXERCISE 13.5
What type of injected dependency allows us to have a new instance of a dependency every time it is requested, regardless of whether we are still dealing with the same HTTP request?

   a   Singleton
   b   Scoped
   c   Transient

EXERCISE 13.6
What type of injected dependency allows us to use the same instance of a dependency only for the duration of an HTTP request's life cycle in our service?

   a   Singleton
   b   Scoped
   c   Transient

Summary

- The controller layer is the outer layer in terms of architecture when considering a repository/service pattern. A controller can accept HTTP requests and communicate with external systems. If we could not accept or talk with external systems, nobody could use our service.
- An HTTP request always contains headers (CORS, authentication, etc.) and sometimes a body (JSON or XML).

- An HTTP response always contains headers, an HTTP status code (200 OK, 404 Not Found, etc.), and sometimes a body.
- ASP.NET's `IActionResult` interface allows us to easily return HTTP responses from methods. This allows us to write clear and concise code that everybody can understand.
- Coding to interfaces is a clean code principle that promotes the use of generic constructs over limiting concrete classes. This allows us to adhere to the Open/Closed Principle and easily extend our code without changing the existing class.
- Middleware is any code that we execute before dealing with a provided HTTP request in a controller's endpoint method. We can use middleware to execute things such as authentication checks, dependency injection, and routing.
- When injecting a dependency in middleware, you have the option of three types of injected dependencies: singleton, scoped, and transient. A singleton dependency mimics the singleton design pattern and guarantees all requests operate on a single instance of an injected dependency. With scoped, the injected dependency is shared across the same request but not across multiple requests. With transient, a new instance of a dependency is instantiated every time it is requested by a constructor.
- To route an HTTP request to an endpoint, we have to set up routing in middleware and add routing attributes to both the controller class and the methods. This allows granular control over what our routes should look like.
- There are `HttpAttribute` routing method attributes for most common HTTP actions. You can either use them as is or provide an additional route and use path parameters.

JSON serialization/
deserialization and
custom model binding

This chapter covers

- Serializing and deserializing JSON data
- Using the [FromBody] argument attribute to magically deserialize JSON data
- Implementing a custom model binder using the IModelBinder interface
- Generating an OpenAPI specification on the fly at run time

This is it. The last refactoring chapter. Throughout this book, you refactored an existing codebase from the ground up. We learned about test-driven development, how to write clean code, and tips and tricks for C#. Figure 14.1 shows how far we've come on our journey together.

In this chapter, we'll implement the last controller: BookingController (section 14.1). After that, we'll do some manual testing and acceptance testing against the OpenAPI specification from FlyTomorrow. We'll also set up Swagger middleware to generate an OpenAPI specification on the fly (section 14.2). This is an optional but a very useful technique to know because Swagger helps us with our acceptance testing.

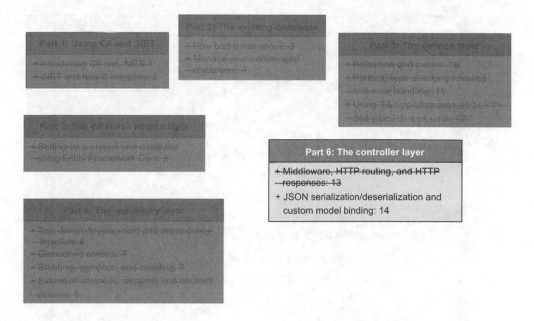

Part 1: Using C# and .NET
+ Introducing C# and .NET: 1
+ .NET and how it compiles: 2

Part 2: The existing codebase
+ How bad is this code?: 3
+ Manage your unmanaged resources!: 4

Part 5: The service layer
+ Reflection and mocks: 10
+ Runtime type-checking revisited and error handling: 11
+ Using IAsyncEnumerable<T> and yield return: 12

Part 3: The database access layer
+ Setting up a project and database using Entity Framework Core: 5

Part 4: The repository layer
+ Test-driven development and dependency injection: 6
+ Comparing objects: 7
+ Stubbing, generics, and coupling: 8
+ Extension methods, streams, and abstract classes: 9

Part 6: The controller layer

+ Middleware, HTTP routing, and HTTP responses: 13
+ JSON serialization/deserialization and custom model binding: 14

Figure 14.1   In the previous chapters, we implemented the database access, repository, and service layers, and `FlightController` class. In this chapter, we'll finish the job and implement the `BookingController` class.

14.1 *Implementing the BookingController class*

In chapter 13, we learned how to implement a controller (`FlightController`) and added some HTTP `GET` methods (`GET /Flight` and `GET Flight/{FlightNumber}`). In this section, we'll build on that knowledge and implement the `BookingController`. The `BookingController` is the entry point and gateway for FlyTomorrow to create a booking with Flying Dutchman Airlines. With this controller, we'll complete our implementation of the FlyingDutchmanAirlinesNextGen service and start providing some actual revenue value to the company. After all, if people cannot book seats on our flights, we can't make money from oversized bags, snacks, and lottery tickets on board.

Let's take one more look at the contract between Flying Dutchman Airlines and FlyTomorrow to see what endpoints the `BookingController` class should have, shown in figure 14.2.

As you can see, we have the following three endpoints to implement:

- `GET /Flight`
- `GET /Flight/{FlightNumber}`
- `POST /Booking/{FlightNumber}`

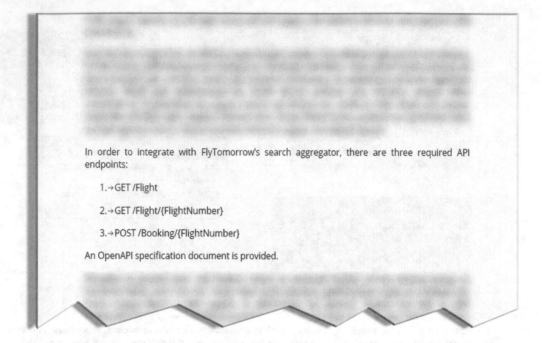

In order to integrate with FlyTomorrow's search aggregator, there are three required API endpoints:

1.→ GET /Flight

2.→ GET /Flight/{FlightNumber}

3.→ POST /Booking/{FlightNumber}

An OpenAPI specification document is provided.

Figure 14.2   The, by now, well-known contract between FlyTomorrow and Flying Dutchman Airlines. Endpoints 1 and 2 were implemented in chapter 13. In this chapter, we'll implement endpoint 3.

In chapter 13, we implemented endpoints numbers 1 and 2. That leaves only the third endpoint for us now. The first two endpoints live inside a FlightController class, but the third requires us to implement a BookingController class.

The previous two endpoints also did not require us to process any provided JSON body. Sure, we had a path parameter in the GET /Flight/{FlightNumber} endpoint, but it constrained the flight number data to whatever a path parameter can accept. With a POST, we need to accept the data that was posted to the endpoint. We'll look at how to do this in section 14.1.2.

Before we do that, however, let's create our (by now) standard skeleton class: BookingController. We know from section 13.3 that for the CLR to pick up our controller class as a viable routing end station, we need to have the BookingController derive from the Controller class and add the [Route] class attribute as follows:

```
[Route("{controller}")]
public class BookingController : Controller { }
```

14.1.1 Introduction to data deserialization

Let's unravel the details around the `POST /Booking/{flightNumber}` endpoint and look at the data we can expect to be passed into our service (figure 14.3).

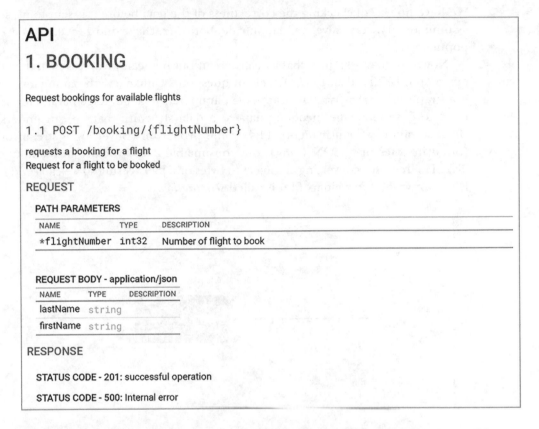

Figure 14.3 The `POST /Booking/{flightNumber}` endpoint accepts an HTTP body containing the first and last name of the customer that wants to book the given flight. It returns a 201 or 500. This is a screenshot from a generated OpenAPI specification.

The `POST /Booking/{flightNumber}` combines two ways of providing data to the controller: a path parameter (`flightNumber`) and a JSON body containing two strings: first and last names. We can model this data in JSON as follows:

```
{
  "firstName" : "Frank",
  "lastName"  : "Turner"
}
```

Of course, nothing stops users from filling out the fields incorrectly and providing full names in both fields as shown here:

```
{
    "firstName" : "Pete Seeger",
    "lastName"  : "Jonathan Coulton"
}
```

We have no way of checking the correctness of the data before it is sent to us, so let's assume a (very, very naïve) validation rule: both firstName and lastName need to be populated.

Now, you may ask, "Jort, that is really great. But how can we access such data inside our methods?" To that, I say, "Excellent question." Unlike a path parameter, we cannot simply add firstName and lastName parameters to a method's parameter list. We need to deserialize the incoming data to a data structure that we can understand. Deserialization, shown in figure 14.4, is the process of converting a stream of data (often in bytes or a JSON string) to a consumable data structure in memory or on disk. The reverse (converting an object to bytes or a JSON string so we can send it over HTTP or write it to a binary file) is called *serialization*.

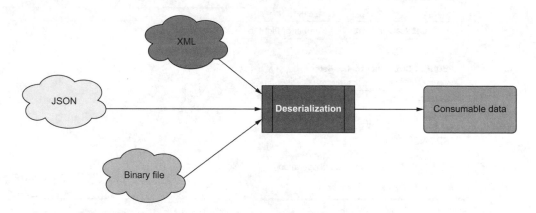

Figure 14.4   Deserialization takes streams of data such as XML, JSON, and binary files and turns them into consumable data, often stored in data structures. This allows us to work with serialized data.

Because the HTTP request's body comes through the wire serialized (as a JSON string in our case), and we need to access its body information, we have to deserialize the body into some sort of defined structure.

To deserialize data, we use the following two concepts:

- A data structure (usually a class) with an appropriate structure to deserialize the data
- Model binding using the [FromBody] argument attribute (model binding is also referred to as data binding)

Let's start by providing ASP.NET with a data structure into which to deserialize the provided body. The best way to do this (because it is the most organized) is to create a

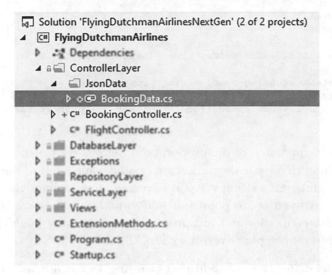

Figure 14.5 The `BookingData` class is added to the new JsonData folder in the ControllerLayer folder. Keeping the JsonData classes inside the ControllerLayer folder aids us in making sure our codebase is organized.

class or struct to hold our data. Even though we just want to store the data, we also want to do some validation on the provided data, so, we use a class. We store this new class in a new folder, ControllerLayer/JsonData, and name the file BookingData.cs, as shown in figure 14.5 and the next code snippet.

```
public class BookingData {
  public string FirstName { get; set; }
  public string LastName { get; set; }
}
```

When all is said and done, the `BookingData` class should be populated with the data provided by the external system calling the endpoint. We also want to do some validation on the properties: if the provided string is null or empty, do not set the property to the provided string but throw an `InvalidOperationException` (alternatively, an `ArgumentNullException` would also be appropriate). We'll also set a message on the exception, telling people what we couldn't do: set either `FirstName` or `LastName`. Rather than duplicating that same validation twice (once for both properties' setters), we can create a private method to do the validation and just call that. To add a body to the setter, we need to also provide one for the getter. This leads to the needed creation of a backing field as well, as shown in the next listing.

Listing 14.1　BookingData.cs

```
private string _firstName;
public string FirstName {
  get => _firstName;
  set => _firstName = ValidateName(value, nameof(FirstName));}
}
```

Returns the backing field's value → (points to `get => _firstName;`)

Backing field for the FirstName property ← (points to `private string _firstName;`)

Sets the value to the backing field ← (points to `set => _firstName = ValidateName(value, nameof(FirstName));}`)

```
private string _lastName;
public string LastName {
  get => _lastName;
  set => _lasttName = ValidateName(value, nameof(LastName));}}
```

Validates the input value

```
private string ValidateName(string name, string propertyName) =>
  string.IsNullOrEmpty(name)
  ? throw new InvalidOperationException("could not set " + propertyName)
  : name;
```

In listing 14.1, we pass in the name of the properties to help us construct the error message on the fly. To do this, we use the nameof expression, which gets us the name of a variable, type, or member as a string that is resolved at compile time. The listing should be easy to follow for you at this point, and you should be able to explain the differences between auto-properties and full properties with backing fields. If you have trouble with the differences, please revisit section 3.3.3.

CONDITIONAL CURLY BRACES   The only odd part of listing 14.1 is the lack of curly braces after the if(IsValidName(value)) conditionals. In C#, if you omit the curly braces after a conditional, the CLR assumes the next statement is the conditional's body and executes it. Note that this is limited to one executed statement. If you have two or more statements that make up a conditional's body, you need to use curly braces.

The last thing we have to do for the BookingData class is provide some unit tests that validate our assumptions around the functionality we just implemented. These unit tests are pretty straightforward, and you should be able to write them yourself. If you get stuck, the following are implementations you can use (we add the test file to the new FlyingDutchmanAirlines_Test/ControllerLayer/JsonData folder):

```
[TestClass]
public class BookingDataTests {
  [TestMethod]
  public void BookingData_ValidData() {
    BookingData bookingData = new BookingData {FirstName = "Marina",
  LastName = "Michaels"};
    Assert.AreEqual("Marina", bookingData.FirstName);
    Assert.AreEqual("Michaels", bookingData.LastName);
  }

  [TestMethod]
  [DataRow("Mike", null)]
  [DataRow(null, "Morand")]
  [ExpectedException(typeof(InvalidOperationException))]
  public void BookingData_InvalidData_NullPointers(string firstName,
  string lastName) {
    BookingData bookingData = new BookingData { FirstName = firstName,
  LastName = lastName };
    Assert.AreEqual(firstName, bookingData.FirstName);
    Assert.AreEqual(lastName, bookingData.LastName);
  }
```

```
[TestMethod]
[DataRow("Eleonor", "")]
[DataRow("", "Wilke")]
[ExpectedException(typeof(InvalidOperationException))]
  public void BookingData_InvalidData_EmptyStrings(string firstName,
➥ string lastName) {
    BookingData bookingData = new BookingData { FirstName = firstName,
➥ LastName = lastName };
    Assert.AreEqual(firstName, bookingData.FirstName ?? "");
    Assert.AreEqual(lastName, bookingData.LastName ?? "");
  }
}
```

How do we populate the `BookingData` class after we receive an HTTP `POST` request? That is where the `[FromBody]` attribute comes in.

14.1.2 Using the [FromBody] attribute to deserialize incoming HTTP data

In section 14.1.1, we created a data structure in which to store deserialized information. Within the context of an HTTP `POST` request, we can usually expect valid information to adhere to our provided OpenAPI specification. In this case, for the `POST` request to be valid, the JSON data needs to be deserialized to the `BookingData` class's properties: `firstName` and `lastName`. If we end up with an incomplete request (the `BookingClass`'s properties have null pointers), we return an HTTP status code of 500. You could also return an HTTP status code of 400 (Bad Request) in this scenario, and that may often be the correct code to return, but let's stick with the provided OpenAPI specification (shown in figure 14.3).

But first things first: how do we get the data deserialized to the `BookingData` class? We can't just add a `BookingData` type to the parameter list and expect it to automatically work. It may sound crazy, but that is actually pretty close to reality! ASP.NET's `[FromBody]` attribute can be applied to a parameter to tell ASP.NET we want to perform model binding to this type. When the CLR routes a payload to an endpoint with such a parameter, it takes the payload's `Body` element and attempts to deserialize it to the given data type.

To request this model binding, simply add "*FromBody type argumentName*" to the parameter list of a method (in our case, let's create a new method in the Booking-Controller class called `CreateBooking` along with an HTTP attribute of `[HttpPost]`) as follows:

```
[HttpPost]
public async Task<IActionResult> CreateBooking([FromBody] BookingData body)
```

By adding the `[FromBody]` attribute to a type of `BookingData` accessible through the body variable, we can now use the data from the HTTP request, as shown in figure 14.6.

It is that simple. Now, some people are not a fan of "magic" in their codebases, and that's fine. Know that by default, ASP.NET is set up to serialize JSON data. If you want

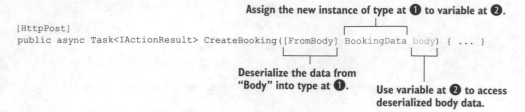

Figure 14.6   Using the [FromBody] attribute. When using the [FromBody] attribute, you can deserialize HTTP JSON data to a specific data structure and access it.

to use XML, you have to add the following lines to a global.asax.cs file (this file, when present, contains global configuration details for your service):

```
XmlFormatter xmlFormatter =
➥ GlobalConfiguration.Configuration.Formatters.XmlFormatter;
xmlFormatter.UseXmlSerializer = true;
```

Let's quickly look at an alternative way of parsing HTTP data to data structures before we continue (and keep using [FromBody]).

14.1.3   Using a custom model binder and method attribute for model binding

Instead of using the [FromBody] attribute to automatically bind HTTP data to a data structure, we can also lift the veil of ASP.NET's magic and implement our own model binder. People often object to using the [FromBody] attribute because it seems to be magically doing things under the hood with no explanation. This section aims to explain that magic.

As a custom model binder, our BookingModelBinder contains information on how we want to bind the given data to our class. Using a custom model binder is somewhat cumbersome but can provide greater control to your data-binding process. To start, let's add a new class to serve as our model binder, as shown in the next listing. This class, BookingModelBinder, needs to implement the IModelBinder interface. The IModelBinder interface is what lets us use the BookingModelBinder to bind the data to the model, which we will do in a bit.

Listing 14.2   The beginnings of a custom model binder

To provide custom model binding, we need to implement the IModelBinder interface.

```
class BookingModelBinder : IModelBinder {
  public async Task BindModelAsync(ModelBindingContext bindingContext){
    throw new NotImplementedException();
  }
}
```

The IModelBinder interface requires us to implement BindModelAsync.

Our `BookingModelBinder` class's implementation has the following four major parts, as shown in figure 14.7:

1 Validate the `bindingContext` input argument.
2 Read the HTTP body into a parsable format.
3 Bind the HTTP body data to the `BookingData` class's properties.
4 Return the bound model.

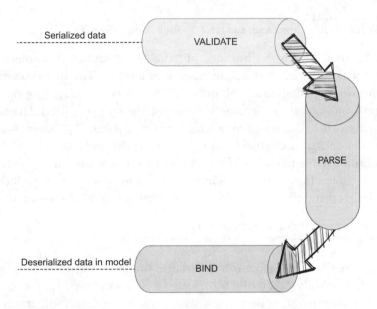

Figure 14.7   When using a custom model binder to deserialize data, we need to validate, parse, and bind our data before returning the data in a bound model. This workflow gives us fine-grained control over the deserializing process.

The first step is also the easiest: we just want to make sure that the `bindingContext` argument isn't tied to a null value as follows:

```
public async Task BindModelAsync(ModelBindingContext bindingContext) {
  if (bindingContext == null) {
    throw new ArgumentException();
  }
}
```

For step 2 (read the HTTP body into a parsable format), we need to access and then handle the HTTP body information.

Luckily, we can access everything we need about the incoming HTTP request through the provided `ModelBindingContext` instance. The classes we are looking for are `HttpContext` and `HttpRequest`. They contain properties tied to all expected elements (body, headers, and the like). The `Request` class provides us with an instance of `PipeReader`, which has access to the serialized body element. The `PipeReader` class is part of the `System.IO.Pipelines` namespace. `System.IO.Pipelines` contains classes (most importantly, `Pipe`, `PipeWriter`, and `PipeReader`) that help with high-performance input/output (IO) operations.

To retrieve and use the `PipeReader` so we can get one step closer to the body data, we use the `Request.BodyReader` property and call its `ReadAsync` method as follows:

```
ReadResult result = await
    bindingContext.HttpContext.Request.BodyReader.ReadAsync();
```

The `ReadAsync` method returns an instance of `Task<ReadResult>`. This object contains three properties: `IsCompleted`, `IsCanceled`, and `Buffer`. The first two are used for checking whether the reading of the provided data was completed or canceled. The third is where our data lives. Because we are dealing with serialized data and an asynchronous process, the data is stored in a buffer of type `ReadOnlySequence<byte>`. It is this buffer that contains the actual bytes representing the body data. Typically, the buffer contains only one "segment" of data, so we can retrieve the first `Span` (a `Span` represents a contiguous chunk of data). Then, we need to deserialize that data back into a readable JSON string. We do that by using the `Encoding.UTF8` class as follows:

```
ReadOnlySequence<byte> buffer = result.Buffer;
string body = Encoding.UTF8.GetString(buffer.FirstSpan);
```

Now that we have the JSON string, we can deserialize the JSON string into our model (step 3: bind the HTTP body data to the `BookingData` class's properties). C# has some solid JSON functionality through the `System.Text.Json` namespace, which was introduced (and comes installed by default) in .NET 5. To deserialize a JSON string into a `BookingData` struct, we just have to call `JsonSerializer.Deserialize<T>` and give it the type we want to reserialize into as the generic type parameter (`BookingData`) and the JSON string we want to deserialize (body), as shown here:

```
BookingData data = JsonSerializer.Deserialize<BookingData>(body);
```

This deserializes the values coming out of the body to the appropriate types for their respective properties on the `BookingData` struct.

The last step (step 4) is to return the bound model. You may have noticed that the return type of the `BindModelAsync` method is `Task`. We cannot change the return type to be `Task<BookingData>` because we are bound to implement the `IModelBinder` interface. But, we have another way to get the new `BookingModel` instance to the endpoint method: by using the `ModelBindingContext` class's `Result` property, as shown here:

```
bindingContext.Result = ModelBindingResult.Success(data);
```

If we add that to the end of our method, we can rest assured that our instance of `BookingData` is passed to the controller—another piece of magic. As you continue your C# journey, you will encounter many such pieces of magic. But, if you drill down far enough, you can usually figure out what is going on underneath the covers. In the words of Harry Potter's Vernon Dursley, "There's no such thing as magic!"

That wraps up the `BookingModelBinder` class, but what about the endpoint method? Because we can't use the `[FromBody]` attribute, what do we do instead? It is actually fairly similar. We add a `[ModelBinder(typeof([custom binder]))]` attribute to the parameter as follows:

```
[HttpPost]
public async Task<IActionResult>
➡ CreateBooking([ModelBinder(typeof(BookingModelBinder))]
➡ BookingData body, int flightNumber)
```

Although definitely more involved than simply slapping on the `[FromBody]` attribute, we can understand this argument attribute through our knowledge of `[FromBody]`. See the next listing for the complete code.

Listing 14.3 Completed `BookingModelBinder` custom model binder class

```
class BookingModelBinder : IModelBinder {
  public async Task BindModelAsync(ModelBindingContext bindingContext) {
    if (bindingContext == null) {
      throw new ArgumentException();
    }

    ReadResult result = await
➡ bindingContext.HttpContext.Request.BodyReader.ReadAsync();
    ReadOnlySequence<byte> buffer = result.Buffer;

    string bodyJson = Encoding.UTF8.GetString(buffer.FirstSpan);
    JObject bodyJsonObject = JObject.Parse(bodyJson);

    BookingData boundData = new BookingData {
      FirstName = (string) bodyJsonObject["FirstName"],
      LastName = (string) bodyJsonObject["LastName"]
    };

    bindingContext.Result = ModelBindingResult.Success(boundData);
  }
}
```

The code you saw in this section is not required (and in fact not used) going forward. It is merely an excellent tool for you to know but overkill for our use case.

14.1.4 *Implementing the CreateBooking endpoint method logic*

With the model binding out of the way (and we go back to using the `[FromBody]` attribute), we can now focus on the meat of the `CreateBooking` method: the logic that calls the necessary service methods to create a booking in the database. Let's recap what the general steps are to create a booking, as shown in figure 14.8:

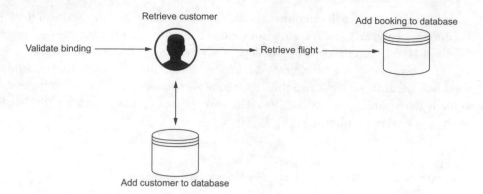

Figure 14.8   Creating a new booking in the database involves validating our model binding, retrieving (and adding if appropriate) a customer, retrieving the flight, and then creating the booking in the database. With this workflow, we always have all the information we need in the database.

1 Validate our data binding.
2 Make sure we have the provided customer in the database. If we do not, add the customer to the database.
3 Make sure the flight the customer wants to book exists.
4 Request a new entry in the `Booking` table containing the new booking.

Because we implemented the service and repository layer methods already, all these items should be very easy to implement. Let's start with the only somewhat tricky one: validating our data binding. To make sure our instance of `BookingData` is in a valid state, we need to define what that means. The instance is considered valid if both the `FirstName` and the `LastName` properties are set to a valid, nonempty string. If this is not the case, we don't want to do any processing. We already have logic in the `BookingData` class that makes sure we assign only valid names to the properties. If the passed-in name is not valid, the property remains unset. We do not want to use the instance in this case.

ASP.NET gives us access to the `IValidatableObject` interface. This interface allows us to define validation rules for the CLR to run through at the creation of the instance. If the validation rules are found to be broken, ASP.NET sets to `false` a Boolean property on the `ControllerBase` class: `ModelState.IsValid`. We can check that property in our controller to make sure the object we are using is valid. To implement the `IValidatableObject` interface, we need to do the following:

- Add the `IValidatableObject` interface to the `BookingData` class.
- Implement the required `Validate` method to validate the property values and handle any errors.

That doesn't sound too bad. Adding the interface to the class is easy, as shown next:

```
public class BookingData : IValidatableObject
```

Because the `BookingData` class now says it implements the `IValidatableObject` interface, we should actually do so. The interface tells us we *need* to implement a method called `Validate`, so let's hop right on that as follows:

```
public IEnumerable<ValidationResult> Validate(ValidationContext
    validationContext) {}
```

Remember that when we implement an interface, we have to implement any methods on that interface in our implementation class. We cannot change the method's signature because that would break our promise to the compiler and the interface to implement all methods on the interface. So, what do we do with the `Validate` method? The CLR calls the `Validate` method when the object is instantiated, and determines (based on the provided validation rules) how to set the `ModelState.IsValid` property. The return type (`IEnumerable<ValidationResult>`) allows us to return a data structure (implementing the `IEnumerable` interface, containing instances of `Validation-Result`) with no, one, or multiple errors. We can access these errors in the controller and return them to the customer.

What does this look like? Well, we need to instantiate a new type of `IEnumerable <ValidationResult>`, verify that our properties are set to an appropriate value (we already check whether the names they are set to are valid through the property's setters at model-binding time, but they can still be null values), add errors to the return data structure if a problem arises, and return the list of errors, as shown in the next listing.

Listing 14.4 BookingData's `Validate` method

```
public IEnumerable<ValidationResult> Validate(ValidationContext
➥ validationContext) {
  List<ValidationResult> results = new List<ValidationResult>();
  if (FirstName == null && LastName == null) {
    results.Add(
➥ new ValidationResult("All given data points are null"));
  } else if (FirstName == null || LastName == null) {
    results.Add(
➥ new ValidationResult("One of the given data points is null"));
  }
  return results;
}
```

- **Creates an empty list of errors**
- **If they are not both null values, perhaps only one of them is.**
- **Checks if both FirstName and LastName are null values**
- **If both properties are null values, adds an error to the list**
- **If only one of the properties is a null value, adds an error to the list**
- **Returns the list containing errors (if any)**

How do we actually use these errors? Back in the controller method, we should add a check to see if the `ModelState.IsValid` property is set to `true`. If it is, we can continue with our work. But if it is not, we should return an HTTP status code of 500, along with the found error, as follows:

```
[HttpPost]
public async Task<IActionResult>
➥ CreateBooking([FromBody] BookingData body) {
```

```
if (ModelState.IsValid) {
  …
}

return StatusCode((int) HttpStatusCode.InternalServerError,
➥ ModelState.Root.Errors.First().ErrorMessage);
}
```

If we were to query the CreateBooking endpoint with an invalid JSON payload, we would get an HTTP code of 500 along with the found validation error. We now have code that binds the provided JSON data to a model and that validates the resulting model. All we have to do now is to ask the BookingService to create a booking for us and pass on the appropriate information. To do this, we first need to add a backing field and an injected instance of type BookingService and set up the middleware to provide us with this instance at runtime.

First up, let's add the backing field and injected instance (through a constructor) in BookingController as follows:

```
[Route("{controller}")]
public class BookingController : Controller {
  private BookingService _bookingService;

  public BookingController(BookingService bookingService) {
    _bookingService = bookingService;
  }

  …
}
```

Now let's add the dependency injection middleware in Startup. The BookingService class requires injected dependencies of type BookingRepository, FlightRepository, and CustomerRepository. Luckily, we already have an injected (transient) dependency of type FlightRepository, so we just have to add (besides the BookingService) the BookingRepository and CustomerRepository transient instances to the Startup .ConfigureServices method, as shown here:

```
public void ConfigureServices(IServiceCollection services) {
  services.AddControllers();

  services.AddTransient(typeof(FlightService), typeof(FlightService));
  services.AddTransient(typeof(BookingService), typeof(BookingService));
  services.AddTransient(typeof(FlightRepository),
➥ typeof(FlightRepository));
  services.AddTransient(typeof(AirportRepository),
➥ typeof(AirportRepository));
  services.AddTransient(typeof(BookingRepository),
➥ typeof(BookingRepository));
  services.AddTransient(typeof(CustomerRepository),
➥ typeof(CustomerRepository));
```

```
  services.AddDbContext<FlyingDutchmanAirlinesContext>
➡ (ServiceLifetime.Transient);
  services.AddTransient(typeof(FlyingDutchmanAirlinesContext),
➡ typeof(FlyingDutchmanAirlinesContext));
}
```

The last thing we need before we can request the creating of a new booking is the endpoint's path parameter, shown in the next code sample. This parameter maps to the {flightNumber} section of the POST /Booking/{flightNumber} endpoint.

```
[HttpPost("{flightNumber}")]
public async Task<IActionResult> CreateBooking([FromBody] BookingData body,
➡ int flightNumber) {
  if (ModelState.IsValid) {
    …
  }

  return StatusCode((int) HttpStatusCode.InternalServerError,
➡ ModelState.Root.Errors.First().ErrorMessage);
}
```

Let's also do some quick input validation on the flightNumber argument. We can use the IsPositiveInteger extension method to make sure the flight number is not a negative integer as follows:

```
[HttpPost("{flightNumber}")]
public async Task<IActionResult> CreateBooking([FromBody] BookingData body,
➡ int flightNumber) {
  if (ModelState.IsValid && flightNumber.IsPositiveInteger()) {
    …
  }

  return StatusCode((int) HttpStatusCode.InternalServerError,
➡ ModelState.Root.Errors.First().ErrorMessage);
}
```

With that, we can almost call the BookingService.CreateBooking method and create a booking in the database. We just have to concatenate the FirstName and LastName strings (with a space in between), because BookingService.CreateBooking just takes a single parameter of type string representing the customer's name. We should be able to use string interpolation for this. Following the concatenation, we can finally call the service's CreateBooking method as follows:

```
[HttpPost("{flightNumber}")]
public async Task<IActionResult> CreateBooking([FromBody] BookingData body,
➡ int flightNumber) {
  if (ModelState.IsValid && flightNumber.IsPositiveInteger()) {
    string name = $"{body.FirstName} {body.LastName}";
    (bool result, Exception exception) =
➡ await _bookingService.CreateBooking(name, flightNumber);
  }
```

```
    return StatusCode((int) HttpStatusCode.InternalServerError,
➡ ModelState.Root.Errors.First().ErrorMessage);
}
```

The `BookingService.CreateBooking` method returns a tuple containing a Boolean value representing whether the creation of the booking was successful and an exception value set to any exception that was thrown. Based on these return values, we can determine what we want to return to the user as follows:

- If the Boolean is set to `true`, and the exception is null, return an HTTP status code of 201 (Created).
- If the Boolean is set to `false`, and the exception is not null, return an HTTP status code of 500 or 404, depending on the exception type.
- If the Boolean is set to `false`, and the exception is null, return an HTTP status code of 500.

We can easily add these as a couple of conditionals as follows:

```
[HttpPost("{flightNumber}")]
public async Task<IActionResult> CreateBooking([FromBody] BookingData body,
➡ int flightNumber) {
  if (ModelState.IsValid && flightNumber.IsPositiveInteger()) {
    string name = $"{body.FirstName} {body.LastName}";
    (bool result, Exception exception) =
➡ await _bookingService.CreateBooking(name, flightNumber);

    if (result && exception == null) {
      return StatusCode((int)HttpStatusCode.Created);
    }

    return exception is CouldNotAddBookingToDatabaseException
      ? StatusCode((int)HttpStatusCode.NotFound)
      ? StatusCode((int)HttpStatusCode.InternalServerError,
➡ exception.Message);
  }

  return StatusCode((int) HttpStatusCode.InternalServerError,
    ModelState.Root.Errors.First().ErrorMessage);
}
```

Because the `BookingService` returns an exception of type `CouldNotAddBookingTo-DatabaseException` when the flight cannot be found, we can use that to pivot our return status code to a 404.

And at this point, I have some really exciting news: we are all done with implementing our rewrite of the Flying Dutchman Airlines service! Pat yourself on the back and reflect on the (hopefully) many things you learned along the way. Although not a true production-ready reflection of the actual world, this process highlighted a lot of real-world scenarios and decisions. In the next section, we'll verify our work by doing some acceptance testing.

14.2 Acceptance testing and Swagger middleware

There are many ways to verify that your code works as you expect. Throughout the book, we used unit tests as a way to measure functionality expectations. But what do you do when you are at the end of the line? You implemented all your code using TDD-light (we cheated somewhat in the book), and now you want to verify the entire system. You could do something like automated integration tests (tests that run entire workflows in a production codebase; they are often part of a CI/CD system and run nightly). You may also be in the very lucky position to have a QA engineer available to you. But I want to show you a simple way of verifying your code works: acceptance testing.

When we talk about acceptance testing, all we are really saying is, "Match the requirements to our functionality." The requirements we got from the user came in the form of an OpenAPI specification, but they can come in a lot of forms (user stories are another notable requirement format). So, in this section, we'll do acceptance testing in the following two ways:

- We'll take the OpenAPI specification provided by FlyTomorrow and manually test our endpoints (section 14.2.1).
- We'll add an optional Swagger middleware to our service to generate an OpenAPI specification on the fly. We'll compare this generated specification to the provided one. They should match (section 14.2.2).

Acceptance testing before you hand off your product to a client is incredibly important and useful. Wouldn't you want to catch any bugs or incorrect functionality *before* the client does? Because we are testing against the production (deployed) database,[1] we can test only happy path and nondatabase exception scenarios. We don't want to force failures in a production environment. This is where us having unit-tested the failure paths comes in handy because we can still be safe in knowing they work.

14.2.1 Manual acceptance testing with an OpenAPI specification

Before we start testing, let's come up with a methodology and some testing steps that we can follow for all endpoints. We expect all functionality to work fine, especially because we did test the code after implementing it, but we can never be too sure! For our manual testing, I propose we use the following steps:

1 Identify the input requirements.
2 Determine the happy path and nondatabase exception cases.
3 Test!

---

[1] You typically do not want to test against a production database. The reason we do so in this book is because it allows me to provide a publicly deployed database for you to use.

The endpoints we need to test follow:

- `GET /flight`
- `GET /flight/{flightNumber}`
- `POST /booking/{flightNumber}`

So, without further ado, let's begin with the `GET /flight` endpoint, shown in figure 14.9. If we look at the OpenAPI specification, we see that this endpoint can return HTTP statuses of 200 (along with the `flightView` data), 404, and 500.

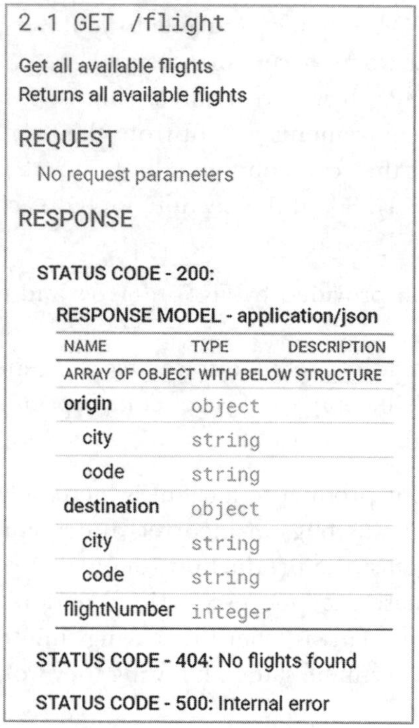

2.1 GET /flight

Get all available flights
Returns all available flights

REQUEST

No request parameters

RESPONSE

STATUS CODE - 200:

RESPONSE MODEL - application/json

NAME	TYPE	DESCRIPTION
ARRAY OF OBJECT WITH BELOW STRUCTURE		
origin	object	
city	string	
code	string	
destination	object	
city	string	
code	string	
flightNumber	integer	

STATUS CODE - 404: No flights found

STATUS CODE - 500: Internal error

Figure 14.9   OpenAPI specification of the `GET /flight` endpoint. This endpoint is used to get information on all flights in the database. This is a screenshot from a generated OpenAPI specification.

Because this is just a `GET` call, and there are no path parameters or other inputs that need validating, the only happy path (or non-database-related exception) case is the success case. If we query the `GET /flight` endpoint, we should get details on every flight in the database, as shown in figure 14.10.

```
curl -v http://localhost:8081/flight
*   Trying ::1...
* TCP_NODELAY set
*   Trying 127.0.0.1...
* TCP_NODELAY set
* Connected to localhost (127.0.0.1) port 8081 (#0)
> GET /flight HTTP/1.1
> Host: localhost:8081
> User-Agent: curl/7.55.1
> Accept: */*
>
< HTTP/1.1 200 OK
< Date: Sat, 06 Jun 2020 19:40:47 GMT
< Content-Type: application/json; charset=utf-8
< Server: Kestrel
< Transfer-Encoding: chunked
<
[{"flightNumber":"0","origin":{"city":"Groningen","code":"GRQ"},"destination":{"city":"London","code":"LHR"}},{"flightNumber":
"1","origin":{"city":"London","code":"LHR"},"destination":{"city":"Groningen","code":"GRQ"}},{"flightNumber":"2","origin":{"ci
ty":"Groningen","code":"GRQ"},"destination":{"city":"Prague","code":"PRG"}},{"flightNumber":"3","origin":{"city":"Prague","cod
e":"PRG"},"destination":{"city":"Groningen","code":"GRQ"}},{"flightNumber":"4","origin":{"city":"Groningen","code":"GRQ"},"des
tination":{"city":"Basel","code":"MLH"}},{"flightNumber":"5","origin":{"city":"Basel","code":"MLH"},"destination":{"city":"Gro
ningen","code":"GRQ"}},{"flightNumber":"6","origin":{"city":"Groningen","code":"GRQ"},"destination":{"city":"Paris","code":"CD
G"}},{"flightNumber":"7","origin":{"city":"Paris","code":"CDG"},"destination":{"city":"Groningen","code":"GRQ"}},{"flightNumbe
r":"8","origin":{"city":"Groningen","code":"GRQ"},"destination":{"city":"Cardiff","code":"CWL"}},{"flightNumber":"9","origin":
{"city":"Cardiff","code":"CWL"},"destination":{"city":"Groningen","code":"GRQ"}},{"flightNumber":"10","origin":{"city":"Gronin
gen","code":"GRQ"},"destination":{"city":"Edinburgh","code":"EDI"}},{"flightNumber":"11","origin":{"city":"Edinburgh","code":"
EDI"},"destination":{"city":"Groningen","code":"GRQ"}},{"flightNumber":"12","origin":{"city":"Groningen","code":"GRQ"},"destin
ation":{"city":"Cork","code":"ORK"}},{"flightNumber":"13","origin":{"city":"Cork","code":"ORK"},"destination":{"city":"Groning
en","code":"GRQ"}},{"flightNumber":"14","origin":{"city":"Groningen","code":"GRQ"},"destination":{"city":"Oslo","code":"OSL"}}
,{"flightNumber":"15","origin":{"city":"Oslo","code":"OSL"},"destination":{"city":"Groningen","code":"GRQ"}},{"flightNumber":"
16","origin":{"city":"Groningen","code":"GRQ"},"destination":{"city":"Berlin","code":"BER"}},{"flightNumber":"17","origin":{"c
ity":"Berlin","code":"BER"},"destination":{"city":"Groningen","code":"GRQ"}},{"flightNumber":"18","origin":{"city":"Groningen"
,"code":"GRQ"},"destination":{"city":"Lyon","code":"LYS"}},{"flightNumber":"19","origin":{"city":"Lyon","code":"LYS"},"destina
tion":{"city":"Groningen","code":"GRQ"}},{"flightNumber":"20","origin":{"city":"Groningen","code":"GRQ"},"destination":{"city"
:"Luxembourg","code":"LUX"}},{"flightNumber":"21","origin":{"city":"Luxembourg","code":"LUX"},"destination":{"city":"Groningen
","code":"GRQ"}},{"flightNumber":"22","origin":{"city":"Groningen","code":"GRQ"},"destination":{"city":"Salzburg","code":"SLZ"
}},{"flightNumber":"23","origin":{"city":"Salzburg","code":"SLZ"},"destination":{"city":"Groningen","code":"GRQ"}},{"flightNum
ber":"24","origin":{"city":"Groningen","code":"GRQ"},"destination":{"city":"Milan","code":"MXP"}},{"flightNumber":"25","origin
":{"city":"Milan","code":"MXP"},"destination":{"city":"Groningen","code":"GRQ"}},{"flightNumber":"26","origin":{"city":"Gronin
gen","code":"GRQ"},"destination":{"city":"Copenhagen","code":"CPH"}},{"flightNumber":"27","origin":{"city":"Copenhagen","code"
:"CPH"},"destination":{"city":"Groningen","code":"GRQ"}},{"flightNumber":"28","origin":{"city":"Groningen","code":"GRQ"},"dest
ination":{"city":"Belfast","code":"BFS"}},{"flightNumber":"29","origin":{"city":"Belfast","code":"BFS"},"destination":{"city":
"Groningen","code":"GRQ"}},{"flightNumber":"30","origin":{"city":"Groningen","code":"GRQ"},"destination":{"city":"Sorvag","cod
e":"FAE"}},{"flightNumber":"31","origin":{"city":"Sorvag","code":"FAE"},"destination":{"city":"Groningen","code":"GRQ"}},{"fli
ghtNumber":"32","origin":{"city":"Groningen","code":"GRQ"},"destination":{"city":"Norwich","code":"NWI"}},{"flightNumber":"33"
,"origin":{"city":"Norwich","code":"NWI"},"destination":{"city":"Groningen","code":"GRQ"}},{"flightNumber":"34","origin":{"cit
y":"Groningen","code":"GRQ"},"destination":{"city":"Liverpool","code":"LPL"}},{"flightNumber":"35","origin":{"city":"Liverpool
","code":"LPL"},"destination":{"city":"Groningen","code":"GRQ"}},{"flightNumber":"36","origin":{"city":"Groningen","code":"GRQ
"},"destination":{"city":"Toulouse","code":"TLS"}},{"flightNumber":"37","origin":{"city":"Toulouse","code":"TLS"},"destination
":{"city":"Groningen","code":"GRQ"}},{"flightNumber":"38","origin":{"city":"Groningen","code":"GRQ"},"destination":{"city":"Ca
en","code":"CFR"}},{"flightNumber":"39","origin":{"city":"Caen","code":"CFR"},"destination":{"city":"Groningen","code":"GRQ"}}
]* Connection #0 to host localhost left intact
```

Figure 14.10   The return data from a query to the `GET /flight` endpoint. All flights in the database are returned in JSON form. This allows users to quickly process the data.

As you can see, the endpoint returned a lengthy list of information on flights in the database. That does it for the `GET /flight` endpoint. Let's move on to the next (more interesting) endpoint: `GET /flight/{flightNumber}`, whose spec is shown in figure 14.11.

We can see that the `GET /flight/{flightNumber}` uses a path parameter and can return a 200 (along with some data), a 400, or a 404. We can test all these scenarios by requesting a valid flight, a flight with an invalid flight number, and a flight with a flight number that is valid but not in the database, as shown in table 14.1.

Figure 14.11   OpenAPI specification of the `GET /flight/{flightNumber}` endpoint. This endpoint allows the user to get information on a specific flight when given a flight number. This is a screenshot from a generated OpenAPI specification.

Table 14.1   Return data for our manual tests of the `GET /flight/{flightNumber}`

Flight numbers	Returned status	Returned data

19	201	`{`
		`    "flightNumber":"19",`
		`    "origin":{"city":"Lyon","code":"LYS"},`
		`    "destination":{"city":"Groningen",`
		`        "code":"GRQ"}`
		`}`

−1	400	(Bad Request) N/A
500	404	(Flight Not Found) N/A

In table 14.1, all returned data from the endpoint is presented. It looks like we have another passing endpoint on our hands. Now, for the final endpoint: `POST /booking/{flightNumber}`, whose spec is shown in figure 14.12.

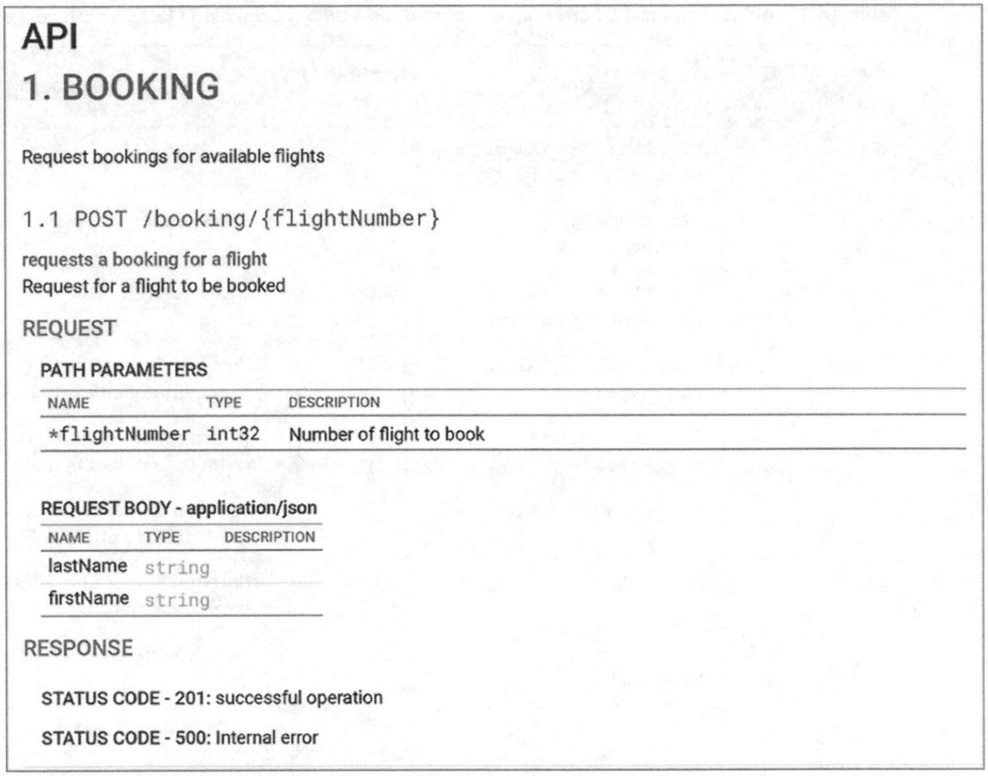

API
1. BOOKING

Request bookings for available flights

1.1 POST /booking/{flightNumber}

requests a booking for a flight
Request for a flight to be booked

REQUEST

PATH PARAMETERS

NAME	TYPE	DESCRIPTION
*flightNumber	int32	Number of flight to book

REQUEST BODY - application/json

NAME	TYPE	DESCRIPTION
lastName	string	
firstName	string	

RESPONSE

STATUS CODE - 201: successful operation

STATUS CODE - 500: Internal error

Figure 14.12   The OpenAPI specification for the POST /booking/{flightNumber} endpoint. This endpoint allows users to book a flight, given a customer name and flight number. This is a screenshot from a generated OpenAPI specification.

The POST /booking/{flightNumber} only has two potential return states (a 201 and a 500), but that is somewhat deceptive. We can force an error from this endpoint in the following ways:

- Pass in a JSON body with empty strings for names.
- Pass in a JSON body missing one or both of the required properties (firstName and lastName).
- Use an invalid flight number.
- Use a flight number for a flight that does not exist.

Table 14.2 shows the inputs and outputs the GET /flight/{flightNumber} gives us. With the data in table 14.2, we can say that all our manual testing passes. We did not see any unexpected output and can safely move on to the last test: generating an OpenAPI file based on the service on the fly and comparing it against FlyTomorrow's version.

Table 14.2   All success and failure responses from the POST /booking/{flightNumber}

Endpoint flight number	Body	Returned status	Returned data
1	firstName : "Alan" lastName: "Turing"	201	(Created) N/A
-1	firstName : "Alan" lastName: "Turing"	400	(Bad Request) N/A
999	firstName : "Alan" lastName: "Turing"	404	(Not Found) N/A
1	firstName : "Alan" lastName: ""	500	(Internal Server Error) "One of the given data points is null"
1	firstName : "" lastName: "Turing"	500	(Internal Server Error) "One of the given data points is null"
1	firstName : "Alan"	500	(Internal Server Error) "One of the given data points is null"
1	lastName: "Turing"	500	(Internal Server Error) "One of the given data points is null"
1	firstName : "" lastName: ""	500	"All given data points are null"
1	N/A	500	"All given data points are null"

14.2.2 *Generating an OpenAPI specification at runtime*

In section 13.3, we discussed middleware and how to use it. We looked at routing and dependency injection. But what if I told you we can generate an OpenAPI specification through a Swagger middleware option (Swagger is the precursor to OpenAPI)? The CLR through ASP.NET creates this OpenAPI specification at runtime, so it always reflects the latest and greatest state of your endpoints. The goal of this section is to generate such a dynamic OpenAPI specification and compare it with the OpenAPI specification we got from FlyTomorrow.

> **NOTE**   This section is optional and requires the installation of a third-party C# library. Generating an OpenAPI specification is not a functional requirement for most applications. If you skip this section, you can pick up reading again at the summary.

Because .NET 5 does not come with the functionality to add Swagger middleware, we have to install a third-party library called Swashbuckle. Go ahead and install the Swashbuckle.AspNetCore package through the NuGet package manager (see section 5.2.1). Once we have installed the Swashbuckle.AspNetCore package, we can add the middleware configuration.

We add middleware to the Startup.cs file by changing both the `Configure` method and the `ConfigureServices` method. The setup is simple and works out of the box, as shown in the next listing.

Listing 14.5   Startup with Swashbuckle middleware

```
class Startup {
  public void Configure(IApplicationBuilder app, IWebHostEnvironment env) {
    app.UseRouting();
    app.UseEndpoints(endpoints => { endpoints.MapControllers(); });

    app.UseSwagger();                                    Generates a Swagger file
    app.UseSwaggerUI(swagger =>                           at the default location
   swagger.SwaggerEndpoint("/swagger/v1/swagger.json",
   "Flying Dutchman Airlines"));
  }                                                      Exposes an interactive GUI, pointing
                                                         to the generated Swagger file

  public void ConfigureServices(IServiceCollection services) {
    services.AddControllers();

    services.AddTransient(typeof(FlightService),
   typeof(FlightService));
    services.AddTransient(typeof(BookingService),
   typeof(BookingService));
    services.AddTransient(typeof(FlightRepository),
   typeof(FlightRepository));
    services.AddTransient(typeof(AirportRepository),
   typeof(AirportRepository));
    services.AddTransient(typeof(BookingRepository),
   typeof(BookingRepository));
    services.AddTransient(typeof(CustomerRepository),
   typeof(CustomerRepository));

    services.AddDbContext<FlyingDutchmanAirlinesContext>
   (ServiceLifeTime.Transient);

    services.AddTransient(typeof(FlyingDutchmanAirlinesContext),
   typeof(FlyingDutchmanAirlinesContext));

    services.AddSwaggerGen();                 Adds Swagger
  }                                           to middleware
}
```

By adding the Swagger setup to both the `ConfigureServices` and `Configure` methods, the CLR knows to scan the service at launch and request a Swagger file to be generated based on that information. To test this out, all we have to do is launch the service and navigate to the `SwaggerUI` endpoint: `[service]/swagger`.

In figure 14.13, you see the resulting Swagger UI generated by the Swagger middleware.

Figure 14.13   The autogenerated OpenAPI specification of the Flying Dutchman Airlines service. We can use this to double-check our work against FlyTomorrow's OpenAPI specification.

On the surface, this looks pretty good, albeit a bit sparse. Let's investigate further and see if we are missing any information. By expanding the GET /{controller]/[flight-Number} section, we can see in figure 14.14 that it generated only the return information for a status code 200.

The thing is that we know for a fact that we added logic to the appropriate endpoint method to return more than just a 200. What happened here? You often encounter this situation: for whatever reason, the CLR could not automatically determine all the return status codes. But, luckily, we can add a method attribute to the appropriate method that tells the CLR what return codes the method returns as follows:

```
[HttpGet("{flightNumber}")]
[ProducesResponseType(StatusCodes.Status200OK)]
[ProducesResponseType(StatusCodes.Status404NotFound)]
[ProducesResponseType(StatusCodes.Status400BadRequest)]
public async Task<IActionResult> GetFlightByFlightNumber(int flightNumber) { … }
```

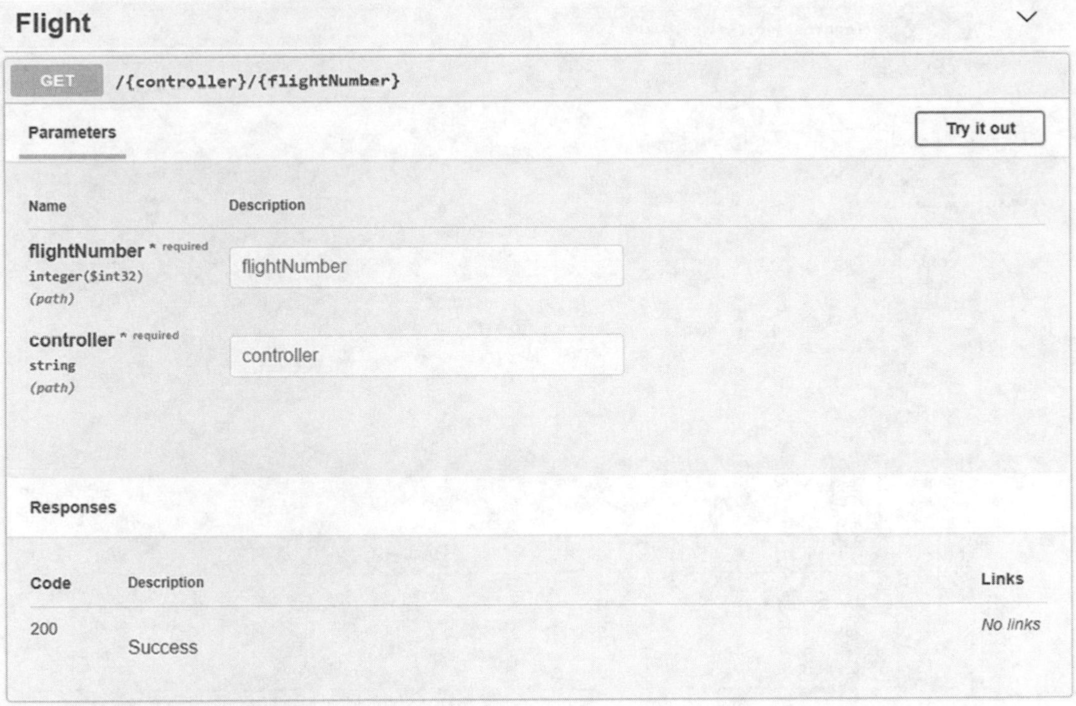

Figure 14.14 The expanded GET /Flight/{FlightNumber} OpenAPI information generated at the launch of the service. This seems to be missing some return information that we added to the controller.

If we now compile and launch the service again, we see the Swagger UI has changed (as shown in figure 14.15).

That looks good. To make sure the other two endpoints (GET /Flight and POST /Booking/{flightNumber}) have the correct information, go ahead and add the appropriate method attributes to their respective endpoint methods. After that, we can compare our generated OpenAPI to the one provided by FlyTomorrow.

COMPARING OPENAPI SPECIFICATIONS: GET /FLIGHT

Perhaps the easiest endpoint to compare in terms of OpenAPI specifications is the GET /flight endpoint, shown in figure 14.16. It does not take in a body (GET requests cannot contain a body), and it returns a 200 along with any data it finds, a 404 if no data was found, or a 500 in case of trouble.

Figure 14.16 shows us clearly that all return codes are accounted for in the auto-generated OpenAPI specification for the GET /flight endpoint.

COMPARING OPENAPI SPECIFICATIONS: GET /FLIGHT/{FLIGHTNUMBER}

The second endpoint we look at is the GET /Flight/{flightNumber} endpoint. This endpoint is very similar to the GET /flight endpoint but introduces the concept of a

GET	/{controller}/{flightNumber}		

Parameters   Try it out

Name	Description
flightNumber * required integer($int32) (path)	flightNumber
controller * required string (path)	controller

Responses

Code	Description		Links
200	Success		No links
400	Bad Request		No links
404	Not Found		No links

Figure 14.15   The expanded `GET /Flight/{FlightNumber}` OpenAPI information was generated at the launch of the service with the correct return statuses. It is important to reflect your API truthfully in an OpenAPI specification so you do not lead people down the wrong road.

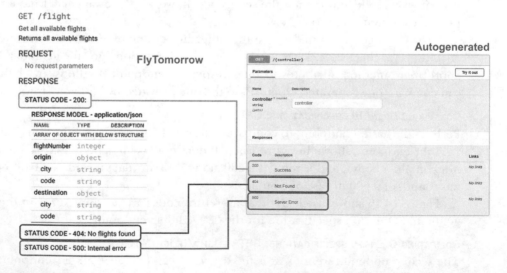

Figure 14.16   Comparing the FlyTomorrow and the autogenerated OpenAPI specification for `GET /Flight`. This is one way to verify our work against a customer specification.

path parameter. Let's see in figure 14.17 how our generated OpenAPI specification stacks up against the FlyTomorrow specification.

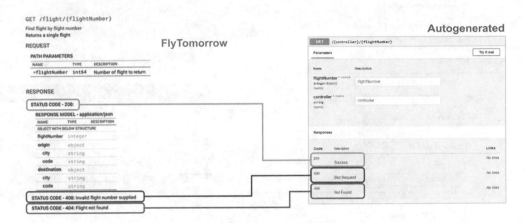

Figure 14.17 Comparing the FlyTomorrow and the autogenerated OpenAPI specification for `GET` `/Flight/{flightNumber}`**. By comparing the two specifications, we can be sure we did a good job.**

Once again, the returned statuses look to be the same in both the FlyTomorrow and the autogenerated OpenAPI specification. Great, let's move on to the final endpoint.

COMPARING OPENAPI SPECIFICATIONS: POST /BOOKING/{FLIGHTNUMBER}

The final endpoint we implemented was the `POST /Booking/{flightNumber}`. This endpoint combined a `POST` request plus a body with a path parameter. The endpoint method had to do JSON deserialization and serialization of data coming in and out of the service. Let's have a look at how we did (figure 14.18).

The image in figure 14.18 is encouraging but not quite what we want to see at this stage. We can see that the 201 and 500 status codes map correctly, but it turns out we implemented a 404 return status. This return was not necessary per the FlyTomorrow OpenAPI specification. Now, there is something to be said for keeping this return status because there is a possibility that the developers at FlyTomorrow would like to have it. On the other hand, it is often best to stick to the customer requirements fairly tightly. In that vein, the last task in this book for you is to change the `BookingControl-ler` to not return the 404 (if you get stuck, see the source code). As a bonus challenge: Swagger has the functionality to specify descriptions along with return codes. Research and implement this.

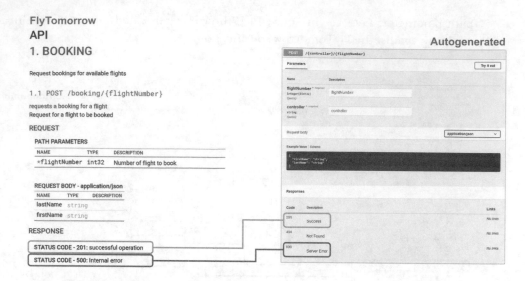

Figure 14.18   Comparing the FlyTomorrow and the autogenerated OpenAPI specification for POST /Booking/{flightNumber}. **If we did not compare the two specifications, we may have missed the need for the 404 Not Found return and shipped incorrect code to the customer.**

14.3   The end of the road

Congratulations! You did it. You reached the end of the book. I hope you thoroughly enjoyed the material and learned a new thing or two. If you want to continue your C# journey, I suggest you look at Jon Skeet's *C# in Depth* (4th edition; Manning, 2019), Dustin Metzgar's *.NET Core in Action* (Manning, 2018), Andrew Lock's *ASP.NET Core in Action* (2nd edition; Manning, 2021), and Jeffrey Richter's *CLR via C#* (4th edition; Microsoft Press, 2012). Appendix E contains a list of various resources (books, websites, articles) recommended in this book.

Lastly, I want to leave you with a quote from the eminent Donald Knuth:[2]

> *If you find that you're spending almost all your time on theory, start turning some attention to practical things; it will improve your theories. If you find that you're spending almost all your time on practice, start turning some attention to theoretical things; it will improve your practice.*

---

[2] Donald Knuth is an American computer scientist, famous for his books in *The Art of Computer Programming* series. He is the recipient of the 1974 ACM Turing Award (the computer world's equivalent of the Academy Awards/Pulitzer Prize/Nobel Prize), was instrumental in the popularization of asymptotic notation, and is professor emeritus at Stanford University. His (excellent) personal website is https://www-cs-faculty.stanford.edu/~knuth/.

Summary

- JSON data coming in from an HTTP request is serialized. This means that the data is not in a format that we can directly use. We need to deserialize this data before we can operate on it.
- To deserialize JSON data, we can use either the [FromBody] argument attribute or implement a custom model binder. Deserializing data is what allows us to put incoming JSON or XML data in a usable data structure.
- You can use the IModelBinder interface to implement a custom model binder. This is useful when you want to have more control over how data is serialized into your models.
- By using the ModelState.IsValid check, we can verify that no errors were found during model binding. This is most useful when combined with a custom model binder, because you can precisely define when a model is not valid in that situation.
- You can generate an OpenAPI specification of your service at launch by adding Swagger middleware to your configuration. This is helpful with acceptance testing and to make sure you are implementing the correct endpoints.

appendix A
Exercise answers

This appendix provides answers to the exercises as found in the book as well as explanations of the answers.

Chapter 2: .NET and how it compiles

Exercise number	Answer	Explanations
2.1	d	AmigaOS is an operating system originally developed for the Amiga PC. Its last major release was in 2016. It is not supported by .NET 5.
2.2	c	
2.3	d	
2.4	a	
2.5	b, a	
2.6	e	
2.7	c	
2.8	a	

Chapter 4: Manage your unmanaged resources!

Exercise number	Answer	Explanations
4.1	False	Attributes can be applied to methods, classes, types, properties, and fields.
4.2	True	
4.3	False	Enumerations are created with the enum keyword.
4.4	a, d	Only a Hufflepuff would write connection strings on a sticky note.
4.5	b	
4.6	a	
4.7	c	
4.8	True	
4.9	False	

Chapter 5: Setting up a project and database with Entity Framework Core

Exercise number	Answer	Explanations
5.1	b	
5.2	a	
5.3	a, d	Tomcat is an open source implementation of Java Servlet (similar to WebHost); JVM is the Java Virtual Machine (similar to the CLR).
5.4	True	
5.5	See below the table for answer	
5.6	One per database entity	

Answer to exercise 5.5: There are a variety of ways to solve this exercise as a one-liner. You can pick from a variety of access modifiers, method names, and variable names. Two constants remain, however: the return type needs to be of type integer, and we need to return the product of the two integer input arguments as follows:

```
public int Product(int a, int b) => a * b;
```

Chapter 6: Test-driven development and dependency injection

Exercise number	Answer	Explanations
6.1	c	Answer B ("Don't perform the same logic in two separate places") describes the Don't Repeat Yourself (DRY) principle.
6.2	True	In the book, however, we use TDD-lite where we sometimes break this rule.
6.3	False	Test classes must have an access modifier of `public` to be used by a test runner.
6.4	c	
6.5	False	LINQ allows us to perform queries on collections by using SQL-like statements and methods.
6.6	a	
6.7	b	
6.8	True	
6.9	a	
6.10	True	

Solution to the exercise found in section 6.2.8:

```
[TestMethod]
public async Task CreateCustomer_Success()
{
    CustomerRepository repository = new CustomerRepository();
    Assert.IsNotNull(repository);

    bool result = await repository.CreateCustomer("Donald Knuth");
    Assert.IsTrue(result);
}


[TestMethod]
public async Task CreateCustomer_Failure_NameIsNull()
{
    CustomerRepository repository = new CustomerRepository();
    Assert.IsNotNull(repository);

    bool result = await repository.CreateCustomer(null);
    Assert.IsFalse(result);
}

[TestMethod]
public async Task CreateCustomer_Failure_NameIsEmptyString()
{
    CustomerRepository repository = new CustomerRepository();
    Assert.IsNotNull(repository);
```

```
        bool result = await repository.CreateCustomer(string.Empty);
        Assert.IsFalse(result);
}

[TestMethod]
[DataRow('#')]
[DataRow('$')]
[DataRow('%')]
[DataRow('&')]
[DataRow('*')]
public async Task CreateCustomer_Failure_NameContainsInvalidCharacters(char
➥ invalidCharacter)
{
        CustomerRepository repository = new CustomerRepository();
        Assert.IsNotNull(repository);

        bool result = await repository.CreateCustomer("Donald Knuth" +
          invalidCharacter);
        Assert.IsFalse(result);
}
```

Chapter 7: Comparing objects

Exercise number	Answer	Explanations
7.1	Write a unit test that uses the exception found method attribute.	
7.2	b	
7.3	Exception	You can also derive a custom exception from a different Exception (custom or not) that inherits from the Exception class.
7.4	c	A and B can be default values for the underlying type of the collection, so they are correct in some cases.
7.5	c	When comparing value types, the equality operator compares their values against each other.
7.6	a	When comparing reference types, the equality operator compares their memory address against each other.
7.7	True	
7.8	a	When overloading an operator, you also need to overload its counter operator.
7.9	False	Perfect randomness does not exist in computing.
7.10	False	Perfect randomness does not exist in computing.
7.11	True	

Chapter 8: Stubbing, generics, and coupling

Exercise number	Answer	Explanations
8.1	c	
8.2	False	Two classes that are heavily dependent on each other signifies tight coupling.
8.3	a	
8.4	c	
8.5	False	Strings are immutable. Every change that is made to a string results in a new memory allocation, with the resulting string stored into that spot in memory.
8.6	False	You have to `override` the base class's methods.
8.7	a	The DRY principle stands for the Don't Repeat Yourself principle. The Phragmén–Lindelöf principle deals with boundedness of a holomorphic function on an unbounded domain.
8.8	b	
8.9	c	
8.10	False	Generics can be used with classes, methods, and collections.
8.11	False	
8.12	False	
8.13	True	
8.14	b	
8.15	False	If you do not declare a `default` case in a `switch` statement, and no other cases are matched, no execution will take place within the `switch` statement.

Chapter 9: Extension methods, streams, and abstract classes

Exercise number	Answer	Explanations
9.1	b	
9.2	a	
9.3	False	You can use the `[DataRow]` method attribute with as many data points as you want.
9.4	b	
9.5	False	

Exercise number	Answer	Explanations
9.6	False	An abstract class can contain both abstract and regular methods.
9.7	False	
9.8	True	

Chapter 10: Reflection and mocks

Exercise number	Answer	Explanations
10.1	b	
10.2	False	The repository layer typically interacts with a database through a database access layer when using an ORM.
10.3	True	
10.4	True	
10.5	a	
10.6	c	We never want to delete code without worrying about the side effects. When encountering commented-out code, do your due diligence to figure out why it is there. There better be a really good excuse or else delete it. Ninety-nine percent of the time, you can delete the code without issue.
10.7	d	
10.8	a	
10.9	True	
10.10	c	
10.11	True	While there is still some coupling between the controller and the repository, this is looser coupling when compared to the controller directly calling the repository.
10.12	False	This is the functionality of a stub.
10.13	False	The InternalsVisibleTo allows you to expose an assembly's internals to a different assembly.
10.14	c	
10.15	True	
10.16	b	
10.17	a	[MethodImpl(MethodImplOptions.NoInlining)] can be applied only to methods.

Chapter 11: Runtime type checking revisited and error handling

Exercise number	Answer	Explanations
11.1	False	
11.2	c	
11.3	a	Only a service is allowed to call a repository. A repository should not call another repository.
11.4	True	
11.5	b	
11.6	False	The discard operator can still result in memory allocation.
11.7	a	The first `catch` block is entered because an `ItemSoldOut-Exception` can be used as an `Exception` type.
11.8	a	

Chapter 12: Using IAsyncEnumerable<T> and yield return

Exercise number	Answer	Explanations
12.1	True	
12.2	False	We would likely need to implement the `InventoryService`, though.
12.3	b	
12.4	a	
12.5	Yes	The `Dragonfruit` class can set the `IsFruit` property because the `IsFruit` property has an access modifier of `protected`. With a `protected` access modifier, the owning class and its children (derived classes) can access the property. The `Dragonfruit` class derives from the `Fruit` class.
12.6	True	
12.7	True	
12.8	False	When you add a constructor to a struct, you need to set *all* properties present on the struct or the compiler will not compile your code.

Chapter 13: Middleware, HTTP routing, and HTTP responses

Exercise number	Answer	Explanations
13.1	True	
13.2	c	
13.3	a	
13.4	True	
13.5	c	
13.6	b	

appendix B
Clean code checklist

You can use this short checklist when encountering code that you are unfamiliar with or while writing new code. This checklist is not meant to be exhaustive and is merely a starting point for your own research.

GENERAL

- My code reads like a narrative. I write code for humans, not machines.
- I document my code only when necessary. My code should speak for itself.
- I provide clear instructions on how to build and release my codebase. Where appropriate, I provide working build scripts/makefiles or CI/CD setup instructions.
- I use native functionalities instead of implementing my own libraries, unless for a very good reason.
- My code is consistent in its design patterns, documentation, and naming conventions. I do not change things mid-development and go against established patterns.
- I have added logging to my application, so I or other developers can debug when things go awry.

CLASSES

- My class has the strictest access modifier possible.
- My class is named accurately.
- My class performs operations on only one specific object and, therefore, adheres to the single-responsibility principle.
- My class lives in the right folder within my project.
- If I struggle with implementing my class, I take a step back and come up with a brief description of the class and its intended functionality. This refocus can help write cleaner code. If my class should do multiple things, I split it up.

METHODS

- My method has the strictest access modifier possible.
- My method is named accurately and correctly describes the logic within (leaving nothing out).
- My method performs only one general operation or collects information from other methods related to its operations. It adheres to the single-responsibility principle.
- If my method has a public access modifier, I do not perform any operations within the method. The public method calls other, smaller, methods and organizes the outputs.
- I have unit tests backing my method. The unit tests should cover the major success and failure logic branches.

VARIABLES, FIELDS, AND PROPERTIES (VFP)

- My VFP types are of the most abstract type possible. If I can use an interface instead of a concrete type, I use the interface. This promotes polymorphism and the use of the Liskov substitution principle.
- I do not have any "magic numbers" assigned to a variable.
- Whenever possible, I restrict my VFPs to the tightest access modifier possible. If a VFP can be made read only, I make it read only. If a VFP can be made a constant, I make it a constant.
- I always validate my input arguments. This protects me against unwanted null pointer exceptions and operating on data in an invalid state.
- I use enums and constants instead of string literals where appropriate.

TESTING

- I always provide appropriate unit tests to my code.
- I follow test-driven development where possible.
- I am not focused on code coverage. My goal in testing is to protect against unexpected side effects and to validate my assumptions about the requirements and existing code.
- If one of my changes breaks a test, I fix the test.
- I always write the least amount of code necessary to satisfy all tests. Any extraneous lines increase the amount of code to maintain.

appendix C
Installation guides

This appendix contains quick installation guides for the following:

- .NET Framework 4.x
- .NET 5
- Visual Studio
- Visual Studio for Mac
- Visual Studio Code

.NET FRAMEWORK 4.X (WINDOWS ONLY)

The .NET Framework is supported only on Windows. To install the latest version of .NET Framework 4, go to https://dotnet.microsoft.com/download/dotnet-framework, and select the top option from the list of releases. Please note that the minimum .NET Framework version you need to run to support the supplied source code for this book is .NET Framework 4.8. When you click on a release, you are brought to the download link page for that release. Click Download .NET Framework 4.[version] Developer Pack. This will download an installer that you can run to install .NET Framework on your machine.

.NET 5 (WINDOWS, LINUX, AND MACOS)

.NET 5 is supported on Windows, Linux, and macOS (64-bit only). To install the latest version of .NET 5, navigate to https://dotnet.microsoft.com/download/dotnet/5.0, and select the latest SDK release. At the time of writing, the latest release is SDK 5.0.203. When you click on the appropriate release, you are directed to the download page of the respective release. There is also an option to download the binaries for all platforms if you wish to do so. Running the downloaded installer installs .NET 5 on your platform.

VISUAL STUDIO (WINDOWS)

Visual Studio is the premier IDE for developing C# on Windows. Visual Studio comes in the following three flavors:

- Community
- Professional
- Enterprise

The Community Edition is free and allows you to develop (commercial) software unless you are part of an organization (and doing work for that organization) with more than 250 PCs or over 1 million US dollars in annual revenue. There are some feature differences between the three editions, but everything we do in this book can be done using Visual Studio Community.

To download Visual Studio Community, visit https://visualstudio.microsoft.com/vs/, and select Visual Studio Community from the Download Visual Studio dropdown list. Please make sure that the version is at least Visual Studio 2019 v16.7 because .NET 5 will not function correctly on older versions of Visual Studio (including previous years' releases, such as Visual Studio 2017). When you launch the installer, you are greeted with a host of Visual Studio installation options. These options are called "workloads," and for this book, you want to install the following ones:

- ASP.NET and web development
- .NET Core cross-platform development

By selecting the workloads, a download button is enabled in the bottom right-hand corner. Click this, and Visual Studio will be installed with the selected workloads. Please note that Visual Studio routinely takes over 8 GB to install.

VISUAL STUDIO FOR MAC

Visual Studio for Mac is a separate product from Visual Studio. It is Microsoft's attempt to bring the Visual Studio experience to macOS. To install Visual Studio for Mac, visit https://visualstudio.microsoft.com/vs/mac/. Click the Download Visual Studio for Mac button, and run the downloaded installer. You are now ready to use Visual Studio for Mac. Other IDEs on macOS to consider are VS Code and JetBrains' Rider. Please make sure you are always using the most up-to-date version of Visual Studio for Mac.

VISUAL STUDIO CODE (WINDOWS, LINUX, MACOS)

You do not have to use Visual Studio with this book or in your daily work. In theory, you can use any editor with C# and compile through the command line. In practice, this is a bit painful. Microsoft has developed a light-weight alternative to Visual Studio in Visual Studio Code. It is free and functions more like a text editor than a fully fledged IDE. To download Visual Studio Code, visit https://code.visualstudio.com/, and click the Download for [platform] button. Run the installer, and then, Visual Studio Code is ready for use. When you write C# code (or open a C# solution) for the first time in Visual Studio Code, it will prompt you to download a C# package. Accept this prompt, and you will be able to use Visual Studio Code (or VS Code) with C#.

RUNNING THE FLYING DUTCHMAN AIRLINES DATABASE ON YOUR LOCAL MACHINE

If you do not want to (or cannot) use the deployed database for the Flying Dutchman Airlines project in the book, you can run the SQL database in a local instance of SQL Server.

To do this, you need the following installed:

- SQL Server Developer Edition
- Microsoft SQL Server Management Studio

To download SQL Server, please visit https://www.microsoft.com/en-us/sql-server/sql-server-downloads, and download the Developer version of SQL Server. After installing SQL Server, you can move on to installing SQL Server Management Studio (SSMS) from https://docs.microsoft.com/en-us/sql/ssms/download-sql-server-management-studio-ssms?view=sql-server-ver15. Both SQL Server Developer and SSMS are free.

After SSMS is installed, if you have not done so already, please create a new local SQL Server instance through SQL Server. To install a new local SQL Server instance, open the SQL Server Installation Center that was installed alongside your SQL Server Developer Edition application. In the installation center, click Installation > New SQL Server Stand-alone Installation or Add Features to an Existing Installation.

Follow the installation wizard, noting the login credentials you give your SQL Server instance. You need this information to connect to the SQL Server instance.

Now launch SSMS. You are greeted by a connection dialog where you can browse for your SQL instance and fill in your connection information. After connecting, you are greeted by the SSMS primary screen. Here, in the Object Explorer, right-click Databases, and select Import Data-Tier Application.

Clicking the Import Data-Tier Application context menu option brings up a wizard that lets you import the provided Flying Dutchman Airlines database. In the Import Settings window, select Import from Local Disk and browse to the database file (FlyingDutchmanAirlinesDatabase.bacpac). In the following window, you can rename the database if you wish. After going through the wizard, the database should be imported and ready to use with the code in this book.

There is a chance that your database import will fail. This usually is because of a mismatch between the contained database settings in Microsoft Azure and SSMS. If the import fails, please run the following command on the main database in your SQL instance (automatically generated for you):

```
sp_configure 'contained database authentication', 1; GO RECONFIGURE; GO;
```

Some people have reported that syntax issues around the GO keyword sometimes arise. If you run into issues with the previous command, this next command should work for you instead:

```
EXEC sp_configure 'contained database authentication', 1; RECONFIGURE;
```

One last note: whenever you encounter a connection string in the book, make sure you replace it with the correct connection string for your local SQL instance copy of the database.

appendix D
OpenAPI FlyTomorrow

The OpenAPI specification in this appendix reflects the OpenAPI specification we received from FlyTomorrow. This OpenAPI specification guides the refactor and rewrite of the Flying Dutchman Airlines service throughout the book.

```
OpenAPI FlyTomorrow.com
openapi: 3.0.1
info:
  title: FlyTomorrow required endpoints
  description: This OpenAPI file specifies the required endpoints as per
    the contract
    between FlyTomorrow.com and Flying Dutchman Airlines
  version: 1.0.0
servers:
- url: https://zork.flyingdutchmanairlines.com/v1
tags:
- name: flight
  description: Access to available flights
- name: booking
  description: Request bookings for available flights
paths:
  /flight:
    get:
      tags:
      - flight
      summary: Get all available flights
      description: Returns all available flights
      operationId: getFlights
      responses:
        200:
          description: ""
          content:
            application/json:
              schema:
                type: array
```

```
              items:
                 $ref: '#/components/schemas/Flight'
          404:
            description: No flights found
            content: {}
          500:
            description: Internal error
            content: {}
  /flight/{flightNumber}:
    get:
      tags:
      - flight
      summary: Find flight by flight number
      description: Returns a single flight
      operationId: getFlightByFlightNumber
      parameters:
      - name: flightNumber
        in: path
        description: Number of flight to return
        required: true
        schema:
          type: integer
          format: int32
      responses:
        200:
          description: ""
          content:
            application/json:
              schema:
                $ref: '#/components/schemas/Flight'
        400:
          description: Invalid flight number supplied
          content: {}
        404:
          description: Flight not found
          content: {}
  /booking/{flightNumber}:
    post:
      tags:
      - booking
      summary: requests a booking for a flight
      description: Request for a flight to be booked
      operationId: bookFlight
      parameters:
      - name: flightNumber
        in: path
        description: Number of flight to book
        required: true
        schema:
          type: integer
          format: int64
      requestBody:
        content:
          application/json:
            schema:
```

```
                    $ref: '#/components/schemas/Customer'
            required: true
          responses:
            201:
              description: successful operation
            500:
              description: Internal error
              content: {}
components:
  schemas:
    Airport:
      type: object
      properties:
        city:
          type: string
        code:
          type: string
    Customer:
      type: object
      properties:
        firstName:
          type: string
        lastName:
          type: string
    Flight:
      type: object
      properties:
        flightNumber:
          type: integer
          format: int32
        origin:
          $ref: '#/components/schemas/Airport'
        destination:
          $ref: '#/components/schemas/Airport'
```

appendix E
Reading list

.NET CORE

- Metzgar, Dustin, *.NET Core in Action* (Manning, 2018).

.NET STANDARD

- .NET Standard specification. The latest version of this document can be found at github.com/dotnet/standard/tree/master/docs/versions.

ASP.NET

- Lock, Andrew, *ASP.NET in Action* (2nd edition; Manning, 2020).

C#

- Standard ECMA-334 C# Language Specification. The ECMA standard specification is always a couple of versions behind the latest released language version. It can be found at ecma-international.org/publications/standards/Ecma-334.htm.
- Wagner, Bill, *Effective C#* (2nd edition; Microsoft Press, 2016).
- Skeet, Jon, *C# In-Depth* (4th edition; Manning, 2019).

COM/INTEROP

- Clark, Jason, *Calling Win32 DLLs in C# with P/Invoke* (MSDN Magazine; July 2003). https://docs.microsoft.com/en-us/archive/msdn-magazine/2003/july/net-column-calling-win32-dlls-in-csharp-with-p-invoke.
- Clark, Jason, *P/Invoke Revisited* (MSDN Magazine; October 2004). https://docs.microsoft.com/en-us/archive/msdn-magazine/2004/october/net-column-p-invoke-revisited.

COMMON LANGUAGE RUNTIME (CLR)

- Richter, Jeffrey, *CLR Via C#* (4th edition; Microsoft Press, 2012).

COMPILERS

- Aho, Alfred V., Monica S. Lam, Ravi Sethi, and Jeffrey D. Ullman, *Compilers: Principles, Techniques, and Tools* (2nd edition; Pearson Education, 2007).

CONCURRENT PROGRAMMING

- Duffy, Joe, *Concurrent Programming on Windows* (Addison-Wesley, 2008).

DATABASES AND SQL

- Cornell University, *Relational Databases Virtual Workshop* at https://cvw.cac.cornell.edu/databases/.
- Takahashi, Mana, Shoko Azumas, and Trend-Pro Co., Ltd., *The Manga Guide to Databases* (No Starch Press, 2009).
- Hunt, Andrew, and Dave Thomas, *The Pragmatic Programmer* (Addison Wesley, 1999).

DEPENDENCY INJECTION

- Fowler, Martin, *Inversion of Control Containers and the Dependency Injection Pattern* (https://www.martinfowler.com/articles/injection.html).
- Martin, Robert C., *OO Design Quality Metrics, An Analysis of Dependencies* (https://groups.google.com/forum/#!msg/comp.lang.c++/KU-LQ3hINks/ouRSX-PUpybkJ).
- Van Deursen, Steven, and Mark Seemann, *Dependency Injection Principles, Practices, and Patterns* (2nd edition; Manning, 2019).

DESIGN PATTERNS

- Gamma, Eric, Richard Helm, Ralph Johnson, and John Vlissides, *Design Patterns: Elements of Reusable Object-Oriented Software* (Addison-Wesley, 1994).
- Martin, Robert C., and Micah Martin, *Agile Principles, Patterns, and Practices in C#* (Prentice Hall, 2006).
- Freeman, Eric, Elisabeth Robson, Kathy Sierra, and Bert Bates, *Head First: Design Patterns* (O'Reilly, 2004).

ENIAC

- Dyson, George, *Turing's Cathedral: The Origins of the Digital Universe* (Vintage, 2012).

GENERICS

- Skeet, Jon, *C# In-Depth* (4th edition; Manning, 2019).

GRAPH THEORY

- Trudeau, Richard J., *Introduction to Graph Theory* (2nd edition; Dover Publications, 1994).

HASHING

- Wong, David, *Real-World Cryptography* (Manning, 2021).
- Knuth, Donald, *The Art of Computer Programming Volume 3: Sorting and Searching* (2nd edition; Addison-Wesley, 1998).

HTTP

- Pollard, Barry, *HTTP/2 in Action* (Manning, 2019).
- Berners-Lee, Tim, *Information Management: A Proposal* (French Conseil Européen pour la Recherche Nucléaire; CERN, 1990).
- Berners-Lee, Tim, Roy Fielding, and Henrik Frystyk, *Hypertext Transfer Protocol—HTTP/1.0* (Internet Engineering Task Force; IETF, 1996).

KUBERNETES AND DOCKER

- Lukša, Marko, *Kubernetes in Action* (2nd edition; Manning, 2021).
- Stoneman, Elton, *Learn Docker in a Month of Lunches* (Manning, 2020).
- Davis, Ashley, *Bootstrapping Microservices with Docker, Kubernetes, and Terraform* (Manning, 2020).

MATHEMATICS

- Knuth, Donald, *The Art of Computer Programming, Volume 1: Fundamental Algorithms* (Addison Wesley Longman, 1977).
- Hofstadter, Douglas R., *Gödel, Escher, Bach: An Eternal Golden Braid* (Basic Books, 1977).
- Alama, Jesse, and Johannes Korbmacher, *The Stanford Encyclopedia of Philosophy, The Lambda Calculus* (https://plato.stanford.edu/entries/lambda-calculus/).
- Conery, Rob, *The Imposter's Handbook: A CS Primer for Self-Taught Programmers* (Rob Conery, 2017).

MATLAB

- Hamming, Richard, *Numerical Methods for Scientists and Engineers* (Dover Publications, 1987).
- Gilat, Amos, *MATLAB: An Introduction with Applications* (6th edition; Wiley, 2016).

MICROSERVICES

- Gammelgaard, Christian Horsdal, *Microservices in .NET Core* (Manning, 2020).
- Newman, Sam, *Building Microservices: Designing Fine-Grained Systems* (O'Reilly Media, 2015).
- Richardson, Chris, *Microservices Patterns* (Manning, 2018).
- Siriwardena, Prabath, and Nuwan Dias, *Microservices Security in Action* (Manning, 2019).

OPCODES AND ASSEMBLY

- BBC Bitesize: Computer Science—Binary and Data Representation (instructions) at https://www.bbc.co.uk/bitesize/guides/z2342hv/revision/1.

RED-BLACK TREES

- Cormen, Thomas H., Charles E. Leiserson, Ronald L. Rivest, and Clifford Stein, *Introduction to Algorithms*, chapter 13, "Red-Black Trees" (3rd edition; Massachusetts Institute of Technology, 2009).
- Galles, David, red/black tree visualizations; https://www.cs.usfca.edu/~galles/visualization/RedBlack.html (University of San Francisco).
- Wilt, Nicholas, *Classic Algorithms in C++: With New Approaches to Sorting, Searching, and Selecting* (Wiley, 1995).

REFACTORING

- Fowler, Martin, *Refactoring: Improving the Design of Existing Code* (Addison-Wesley, 1999).

SEPARATION OF CONCERNS

- Dijkstra, Edsger, *The Role of Scientific Thought* in *Selected Writings on Computing: A Personal Perspective* (Springer-Verlag, 1982).
- Martin, Robert C., *Clean Code: A Handbook of Agile Software Craftsmanship* (Prentice-Hall, 2008).
- Constantine, Larry, and Edward Yourdon, *Structured Design: Fundamentals of a Discipline of Computer Program and System Design* (Prentice-Hall, 1979).

THE SINGLE-RESPONSIBILITY PRINCIPLE

- Martin, Robert C., *The Single-Responsibility Principle* (https://blog.cleancoder.com/uncle-bob/2014/05/08/SingleReponsibilityPrinciple.html).

THE LISKOV PRINCIPLE

- Liskov, Barbara H., and Jeannette M. Wing, *A Behavioral Notion of Subtyping* (ACM Transactions on Programming Languages and Systems [TOPLAS], 1994).

UNIT TESTING

- Khorikov, Vladimir, *Unit Testing Principles, Practices, and Patterns* (Manning, 2020).[1]
- Osherove, Roy, *The Art of Unit Testing* (2nd edition; Manning, 2013).
- Kaner, Cem, James Bach, and Bret Pettichord, *Lessons Learned in Software Testing: A Context-Driven Approach* (Wiley, 2008).

---

[1] The author was one of the technical reviewers for Vladimir Khorikov's *Unit Testing Principles, Practices, and Patterns*.

VISUAL STUDIO

- Johnson, Bruce, *Professional Visual Studio 2017* (Wrox, 2017).
- ———— *Essential Visual Studio 2019: Boosting Development Productivity with Containers, Git, and Azure Tools* (Apress, 2020).[2]

---

[2] The author was the technical reviewer for Bruce Johnson's *Essential Visual Studio 2019: Boosting Development Productivity with Containers, Git, and Azure Tools* (Apress, 2020).

index